Prelude to Tragedy

Prelude to *Tragedy*

Vietnam, 1960–1965

Edited by Harvey Neese and John O'Donnell

NAVAL INSTITUTE PRESS
Annapolis, Maryland

Naval Institute Press
291 Wood Road
Annapolis, MD 21402

Library of Congress Cataloging-in-Publication Data
    Prelude to tragedy : Vietnam, 1960–1965 / edited by Harvey Neese
    and John O'Donnell.
        p.   cm.
    Includes bibliographical references and index.
    ISBN 1-55750-491-1 (alk. paper)
      1. Vietnam—Politics and government—1945–1975. 2. Vietnamese Conflict,
    1961–1975—United States. 3. Vietnam (Republic)—Foreign relations—United
    States. 4. United States—Foreign relations—Vietnam (Republic). 5. United
    States—Foreign relations—1963–1969. I. Neese, Harvey, 1934– II. O'Donnell,
    John, 1935–

DS556.9 .P74 2000
959.704'31—dc21

                                    00-063837

Printed in the United States of America on acid-free paper ∞
07 06 05 04 03 02 01 00   9 8 7 6 5 4 3 2
First printing

Unless otherwise noted, photographs are from individual
contributors' collections.

Contents

Foreword

Vladimir Lehovich and I arrived at Tan Son Nhut air base in Saigon on the evening of 26 May 1963. We were both new foreign service officers, and we had been together for a year—first in the State Department's foreign service basic training course, then in Vietnamese language school in Washington and in area training at the University of California. We had been given special assignments in Vietnam with the Office of Rural Affairs, a newly formed group within the foreign-aid mission.

It was unusual to assign FSOs to the foreign-aid program, but U. Alexis Johnson, then the deputy undersecretary of state for political affairs, had decided to diversify the foreign service experience. And as French-speaking bachelors, Vlad and I were the first two FSOs chosen. This seemingly minor personnel decision was to determine the rest of my governmental career.

We were met at the airport by Ralph Boynton, an administrative officer of the Rural Affairs team, and by Tony Lake and his wife. Vladimir and I had entered the foreign service in the same class as Tony, who had gone to Saigon a few months earlier to work in the embassy. As we stepped off that airplane into the swampy evening heat of Vietnam, it was good to see two familiar faces. Boynton immediately told us to take off our ties. "This is a shirtsleeves outfit," he said. "A can-do operation."

We were given an apartment in Saigon. Within two weeks of our arrival, at a nearby intersection, there occurred one of the seminal events of that year, indeed of the entire conflict: a Buddhist monk named Thich Quang Duc self-immolated to protest the regime of Ngo Dinh Diem. This was only the beginning of a series of events that would culminate with Diem's overthrow and assassination on 1 November 1963, an event that transformed the nature of our involvement in Vietnam.

Rural Affairs was an unorthodox, entrepreneurial organization run by a charismatic thirty-four-year-old American named Rufus Phillips. In the eyes of the two newest and youngest members of his team, Phillips was a mystery. A former army officer, he had been in Vietnam during the mid-1950s and had developed an exceptionally close relationship with Diem and his family. Rufus seemed to know all sorts of secrets, none of which he was about to share with a pair of very junior foreign service officers. He had been a young protégé of perhaps the most famous American operative in Southeast Asia, Col. Ed Lansdale, the model for Graham Greene's "Quiet American" and for Col. Edwin B. Hillandale in William Lederer and Eugene Burdick's bestseller, *The Ugly American*. Phillips was a large physical presence with an infectious, boyish grin. His slow Virginia drawl did not disguise his energy and quick mind. Rufus seemed to us the epitome of President Kennedy's new generation-a Yale man with military and intelligence experience, deeply committed to his job and absolutely convinced of the importance of improving the lives of the Vietnamese and defeating the Viet Cong.

I do not think Rufus knew what to do with us at first, so he made me an assistant to George Melvin, one of Rufe's regional field officers. A crusty old guy (he was in his early fifties, which seemed old to me at the time), Melvin had also served in Indo-China in the 1950s with the sainted Lansdale. From May to September 1963, I traveled all over the country with Melvin, assessing the pacification program. We went from the mangrove swamps of the Ca Mau Peninsula, where I saw my first casualties, to the highlands, where we drank fermented rice wine with Rhade tribesmen in a raised Montagnard lodge near Ban Me Thuot.

In the fall of 1963, a minor crisis in the lower Mekong Delta afforded me a unique opportunity. The province chief of Ba Xuyen, Lieutenant Colonel Chieu, and the American in charge of Rural Affairs, Bob Friedman, had gotten into an argument, and to show his anger at Chieu, Phillips had pulled Friedman out. Without realizing how "nervy" I was, I asked Phillips and Melvin to let me replace Friedman. I guess Phillips thought that it would be even more insulting to Chieu than leaving the post empty if he sent a twenty-two-year-old to Ba Xuyen. So he sent me there as the senior American civilian in the pacification program, and I became part of a triumvirate, administering American aid to the Strategic Hamlet Program in Ba Xuyen with Chieu and the Military Assistance and Advisory Group adviser, an army major named Peterson. Like I said, I was twenty-two.

Chieu must have been amused when I arrived in Soc Trang, the province capital. Looking now at old photographs, I realize how young I looked and was. We dispensed money, cement, cooking oil, roofing wheat, barbed wire, and various other goods to the villagers. We trained and armed the hamlet militia, paid to relocate families, tried to start self-help programs, built schools, and trained province officials. This was, I thought at the time, foreign aid at its very best—direct assistance to the people. I wondered why this program was considered so revolutionary; I had assumed that aid programs always worked this way, although in fact most aid was (and still is) highly programmatic and delivered through cumbersome systems. Rufus's group—the "shirtsleeves outfit"—bypassed all that and provided aid directly to the peasants.

At first, young and inexperienced, I was optimistic. I thought we were accomplishing something. But even then, I could see the difficulties we faced. On 8 November 1963, after only seven weeks in Soc Trang, I wrote to a friend back in Washington:

> I feel we've made some real progress in our programs. But it is very tough, and everything is immensely more difficult than it should be. . . . In the last two months, the Viet Cong have extended their control [throughout the Ca Mau Peninsula] and it's now beginning to look desperate to the south of here. In Ba Xuyen itself, however, there are areas where we can and do work. The southern part of this province is almost unmovable hell right now, and in every one of the eight districts there is a large number of VC units. Intelligence estimates for Ba Xuyen carry about 3000 armed hardcore VC. This must be added for a truer picture: while we claim that we control 61% of the population through the Strategic Hamlet Program, we concede to the VC control of over 50% of the land area, with over 135,000 people in it. That is quite a nice little base for the VC to operate within.

I soon learned that many areas in the Delta that Washington maps showed as under government control often were not. Sometimes when I asked Chieu to visit a particular hamlet or village that was shown on our official maps as Saigon-controlled, he would tell me that we could not go there until he got a battalion of troops to escort us. "Well then," I'd say, "it isn't very safe, is it?" The fact that the military was reporting most of these areas as under control puzzled me at first, and later it disturbed me deeply. We were deceiving ourselves, which would make formulating the right policy all the harder. It was my first glimpse of what was later called "the credibility gap."

"When one gets so deeply involved," I wrote in another letter, dated 11 December 1963, "one begins to hope for some sign of improvement, or at least some real commitment on the part of the Vietnamese. My job overseeing the AID program in Ba Xuyen puts me continually in the position of advocate of plans and projects that seek to make a reality out of the clichés that everyone pays lip service to. I don't mind this (actually enjoy it) but it is sometimes tiring to try to get the Vietnamese to do something which, after all, is for their own good (or so we think)."

The failures and inefficiencies of our pacification efforts in Ba Xuyen were not unique; they illustrated a wider problem throughout South Vietnam. Phillips, perhaps the most knowledgeable civilian official then in Vietnam, was rightly admired for his energy, optimism, and idealism. As Lansdale's protégé, he believed deeply in winning the hearts and minds of the people by building schools and health clinics, training, and other forms of tangible aid. But by the summer of 1963, Rufus began to see that what we were doing was not succeeding, particularly in the Delta.

He expressed his concern directly, and memorably, to President Kennedy in September 1963, when he accompanied a senior American diplomat, Joe Mendenhall, and Maj. Gen. Victor "Brute" Krulak back to Washington to brief the president and the National Security Council. Mendenhall's and Krulak's opinions on our progress in Vietnam could not have been more different—Mendenhall (an FSO and the former number two in the Saigon embassy) believed that the war effort was doomed politically if Diem remained in power, while Krulak (the Joint Chiefs special representative on counterinsurgency) said the war was being won militarily. Rufus directly challenged the military's reporting.

Back in Vietnam we heard only rumors and second-hand accounts of what had happened in Washington. But I now know that Rufus had growing doubts. He had lost confidence in Diem, to whom he had once been so close. Nhu turned on Rufus publicly, until Diem toned down the attacks. His frank assessment of the bleak situation—and the military's inability to report accurately—had poisoned his relationship with Military Assistance Command, Vietnam. By 1964, Rufus had gone back to Virginia for a career in business and politics. Rural Affairs went on under George Tanham and Sam Wilson. But it became more a bureaucracy than a crusade. We had seen the best of it. I soon went on to another, more routine assignment in the embassy.

In retrospect I think that what we were doing in Rural Affairs had little chance of success. Our efforts failed not for lack of effort or good intentions, but because our work was part of a larger policy that was fundamentally flawed. Our troubled policy was not apparent to me at the time, of course; I was young and loved my job. I did not discover until later that what we were doing was not working—success was elusive and, given the limitations on our policy and the weaknesses of the Saigon government, perhaps unachievable.

As a personal experience, however, my work in Rural Affairs was seminal.

It gave me an on-the-ground view of the opportunities and limitations of America's efforts in Vietnam and, by extension, elsewhere. My work in Vietnam shaped the rest of my career. I had started in 1963 at the lowest level of the American bureaucracy dispensing village tool kits and wheat. By the time I got to the Johnson White House in 1966 and the Paris Peace Talks with North Vietnam in 1968, my experience had given me a perspective that few of my colleagues had. In 1995, when I went to Dayton, Ohio, as chief negotiator in the talks that ended the war in Bosnia, Vietnam's lessons were still with me—and guided me enormously.

Vietnam's lessons remain with me. And I see still in memory many of my friends and colleagues from that time—Jay Ruoff, Bert Fraleigh, Frank Wisner, Earl Young, Dave Hudson, Oggie Williams, Bob Dunn, Harvey Neese, Col. Napoleon Valeriano, my Vietnamese assistant Duong, and the unforgettable Lt. Col. Charles T. R. Bohannan, U.S. Army (Ret.). Moreover, there were numerous Vietnamese who gave so much to this effort. Their side has received little notice and deserves attention. All of us, American and Vietnamese, surrounded Phillips, this dazzling, charismatic young man.

I will always be grateful for this experience.

Ambassador Richard Holbrooke

Contributors

Bert Fraleigh was born in Toronto, Ontario, in 1920. He graduated in sciences and civil engineering from the University of Alaska, Fairbanks. Fraleigh later served with the U.S. Army Engineers Department as a civilian and with the U.S. Navy in World War II. After the war, he rose to senior positions in American assistance programs, often advising national leaders in China, Taiwan, Hong Kong, Laos, South Vietnam, and the Philippines, and he had special assignments in Korea, Indonesia, and Okinawa. He was the last American official to leave China after the communist takeover in 1949, through the assistance of the future premier, Chou En-lai. For his work Fraleigh was nominated in 1957 for the State Department's Flemming Award for the ten outstanding men in federal service under age forty. After retiring in 1976 from federal service, Fraleigh entered the private sector and taught international business as a visiting professor at the Milwaukee School of Engineering, where he received his doctorate. Fraleigh speaks and writes Chinese fluently. His wife of nearly forty years, Jean, is a noted Chinese artist and art collector.

Hoang Lac was born in Nam Dinh, Vietnam, in 1927, and he graduated from the National Military Academy at Dalat in 1950. Until 1954, he served with Vietnamese units assigned to the French army, eventually becoming a regiment commander. After leaving the French army, he joined the Army of the Republic of Vietnam (ARVN), where he served as a regiment and division commander and as Inter-Arms Presidential Brigade commander. He also served as province chief of Kien Giang and as special commissioner of Military Region III and Saigon Capital Military District. From 1961 to 1963, he was the operational director for the Inter-Ministerial Committee of the Strategic Hamlet Program. He later became director general of reconstruction, a post he held until 1968, when he was promoted to brigadier general and appointed deputy minister of revolutionary development. In 1969, he became a major general and commander of Quang Trung National Military Training Center. From 1972 to 1975, he served as deputy commanding general of Military Region I. Lac is also the author of three books on the Vietnam War. He is married, has four children, and currently resides in Houston, Texas.

Lu Lan was born in 1926 in Quang Tri Province, in a village three kilometers south of the seventeenth parallel. He is a native of Trieu Phong District, where Le Duan, successor to Ho Chi Minh, was raised. In 1945, Lu Lan joined the Viet Minh in the League for the Independence of Vietnam, but he was discharged in 1947 by the provincial Resistance Committee for reasons of social class. He entered the National Military Academy at Dalat in 1950 and graduated a year later. When communist North Vietnam was established in 1954, he chose to remain in the anticommunist South. Three years later, Lu Lan attended the U.S. Military Command and General Staff College at Fort Leavenworth, Kansas. In 1958, he was appointed deputy chief of staff for operations and training of the ARVN Joint General Staff (J3), and from 1962 until 1966, Lu Lan was commanding general for three army divisions. From 1967 to 1973, Lu Lan held a number of important positions in the ARVN, including commandant general of the Command General Staff College; chief of Central Training Command, Saigon; commanding general, ARVN II Corps Tactical Zone; and inspector general of ARVN. In 1973, Lu Lan was the superintendent of the ARVN National Defense College in Saigon, a post he held until 1975, when he was admitted to the United States as a refugee. Ten years later he became a naturalized American citizen. He retired in 1995, after eighteen years of service to the State of Virginia.

Harvey Neese graduated from the University of Idaho in 1958 with a bachelor of science degree in agriculture and started work on a master's degree in animal husbandry. Halfway through the degree, he became tired of school and, by a freak turn of events, landed a volunteer position in South Vietnam in March 1959 with International Voluntary Services (IVS), one of the models for the Peace Corps. He spent some fourteen years in Southeast Asia, including about six years in South Vietnam and four years in Laos. He worked directly with the U.S. Operations Mission (USOM) in South Vietnam in the early 1960s and was later involved with a USOM project in Laos. He was in Laos in 1975, trying to locate a wild cattle species from northern Cambodia, when the Lao communists took over. He and his family escaped unharmed, crossing the Mekong River in a small boat with other escapees. In 1985, after years of consulting on agricultural projects around the world, Neese became field director and later director of the Post Harvest Institute for Perishables, an international agricultural institute at the University of Idaho that advises developing countries around the world. Neese lives in Troy, Idaho, with his wife, Winnie, originally from Singapore. They have two daughters, Delia Renee and Dena Sarita.

John O'Donnell was born in 1935 on a sugar plantation in Waialua, Hawaii. He graduated from Stanford University in 1956 with majors in economics and history. After college, he entered the U.S. Army and served in the Psychological Warfare Unit as an area studies specialist for Cambodia and Laos. Military assignments took him to the Philippines, Thailand, South Vietnam, and a six-month stint in Laos working with the Royal Lao army. Upon completion of his military service in 1959, he attended graduate school at the University of Hawaii then took a job in the private sector.

In October 1962, he joined the Agency for International Development (AID) as a provincial representative in South Vietnam. Subsequent AID assignments over a thirty-year foreign-service career included the following: rural development work in Peru; an assignment with the University of Hawaii Asia Training Center preparing AID personnel for field assignments in Southeast Asia; work with the U.S. counterinsurgency program in Thailand; senior-level positions in agriculture and rural development in Guatemala, Peru, and Ecuador; and management of worldwide technical planning and support services in AID's headquarters in Washington. He was appointed to AID's Senior Foreign Service in 1982 and retired in 1991. During his career, he was decorated by the governments of South Vietnam and Peru and received other honors from AID and the countries in which he served. Since retirement, he has worked part-time as a consultant to AID, primarily in Latin America, in a variety of program design and evaluation assignments. O'Donnell lives in Great Falls, Virginia, with his wife, Sharon, and two daughters, Erin and Meghan.

Rufus (Rufe) Phillips was born in Middletown, Ohio, in 1929 and raised in rural Virginia. He graduated from Yale in 1951 and attended the University of Virginia Law School, which he soon abandoned for an assignment with the Central Intelligence Agency (CIA). When a proposed assignment fell through, he enlisted in the U.S. Army. He graduated from Officers Candidate School at Fort Benning, Georgia, in fall 1953 as a second lieutenant, then attended paratrooper jump school, also at Fort Benning, and was assigned to Korea in spring 1954. Because of his paramilitary background and some proficiency in French, he was transferred to the U.S. Military Assistance Advisory Group in South

Vietnam and assigned to the semicovert Saigon Military Mission, under the already legendary Col. Edward G. Lansdale. He arrived in Saigon on 8 August 1954, just before the Geneva Accords went into effect. He remained in South Vietnam until 1956, when he went to Laos to help initiate a Lao government civic-action program. For his service as an adviser to the Saigon Military Mission in South Vietnam, he received the CIA's Medal of Merit.

In June 1962, AID in Washington asked him to evaluate the economic aid mission's role in the counterinsurgency efforts in South Vietnam. Based on his evaluation, the Office of Rural Affairs was created, along with a counterinsurgency program, and he was recruited to lead the office, which he directed until November 1963. From 1965 through 1968, while running his family's engineering consulting firm, he served as a consultant to the U.S. State Department on South Vietnam, spending about a month in Saigon each year assisting General Lansdale's belated mission. He also became a source for Vice-President Hubert Humphrey's views on South Vietnam. After a foray into politics in the 1970s, Phillips works today as an airport planning and design consultant. He resides in McLean, Virginia, with his wife, Barbara. They have two sons, two daughters, and three grandchildren.

George Tanham grew up in Tenafly, New Jersey. After graduating from Princeton University in 1943, he joined the U.S. Army and served in Europe during World War II. He was awarded the Silver Star twice, the Air Medal, and the Purple Heart. He was also awarded the croix de guerre by the French government. After the war, Tanham received a doctorate in history from Stanford University, and later became a tenured professor at the California Institute of Technology. In 1955, Tanham joined the RAND Corporation full time. The next year, RAND sent him to Paris to study the Viet Minh, who had just defeated the French in Indo-China. Tanham spent the next eight months poring through French records of the war, including some of the most highly classified documents. His report was eventually declassified and published, one of the first books on the subject of communist insurgency by an American.

In 1958, Tanham made his first trip to South Vietnam. In 1961, he served as the U.S. representative for a Southeast Asia Treaty Organization (SEATO) study on countersubversion in Southeast Asia, and he often visited South Vietnam for the Department of Defense. In 1964, Tanham was appointed associate director of USOM to South Vietnam, heading the Office of Rural Affairs. The next year, however, he resigned in protest of the USOM director's antirural development position and returned to RAND as deputy vice-president. In

1968, Tanham was appointed special assistant for counterinsurgency with the rank of minister to the American ambassador in Thailand. While in Thailand, he served as chairman and U.S. representative to a second SEATO study group on countersubversion. He returned to RAND in 1970, where he served for the next five years as both a corporate vice-president and vice-president of RAND's Project Air Force Division. He retired from RAND in 1982. Tanham has published several books on insurgency, and more recently, he has published two books on India. He is currently working on a study of Pakistani strategic thinking. He lives in Washington, D.C., and Strasburg, Virginia.

Tran Ngoc Chau was born in 1924 in the imperial capital city of Hue in Central Vietnam. In 1943, he joined the National Salvation Youth, a secret intelligence group organized by the Viet Minh to undermine the authority of both the French and the Japanese in Vietnam. In 1945, Chau joined the Liberation Army to fight the French colonialists. He left the Viet Minh in 1949 and offered his allegiance to the State of Vietnam. Soon after his defection, he joined the first class at the new National Military Academy and, after graduating, served briefly as an instructor and then as a battalion commander on the front line. After the war ended in 1954, Chau was appointed the first Vietnamese commandant of the Cadet Corps at the National Military Academy in Dalat. In 1956, he was in the first class of Vietnamese officers to graduate from advanced infantry training at Fort Benning, Georgia.

Chau became province chief of Kien Hoa in 1962, and soon thereafter he was promoted to lieutenant colonel. A year later, at the height of the Buddhist crisis, President Diem appointed him mayor of Da Nang and governor of the Quang Nam–Da Nang area. After the 1963 coup toppled the Diem government, he returned as province chief to Kien Hoa. In 1965, he was appointed national director of the Revolutionary Development Cadres and commandant of the training center in Vung Tau. He resigned in 1966, retired from the army, and returned to Kien Hoa Province, where he ran for a seat in the National Assembly and won by a large margin. He was then elected secretary general of the lower house of the National Assembly.

In 1968, Chau called for the recognition of the National Liberation Front, the political arm of the Viet Cong, as a first step toward negotiations with the communists. In February 1970, he was arrested by the Thieu government and charged with sedition. He spent four years in jail and was released just before the fall of Saigon to the communists. He was arrested again in 1975 and imprisoned by the communist government until late 1978. In February of the next

year, Chau escaped from Vietnam with his family by boat. After many
months in Malaysia and Indonesia, and with the help of American friends,
he came to the United States. In 1985, Chau took a job as a project manager with a small computer graphics company in Van Nuys, California. That
same year, he and his wife, plus six of their seven children, were granted
American citizenship.

Prelude to Tragedy

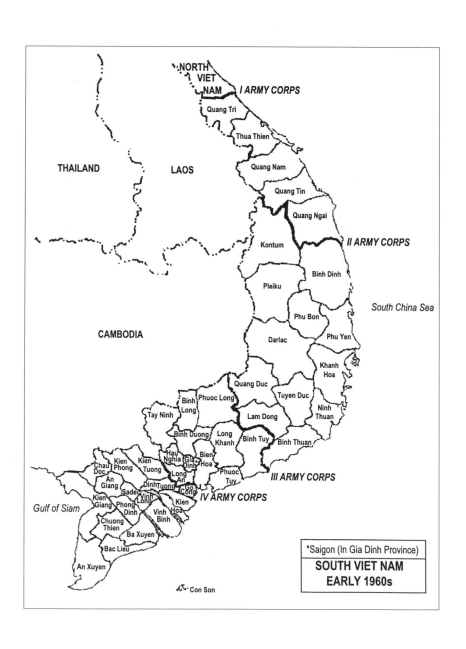

NORTH
VIET
NAM

I ARMY CORPS

Quang Tri

Thua Thien

THAILAND

LAOS

Quang Nam

Quang Tin

Quang Ngai

II ARMY CORPS

Kontum

Binh Dinh

Pleiku

South China Sea

Phu Bon

CAMBODIA

Darlac

Phu Yen

Khanh
Hoa

Quang Duc

Binh\Phuoc Long
Long

Tuyen Duc

Ninh
Thuan

Tay Ninh

Lam Dong

Binh Duong   Long   Binh Tuy   Binh Thuan
             Khanh

Hau\
Nghia\Gia   Bien
Kien\Phong   Kien   Dinh Hoa
Chau\   Tuong   Long\   Phuoc
Doc\   An   Dinh\Tuong   Tuy
         Giang\Sadec\   Go\   *III ARMY CORPS*
Kien\   Dinh   Cong
Giang\Phong   Vinh\   Kien   *IV ARMY CORPS*
        Dinh   Long\   Vinh\   Hoa
Chuong\   Binh
Thien

Gulf of Siam

Ba Xuyen

Bac Lieu

An Xuyen

🦅 Con Son

Saigon (In Gia Dinh Province)

**SOUTH VIET NAM
EARLY 1960s**

Introduction

In his account of U.S. involvement in South Vietnam, *In Retrospect: The Tragedy and Lessons of Vietnam,* former Secretary of Defense Robert McNamara acknowledges that the key decision makers at the highest levels of the U.S. government, including President Kennedy, Secretary of State Dean Rusk, McGeorge Bundy, the president's assistant for national security affairs, and Gen. Maxwell Taylor, chairman of the Joint Chiefs of Staff, were "setting policy for a region that was terra incognita."[1] He adds, "Our government lacked experts for us to consult to compensate for our ignorance."[2]

Given this admission, it is astonishing that this lack of knowledge did not stop McNamara and other top decision makers from blundering forward in their ignorance and hubris to create the debacle that we came to know as the Vietnam War. The sad truth is that in the initial stages of U.S. involvement in South Vietnam in the early 1960s, there were many individuals with experience in Asia and in dealing with communist revolutionary warfare who were not consulted or whose advice was ignored or dismissed.

One of America's most knowledgeable experts on communist insurgency in Southeast Asia and how to deal with it was Maj. Gen. Edward Lansdale, who occupied a key position in the Pentagon when McNamara became secretary of defense. Lansdale had earlier been the principal adviser to President Magsaysay during the insurgency by the communist Huks in the Philippines in the early 1950s and to President Ngo Dinh Diem during his successful struggle to keep South Vietnam free and stable after the 1954 Geneva Accords.

In 1961, at the beginning of his administration, President Kennedy was so impressed by Lansdale's grasp of the situation in South Vietnam that he wanted to send him there as ambassador.[3] Unfortunately, Rusk blocked Lansdale's appointment because of his own uneasiness and because of firmly entrenched opposition in the State Department and elsewhere.[4] During the same period,

1

before the United States became deeply involved, Lansdale made a special effort to try to explain the situation in South Vietnam and the communist insurgency to McNamara, who, with his mind set against concepts that couldn't be reduced to numbers, refused to listen. In his book, McNamara dismisses Lansdale with the comment that he "was relatively junior and lacked broad geopolitical expertise."[5] In fact, Lansdale was light-years ahead of McNamara in understanding Southeast Asia and communist revolutionary warfare.[6] There were others, including some of the authors of this account.

This book brings together the firsthand accounts of eight individuals, Americans and Vietnamese, who were intimately engaged in counterinsurgency operations in South Vietnam at the national, provincial, and village levels at the beginning of the increased U.S. involvement in that country in the early 1960s. During this period, fateful decisions were made that led the United States and South Vietnam down the slippery slope to shameful defeat in 1975.

In this early period, there were knowledgeable people who, if heeded, and effective Vietnamese–U.S. programs that, if supported, might have led to a very different turn of events in South Vietnam. We believe that if U.S. decision makers had sought and followed the advice of experts like General Lansdale and others who are represented by the contributing writers of this book, then the Buddhist crisis, the coup against President Diem, the subsequent disintegration of the Vietnamese government at all levels, and the massive introduction of U.S. combat troops, beginning in 1965, might never have taken place. The real tragedy of the Vietnam War is that it *didn't have to happen.*

This account is restricted to the early 1960s and does not address the many military and political issues that flowed from the decision to commit U.S. combat troops in 1965. These issues are the subject of many other books. Our intention is to shed light on what happened in the early days of the U.S. participation in South Vietnam that led to our becoming engaged on the losing end of an unpopular land war in Asia.

A brief chronology of key events in the early 1960s will help to provide the context for the personal accounts that follow.[7] As President Eisenhower left office in 1961, he warned incoming President Kennedy that Laos was the key problem area in Southeast Asia, and he did not mention South Vietnam. Shortly after his inauguration, Kennedy was made aware of the seriousness of the problems in South Vietnam in a lengthy memo that had been prepared by Lansdale, then a brigadier general, who had just returned from a visit to the area.[8]

Kennedy's attention was then diverted for a time by events in Cuba (the Bay of Pigs fiasco in April 1961) and Laos (the Geneva Convention in May 1960), but in October 1961, Kennedy dispatched Gen. Maxwell Taylor and Deputy

Special Assistant for National Security Affairs Walt Rostow to South Vietnam to provide him with an assessment of the situation there.

Based on the information he received from the Taylor-Rostow report, Kennedy authorized a substantial increase in U.S. assistance to the Diem administration, including the assignment of U.S. military advisers down to the sector (provincial) level.[9] In February 1962, the U.S. Military Assistance Advisory Group (MAAG) in South Vietnam was upgraded to the U.S. Military Assistance Command, Vietnam (MACV), and by mid-1962, the number of American military advisers in country had been increased from seven hundred to twelve thousand.

On 17 April 1962, the Vietnamese government established the Strategic Hamlet Program as the principal vehicle for dealing with the Viet Cong (Vietnamese communists) insurgent threat in the rural areas. Based on the recommendations of Rufus Phillips and Bert Fraleigh in July 1962, the U.S. Operations Mission (USOM) established the Office of Rural Affairs (RA) to provide material and advisory assistance to the Strategic Hamlet Program, assigning USOM provincial representatives to work with province chiefs and U.S. military sector advisers in carrying out the counterinsurgency program in each of South Vietnam's forty-plus provinces.

Progress was made against the Viet Cong in late 1962 and early 1963 as Vietnamese and American efforts were concentrated on implementing the Strategic Hamlet Program. In May 1963, South Vietnamese troops and police fired on Buddhist demonstrators in the city of Hue, precipitating the Buddhist crisis that became the dominant preoccupation of both the U.S. and the Vietnamese governments in the ensuing months, capped by the attack on Buddhist temples by forces controlled by Ngo Dinh Nhu on 21 August 1963.

These moves by the Diem administration enraged the Buddhists and many in the South Vietnamese military. A plot of a coup d'état against President Diem was started by a group of Vietnamese generals and supported by Ambassador Henry Cabot Lodge, who had arrived in Saigon the day after the attack on the Buddhist temples. After much communication back and forth between Saigon coup plotters and Washington, with some false starts, the coup was launched on 1 November 1963. President Diem and his brother Nhu were captured and assassinated by Vietnamese army forces the next day. The triumvirate of Generals Duong Van Minh, Tran Van Don, and Le Van Kim assumed power but was not able to govern effectively and was ousted in a coup by Gen. Nguyen Khanh on 30 January 1964.

As a result of the fall of Diem and the subsequent failure of the military triumvirate, the government apparatus in Saigon and in the provinces was in total disarray. The Viet Cong took advantage of the chaos and struck hard against the Strategic Hamlet Program in the rural areas. After a U.S. Navy incident with North Vietnamese patrol boats in the Gulf of Tonkin on 2 August 1964, Congress passed a resolution on 7 August giving President Johnson extraordinary powers to act in Southeast Asia. After a series of Viet Cong attacks on U.S. installations in early 1965, the United States sent the first combat troops (two marine battalions) to South Vietnam on 8 March 1965. By December, the U.S. troop strength had reached almost two hundred thousand.[10]

In revisiting the period from the 1961 decision to commit increased U.S. assistance to President Diem's beleaguered government until the introduction of U.S. combat troops in early 1965, we have assembled the personal accounts of five Americans and three Vietnamese who lived through those turbulent times. They are representative of a much larger group, Americans and Vietnamese, who worked in South Vietnam before and during the early 1960s. This is a story of their struggles, successes, and frustrations as they worked to promote security, democracy, and development to thwart a clever and determined enemy. At the national level, Rufus (Rufe) Phillips and Bert Fraleigh, and later George Tanham, led the Office of Rural Affairs in the American economic aid mission. Col. (later Maj. Gen.) Hoang Lac was the principal Vietnamese staff officer for the Strategic Hamlet Program. They worked closely together to carry out the Vietnamese government's counterinsurgency efforts in the early 1960s.

Col. (later Lt. Gen.) Lu Lan held the critical position of deputy chief of staff for operations and training at the Army of the Republic of Vietnam (ARVN) Joint General Staff in early 1958. This was when U.S. high-level military brass overruled the objections of experienced Vietnamese officers like Lu Lan, who had fought both with and against the Viet Minh, to make the Vietnamese army a mirror image of conventional U.S. military forces. Vietnamese army efforts were then focused on search-and-destroy operations rather than on protection of the civilian population.

In the upper Mekong Delta, in Kien Hoa Province that was riddled with Viet Cong supporters, Lt. Col. Tran Ngoc Chau, supported by USOM Rural Affairs Provincial Representative John O'Donnell, led an imaginative and aggressive counterinsurgency campaign. These efforts brought large segments of the rural population over to the side of the Vietnamese government and served as the prototype for pacification programs elsewhere.

At the village level, Harvey Neese, a former volunteer for International Voluntary Services, a nonprofit, private organization, worked with the rural population throughout South Vietnam. He helped bring real economic progress to the grassroots level through a nationwide pig-and-corn program and other village-level projects. The common thread, running through these personal accounts, is an appreciation of the complexities of South Vietnam and the principles and practicalities of grassroots political and economic development and security. Unfortunately, the knowledge, experience, and advice of these individuals and others like them were not sought by U.S. policymakers or were dismissed or discredited when offered.

The real lesson of South Vietnam was the absolute necessity of identifying knowledgeable, experienced, and motivated individuals on both the Vietnamese and the U.S. sides. The next important step was to use them and their understanding of Vietnam and communist revolutionary warfare to shape and implement an effective counterinsurgency strategy that recognized the primacy of political, psychological, and economic considerations in winning the support of the rural population. A corollary lesson was that this strategy could not be implemented effectively by a massive U.S. bureaucracy. To be successful, it had to be done on a direct advisory and supportive basis, using a relatively small number of skilled and knowledgeable Americans working in partnership with the Vietnamese. In such a strategy, the military had a critical role to play in protecting the villagers against attack by the insurgents. Unfortunately, this was too often a weak link in the early counterinsurgency program.

Earlier counterinsurgency efforts in the Philippines and Malaya, which applied many of these same principles, had been successful. We believe that if the United States had pursued a strategy similar to the one it employed in the Philippines in the early 1950s (similar to the approach used by the British in Malaya in the 1950s) and had assigned a small advisory group headed by a proven leader such as Ed Lansdale to work with President Diem starting in 1961, the Vietnamese government would have had a reasonable chance of containing and perhaps defeating the communist insurgency in the South without the commitment of U.S. combat troops.

If McNamara and other high-level policymakers had understood and followed such a strategy, rather than conventionally militarize and Americanize the struggle as they did, the events that followed might have been very different.

Notes

1. Robert McNamara, *In Retrospect: The Tragedy and Lessons of Vietnam* (New York: Times Books, 1995), 32.
2. Ibid.
3. See William J. Rust, *Kennedy in Vietnam* (New York: Charles Scribner & Sons, 1985), 26, 27.

4. See Cecil B. Currey, *Edward Lansdale: The Unquiet American* (Boston: Houghton Mifflin, 1988), 228; see also Rust, *Kennedy in Vietnam*, 27.

5. McNamara, *In Retrospect*, 32.

6. The following quote, from a memorandum from the deputy special assistant for national security affairs (Walt Rostow) to the president dated 6 December 1961, gives an idea of the high regard in which Lansdale was held in some quarters: "A final direct word from me on South Viet Nam as a member of your personal staff. . . . it is crucial that we free Ed Lansdale from his present assignment and get him out to the field in an appropriate position. He is a unique national asset in the Saigon setting; and I cannot believe that anything he may be able to do in his present assignment [working on Cuba] could match his value in Southeast Asia. On this matter you may have to have a word with the Attorney General [Robert Kennedy, who was directing the administration efforts against Castro]." See U.S. Department of State, *The Foreign Relations of the United States, 1961–1963*, vol. 1, *Vietnam, 1961* (Washington, D.C.: U.S. Government Printing Office, 1988), 719.

7. The information in the chronology of events that follows is taken largely from the "Chronology," which appears in Stanley Karnow, *Vietnam: A History* (New York: Viking, 1983), 678–80.

8. See U.S. Department of Defense, *United States—Vietnam Relations, 1945–1967*, book 11 (Washington, D.C.: U.S. Government Printing Office, 1971), 1–12 for the text of the 17 January 1961 memorandum from General Lansdale to Secretary of Defense Thomas S. Gates Jr. following Lansdale's visit to South Vietnam from 2 to 14 January 1961. In the report, Lansdale recommends that "the U.S. should recognize that Vietnam is in a critical condition and should treat it as a combat area of the cold war, as an area requiring emergency treatment." In a memorandum from McGeorge Bundy to Dulles, Rusk, and McNamara inviting them to a meeting with President Kennedy on 27 January 1961, Bundy reported that the meeting was called to discuss Cuba and Vietnam, the latter because of the president's "keen interest in General Lansdale's recent report and his awareness of the high importance of this country." See *The Foreign Relations of the United States, 1961–1963*, vol. 1, *Vietnam, 1961*, 13.

9. See *The Foreign Relations of the United States, 1961–1963*, vol. 1, *Vietnam, 1961*, 477–532 for the text of the Taylor Mission Report.

10. See also the appendix, "America's Involvement in Vietnam," for a brief overview of events in Vietnam before 1961.

Before We Lost in South Vietnam

Rufe Phillips

"Did you two gentlemen go to the same country?"
> Question by President Kennedy after a National Security Council briefing attended by Rufe Phillips on 12 September 1963, to two officials, one civilian, the other military, who had just returned from a fact-finding trip to South Vietnam

You could say that I grew up in South Vietnam, not from boyhood to the age of maturity, which was then twenty-one, but for that crucial middle-twenties and early thirties period when you really grow up. I first came to Vietnam in uniform, a green second lieutenant, fresh out of infantry Officers Candidate School and paratrooper jump school, with a brief stay in Korea.

It was 8 August 1954, three days before the Geneva Accords went into effect (the division of Vietnam into North and South) and two days before my twenty-fifth birthday. I arrived in Saigon to become a member of what was known as the Saigon Military Mission, headed by Col. Edward G. Lansdale. I was there first as a military officer detailed to the Central Intelligence Agency (CIA) and then as a civilian, with a couple of years in Laos. In 1959, I left government service and joined my father in a private engineering business.

In 1962, I was called back into service by the Kennedy administration, this time as director of Rural Affairs in the United States Operations Mission (USOM) in Saigon, America's foreign aid agency. I was sent to Saigon to reorganize the U.S. assistance program and get it involved in supporting the counterinsurgency struggle of the South Vietnamese. I stayed in South Vietnam until my father died of cancer and President Ngo Dinh Diem was assassinated in November 1963, when I returned home with my wife, Barbara, and our two small children to take over the family business. I continued as a consultant to the U.S. State Department, and in 1965, 1966, and 1967 I returned to South Vietnam for brief periods to try to help the ill-fated Lansdale Mission, which was assigned to the American embassy in Saigon. I last visited South Vietnam in 1968, just before Lansdale returned to the United States.

I was twenty-four when I arrived and thirty-nine when I left Saigon for the last time. Now, more than forty years after I first breathed the pungent air of Saigon and traveled down those Mekong Delta canals that stretch over the horizon, what occurred there is just as vivid in my mind as if it had all happened yesterday. How was it to have devoted the largest share of fourteen years of your life to trying to help a people save themselves and their country from the scourge that was communism? That is the question people might ask. I can say that it was often inspiring, sometimes rewarding, but in the end deeply discouraging and frustrating because the effort failed.

It is my deeply held belief that it need not have failed had we helped the Vietnamese in the right way, a way that many at the working level in South Vietnam understood but that never got a significant hearing higher up. There seemed to be willful ignorance and an almost boundless arrogance on the part of too much of America's leadership. And the farther away from Saigon you were, the worse it got. But it was all too prevalent at the upper levels in Saigon as well.

No one personified these qualities more in the 1960s than Secretary of Defense Robert McNamara. Reading his book, *In Retrospect: The Tragedy and Lessons of Vietnam,* brought back to mind my experiences in South Vietnam and my encounters, one might say confrontations, with him and with others often as ignorant but usually not as arrogant.

The successful approach to helping the South Vietnamese build a nation while confronting communist subversion in the early 1954 to 1956 days became increasingly marginalized as time went on. That approach had three main thrusts: political, military, and economic-social. And there was another important characteristic of the earlier American approach to working with the Vietnamese—informed and imaginative persuasion based on mutual trust rather than dictation.

What happened afterward politically was perhaps best characterized by Dan Van Sung, a Vietnamese journalist and member of the Front for Democratization, which had been formed in Saigon in the early 1960s. He said, "The anti-communist fight in Viet Nam is seventy-five percent political and twenty-five percent military. Yet everything American is directed to the twenty-five percent." "The way out," he said, "is not by an abandonment [by the Americans] but, on the contrary, by going deep into every local revolutionary problem and helping solve them using principles of justice and freedom, perhaps infusing them with the revolutionary spirit of 1776 from which the United States herself was born and developed." The United States, he went on to say, seemed to know how to fight communism, "only with bombs and dollars," and, "instead of assuming the role of leader," we had become "a mere purveyor of means."

What happened militarily was most clearly expressed by Father Nguyen Loc Hoa, a Vietnamese priest of Chinese origin, when he received the Magsaysay award, Asia's Nobel Prize, in 1964 for "his extraordinary valor in defense of freedom, strengthening among a beleaguered people the resolution to resist tyranny." With civilian volunteers recruited off the streets of Saigon, he had started a hamlet and created a secure area in the most insecure part of South Vietnam, Ca Mau.

Father Hoa began by asking, "Why are we not winning in Vietnam? My answer is simple. The misplacement of the order of importance. The Magsaysay way is winning the people first, winning the war second. I am afraid that in South Vietnam today the order is reversed. Weapons are important. Fighting is necessary to protect the people from being physically harmed by the communists. Our offense must rely solely on winning the people, because as soon as the people understand what communism means, and as soon as they have faith in our ability to protect them, and as soon as they have confidence in our integrity, the battle is won." He then went on to say, "When fought as a conventional war, we really have no chance to win. How can we expect a young man to fight for us when his aged father was killed by artillery fire? . . . How can we claim to be with the people when we burn their homes simply because those houses happen to be in communist controlled territory?"

In 1962, a social and economic effort was initiated in the rural areas by the Vietnamese and a small group of Americans in the economic aid mission, or USOM, with help from American civilian and military advisers in the provinces. How the effort was handled on a low-key basis of mutual trust with the Vietnamese and how it was succeeding are described in this and other contributions to this book. However, this effort never received the political underpinning or the military support that was needed.

Saigon Snake Pit—1954

The period from 1954 to 1956 has received little in-depth historical attention, being regarded mainly as a time in which America deepened its commitments, tied its fortunes to President Ngo Dinh Diem, and carried out covert activities in the North in contradiction to the Geneva Accords. The covert activities were highlighted in the *Pentagon Papers* as significant, but to those of us who were the actors on the ground during those years, the attempt to make things difficult for the North Vietnamese was a sideshow to the birth of an independent South Vietnam. The fact that it received so much attention in the *Pentagon Papers* only confirmed the made-in-Washington viewpoint of the Pentagon "whiz kids" who had compiled them.

A brief recounting of events will set the scene for 1954 and the beginning of the U.S. Saigon Military Mission. After Dien Bien Phu fell to the communists on 7 May 1954 and the Geneva Conference opened the next day, the noncommunist Vietnamese government resigned. Ngo Dinh Diem, who came from a prominent Central Vietnam mandarin family, was the only noncommunist leader left with the impeccable credentials of having never cooperated with the French, whom the communists and nationalists were trying to drive from Vietnam. His elder brother, Khoi, had been killed by the communists in 1945 in their campaign to eliminate rival nationalist leaders. Diem was captured by Ho Chi Minh in that same year, and after a face-to-face confrontation in which he refused to join the Viet Minh, he escaped. Assassins were subsequently dispatched to find him, but he had fled to a Montagnard village (Montagnards live in the mountainous areas of South and North Vietnam but ethnically are from Indonesian stock), thus escaping death by a hair.

On 20 and 21 July, which ironically followed France's Bastille Day by just a few days, the Geneva Accords were signed, cutting Vietnam into North and South. The South Vietnamese had walked out in bitterness and shame. On 7 July, Ngo Dinh Diem was appointed prime minister of South Vietnam by Emperor Bao Dai with full powers as a last gesture to Vietnamese nationalism in what was universally thought to be a losing cause.

Diem arrived in Saigon in early July. He found that the French were still occupying the Governor General's Palace and that the Palace Guard was under hostile control of the Binh Xuyen, a gangster sect. Bao Dai, whiling away his time on the French Riviera but needing funds, had sold control of the National Police and hence of Saigon to the Binh Xuyen a year before for the equivalent of several million dollars. The Binh Xuyen consequently controlled all gambling, prostitution, and opium trade in what was a wide-open city.

In this atmosphere, a series of serious challenges to Diem arose from every quarter of a fractious society in despair over losing half the country while still trying to emerge from eighty years of French "divide-and-rule" colonialism. The South Vietnamese government existed in name only, a collection of French-trained civil servants sitting in their offices waiting for French orders that no longer came, while the army was a disorganized mob, with whole units deserting in the North and finding their way back to their home villages in the South.

A Vietnamese air force officer, Nguyen Van Hinh, who was at the same time the Vietnamese armed forces chief of staff and a French citizen with the rank of general in the French Air Force, began busily plotting a coup against Diem shortly after Diem's arrival. As time went on, it was clear that the coup attempt had the support of, and was even instigated by, some of the French colonial office diehards who remained in Saigon. During that period, two powerful religious sects, the Cao Dai and the Hoa Hao, began to believe that their armed "fiefdoms," which the French had helped create, might be threatened by Diem's known incorruptibility, a characteristic of Diem that was even more threatening to the Binh Xuyen.

Few gave the South more than six months to survive; it was supposed to collapse into anarchy. One of my first assignments was to try to obtain some medical kits from the U.S. assistance mission to give to a psychological-warfare company of the Vietnamese army for distribution in the countryside. I was told by an American official that it was useless to give the kits to the Vietnamese army because they were sure to fall into communist hands in a few months.

It was into this snake pit that Colonel Lansdale and the handful of Americans who made up his team began their work. There were about ten of us in the initial group that constituted what was called the Saigon Military Mission, as distinct from the regular CIA station. Nearly all of us had military or paramilitary backgrounds, and only one had any previous experience in Vietnam. Our group, while headed by Lansdale as an Air Force officer, was officially assigned to the U.S. Military Assistance Advisory Group MAAG under Gen. John T. (Iron Mike) O'Daniel.

I was so inexperienced about what I could do to be useful that it took some time for me to realize what a privilege it was to work for Lansdale, the most imaginative and able American who ever tried to help the Vietnamese, or to understand what he really wanted me to do. I remember another team member, perplexed like the rest of us, asking Lansdale one day what our mission was, to which he replied with deceptive simplicity, "Find out what the Vietnamese people want and then help them get it."

Before coming to Vietnam, Lansdale had helped the Filipinos defeat the communist Huks. He assisted President Magsaysay in developing his pacification

Ed Lansdale *(left)*, America's best-known counterinsurgency expert, chats with Lou Conein, CIA operative and Southeast Asia specialist, in Saigon, 1956. *Ogden Williams*

approach of "all-out friendship or all-out force" toward the Huks, while at the same time making Philippine democracy work by ensuring honest elections. Lansdale was sent to Saigon at the beginning of June 1954 by Allen Dulles, head of the CIA, with the full blessing of his brother, Foster, then secretary of state, and Admiral Radford, chairman of the Joint Chiefs of Staff (JCS). Lansdale's official orders were brief, encapsulated in a one-sentence message, "Save South Viet Nam," and ending with a cryptic and unusual, "God bless you."[1]

Working with Colonel Lansdale

I met Lansdale when he came to a hotel room at the Hotel Majestic on Saigon's waterfront to brief his staff about a week after we had landed. We had been put up there temporarily because there was nowhere else to stay. I knew next to nothing about him, except for vague reports from some of the team who had been assigned from Washington that he had achieved miracles in the Philippines.

He came into the room quietly, asking us to sit on the twin beds and the few available chairs. He was forty-six years old, of medium height and build, and dressed in khaki shorts, kneesocks, a short-sleeved uniform shirt, and an Air Force officer's hat worn at a slight rakish angle. I noticed a high forehead, penetrating eyes, a throat with a prominent Adam's apple, and a clipped mustache. He was military in manner but had a jaunty air. His pattern of speech was informal. He spoke in a characteristically soft voice that radiated warmth and confidence. There was an easy and collegial style about him.

I remember him raising his voice slightly to be heard over the "swopping" sound of the ceiling fan that kept the heat and humidity marginally bearable. Our mission, he said, was to help save South Vietnam. The stakes were high and the odds difficult. He said that the situation was very fluid, that he would move us into more permanent housing as soon as possible, and that he would be interviewing us individually for specific assignments but had no precise timetable. He radiated determination that generated confidence, but at the same time it was clear that he had not yet quite figured out how to use us. He left me with a mixture of confusion and hope that I might make a difference. Doing what, I knew not. Under Lansdale, I gradually learned how a people-first struggle against the communists could really work and how it was the only way a country might defeat a so-called communist people's war. Lansdale had a low-key way of listening to the South Vietnamese and feeding their own ideas back to them in the form of suggestions for action that were practical but that built popular support. It was clear that he was there to help them without thinking of himself or his career, and it became clear that he was willing to risk that career for them if necessary.

I also learned how to listen to and work with the Vietnamese, not as an outsider but as a compatriot they came to trust. I was moved by their patriotism and their passion for their country, feelings I took for granted about my own. I came to understand that the freedom and the sense of well-being that I enjoyed as an American was not a gift but a privilege to be fought for and to be shared. I came to believe that freedom was truly indivisible. My convictions deepened as I got to know the many Filipino volunteers who were also there to help the South Vietnamese. I had the privilege of meeting their president, Ramon Magsaysay, who personified a democratic government that Filipinos were willing to risk their lives for. They understood that what came first for him was them, the Filipino people, not himself. This was the Magsaysay spirit. It permeated the Filipinos I knew, and I shared Lansdale's conviction that it could help set a fire within the Vietnamese.

Lansdale wanted the Magsaysay spirit to spread to South Vietnam, and it did. How it happened is recounted accurately in Lansdale's book, *In the Midst of Wars*. What really made a difference in the turn of events was Lansdale's political advice to President Diem and his good offices as a catalyst and intermediary to help the Vietnamese nationalists unite. To that point, all Vietnamese political experience had been underground, against the French and against the communists. There was little trust among nationalist groups, even though they shared the same aspirations.

It was also Lansdale's willingness to stick his neck out by reporting the facts about the miniwar in Saigon in April 1955, which had been started by the Binh Xuyen. This struggle eventually engulfed dissident elements of the Cao Dai and Hoa Hao as well, but it was won by the Vietnamese army with popular support. By reporting the facts, Lansdale defied a mistaken American ambassador, Gen. Lawton Collins, and the embassy staff who wanted to abandon Diem and give in to the sects. The Vietnamese understood that what was really at stake was their final independence from the French, who were so obviously behind the sect rebellion. They also came to understand that Lansdale was willing to risk not only his career but also, if necessary, his life for their cause. In the process, Lansdale and his team became brothers-in-arms with the Vietnamese.

Lansdale and his team, acting as a catalyst, spurred Vietnamese government actions that successfully resettled almost a million refugees who had fled the North, demobilized and took care of veterans, reoccupied and pacified vast territories that the communists had ruled for nine years, moved the government out into the villages, and laid the foundations for democratic self-government.

Pacification-Reoccupation

I became involved in a cause much larger than myself. In a very short time for a very junior officer, I was given significant responsibilities. In late 1954, I helped draft a National Security Action Policy for Diem to proclaim, which set up the framework for the Vietnamese government to reoccupy and pacify vast areas of South Vietnam. These areas had long been under communist control but had to be evacuated by them in compliance with the Geneva Accords.

Beginning early in 1955, I was the only American liaison with a Vietnamese army force that reoccupied the Ca Mau Peninsula at the very tip of South Vietnam, as the communist Viet Minh evacuated their troops from that area to the North and the French evacuated Hanoi. Then in early April, I became the only American adviser to a two-division-sized Vietnamese army reoccupation and pacification of the Viet Minh–controlled Interzone V in Central Vietnam. (Historically, Central Vietnam was a distinct region of unified Vietnam. Central Vietnam in this book refers to the northern sector of South Vietnam.) Interzone V had been occupied and controlled by the communists for nine years and covered most of Quang Ngai and all of Binh Dinh Provinces to the south of Hue. Interzone V was the last stronghold of the communists to be turned over to the fledgling South Vietnamese government. At the same time, the French evacuated their last outpost in the North, the port of Haiphong.

Looking back, I can see clearly that this came about not because I was some kind of boy genius, far from it, but because the Vietnamese trusted me as a friend who had learned how to work with them as an equal, not as a superior, and who wanted only to help them help their own people. At one point in 1955, my presence as the only adviser with the Vietnamese army in its reoccupation operations was challenged by the French members of the Joint Military Mission of which I was a part. (The Joint Mission had been formed in late 1954 in the hopes that the Americans and the French could work together to advise and support the Vietnamese armed forces.) The French asked the Vietnamese to accept a French liaison officer and were told by the Vietnamese that they didn't want any foreigners along. When the French objected, saying, "But Phillips is not Vietnamese," the Vietnamese replied, "Yes, but he's our friend."

In later years, I would recount how the Vietnamese under Col. Le Van Kim had so trained their two army divisions for the reoccupation of Interzone V in Quang Ngai and Binh Dinh that there was not a single incident between the thousands of soldiers and civilians who had come in contact with one another as the occupation moved southward for a month. I remember seeing how hesitant people were at first to have any contact with the Vietnamese soldiers, conditioned as they were by Viet Minh propaganda about how they would be pillaged and raped. Then I watched in amazement as the operation progressed farther south and how the people began coming out of their houses and voluntarily giving the soldiers water while vocally cheering them on. Few would believe it.

Just two weeks after the reoccupation was complete, President Diem visited Qui Nhon in Binh Dinh Province at the southern end of the Interzone in Central Vietnam and received a tremendous welcome. This was the payoff for the work I had done in drawing up, together with the Vietnamese, the rigorous indoctrination course in troop behavior and civic action that had been given to the soldiers who participated in the operation. Colonel Kim and I became lifelong friends as a result of our working together on that operation.

This was the spirit in which we worked at the time, and most of what we and the Vietnamese tried went right. Then the country south of the seventeenth parallel achieved full independence when the French forces, which had been regrouped from north to south, finally departed in early summer 1955.

Much more important to the Vietnamese psyche than Diem's consolidation of power during this time was his taking over assumption of the mantle of Vietnamese nationalism from Ho Chi Minh by ridding South Vietnam of the last

vestiges of French colonialism. Nationalism, which had sustained the com-
munist-run Viet Minh against the French, was no longer their exclusive
property. By opposing and defeating the attempted takeover by the sects that
had overt French backing, Diem received both credit and immense popular
support. His platform had always been independence and nationalism. His
government had no taint of collaboration with French colonialism. Ho Chi
Minh had been responsible for the French leaving half the country, the North,
but Diem had gotten them all the way out. Thus, out of the post-Geneva chaos
in the South, Diem emerged as a formidable rival, while the North became
mired in a drastic Stalinist land-reform purge of even the smallest village
landowners. By 1956, this had sparked serious peasant revolts in the North.

Working with Diem and Fellow Americans

Diem's main limitations were his essentially reclusive personality and his lack
of experience in anything but the underground politics of resistance against
the French and the Viet Minh. Diem needed advice in developing a political cause beyond nationalism that could capture the imagination and loyalty
of the Vietnamese people.[2] That cause was democracy, in which Diem
believed in the abstract but about which he knew little in practice. Lansdale tried to help him and might have succeeded had he not been frustrated
by our own policymaking establishment. As time passed, Lansdale was no
longer on the scene, and there was much less understanding and trust from
the more formal American side. Diem began to rely more and more on his
family, particularly his brother Nhu, with the result that his approach became
more and more authoritarian.

As Diem emerged, so did a conflict among the Americans that proved more
basic and long-lasting than I perceived at the time. It originated in Saigon but
was echoed in Washington, and it grew until it became an embedded disconnect between reality in South Vietnam and its true needs and the perceptions
of the policymakers.

As the conflict began, arrayed on one side were the few who had actually
participated in defeating a communist insurgency, using democracy as a
weapon; these Americans had unconventional ideas of what to do and had an
understanding of the Vietnamese that was deep and sincere enough to earn
their trust. On the other side were the many whose experience and outlook
were limited to ordinary diplomacy and to conventional military and intelligence operations; it was often a measure of their mettle if they were seen as
imposing their ideas on the Vietnamese, and for them, bureaucratic preroga-
tives were of prime importance.

As the Vietnamese listened to, and trusted, Lansdale and his team, personal jealousies intensified this conflict on the American side. Added in the balance, at the Washington level, were those caught up in the hubris of their own infallibility as part of the importance of their past or present prestigious positions. After all, a McNamara must have thought that if he could run Ford Motor Company he could certainly tell the Vietnamese what to do. For Ambassador Henry Cabot Lodge, after persuading Eisenhower to run for president, telling the Vietnamese what to do politically was a piece of cake. Then there were those who fancied themselves practitioners of realpolitik, convinced that events and people in South Vietnam could be manipulated as part of a larger, geopolitical strategy. And there was a legion of those who played games of self-advancement and bureaucratic self-protection at all levels.

These American internal conflicts would persist with disastrous effects. Because of his unique insights and relationships with the Vietnamese, Lansdale became classified as a lone wolf, not a team player. Too often the so-called team was ignorant and wrong. With McNamara, the hubris of wrongheadedness and the disconnect with Vietnamese reality reached its apogee.[3]

American Mistakes with President Diem

There was a real opening in 1955 and 1956 for the establishment of democratic institutions had the United States possessed the understanding and the will to insist when Diem was most open to advice. Few Americans understood then that there would be a continuing struggle for popular allegiance in the South and that democracy was the indispensable cause if the communists were to be successfully resisted. This was Lansdale's principal thesis. He tried to focus policy behind that idea and to prevent mistakes, but there were two key policy issues on which he was overruled.

The constitution adopted by South Vietnam in 1956, with prospects for democratic growth, was a particular Lansdale goal. He was way ahead of his time, believing that the only way communism could be defeated was by offering the Vietnamese people something better, democracy. He understood the limitations of Diem's personality, so he wanted to put Diem within a constitutional framework that would oblige him to learn how to govern democratically.

Lansdale had arranged for a Filipino constitutional lawyer, Johnny Orendine, to help Diem draft a constitution. The original draft incorporated an independent judiciary, as well as a true division of powers between an elected president and an elected congress. Lansdale believed that these limits on presidential power, rather than being a hindrance to effective government, would oblige Diem to govern democratically and thus engender a more permanent foundation of popular support. When Diem balked at the independent judiciary and wanted to limit congressional powers, the American ambassador, Frederick Reinhardt, refused to support Lansdale in his efforts to convince Diem that a more balanced constitution was in his country's best interest. Reinhardt, echoing Washington sentiment, thought that constitutional checks and balances would make Diem too weak to govern effectively. Facing the North and developing the country required a strong leader.

Lansdale understood Diem's limitations and wanted to make it necessary for him to reach out to other power centers and nationalist leaders in order to govern. It was a difficult concept for those to understand who did not have Lansdale's subtle and intimate understanding of the difficulties of creating a democratic process with leaders whose experience was in secret revolutionary and autocratic politics. Nor was there any conviction among most American officials that it was necessary, while to Lansdale the creation of a cause worth fighting for was what the struggle against the communists would continue to be all about. He believed deeply that the cause was democracy. His convictions had been reinforced by the course of events in the defeat of the Huks in the Philippines and by his conversations with a broad spectrum of Vietnamese nationalists with deep democratic feelings.

A second serious mistake was that American support was given to Diem's brother and political confidant, Ngo Dinh Nhu, to create and develop a secret, elite political party called the Can Lao. It was almost a carbon copy of the communist party as an organizational weapon. Lansdale understood that such a movement, secretly controlled by Nhu, would become a divisive, rather than a unifying, force. He wanted Diem to act as a nonpartisan leader, to rally other Vietnamese nationalists and sect leaders around him in a government of national unity.

Nhu's idea was to create a loyalist core following and play divide and rule with the sects and other Vietnamese nationalists. Lansdale went all the way to the top in Washington, to Allen and Foster Dulles, to argue his case. He was told that he was being naive, that Diem had to be strong, and to be strong he had to have his own political party. Unfortunately, this policy helped to give Nhu, over time, the controlling influence in Diem's government, dividing rather than uniting Vietnamese nationalists and significant segments of the army as well. That mistake would haunt the Diem regime and American policy until Diem was overthrown and assassinated in 1963.

President Ngo Dinh Diem (*center*) visits Qui Nhon in Binh Dinh Province, 1955. Col. Le Van Kim (*behind Diem in bush hat*) was instrumental in the overthrow of Diem in 1963.

From today's perspective, the power of democratic ideas as a better alternative to communism and American insistence and interference on behalf of these ideas seem almost commonplace. But while enunciated back then as a rationale for opposing communism and as a mantra that democracy was superior to all other forms of government, this concept was seldom applied in practice when the choice was between supporting a noncommunist authoritarian regime and trying to develop a democratic alternative. This was not understood at the time and was seldom, if ever, a guiding principle of American policy. The support given to the Can Lao was a precise case in point.

Contributing to American mistakes was the conviction that by 1956, with Diem in firm control, South Vietnam was saved from communism. American policy and support could be turned over to a more conventional American country team to be implemented through diplomacy and standard military and economic aid programs. Diem would be helped to defend against an open invasion from the North, while the South would be industrialized to solve its balance-of-payment problems.

New Role for the Vietnamese Army

In that same period, the Vietnamese army was removed from its territorial (local) security role in the countryside. It had grown into this role as a result of the reoccupation and pacification operations in former communist areas and against the sects. It was instead organized into an army of regular divisions to defend against the danger of an overt conventional invasion across the seventeenth parallel by the North Vietnamese. Nothing effective was organized and trained to take over local security from the army. The Civil Guard became the subject of a deep dispute between the head of MAAG, Gen. Samuel T. Williams, and President Diem on the one hand, both of whom wanted to see MAAG take over the training and advisory role, and on the other hand, Ambassador Elbridge Durbrow and USOM, who wanted to keep responsibility for the Civil Guard, which they saw more as a national police force. The result was that next to nothing was done to fill the security vacuum left by the army when it stopped ensuring security in the countryside.

First Civic Action Program—1955

In 1955, the Vietnamese started a program called Civic Action. Lansdale assigned me to help with this new program after my stint as an adviser to the reoccupation operation in Central Vietnam was over. A former Viet Minh, Kieu Kong Cung, had been put in charge by Diem. Cung's background made an interesting but not unusual story. Cung had been a lowly lieutenant in the French army at the beginning of World War II. He recalled later having been in the French mess hall when word came that France had surrendered. The French officers stood up and sang the "Marseillaise" with tears in their eyes. He remained seated, realizing, he said, that their cause was not his, for he was Vietnamese. He resigned his commission. Then at the end of the war he joined, without any ideology except nationalism, the Viet Minh popular front in the South. Because he had some military experience, he became the leader of one of several units that resisted in 1946 when the French returned.

He stayed with the Viet Minh, and by 1951 had risen to the rank of brigadier general, but he refused to join the Communist Party. He was a nationalist but did not believe in communism. His refusal created suspicion that extended, he said, all the way up to Gen. Vo Nguyen Giap, military head of the North Vietnam Army. A secret list was prepared of noncommunists to be purged. Warned by friends in the party that he was at the point of being arrested, he deserted in secret from his command, which was near the Chinese border. He gathered his wife and two small children in the middle of the night, and with false identity papers as a peasant farmer, he spent a year making his way slowly to the south, evading both the French and the communists.

Cung had gone underground in 1952 in a village in the Mekong Delta where his wife had family. There he farmed as just another peasant. In 1954 after Diem returned, Cung was attracted by what he knew of Diem, who had a national reputation. He waited to see what Diem would do, and when it became apparent that Diem would fight for his beliefs, he volunteered. In Diem, he told me, he found a true Vietnamese nationalist whom he wanted to help.

When I first met Cung, he was wearing black pajamas, just like the teams he was beginning to train to go into the villages. He was stocky for a Vietnamese, with a square face and crew cut. He seemed shy when I first met him, but it was more than personality. I learned that he had had little to do with Westerners since his early days in the French army, and it was difficult for him to trust anyone with a white skin.

The basic idea of Civic Action was to extend government into the rural areas, to give medical assistance, to help rebuild villages that had been destroyed or neglected by war, and to organize support for the new nationalist government. I helped with the training program because some of his people had been sent to the Philippines to see how Civic Action was done there. After I had earned his confidence, Cung and I worked up a training-and-operations program for which Lansdale was able to get some initial seed money from the CIA, in addition to the very limited Vietnamese funds available. The basic idea was that the teams would bring tangible economic help to the villages, as well as establish a government presence. I was to help them get started and then turn over support of the program to the American economic aid mission.

By mid-1956, there were over a hundred Civic Action teams in the field. Although these teams were helpful to villagers, they were very short of tangible supplies, tools, medicines, and other items that the population, deprived by nine years of war, badly needed. In one village I visited north of Saigon, the team had just started work. As an ice breaker, simple medicines from a village first aid kit were being used to help people long denied any medical help. One urgent need was for help in redigging an old irrigation ditch that had been abandoned during the war. I found a village force with team members busily digging out the ditch. The team leader told me later that he planned to continue helping the villagers until he had their confidence before putting out any propaganda about the government. I was impressed with the team's spirit and its approach, but it needed more tools and more medicines, as well as some money for local building materials such as cement.

To be truly effective, the program required much more support than either the CIA was prepared to give or the Vietnamese government could provide. Based on what I had learned about American support for community development in India and other countries, I helped Cung draft an entire program that called for American community-development advisers and a budget for village tools, health kits, school kits, sewing machines, and other self-help items. Team pay would come from the Vietnamese.

U.S. Official Doesn't Get It

After much persuasion, Cung reluctantly agreed to present his program to Leland Barrows, the USOM director, and his staff. The meeting was arranged in early 1956 at USOM headquarters by Lansdale. I had met Barrows and some others of his staff before and had even gotten some medical kits from the public health chief. He was no longer the same person who, in 1954, had thought such kits would all be turned over to the communists.

Cung was a proud man and did not like asking for help. He began his presentation somewhat haltingly but in excellent French, and I translated for him. He explained that as a result of the war, a vacuum of government existed in the countryside. Based on his knowledge of how the communists worked, he said, they would fill it if the government did not. The purpose of his teams, he explained, was to help the villagers develop themselves and their villages and thus earn for the government their trust and support. He had heard of successful American assistance elsewhere for this type of community development, he said, and he invited American community development advisers to participate.

After his presentation, I could tell from the tenor of the questions that the Americans present didn't get it. "Why is Civic Action even needed?" Barrows wanted to know. "Couldn't what the teams are doing be taken over by regular civil administrators? Wouldn't it be more appropriate to train the existing civil administration?" Cung pointed out that the civil administrators had no experience in working with villagers; their dress in white sharkskin suits was an all-too-vivid reminder to the villagers of colonialism. He and his teams all dressed in the standard black pajamas of the typical Vietnamese peasant. I pointed out that the civil administration was almost nonexistent except for holdovers from the French days when they were dependent on receiving orders from their French superiors. "It would take years to get a completely new civil administration on its feet," I said. "There isn't time."

I saw that Barrows and his staff didn't understand the condition of Diem's nascent government or the situation in the countryside, and they had no sense of urgency. Later, Lansdale appealed directly to Barrows and then to Ambassador Reinhardt, but to no avail. At the same time, the CIA was insisting that this was an economic program, not a traditional CIA operation.

The prevailing view in the USOM economic aid mission was that priority had to be given to industrialization and to large infrastructure projects. The purpose was to have the Vietnamese make things they were then importing so that U.S. assistance could be reduced. Lansdale and I pleaded in vain that the struggle was not over; what would matter in the long run were the people in the countryside. We were convinced that the government had to put down roots, or the communists would. I knew firsthand from my experience in the reoccupation operations of 1955 that the communists had taken more than twenty thousand youngsters from Ca Mau in the very south and Interzone V in the center with them to North Vietnam when they evacuated. It was certain they would return after indoctrination as dedicated communists.

The noncommunist side had to offer a better alternative in the villages and make it real before these youths returned. To the new team of diplomats, the economic advisers, and much of the military advisory group, it was like baying at the moon. There was no sense of urgency, only complacency that Diem had won, which meant that the American mission could settle in to do what it traditionally did in other countries.

I also had the distinct impression that the regular American assistance types thought that the CIA had no business supporting such a program in the first place, and if the agency had supported it, it was not the kind of program that the USOM economic aid mission should in principle take over. Never mind that the same economic aid agency was supporting community-development programs in other developing countries that were similarly rural in nature. These suspicions were never voiced, but I could sense the undercurrent.

That was how it was. The American aid mission would continue to operate until mid-1962 without making any significant direct contribution to the well-being of the vast majority of the Vietnamese who lived in the countryside. That's how Diem came to feel that he could not count on American aid personnel to understand anything except their traditional commodity support, infrastructure, and industrial-development programs.

U.S. Ambassador Is Hostile to Diem

Within a few years after 1956, the communists began to resuscitate the guerrilla war by assassinating local government officials. The Civil Guard, which was to be mobilized and trained to replace the Vietnamese army in its territorial security role, never received much effective advice or assistance. Civic Action, lacking an effective economic component, became mainly a propaganda effort. Trust between the Vietnamese leadership and the Americans evaporated.

The American ambassador who had replaced Reinhardt in 1957, Elbridge Durbrow, became personally hostile to Diem and openly campaigned within the diplomatic community to pressure Diem to change his policies.[4] Although most of Durbrow's objectives of getting Diem to broaden the participation of other political parties and groups in his government were laudable, the tactics he used were counterproductive. By openly campaigning within the diplomatic community, including the French, to bring pressure on Diem, he wound up inadvertently encouraging an abortive coup in November 1960. Although it was not clear who would win, Durbrow sat on the fence. When it failed, Vietnamese distrust of Americans became pervasive on all sides, and Ngo Dinh Nhu became even more influential with Diem, his brother.

In the year before the attempted 1960 coup, when security began to deteriorate and political alienation began to mount, Diem requested repeatedly that Lansdale be sent to Saigon as an adviser. The State Department, on Durbrow's urging, turned it down. Durbrow even went so far as to support his objections by cabling that "Lansdale is not expert [on] antiguerrilla activities."

In the last few years of the Eisenhower administration, Vietnam policy was in a caretaker mode while security in the Vietnamese countryside deteriorated as the Viet Cong (VC) stepped up their efforts. It was reported that as proof of the complacency, when Eisenhower talked to Kennedy about international problems during the 1960 inauguration, he spoke at length about Laos but reportedly said little about South Vietnam.

Counterinsurgency Becomes Barbed Wire and Body Counts

In January 1961, the new Kennedy administration inherited not only an immediate crisis in Laos but also an unanticipated one in South Vietnam. The crisis had festered largely unnoticed by the White House because the State Department bureaucracy, which had taken over after John Foster Dulles's death, appeared to have been mainly intent on protecting its reputation and that of Ambassador Durbrow.

Lansdale visited South Vietnam from 2 to 14 January 1961. In December 1960, the situation had grown so critical that the State Department and Ambassador Durbrow combined could no longer keep him away. This visit resulted in a memorandum to Secretary of Defense Thomas S. Gates Jr., which Walter Rostow, counselor of the Department of State and chairman of the Policy

Council, placed on President Kennedy's desk and which he read excitedly shortly after taking office in 1961.[5] He called in Lansdale for a high-level meeting, praised him for his report, and told him he wanted to appoint him as ambassador to South Vietnam. This appointment was blocked by Secretary of State Dean Rusk, who reportedly threatened to resign, so vehement were the objections to Lansdale by some of Rusk's Foreign Service advisers. Lansdale's struggle with Durbrow and his having overturned the position of the embassy staff against Diem during the Saigon miniwar of 1955 had borne bitter fruit.

President Kennedy did decide to make South Vietnam a test case for defeating Khrushchev's doctrine of Wars of National Liberation. The means would be counterinsurgency.

The concept of counterinsurgency, which Lansdale had created within the Pentagon as an unconventional approach to defeating Wars of National Liberation, was proclaimed as administration doctrine in 1961. Neither Secretary of Defense McNamara and Gen. Maxwell Taylor, chairman of the Joint Chiefs of Staff, nor most regular military officers understood the program's emphasis on a people-first approach. Thus, it became a more traditional military assistance program, focusing on logistics and placing advisers with Vietnamese army units. These would conduct conventional search-and-destroy operations against Viet Cong units with little regard for the population. Progress started to be measured in numbers of rolls of barbed wire delivered and the now-infamous McNamara body counts.

Revisiting South Vietnam—1962

After leaving South Vietnam in 1956, I returned in 1962. I had received a telephone call toward the end of May that year from Rutherford Poats in the newly renamed Agency for International Development, or AID (this was a name change from the previous International Cooperation Administration, or ICA, although local missions were still called U.S. Operations Missions). Poats asked me to come in for a discussion about South Vietnam. I did. It turned out that Poats was the deputy director for the Far East in AID. He asked if I would be willing to go to South Vietnam to survey the aid program and to determine how it could be reorganized to support counterinsurgency, which had become the Kennedy administration's buzzword for its efforts in South Vietnam. He said I had been recommended by a number of people as someone who understood the civil side of counterinsurgency. I got the distinct impression that AID was under strong pressure to come up with something different. Sy Janow, the director for the Far East Bureau in AID, also made a personal appeal.

I called Lansdale, who was then in the Pentagon, to ask his advice. As it turned out (he never told me in advance), he was the main source for recommending me. He thought I could make a real contribution and urged me to go. After talking to my wife and then to my father, who was vehemently opposed, I agreed to go. I suppose my father could see what was going to happen, that I would become as deeply committed to the Vietnamese cause as I had been earlier. When I agreed to go, I insisted that Bert Fraleigh, a regular AID employee whom I had known in Laos as extraordinarily effective, join me from Taiwan, where he was then posted.

When Bert and I arrived in Saigon in July 1962 for almost a month, the Vietnamese, from President Diem on down, opened all doors for us. We could go anywhere, see anything, and talk to anybody, which we did. Secretary of Defense Nguyen Dinh Thuan, who had been one of my closest friends during the early days, was particularly helpful. I felt a resurgence of that earlier spirit of trust. I focused on what the Vietnamese were already doing, which was the Strategic

High-level visitors from Washington visit Vinh Binh Province in 1963. *(From left)* Mike Forrestal, National Security Council; Roger Hilsman, assistant secretary of state; the Vinh Binh province chief; Bill Trueheart, deputy chief of mission, South Vietnam; a Vietnamese official; Rufe Phillips, director of USOM Rural Affairs; Col. Hoang Lac, Strategic Hamlet Program; and Col. Carl Schaad, Military Assistance Advisory Group. *Vinh Binh provincial photographer*

Hamlet Program, and how it could be supported and improved by AID's participation. This program was concerned with hamlets' self-development and self-defense. There were things wrong with the way the program was being carried out, particularly the use of forced resettlement in parts of the Mekong Delta, but the basic principles of hamlet self-development and self-defense were correct. Bert focused on the actual assistance programs that we might carry out in the countryside and how they could be effectively delivered.

We very quickly found out that although the government had given the province chiefs some funds for the program, the money was not being used because it was subject to preaudit. To purchase tin roofing for a hamlet school, for example, the province chief had to get three bids, send them to Saigon for approval, and wait weeks and sometimes months for approval. When approval came, the price had often changed, so the funds never were used. Or if the province chief went ahead on his own, he had to falsify his records.

A Counterinsurgency Proposal to Diem

We could see that the Strategic Hamlet Program and its accounting system could never be made to work without massive changes in bureaucratic regulations and mind-set. At the same time, in Phu Yen Province in Central Vietnam, a special combined military-civil operation had been set up with American support. Col. Lucien (Lou) Concin, a cohort from the 1954 days in Vietnam, was back working for the CIA and had ransacked our old national security program files to develop the idea for what was called Operation Sea Swallow in Phu Yen. A joint American–Vietnamese committee had been created at the province level to expedite support for the program and to authorize local expenditures, which included American funds. A regiment of the Vietnamese army had been permanently assigned to provide backup security in the province, which was essential for keeping the regular Viet Cong units from coming down out of the mountains and overwhelming the hamlet militia. This seemed to be working well.

Borrowing this as a model, Bert and I came up with the idea of setting up joint American–Vietnamese committees in all the provinces to authorize spending for the Strategic Hamlet Program without recourse back to Saigon. To administer this unorthodox type of American assistance, we recommended a new and separate office within the AID mission. The head would have the status of assistant director within the AID mission, with a small Saigon staff and with representatives in each of the provinces. Provincial representatives, or prov reps, would live on the local economy, have no office or staff beyond an interpreter, and work directly with Vietnamese province chiefs and the American military adviser, who would also be a member of the provincial committee.

The whole mechanism was a considerable abrogation of Vietnamese sovereignty, so I personally explained it to Minister of Defense Thuan and then to President Diem himself. President Diem and Thuan approved the proposal with one verbal condition; I had to return to South Vietnam to administer the program.

My meeting with Diem in 1962, the first since 1957, was memorable. I had returned from Laos in 1957 to ask for Vietnamese help in training Lao Civic Action teams that the Lao were then recruiting. I remember Diem questioning me closely about my impressions of Laos and his very positive reaction to me personally because of the Lansdale association and to my request for assistance.

This time I was not sure what the reception would be. Relations with Americans had deteriorated so badly in the interim. I knew from many conversations with Lansdale, from my own limited contact with him, and from other Vietnamese that Diem was a very complex person. He was inherently shy and often appeared diffident, but he was a passionate Vietnamese nationalist with immense inner self-confidence. In physical appearance, he was short and stocky, with a head that appeared too large for his body. He had a bland, often impassive face. He exhibited tremendous nervous energy as he chain-smoked endlessly while speaking in rapid-fire French. His English was workable, but he preferred not to use it.

He received me with a wide smile, somewhat like a lost son, I thought. His eyes were warm. I gave him a brief note of greetings from Lansdale with a "you remember Rufus Phillips" introduction to it. He recalled instantly not only my 1957 visit but also his trip to Qui Nhon in Binh Dinh Province in 1955 with me. Some moments were spent inquiring about Lansdale. He asked whether I thought Lansdale might be coming out. This evolved into a discussion on how much Diem would like him to return to assist Ambassador Frederick Nolting. Was there any way I could help with this? I said I would try, and later while I was still in Saigon, I did raise the request with Ambassador Nolting but got no reaction beyond him saying he would think about it.

I explained my mission to the president and told him my observations about what I had seen in the provinces of the Strategic Hamlet Program. He listened attentively and said I must see his brother Nhu and give him these same observations. Nhu, he said, was following the program very closely. I explained the idea of the provincial committees and how this idea was already working in Phu Yen to expedite the use of American funds. He nodded, which I took for agreement (later I would check back with Thuan to make sure Diem understood and approved). I also told him about a real problem I had encountered with assistance for Montagnard refugees, who had fled their villages under pressure from the Viet Cong. Diem had ordered that rice be sent to the provinces where they had congregated, but the rice was not being distributed, apparently because the province chiefs had not received specific authority to do so.

As soon as he heard this, Diem stopped our conversation, called in Vo Van Hai, his private secretary and an old friend from the Lansdale days, and directed him to send an urgent telegram to the concerned province chiefs ordering that the rice be given to the Montagnards immediately. He thanked me for letting him know about the situation and said he knew that some of the province chiefs were too dependent on authority. He then launched into a lengthy description of the various Montagnard tribes involved.

This whole meeting took about four hours, of which a lot of time was a monologue on his part. In later meetings with the president, which we had periodically after I returned as assistant director to administer the program that Bert and I were in the process of creating, he would display an impressive intellect and an incredibly encyclopedic knowledge of every province in South Vietnam and of practically every Vietnamese family. If I said that I had met a particulary province chief who seemed to be doing a good job, he would say something like, "Oh, yes, his grandfather was so and so and his father was so and so and his family was originally from Hue but moved to Saigon around 1920," and so on.

Diem's monologues were undoubtedly mind-numbing for some of the diplomats who had to talk to him because he thought, probably rightly so, that most Americans didn't understand much about South Vietnam. I was younger and knew something about the country and his personality, so I just let him go on until we got through whatever was on his mind. If there was something I wanted to bring up, I would wait for the opportunity and do so. He always listened to my observations with a great deal of interest and attention and would act on any suggestions I might have.

After several interjections from me that I was taking too much of his time, the meeting came to an end. He said, "I hope you are returning to help us." I said I had to talk to my family, but I would do my best. He said, "We need you." All I could say was, "Yes, Mr. President."

Ngo Dinh Nhu, the President's Brother

Ngo Dinh Nhu had a very different personality from his brother. He was slight in build, but he had a similarly outsized head and was very intellectual in his discourse. He was friendly when I met him but more aloof than his brother. It quickly became apparent that he liked to philosophize about the Strategic Hamlet Program as he traced what he saw as its roots in ancient Vietnamese history, beginning with resistance to Chinese incursions into Vietnam. We had a long discussion about how the program was supposed to be implemented, and he listened to my observations with a great deal of interest. When I expressed concern about resettlement, he said he knew that some of the province chiefs had gone too far, but he had told them that he was opposed to forcible resettlement. He also said he knew that some were exaggerating their progress, and that was wrong, too.

Nhu talked about his own trips to the provinces, which he said were made informally without an entourage (I was able to verify later that he had in fact made provincial visits in this manner). His observations about what he had seen were quite specific and made sense. I was encouraged that he seemed as practical as he did about the program, which made me hopeful that a working relationship could be established with him. However, I knew of some of his more irrational tendencies and his disposition to paranoia and distrust, so my meeting with him was less frank on my part than it was with President Diem.

Vietnamese Want Lansdale to Return

About this same time, I also met old Vietnamese friends who had become alienated from Diem and Nhu. They told me, often with bitterness, of their disaffection. I saw real political problems, but I hoped that somehow a return of Lansdale could be engineered, possibly with him serving as an assistant to Ambassador Nolting. (I was to broach this subject again with Nolting later in 1962 after I returned to Saigon and received no response.) I could sense there was a political vacuum on the American side, and I could see that although Diem liked Nolting, it was clear without him saying so that he didn't think Nolting understood enough to be of much practical political help. This was confirmed by Vo Van Hai, who also begged me to find a way to get Lansdale back. Nhu had isolated Diem, he said, from outside political advice and had alienated too many other Vietnamese whose support the president needed.

I saw the pitfalls, but I could also see hope. I could not see myself playing Lansdale, but I could see the possibility that something with a democratic essence based on self-defense, self-government, and self-help might be built from the hamlet level up. This might constitute part of that needed political cause, which had not disappeared but had become dissipated. And

I could see that if what I was doing was successful, then perhaps a way would open to get Lansdale back to work on the political situation before anything could go too wrong.

A Decision to Return to South Vietnam

I was in a quandary, having only committed to do the study. I didn't know what my wife, Barbara, would think. But I knew my father's reaction. I would be deserting him when he needed me. He had opposed my earlier work with the CIA in South Vietnam and Laos, and he thought Lansdale was a dangerous pied piper. Later I would learn that he was not well, but he did not tell me at the time.

I explained this to Thuan as a friend and told him I would do my best. In my heart I had pretty well made up my mind if Barbara would come with me. For all the Diem government's problems, and I had been made more aware of them than most Americans, this was the good fight for the sake of the Vietnamese people that I could not miss.

So I returned with Barbara and two small children in early September 1962 to get the Office of Rural Affairs off the ground in earnest and to start supporting and changing the Strategic Hamlet Program. The challenge was to convert it into something in which people in the countryside were real participants rather than objects and through which democratic ways and institutions could begin to blossom. We seized on the hamlet elections as an instrument in this process and decided to make our funding of self-help programs dependent on them. Hamlets would become eligible for self-help funds once a hamlet chief and council had been elected. Fifty thousand piasters (the unofficial currency exchange rate was about seventy piasters to one U.S. dollar at the time) was to be given to each hamlet. This would buy materials for a hamlet improvement project, a well, a school, or a road that was badly needed and for which the hamlet was willing to provide the labor.

Above all, the idea was to insert our Rural Affairs representatives unobtrusively into the mainstream of the Vietnamese government. Here we would be in a position to act as a catalyst to get things done and to serve as nonpartisan participants who could help the Vietnamese channel their efforts in constructive directions. We would work with the Vietnamese as equals and as friends, not as superior advisers. If this sounded like a revival of the Lansdale approach, it was deliberately intended to be so. We would try to take the best Vietnamese ideas of how pacification should work and help these ideas spread. And we would help the Vietnamese and particularly President Diem at the top become more aware of who were the best province chiefs and who were not so good and should be replaced. This would be done not by praising the good or criticizing the bad but by simply reporting the facts as we saw them. This we did, not to the American side alone, but, more important, to the Vietnamese all the way to President Diem.

In guidelines that Rural Affairs published in early 1963 for the provincial representatives, we told them, "You have the most important job in Vietnam." We went on to say, among other things, that the purpose of the Strategic Hamlet Program was to give the Vietnamese people something worth risking their lives to defend and that the job of our provincial representatives was "to help the Vietnamese make their aspirations for a better life come true."

All our provincial representatives, called prov reps, were volunteers, and many were in their early twenties, particularly those we were able to recruit from the International Voluntary Services (IVS). Those from the IVS were

Richard Holbrooke distributes tool kits in Ba Xuyen Province, early 1964.
Richard Holbrooke

young American college graduates, mainly from agricultural schools, mostly Vietnamese speaking, and already working in South Vietnam. In addition, young Foreign Service officers were recruited, just out of Vietnamese language training, at the very start of their careers. The first were Dick Holbrooke and Vlad Lehovich, who arrived in spring 1963. I sent Holbrooke as prov rep to Ba Xuyen, a particularly difficult province in the southern part of the Mekong Delta, where he got things done despite a not very cooperative province chief, while Lehovich, who spoke French as well as Vietnamese, was effective as roving support for one of our regional representatives, Ralph Harwood. Our younger recruits more than made up in enthusiasm, intelligence, and spirit for their lack of experience and soon found themselves being treated as equals and friends by much older Vietnamese majors and colonels who were province chiefs. Perhaps my own experience at having so much responsibility when I was their age back in 1954 made it easy for me to develop confidence in them. And they had no greater champion than my deputy, Bert Fraleigh, who called them his Young Tigers. Most performed magnificently.

Other contributors to this book will describe in more detail the economic and social assistance programs that were started. Among other efforts, a pig-raising program was spread to thousands of families in Central Vietnam in less than two years. One true story will give an idea of the effect.

The Pig Corn Program was aimed initially at getting the poorest farmer in a hamlet to raise improved-breed pigs in a way that was radically different from traditional, thousand-year-old Vietnamese practices. We thought that if the poorest farmer could succeed, then everyone else would want to participate. In one particular hamlet in Quang Ngai Province, Leonard Chang, who had come from Taiwan to provide technical assistance, told of visiting a tenant farmer dressed in rags in his dilapidated straw hut. While explaining the program, Leonard noticed a pile of straw in the corner to which the farmer occasionally spoke. Underneath the straw, Leonard discovered, was the farmer's wife nursing a baby. They were so poor that she had only straw to cover herself against the early morning chill.

After some persuasion, the farmer agreed to try the pig program on rented land. When Leonard returned several months later to find him, the man ran inside his hut and brought back a fistful of piasters with tears in his eyes. It was, he said, the first time in three generations that his family had ever had any money. Now, he had enough to pay back the loan for the pigs, buy the land where his pigpen was located, build a new house next to it, and plant some rice as well. When Leonard told me this story, I knew

Col. Tran Ngoc Chau, chief of Kien Hoa Province and contributing writer *(left),* with Rufe Phillips *(right of Chau)* and Ralph Harwood *(right of Phillips),* leads an inspection tour of his province in December 1962. *Provincial photographer*

we were helping to generate a cause worth defending for the Vietnamese in the hamlets.

Getting Rural Affairs Off the Ground

In getting the assistance program going, I worked intimately with the chief of staff of the Strategic Hamlet Program, a regular Vietnamese army colonel named Hoang Lac. He had been a regimental commander during the reoccupation of Interzone V in 1955. We remembered each other at our first meeting and quickly developed a bond of trust. I would keep him advised of exactly what we saw happening in the provinces. He would bring his concerns to me about how some of the Vietnamese province chiefs were administering the program. He was very concerned about the numbers game some province chiefs were playing, exaggerating the level of completed hamlets and minimizing the adverse effects of forcible resettlement, particularly in the Mekong Delta provinces.

One particular incident, in March 1963, stands out as to how things worked and how Diem and Nhu could be influenced positively to replace bad leadership. Rob Warne, our representative in Vinh Long Province, south of Saigon in the Delta between the Bassac and Mekong Rivers, had reported that Colonel Phuoc, the province chief, was using forced labor to build long walls across the rice paddies and was exaggerating the number of completed hamlets. Rob asked if I could come down to look at the situation. Rob, a young man, had gone to Vinh Long with his even younger wife and two small children and was living on the local economy, as we obliged all our prov reps to do. Colonel Lac warned me before I went that Colonel Phuoc was regarded as one of Ngo Dinh Nhu's favorites.

When I visited Vinh Long, Phuoc proudly showed me the series of long walls he was building. I asked how he thought the walls would keep Viet Cong guerrillas out. He said no, the main purpose was to control the civilian population from moving across the rice fields. If people used the roads, checkpoints would be set up. He said that the first step in pacification was to control the population, then to win popular support. The work parties we saw were all volunteer labor, he claimed, but I had seen enough Vietnamese farmers to distinguish their usual impassiveness from discontent. These were unhappy people. I hid my dismay the best I could.

I returned to Saigon and wrote a concise report to the AID mission director, Joe Brent, with a copy to Colonel Lac. I asked Brent not to distribute it until we saw what happened on the Vietnamese side. Lac briefed Nhu on what I had reported. Nhu called a meeting of the Strategic Hamlet coordinating committee, summoning Colonel Phuoc to appear. Lac knew his man, so he had the Vietnamese air force in the meantime take aerial photographs of the province. At the meeting, Phuoc claimed that I had insulted him during my visit and denied he was building long walls, only walls around the hamlets themselves. Lac then spread out the photographs and asked him to explain what they clearly showed. He couldn't and was immediately reprimanded by Nhu and ordered to stop building the walls. After that incident, Phuoc's deputy took over effective control of the program, while it took some time for Phuoc to be officially relieved because considerable face-saving was involved.

I was told that Nhu made a point of speaking with Diem about this incident. My old friend Vo Van Hai, the president's secretary, later told me that Diem had gained a lot of confidence in us from the way the problem was handled *en famille*, as he had put it. I felt that we were becoming what we needed to become, a partner in what the government was doing in the countryside. It was not true that Diem, or even Nhu in his more rational and less paranoiac moments, was impervious to advice.

U.S. Ambassador Just Doesn't Get It
The fact that the Vinh Long incident had happened quietly spread throughout the American mission. However, its importance seemed to have totally escaped

Ambassador Nolting. Only a month later I learned, almost by accident, that a wrongheaded, high-level policy decision had been made on the American side. In the midst of growing success—with economic assistance under Bert's enthusiastic leadership really beginning to deliver pigs to poor villagers all over Central Vietnam, with hamlet schools being built, self-help projects being carried out, and security gradually improving in many provinces—we had the rug pulled out from under us, or so it seemed.

I was abruptly informed by Director Brent that the ten-million-dollar special piaster fund, which the United States had contributed to the Strategic Hamlet Program and which served as the basis for the joint Vietnamese–American tripartite committees in each province, was going to be discontinued in the next fiscal year. The funding would henceforth be Vietnamese, and the provincial committees would no longer have any say in how the money was spent. It had all been decided, he said. He went on to say that it was time for the Vietnamese to assume this burden themselves.

I was dumbfounded. This was the first time that Rural Affairs had heard that next fiscal year's counterinsurgency funding was to come from the Vietnamese or that doing away with the provincial committees was even being considered. I was enraged. "Who," I asked Brent, "decided it and why weren't we consulted?" Brent said Ambassador Nolting had recommended it, and Washington agreed. Nothing our own staff or the Vietnamese had ever done was to make me as angry.

I wrote a memorandum to Brent to be sent to Ambassador Nolting. It said, among other things, that we were being asked to give up effective U.S. participation in the province-administered counterinsurgency program directed at winning over the people while it was precisely this participation that was making the program successful.

Then I went to see Nolting, who didn't seem to understand why I was so disturbed. I asked, "Do you realize the effect of eliminating the provincial joint committees? They are what is making the Strategic Hamlet Program work." He said, "Yes, but that is what the Vietnamese want; they are complaining about American advisers being too intrusive." He went on to say, "I am certain President Diem will never again accept any arrangement which would decentralize control to a joint committee in the provinces, even if U.S. funds were made available."

I knew Diem and Nhu had complained about some American military advisers criticizing the Vietnamese directly to the American press (this was mainly John Paul Vann, flamboyant former U.S. military adviser and later prov rep for Rural Affairs, after his reports on the battle of Ap Bac were dismissed by his superiors). I had discounted this problem, knowing it had nothing to do with us. And in fact, the whole handling of the Vinh Long walls issue had been a vote of confidence in Rural Affairs. Now it was apparent that Nolting had taken Vietnamese displeasure with the way some Americans were handling themselves, then assumed it applied across the board, and, for harmony's sake, agreed to drop the provincial committees.

I said as levelly as I could to the ambassador, "I think you are wrong, Mr. Ambassador." Then I asked, "Did President Diem or Nhu specifically object to Rural Affairs or its people?" He admitted that they had not. I said I didn't see how he could make the statement that Diem would not accept the provincial committees. I said heatedly, "Why didn't you consult those who have a direct responsibility for this program and let us explain the need to continue the committees? We don't need the provincial committees, the Vietnamese need the provincial committees to make the program work." He said dismissively, "There are larger policy issues involved." Then the conversation ended.

I suddenly realized that Ambassador Nolting, whom I had briefed regularly on what we were doing, really didn't understand what was happening or how things worked in South Vietnam. Without checking further, Nolting had interpreted Vietnamese complaints so broadly that he was willing to take the Americans out of any but a marginal role in the Strategic Hamlet Program, just when we were beginning to make progress. It was unbelievable. I left abruptly without saying another word, before the clash got beyond control. There was nothing further to be gained. (I later learned that he had tried to persuade Diem to keep the provincial committees but that Diem had been opposed. Knowing Nhu's paranoia, I sensed he was behind Diem's position. But that left the question of why those who were best equipped to explain and persuade on this issue were totally left out.)

Trying to Work with American Mistakes
I could understood how Lansdale must have felt back in 1955 and 1956 when key policy decisions were made without his advice. It was hard to stomach the arrogance and stupidity of it. With the full backing of the Rural Affairs staff, I wrote a letter to Sy Janow, our ultimate boss in AID/Washington, saying, "We would fight an uphill battle . . . to make the system work." I went on to say, "Should we be asked to discharge duties under circumstances which become clearly impossible, I shall have no choice but to resign." I sent a copy to Lansdale via a friend. Lansdale urged me to stay on to work something out with the Vietnamese, and Janow expressed full confidence in us and asked me to continue.

Bert and I huddled. We talked to a number of our regional and prov reps who were equally upset. It was apparent the decision was set in concrete and could not be changed. I felt I couldn't abandon the committed team Bert and I had recruited. I had to work it out with the Vietnamese. I had to make a pitch to Nhu that we were an integral part of their program and that it was in their best interests that the provincial committees continue to function even if all the funds were in Vietnamese hands. Rural Affairs was on its own. We knew we could expect no help from above. On the other hand, we didn't want help of the kind that had just been foisted on us.

First, I had a heart-to-heart talk with Lac about the American screw-up. He wanted things to continue the way they were and promised to support this idea with Nhu. I also talked to Thuan, who suggested we invite Nhu to a conference with a delegation of our provincial representatives to give him a chance to explain his concepts and for us to brief him on all our related rural aid efforts, such as the Pig Corn Program, the hamlet schools, and so on, and on how we worked in the provinces. The meeting was a success. Nhu made a presentation to us, which I translated from French to English for our group.

Nhu was frank and admitted that many province chiefs had gone too fast and made mistakes. I translated for Bert, who presented all the economic and social-hamlet support programs that were under way. We described how the provincial committees actually worked. As the discussion went on, I think it became clear that we were an integral part of the hamlet program and that what we were doing was to help the program succeed. Afterward, I learned that Nhu was happy with the meeting and was apparently impressed by the obvious sincerity of our people.

I went on to brief President Diem personally and to tell him that we were going to prepare reports on the status of the Strategic Hamlet Program on a province-by-province basis and give him a copy of our report. This we did in July and September, writing it in French but without changing a word from the American version.

About a month later, both Thuan and Lac told me that Nhu had agreed that the provincial committees would continue to function just as they had been, even though the funding would now become Vietnamese. It was a real vote of confidence by the Vietnamese in Rural Affairs. However, my confidence that even the American higher-ups in Saigon, much less in Washington, had any real understanding of what we were doing or how things worked or didn't work in South Vietnam, was badly shaken. Things unfortunately would only get worse in this regard.

Although we succeeded in maintaining our key role in the Strategic Hamlet Program, and the Vietnamese economic and social programs we were supporting were beginning to have a very positive effect, a change was needed in the way counterinsurgency was being waged militarily. We were getting adverse reports from the provinces about Vietnamese troop behavior (burning of villages suspected of harboring Viet Cong) and the adverse effects of the indiscriminate use of firepower. Least effective and often most destructive were the Vietnamese army search-and-destroy operations, which were a focus of the U.S. Military Assistance Command, Vietnam (MACV) advisory support at the division and corps levels. Viet Cong forces were seldom encountered and certainly not destroyed by the bombing and shelling of villages suspected of harboring them. The firepower that accompanied these operations was particularly harmful. Moreover, these efforts were totally unrelated to protecting the strategic hamlets from Viet Cong main-force attacks.

When combined with free-fire zones and bombing raids on suspected Viet Cong villages based on outmoded intelligence, most military operations were at best not winning any civilians to the government side. They were in fact helping to recruit many new Viet Cong. To question these tactics openly would have brought Rural Affairs into direct confrontation with Gen. Paul Harkins, chief of MACV, on a subject about which we, as civilians, were not considered qualified to speak.

Beginning in spring 1963, we passed reports from our provincial representatives and their military counterparts to Maj. Gen. Richard (Dick) Stilwell at MACV on an informal basis. These reports detailed abuses of the civilian population by Vietnamese units. But nothing happened. As time went on, it was clear the U.S. military mission was not insisting on changes but was in fact deeply involved in some of the most harmful activities. Among these were deployment of U.S. aircraft and pilots to bomb and strafe villages, using information based on Vietnamese intelligence about the presence of Viet Cong units often days, if not weeks, old. We also learned that the rules of engagement for American helicopter pilots permitted them to respond in-kind if fired on from a particular village. There were specific examples of the Viet Cong deliberately provoking our helicopters to return fire. This tactic was used for recruiting followers; the more civilians killed, the better for the Viet Cong because more relatives and friends could be won over to their side.

Rather than directly confront the U.S. military establishment, I wanted to speak with Minister of Defense Thuan to see what could be done on the Vietnamese side to question these practices. At the time, however, the Buddhist crisis was completely occupying the higher levels of the Vietnamese government.

In May 1963 Office of Rural Affairs staff members meet with Counselor Ngo Dinh Nhu, the president's brother, to discuss the American role in counterinsurgency. Ngo Dinh Nhu *(extreme left)*, Rufe Phillips *(right of Nhu)*, Bert Fraleigh *(right of Phillips)*, and other Rural Affairs officers. *Presidential Palace photographer*

Finally, as Ambassador Nolting was about to be replaced by Lodge, I raised the issue in a direct memorandum to him in early August, called "Bombs, Rockets, Shells, Popular Support and the U.S. Interests." I pointed out that everyone was saying that winning the support of the people was the only way to win a counterinsurgency, but what it really meant, I said, was that, "so long as actions taken in the war contribute to winning the people, they contribute to winning the war. When they do not contribute to winning the people, they contribute to losing the war."

I mentioned that another point of view seemed all too prevalent in practice: "Those who do not support the government, or who are not in government-controlled areas, must suffer for this (after all, war is hell), and after suffering enough they will either blame the VC for their suffering, or will come over to government controlled areas to escape the bombs, shells, etc., which are their lot when the VC are around."

A number of Vietnamese officers, province chiefs, and American military provincial advisers, I said, had a contrary view based on daily contact with the population treated in this fashion, "that the practice of attacking villages invariably generates more recruits than casualties for the VC." I went on to say that these were not isolated incidents and that there were two reasons consistent with American principles why we should neither countenance nor support such actions.

These reasons were that "no one should be punished for actions beyond his control or forced on him by fear of his life; and when any punishment is possibly unjust, as well as excessive, it is certain to create hatred for those that inflict it." My recommendation was, as a first step, that we "absolutely prohibit any attacks by U.S. aircraft or pilots on any targets where the absence of women and children cannot be positively determined," which meant, I said, "inhibiting them from any attacks on houses or villages." And I recommended the discontinuance of the so-called free-fire zones that could be shelled or bombed indiscriminately.

At the end of the memo, I concluded, "This war is not an isolated phenomenon. The actions which we take, or support, here in Viet Nam, must be viewed in that context, and as they may be made to appear long after our major involvement here has ended."

The latter statement was more prophetic than I could have ever imagined at the time, but like so much else that might have influenced positive change, it got lost in the ever more consuming Buddhist crisis.

Through a twist of fate, I would later confront Secretary of Defense McNamara on the effectiveness of the military side of the war effort, which only echoed what many of us had seen on the ground from the very beginning.

Buddhist Crisis and Downfall of Diem

By spring 1963, significant progress was being made with the Strategic Hamlet Program, with the focus becoming one of consolidation and development. Unfortunately, this progress was overcome by a major political crisis over the Vietnamese government's handling of the Buddhists. This began with an unfortunate incident in which the army fired on Buddhist demonstrators in Hue. This was a crisis in which Diem's brother Nhu played a crucial and particularly disastrous role. At the time, Diem still had considerable prestige as an unsullied nationalist despite North Vietnamese attempts to portray him as an American puppet. As the Buddhist crisis deepened, the United States had a last opportunity to intervene to save Diem while helping him regain broad nationalist support, but U.S. involvement required more understanding and deftness than the Kennedy administration possessed. Out of ignorance, preoccupation with stability, dislike of the Nhus, and fear of an unstable Nhu negotiating with the North, the United States encouraged a military coup that created a disastrous political vacuum. No serious attempt was ever made to separate Nhu from Diem.[6]

Without recounting all the details of the downward spiral of the Diem government, several events stand out. One was the incomprehensible fact that Ambassador Nolting decided to go on home leave just when the crisis deepened and began to spin out of control, leaving Diem with no American intermediary at the top for whom he felt even minimal trust.

The other was that Nhu became a complete hawk on the issue of how to deal with the Buddhists, leaving others, such as Vo Van Hai, Secretary Thuan, and even General Cao, the Cao Dai delegate whom Diem had appointed as part of a commission to resolve the crisis, with no influence. Attention was visibly being diverted on the Vietnamese side from the counterinsurgency effort. I became more involved than I wanted to be, urging a peaceful resolution to my own Vietnamese contacts and actually developing, at Cao's request, a written plan to address Buddhist grievances by concrete actions for his commission to recommend to Diem. It was all to little avail because Nhu was taking an increasingly hard line and swaying Diem. I even went to the deputy chief of the American mission, Bill Trueheart, to plead at Thuan's and Vo Van Hai's request that some way be found to get Lansdale out to South Vietnam, even temporarily, to help Diem resolve the crisis. Trueheart was not unsympathetic, but he didn't see how it could be done unless Diem himself requested it. That seemed very unlikely, because such a request would have been a significant admission of weakness on Diem's part. I didn't even try it.

On 22 August, Ambassador Henry Cabot Lodge arrived to replace Nolting. The infamous raid on the pagodas, ordered by Nhu and executed by the Vietnamese Special Forces, had just occurred, which threw everyone into a state of shock. Diem had told Nolting before he left that no violence would be committed against the Buddhists.

At the time, I received word from Lansdale that he had briefed Lodge and particularly his main assistant, Col. John M. (Mike) Dunn, and that I should try to help Lodge understand what was really going on. I made a concerted effort to work with Dunn, who had sought me out immediately upon arrival. I felt I might have some positive influence over events that were clearly now getting out of hand.

In this crisis, I was greatly helped by one of the more unconventional members of the Rural Affairs staff, Lt. Col. Charles T. R. (Bo) Bohannan (retired). I had recruited Bo to help the Vietnamese government conceptualize and start a surrender program (Chieu Hoi) targeted at the Viet Cong, based on the successful Magsaysay model of welcoming and resettling Huk communist returnees in the Philippines. (This program was interpreted as being within the Rural Affairs charter because no one else was doing it.) Bo had been Lansdale's right hand during the campaign against the Huks in the Philippines, had provided the Saigon Military Mission with support during the 1954–1956 days, and had later retired from the CIA.

Bo was about as knowledgeable a counterguerrilla expert as America had, and I used him as a foil for counterproductive ideas (such as population-control efforts involving the placement of national police in every hamlet, which were seductive but harebrained in the South Vietnam context). I also used him as an informal advisory pipeline to the MACV, particularly to the new J-3, General Stilwell, who had known Bo from earlier days. Eventually, we hoped to integrate Vietnamese army strategy and tactics with the population security goals of the Strategic Hamlet Program and to convert ARVN operations into a people-first approach.

In attempting to influence Lodge, I decided to become a source for as much political intelligence as possible about what the Vietnamese leadership, other than Diem and Nhu, was thinking. I felt that if I inserted myself into what was happening and made myself, and Bo by extension, an informal part of Lodge's staff, then I might have a chance to influence events. It became apparent that, with the exception of Nhu and Diem, everyone was aghast at the raid on the pagodas, and this included some of the president's strongest supporters and friends, from Secretary of Defense Thuan on down. The military leadership was particularly appalled by the raid and by the transparent attempt by Nhu, after the fact, to put responsibility for it onto the Vietnamese army. There was even fear that Nhu might take control of the government directly and make Diem a complete figurehead.

I tried to focus Lodge on the idea of disassociating the United States from Nhu and trying to draw a distinction between Nhu and Diem, in hopes of persuading Diem to get Nhu out of the country as the price for continued American support. I felt that if we could bring enough pressure to bear, then Diem might call for Lansdale as the price for letting Nhu go abroad. As strange as it may sound, I believed then (and still do) that Diem trusted Lansdale more than any person—Vietnamese or American—except Nhu.

The Budding Coup against Diem

What I did not realize at the time and which seems more apparent now was that Lodge had apparently decided, before he even came to Saigon, that the only solution was to get rid of both Diem and Nhu. I don't believe he ever conveyed this even to his closest staff. In any case, in his personal papers is an allusion to the Diem regime's being in its terminal stage, which was written after a conversation with President Kennedy that occurred just before he left

Washington. Only this can account for the alacrity with which he interpreted the famous 24 August State Department cable, signed by Rusk, as an order to generate a coup against Diem. The cable had not been coordinated with McNamara and Taylor, who were so angry about it that Kennedy had confided to a friend: "My God, my government is coming apart." The coup attempt then failed to get off the ground, leaving the Kennedy administration to deal with a regime aware that at least some elements of the American mission had backed a coup against it.

Only a few days after Lodge's arrival, I was urgently called to the embassy by Mike Dunn and informed that Lodge had received instructions from Washington (the 24 August cable) to inspire a coup by the Vietnamese army against Diem and Nhu. Dunn asked me what could I do to help. This put me in a quandary. I thought a coup against Diem was a mistake, but I had to play along if I wanted to retain any influence over events. I was close to one of the most influential generals, my old friend Le Van Kim, who had told me earlier that the army was outraged by Nhu. So I arranged for Col. Lou Conein to see Kim. Lou was an old friend from the Saigon Military Mission days who was back in South Vietnam as part of the CIA station. Stemming from that visit and others by Lou, coup plotting by the army began. I did not participate in the meetings, but I knew what was going on.

I was so distraught by this turn of events that I arranged for a secret meeting with Kim through Bui Diem. (Bui Diem was a close friend from the 1954–1956 days who eventually became the longest-serving South Vietnam ambassador to the United States and the author of *In the Jaws of History*.) At this meeting, I pleaded with Kim that if there was a coup, Diem be kept as chief of state. He asked me if that was Lodge's official policy. I answered no, but I said from everything I knew about South Vietnam, it would be the right thing to do. He looked unconvinced. It was the best I could do.

In the week that followed the cable, the Vietnamese army could not get the coup organized, so the organizers called it off. In the meantime, Nhu became aware that some elements of the American mission had backed a coup against the regime. His attitude and particularly that of his wife, Madame Nhu, became more rabid against the Buddhists and unidentified enemies of the regime and was more provocative than ever. Nhu began threatening to initiate talks independently with the North Vietnamese, setting off alarm bells in Washington even if few knowledgeable local observers took this threat seriously.

There was some evidence that Nhu was beginning to plot a countercoup or countercoups. Secretary of Defense Thuan became alarmed about Nhu's sanity after experiencing what he regarded as a paranoiac polemic against the

Americans, the Buddhists, and the army during a meeting at the Presidential Palace. I talked to Lodge about the need for someone like Lansdale to organize a campaign to get Nhu out of South Vietnam. It was like a political campaign, I said, and the campaign needed a campaign manager. He seemed to agree.

Bad News on the Local Front and from Home

At the same time, I had learned in late August that my father was fatally ill with cancer; thus, I needed to return to the United States to meet with my mother. After an exchange of cables, AID/Washington agreed to a trip home for me in early September. Unknown to me, apparently my views on the local situation were wanted at the higher levels of the State Department and the National Security Council.

Just before I was to leave on 10 September, two things happened. Two days earlier, I had been invited just north of Saigon to a II Corps briefing on a sweep that had been conducted in the famous Iron Triangle, a longtime communist-base area that included Cu Chi, the area that became famous for its Viet Cong tunnels. While there, I had a chance to talk to some of the American captains who had been involved as unit advisers, and they told me absolutely nothing was achieved, that no Viet Cong were even encountered.

At this time, I learned that a special two-man mission had been sent out to evaluate whether we were winning the war, and one member, Marine Corps Maj. Gen. Victor (Brute) Krulak from the Pentagon, was at the briefing. I introduced myself to him, then stood in the back as the division adviser described the operation as a victory that had driven the Viet Cong from the area. It was so incredulous that afterward I approached the colonel who had given the briefing and asked him how he could call the operation a victory when, according to his own unit advisers, not a single Viet Cong had been encountered. He said, "But we drove them out." I said, "What do you think is going to happen when our side leaves?" He was nonplussed.

Then the day before I left, I received an urgent call from our prov rep, Earl Young, in Long An Province just south of Saigon. He asked if I could come down for a brief visit because some bad things were happening to the Strategic Hamlet Program in the province. Young and the sector (provincial) military adviser told me that about fifty hamlets in the province had been recently destroyed by Viet Cong company- and battalion-size main-force units. The Viet Cong were invading in force, killing any hamlet defenders who opposed them, rousting the inhabitants from their homes, and making them take down and cut up the barbed-wire defenses and, in many cases, remove the corrugated metal roofs off their houses. This was happening in hamlet after hamlet. When I asked about the security screen the Vietnamese army was supposed to provide, I was told they had been confined to their barracks "for fear of a coup." I told Bohannan and Fraleigh about the visit when I returned to Saigon, but there was no time to write it up because I was leaving the next morning.

Returning to Washington

I left for Washington on the same special plane as Krulak, Joseph Mendenhall of the State Department (the civilian who was to report to Kennedy on the conduct of the war), and John Mecklin, chief of the local U.S. Information Service office. I had been offered a ride at the last moment and reached home late on the night of 10 September. Mecklin would remember that Krulak would not speak to him because of his unfavorable reporting on the local political situation. I was too tired to speak to anybody. When I arrived at home, a message was waiting asking me to report to the office of Assistant Secretary of State Roger Hilsman early the next day.

I met in Hilsman's office with Hilsman and Mike Forrestal of the White House National Security Council (NSC) staff. (Forrestal had made a personal appeal to me back in August 1962 to go back to South Vietnam to administer Rural Affairs—an appeal he said at the time had come from President Kennedy.)

In our conversation, I was told by Forrestal and Hilsman that the special two-man mission consisting of Krulak and Mendenhall would probably be making reports at the upcoming NSC meeting. Both had been sent to South Vietnam to "get the facts" about "Were we winning the war with the Diem regime?"

Krulak, I later learned, had used a World War II relationship with Kennedy, a reputation for innovative tactical thinking, and a facile mind with facts and figures suited to McNamara's mind-set to become his special assistant for counterinsurgency. In that position, he had been able to elbow Lansdale, whom McNamara didn't like or understand, completely out of the picture. Krulak knew little about communist insurgency or South Vietnam and understood even less, as his report would reveal. He had been sent, with a supporting military staff, to find the facts to prove that the war was being won and that no changes were needed.

On the other hand, I knew that Mendenhall was possessed of such an animosity against Diem that he was incapable of objectivity. Under Ambassador Durbrow in Saigon from 1957 to 1961, he had been mainly responsible for Durbrow's ill-conceived and clumsy efforts to reform Diem, which had only reinforced Diem's worst tendencies. In August 1962, he had written an internal memorandum to the deputy assistant secretary of far eastern affairs in which he recommended: "Get rid of Diem, Mr. and Mrs. Nhu and the rest of the Ngo family."[7]

President Ngo Dinh Diem *(center)* visits a hamlet in An Xuyen Province, July 1962.

I sensed from my conversation with Hilsman and Forrestal that Hilsman thought Diem was the problem, and although he and Forrestal shared reservations about the military's rosy view of the war, Forrestal had reservations about whether a coup against Diem was the answer. I told them I thought it was still possible to separate Diem from Nhu.

I was only dimly aware of the sharp split at the top of the administration or of the emotion it was generating. Secretary McNamara and General Taylor believed the war against the Viet Cong was going well enough for the United States to stick with Diem and Nhu. They conceived of the war as mainly a military contest to be won by pure force of arms, for which a stable Saigon regime was the most essential ingredient. The State Department, led by Averell Harriman, undersecretary of state for political affairs, to whom Rusk deferred, thought the outcome hung on the regime's lack of political support. Harriman, supported by Hilsman, was vehemently supporting the replacement of Diem and Nhu. I was unaware that Hilsman wanted to use me to discredit Krulak and to support his own conviction that the regime had to be overthrown. I also did not know that he had been the principal author of the notorious 24 August cable that Lodge interpreted as an order to organize a coup against Diem.

Hilsman and Forrestal asked me to make myself available at the State Department early the next morning for a possible meeting of the National Security Council. I spent the rest of the day with my mother and my father, whose mind was going because of brain cancer, and had no time to contact anyone else. (I later learned that I was under suspicion of having contacted Lansdale in advance of the NSC meeting, but this did not happen.)

Meeting at the NSC with Kennedy

Early on 12 September, I reported to Hilsman's office at the State Department. Hilsman told me the NSC meeting was on for 10:30 A.M. and I should come with him. We arrived early at the Cabinet Room of the White House. I had some time to think about what I wanted to say if I was called on, but I still had no idea if this was really going to happen. I sat toward the rear of the room in seats reserved for the staff. At 10:30, Kennedy strode into the Cabinet Room, flashed a smile, and took his chair along the middle of the conference table between Dean Rusk and Robert McNamara.

"Gentlemen, please proceed," President Kennedy said. McNamara briefly introduced Krulak and Mendenhall as having just returned from South Vietnam and summarized the purpose of their mission. Krulak described his visit to the Mekong Delta and to the area north of Saigon, where he had received briefings on the war from American military advisers at corps and division levels. His report was very favorable. He reeled off statistics about weapons captured and numbers of ARVN offensive operations. "We are winning the war handily," he said, "particularly in the Delta." He concluded that the Buddhist crisis had not affected the Vietnamese officer corps or the conduct of the war and that the war could be won irrespective of the regime's defects.

Mendenhall, in contrast, had visited Saigon and Hue, where he had spoken mainly to Buddhist leaders and to Diem's political opponents, whom he had known from his earlier years in South Vietnam. He said there was widespread hatred of the Diem regime and a virtual breakdown of civil government. "There will be civil war or a large-scale movement to the Viet Cong," he predicted. "Nhu must go if the war is to be won." The implication of his report was that Diem and Nhu were inseparable and that both most go.

Kennedy was incredulous. "Did you two gentlemen go to the same country?" he asked. Hilsman said the two perspectives reflected the difference between a military and a political point of view. Krulak said that Mendenhall had been in the cities, while he had gone to the rural areas. "That's where the war is," he added. Ambassador Nolting, who had been replaced by Lodge, drew a parallel with the year 1961 when there had been hatred of the Diem regime, but it had been dissipated by positive action. National Security Adviser McGeorge Bundy rebutted Nolting.

To me, there was an air of unreality to the discussion. No one there seemed to understand the complexities of South Vietnam or that the conflict was not a conventional war but essentially a political struggle for the loyalty and support of the rural population. This was the other war, the real war, I thought. I was particularly upset at Krulak's report, when I had just been in the Delta. To generate the will to resist the Viet Cong and thus win the population's loyalty and support required that the hamlets serve as the means for improving security and well-being. Most hamlets could defend themselves against local Viet Cong squad and platoon-size attacks but not against main-force assaults. That was the job of the troops of the ARVN, and they were not doing it. Tangible improvements in schools and wells and better crops were happening, but these alone were not enough.

Suddenly, I heard Forrestal's voice saying, "Mr. President, we have with us Rufus Phillips, who is in charge of the Rural Affairs Program in South Vietnam, as you know. I think you ought to hear his views." Kennedy nodded, "Yes, by all means." I knew, as I was thinking, that Lodge had encouraged a coup. I had even met with one of the conspirators. Now it appeared that Nhu might try a bloody coup of his own. What I knew of South Vietnam had convinced me that Diem must be saved as a nationalist symbol who could hold the country together. I felt it was still possible, but this was the last chance. When I was ushered to a chair at the table, Kennedy gave me a warm smile, which encouraged me. Whirling through my mind were two thoughts. "I owe him the truth as I see it." The other was a question: "How can I tell him what I know about South Vietnam in a few minutes?"

"Mr. President," I began, "I am sorry to have to tell you this, but we are not winning the war, particularly in the Delta." At this point, McNamara started shaking his head sideways, a gesture he continued throughout my presentation. I took a deep breath and went on. "I have known South Vietnam since 1954. I have close personal relationships with many Vietnamese in and out of the government, including President Diem and his brother Ngo Dinh Nhu. The problem is Nhu. He has lost the respect of the majority of the civilian and military leadership who would change the government if they saw an alternative. The opinions of the Buddhist leadership, which are violently anti-Diem, are not representative, but there is a general crisis of confidence in the regime shared by civilian and army leaders alike. Our own military advisers are not an accurate source of political information. They are under a directive not to talk politics with their Vietnamese counterparts, and the Vietnamese know it."

Krulak interjected, "Our military officers may not be good on palace intrigue, but they are competent to say whether the war is being won or not, and they say the war is going well."

I resumed. "I have spoken with many Vietnamese political and military leaders such as Secretary of Defense Nguyen Dinh Thuan, President Diem's secretary, Vo Van Hai, Gen. Le Van Kim of the General Staff, and Col. Hoang Lac, who heads the Strategic Hamlet Program. Thuan, the most powerful man in the Diem government after Diem and Nhu, thinks Nhu must leave the country, or there will be chaos. He says security is deteriorating; the government is now losing the war in the Delta. He feels America must act to show it does not support Nhu. We cannot continue to ignore Nhu's actions at the cost of losing Vietnamese respect and support.

"What is needed is a campaign to isolate Nhu and to get him out of the country. The campaign needs a campaign manager. I still believe that Nhu can be split from Diem, but there is only one American who has Diem's confidence and who could persuade Diem to let Nhu go. That man is General Lansdale [Colonel Lansdale had been promoted to general]. Ambassador Lodge agrees that Lansdale should come back. If it doesn't work, no one would be more qualified to help put together a new government. I recommend you send him there as soon as possible."

The president took notes while I spoke. When I finished, he said to me, "Mr. Phillips, I want to thank you for your remarks and particularly for your recommendation concerning General Lansdale."

The president then asked for my specific recommendations for dealing with Nhu. I suggested we cut off CIA aid to Colonel Tung's Special Forces, which had raided the pagodas, and that the U.S. Information Service should stop producing films laudatory of Nhu. We should make it clear that Nhu was the target of our actions. This would isolate him and produce a psychological squeeze for his removal. Kennedy expressed concern that Nhu might precipitate a collapse of the entire country. I said that the army could hold the country together if it had to.

"What do you think of the military situation?" the president asked. "The First, Second, and Third Corps areas are okay," I replied, "but the war effort in the Fourth Corps, the Delta area south of Saigon, is going to pieces. The Strategic Hamlet Program there is collapsing. I was just in Long An Province, where within the past week the Viet Cong destroyed fifty strategic hamlets, forcing the inhabitants to cut the barbed wire defenses and to take the roofs off their houses. ARVN troops, who were supposed to be defending the hamlets, were confined to quarters for fear they might be used for a coup." Hilsman asked whether security had started deteriorating in the Delta before 20 August (the cataclysmic day of the Diem regime's raid on the Buddhist pagodas). I said that it had.

Krulak interrupted again, "Mr. Phillips is putting his views over those of General Harkins, and I take General Harkins's. The Fourth Corps is the most difficult, but we hope to drive the Viet Cong into this area to compress them so they can be destroyed. The war is not being lost militarily."

My God, I thought to myself, Krulak must have gone to the moon—but the moment was too serious to laugh at the absurdity of a Viet Cong "human-type cattle drive" into the Delta. "The strategic hamlets are not being adequately protected," I insisted. "They are being overrun. Furthermore, this is not a military but a political war. It is a war for men's minds more than a war against the Viet Cong, and it's being lost."

John Mecklin spoke next. He said he shared my views and the recommendation about Lansdale but felt I didn't go far enough. He thought we should consider the direct use of American forces in South Vietnam to support the war effort. At this point the meeting broke into an uproar, with General Taylor saying, "No, no, under no circumstances." John McCone, director of the CIA, said that the Vietnamese military would work with Nhu and that the situation was not as ominous as I had reported. Harriman commented that the situation was obviously coming apart, and we could not continue with Diem. There was no consensus. The president was clearly bothered. He asked that the group meet again the next day.

As I left the meeting, the director of AID, David Bell, put his arm around my shoulders and said, "Thanks for telling it as you see it." Outside the White House, it had begun to rain. I slipped on the pavement and cut a deep gash in my shin but didn't feel it—I was numb. I took a cab back to my parents' apartment. Despite the confusion and the lack of understanding, I was encouraged. I had sensed the division and bureaucratic rivalry present in that room. I had seen Krulak's ignorance or ambition, I could not tell which, as well as Mendenhall's prejudices—masquerading as fact, but Kennedy had taken notes only when I had spoken. Maybe he would cut through the bureaucracy and act decisively despite McNamara's clear opposition to what I had said. My mind was in a turmoil. "This might be a real turning point," I thought.

McCone and McNamara Oppose Lansdale to Saigon

Unfortunately, the idea of sending Lansdale to help Lodge was killed, possibly in part by the way Lodge approached it. He sent a "Top Secret, Eyes Only," personal letter to Secretary Rusk on 13 September asking that Rusk show it to President Kennedy. "For maximum security, I am typing it myself and am sending it to you by messenger," he said. "What I ask is that General Lansdale be sent over here at once to take charge, under my supervision, of all U.S. relationships with a change of government here. To function efficiently he must have a staff, and I therefore ask that he be put in charge of the CAS (CIA) station in the Embassy, relieving the present incumbent, Mr. John Richardson."[8] It appeared in Washington that Lodge was attempting an end run around the CIA to replace Richardson with someone he wanted. Naturally, the "eyes only" restriction was not observed.

In a telephone conversation between McCone and Rusk on 17 September, McCone stated he had "no confidence at all" in Lansdale and "could assume no responsibility for the operation." McCone claimed that "this whole thing was built up by him [Lansdale] through Rufus Phillips" and that "Lodge does not know this fellow." Rusk said, "Lansdale denied this," but he called the point "fairly incidental" and went on to say "if [the] Lansdale thing is not appealing to McCone and McNamara . . . it is a small part of it."[9]

In retrospect, it appears that McCone was bitter about the work Lansdale had done for the Kennedys on the ill-fated Operation Mongoose, the purpose of which was to eliminate Castro. It had been initially run out of the White House at Bobby Kennedy's direction without McCone's knowledge, which was not Lansdale's fault. In any case, Lansdale was not CIA career staff.

I could see in the National Security Council meeting that McNamara would probably oppose Lansdale's return because he had shaken his head vigorously when I made that recommendation to the president. McNamara's mind-set rendered him unable to appreciate Lansdale's talents or understanding of South Vietnam. Rusk would have been lukewarm at best because he had opposed President Kennedy's initial attempt to send Lansdale out as ambassador to South Vietnam in 1961. It was another case of the primacy of bureaucratic interests and personal hubris at the top of the administration, with true American and Vietnamese interests taking a backseat.

The opportunity to change direction on the ground was thus lost. With the dispute between the Defense and State Departments' points of view remaining unresolved, Lodge had a green light to continue fanning a coup. Lodge had initially met with Nhu on 2 September to explore what Nhu might be willing to do in terms of leaving the country and received an elliptical response. His response appeared to agree with Lodge that perhaps it would be politically expedient for him to go out of the country, but then he listed reasons why this might not be a good idea.

After repeated requests from Rusk with President Kennedy's backing, Lodge reluctantly had one meeting with Diem on 9 September in which Lodge cited

The chief of Quang Ngai Province *(left)* shares a joke with Rufe Phillips *(right)*, July 1962. *USOM photographer*

harsh comments made in the United Nations and in the U.S. Congress about the Diem government's handling of the Buddhists as justification for telling Diem that "Nhu should go away, not returning at least until [the] end of December—after the [congressional] appropriations had been voted." Diem looked aghast and vigorously objected. The conversation then got into press censorship, and at the end, Lodge reiterated that he hoped very much that "there would be changes in personnel and in policy in order to make continued support of the war possible." There was no discussion, which could have meant anything in practical terms. Lodge's approach thereafter was, as he put it, "silence."

It was the first and last conversation Lodge ever had with Diem about Nhu. On 29 September, McNamara and General Taylor, with Lodge in attendance, met with Diem at the Presidential Palace. Diem was informed by McNamara in blunt terms that continued American aid was at risk because of the government's repressive policies. However, no specific solutions or ideas for resolution that would have made sense in the local political context were raised. None of the American participants knew enough about Diem or South Vietnam to offer ideas that might have had some resonance and that offered a way out without trampling on Diem's nationalism and self-respect. This was the same McNamara who, in a vivid demonstration of ignorance and insensitivity, was to parade around South Vietnam in 1964 while holding General Khanh's hand up in the air, embarrassing both Khanh and the Vietnamese in general, at public rallies and chanting the traditional cry in unintelligible Vietnamese, "Vietnam Cong Hoa Muon Nam" (Republic of Vietnam for Ten Thousand Years), to show American support.

After reviewing the record, which is copiously set forth in the two volumes covering 1963 of *The Foreign Relations of the United States,* published by the Department of State, it can be concluded that no serious effort was made to have a real dialogue with Diem about getting Nhu out of South Vietnam, thus allowing the possibility of restoring Diem's ties with the army and the Buddhists. There was no doubt that it would have been extremely difficult to do this, and indeed it was probably not in the cards unless Lansdale, who had Diem's confidence, had been entrusted with the negotiation.

I remained in Washington for a few weeks after the NSC meeting to take care of family business. During that period, I was asked for advice by Hilsman and Forrestal on how to isolate the Nhus—Madame Nhu and her husband—and whether it was necessary or desirable to send in U.S. troops as recommended by John Mecklin. I responded with brief papers on both subjects. I strongly opposed the introduction of U.S. troops.

Returning to Saigon

Upon my return to Saigon near the end of September, I watched the situation spiral toward disaster, mainly as a bystander. I had been pilloried within MACV for my report about Long An Province and my disagreement with Krulak. MACV turned itself inside out to prove that I was wrong about Long An Province and had relieved the provincial military adviser because he had informed me "about military matters."

During the time I was still in Washington, Lodge had given a cocktail party for some visiting dignitary at which General Harkins heatedly told Bill Trueheart, Lodge's deputy, "I'm going to get that Rufus Phillips." Trueheart, who happened to be with his wife, Phoebe, was so taken aback that he was at a loss for words. Phoebe replied with a charming smile, "But General, he doesn't work for you." When a special mission led by General Taylor and Secretary McNamara came out at the end of September, I was still so controversial that I did not appear personally in any of the briefings that were given by the Rural Affairs staff to McNamara.

McNamara had been given our province-by-province progress reports on the Strategic Hamlet Program by Bill Bundy, his assistant secretary for international security affairs. Bundy also arranged the Rural Affairs briefings. After reading the reports and appearing to listen, McNamara wanted to know why such a detailed appreciation of the Strategic Hamlet Program had not reached him before. His reaction was that the reporting he had been getting was not detailed enough and what was needed was a more comprehensive reporting system. This caused, in typical McNamara fashion, the creation of a reporting system that was so detailed and complicated that it became largely meaningless. Another irony of the visit was that General Taylor went to Long An Province, where he verified all the information I had reported in the 12 September NSC meeting in Washington, including the details of how many miles of barbed wire had been cut up by the intimidated hamlet population on Viet Cong orders.

Partial word of what I had said in Washington had somehow also gotten to Nhu, who now apparently believed that I was one of the American plotters against him. Stories began to appear in the local press about how I was the secret replacement for John Richardson as the new CIA station chief. Even Malcolm Browne of the Associated Press wire service picked up this canard in a news report he filed in Tokyo. At the same time, Madame Nhu's brother was conspiring with the former province chief of Vinh Long (my old nemesis, Colonel Phuoc) to assassinate Americans viewed as being against the regime. He even showed his purported assassination list to an Australian correspondent, Denis Warner, just as Denis was leaving Saigon. Denis called me at 5 o'clock in the morning to meet him at the Givrail (a popular ice cream and coffee shop in Saigon) before his plane took off so he could tell me about it. I was on the list, along with Lou Conein, Mecklin, and Richardson. I promptly reported what Denis had told me to Lodge.

The atmosphere became more and more lurid. I was concerned for the safety of Barbara and our children and obtained some volunteer guards from a Philippine company in Saigon to help guard our house. The company was led by former Magsaysay people. Coup rumors began to fly, and my mother called saying my father was dying. I made arrangements for Barbara and the children to return home, flew back to Washington for his funeral, and then returned alone to see the crisis through, hoping that somehow something could be salvaged when the inevitable coup came. It did, on 1 November 1963. Early in the morning of the next day, Diem was murdered, to our and the Vietnamese army's shame.

I tried to brief the new Vietnamese military leadership on what we were doing and to urge them to preserve the best elements of the Strategic Hamlet Program. With a few exceptions, most seemed more interested in revenge. Many of the hamlet militias, particularly in Central Vietnam, were disarmed while the army tried to reorganize itself. It was time to go home. By chance, I left just before President Kennedy was assassinated, learning about it en route.

In the span of little more than a month, my father had died. Diem and Kennedy had been assassinated. I was exhausted. So much had seemed possible, now it all seemed to be going up in smoke. While taking over the family business to keep it from collapsing, I stayed involved, trying to help over the next four years. But the introduction of five hundred thousand American soldiers into the war, something I had never conceived of in my worst nightmares, changed the arena so radically that there was little anyone not in top leadership could do to help.

Lansdale returned to Saigon in 1965 as an assistant to Ambassador Lodge, but Lodge was unwilling to carve out a strong role for him in the face of opposition from other elements of the American mission, which were by this time huge. Any opening for the Lansdale approach got lost in the enormity of it all as the de facto policy became one of the Americans winning the war militarily and then giving the country back to the Vietnamese. Vietnamization came too late, and a solid political base for continuing the struggle was never built by the noncommunist Vietnamese or among the American public.[10] It was doomed to fail.

Notes

1. Edward G. Lansdale, *In the Midst of Wars: An American's Mission to Southeast Asia* (New York: Harper and Row, 1972), 128.
2. This was a limitation that was shared to a considerable extent by all noncommunist Vietnamese nationalists, none of whom had any experience in open, democratic politics. The price of survival as an independent Vietnamese nationalist was precisely an ability to keep one's activities a secret from both the communists and the French.
3. The apogee was probably reached in 1964, when McNamara, on a trip to Vietnam, toured the countryside with Gen. Nguyen Khanh, raising Khanh's hand in front of assembled crowds of astonished Vietnamese and shouting "Vietnam Cong Hoa Muon Nam." He meant to say "Republic of Vietnam for Ten Thousand Years," a traditional Vietnamese chant, but with his accent, it came out something like, "Ruptured Duck, Lie Down." This would have been funny, except it completely undercut any nationalistic credentials Khanh might have had by making him out to be an American puppet.
4. Ample evidence exists in diplomatic correspondence of this hostility. See U.S. Department of State, *The Foreign Relations of the United States, Vietnam, 1955–1957;* and *The Foreign Relations of the United States, Vietnam, 1961–1963.* On the simplest level, Durbrow appears to have had an impatient personality and a tendency to dictate to people, which was not an acceptable way of dealing with any of the Vietnamese, particularly those who were highly nationalistic and therefore most sensitive to similar earlier behavior by the French. One incident in particular stands out, which was related to me by Joe Reddick, who had been a Lansdale assistant and interpreter in Vietnam from 1954 to 1956. Joe had accompanied

an American delegation, which did not include Lansdale, on a visit to Saigon in 1960 and went to a dinner held by President Diem. During the dinner, Diem expressed his views on the local situation at some length in French, with Reddick serving as interpreter. As Reddick interpreted, Durbrow made a number of caustic remarks in English. Reddick was astonished that Durbrow would be so openly insulting because it was common knowledge that although Diem preferred to speak French, he understood English quite well.

5. For a text of this memorandum, see *United States–Vietnam Relations, 1945–1967,* book 11, 1–12.

6. By a serious attempt to separate Nhu from Diem, I mean an attempt by someone such as Lansdale who could talk to Diem in a brotherly way about such sensitive matters rather than thinly disguised demands made by Ambassador Lodge, who could not help his inbred, imperious manner and had no personal relationship with Diem at all. There seemed to be little official understanding that if Nhu were to leave, he would have to occupy a new position outside the country of some prestige; that Diem's youngest brother, Luyen, a more open personality, would have to serve in a transitional role as personal counselor; and that above all Diem had to have someone among the Americans whom he could trust. Cecil B. Currey, in his biography entitled *Edward Lansdale: The Unquiet American,* relates a conversation Lansdale had with W. Averell Harriman and John Kenneth Galbraith in late summer 1963. Lansdale urged that Galbraith use his good offices to establish a teaching position at Harvard for Nhu. Galbraith was incensed at the idea, and said, "We don't do that at Harvard."

7. *The Foreign Relations of the United States, 1961–1963,* vol. 2, 596.

8. Ibid., vol. 4, 205.

9. Ibid., vol. 4, 240.

10. While pacification succeeded to a considerable extent between 1968 and 1972, as attested to in William Colby's book, *Lost Victory,* the missing element remained a Vietnamese national government with widespread popular support and with nationalist credentials that could compete on a political plane with the North Vietnamese. President Thieu, for all his administrative skills, had none of the popular following or prestige that continuing competition with the communists required. The Vietnamese government remained hollow at the center. The popular cause that Lansdale had tried to help create in the form of participatory government as an alternative to communism worth dying for had not come to pass. On the other hand, one could make the case that had the Americans remained in a strong supporting role instead of completely withdrawing, it might have been possible, even with the limitations of the Thieu government, to have hung on long enough for the opening to China to have provided an opportunity for a modus vivendi in South Vietnam similar to the North-South division of Korea.

Blind Design

Hoang Lac

As a former officer with the Army of the Republic of Vietnam (ARVN), I participated in major battles and political events in South Vietnam for a quarter of a century until the fall of Saigon in 1975. I personally witnessed the changing times and events, as well as the decisions made by top officials, that led to the collapse of South Vietnam.

I had many American friends who shared with me the glory of victories as well as the agony of defeats. My closest and longtime American friend was Richard Stilwell, who became a general in the U.S. Army. I met him in 1960 when we were both colonels. Stilwell then became assistant chief of staff (J3) for the U.S. Military Assistance Command, Vietnam (MACV). Later he became commanding general of the U.S. Army XXIV Corps in the northern part of South Vietnam. Under the command of General Westmoreland, Stilwell and his assistant, General DePuy, were the main architects of America's war effort in South Vietnam.

Stilwell was a general's officer in the purest sense of the word. His heavy workload and hardworking attitude constantly deprived him of much-needed sleep. The differences in our backgrounds and combat experiences obviously resulted in some differences between us. But we had tremendous respect for each other.

Like most other U.S. commanders in South Vietnam, Stilwell was extremely confident in himself and strongly believed in his reasoning that "we have enormous power and great mobility, the NVA [North Vietnam Army] can't sustain the losses, we will wear them down." During a discussion with him, I explained

---

This chapter consists of excerpts from a book entitled *Blind Design* by Hoang Lac and Ha Mai Viet, published in 1996 and condensed by Harvey C. Neese.

my idea that one must start with the basic philosophy of "Know Your Enemy"—that is, the strengths and weaknesses of Gen. Vo Nguyen Giap, the commander in chief of the NVA. Giap simply followed Mao Tse-tung's rules of warfare verbatim. We had to understand that the Viet Cong could not be destroyed nor paralyzed by conventional tactics. If we fought the same way that the French did during the first Indo-China War (1946–1954), we could win every battle and yet not win the war. Americans, far from home, could not fight and win a protracted attrition war. Stilwell was unable to see my point of view.

When we met again in 1988, thirteen years after the fall of South Vietnam, Stilwell was retired from the military and was working as an assistant to Secretary of Defense Caspar Weinberger. We talked about the old days, and he sadly admitted that "we made mistakes in Vietnam."

Although our cowritten book, *Blind Design,* deals with the period from 1954 through 1975, the condensed section prepared for this book is concerned with the events leading up to, and during, the critical years between the commitment of the American support to the government of South Vietnam in 1961 and the introduction of U.S. combat troops in 1965.

Ho Chi Minh, Consummate Revolutionary

To understand the origins of the Vietnam War, it is important to understand the personality and motivation of North Vietnam's leader, Ho Chi Minh. Ho's real name was Nguyen Sinh Cung, later changed to Nguyen Tat Thanh. Ho also used at least twelve other aliases, such as Ly Thuy and Nguyen Ai Quoc. Ho joined the French Communist Party in 1920. He lived in London, New York, and then Paris. In Paris, Ho made contact with Karl Marx's son-in-law, Jean Longuet, and he went to the USSR for training. The USSR sent Ho to Quang Chau, China, in 1925 to be an interpreter for a Mr. Borodine, who was a Soviet representative in China. Ho was honored as a "Cominternchik," which was the Communist International recognition for a foremost faithful member. He was also given a Russian name, Linov.

In 1930, Ho organized the Indo-China Communist Party. Under the name Sung Wen, Ho secretly went to Thailand to establish contact with the Asian branch of the Communist International. In Ho's first writing was the following excerpt: "The Third International is a worldwide Communist Party; those national branches are to listen and obey the common plan and common rules. For the world's proletariat revolution to succeed, we must follow Marxism and Leninism."

Ho's lifetime of power was gained from using various cunning tactics. He lured his opposition into alliances and destroyed them one after another. Examples are the Viet Minh Front (1945), Tan Trao Conference (1945), August Revolution (1945), Provisional Government (1945), Coalition Nationalist Government (1946), Front for Liberation of South Vietnam (1960), and the Provisional Government of South Vietnam (1969).

Before his death, Ho showed his true treacherous self. He wrote in his will his wish for the unification of Vietnam, the building of an international proletariat, and his reunion with his spiritual godfathers, Marx and Lenin.

Ho Chi Minh and the American OSS

In 1944, Ho contacted America's Office of Strategic Services, or OSS (predecessor of the Central Intelligence Agency, or CIA), to supply information on Japanese military activities in China and Indo-China. Ho was the Third International's dream: tricky, cunning, and phony but always hiding under the cover of a patriot with gentle manners and oratory skills. Ho won the trust of American Maj. Archimedes Patti of the OSS, who provided him with military uniforms and arms. In his report to Washington, Patti explained that Ho was an enthusiastic patriot. The OSS named his group Lucius.

When the Japanese surrendered on 15 August 1945, Ho, in collaboration with Vo Nguyen Giap, quickly gained control of the government of Tonkin, or the northern sector of Vietnam. In a 2 September 1945 meeting, Ho delivered the Declaration of Independence speech at Ba Dinh Square, Hanoi. Ho invited Major Patti to be among the honored guests. In the speech, Ho quoted liberally from Thomas Jefferson and the French revolutionary Declaration of the Rights of Man (probably to appease the United States and its powerful allies). The U.S. presence deviously portrayed to the Vietnamese people and to the world that Ho was prodemocratic.

In summer 1946, on his journey to France, Ho had sent a letter to President Truman to request U.S. recognition of free Vietnam, citing his contribution to the war against the Japanese and suggesting that Vietnam should enjoy the same status as the Philippines. Seven other subsequent letters from Ho were sent with no acknowledgment from U.S. officials.

Dividing Vietnam into North and South

After the victory against the French at Dien Bien Phu in 1954, the Vietnamese communists (Viet Minh) planned to take over all of Indo-China, but the plan was not approved by the leaders of the USSR and the People's Republic of China (PRC). The USSR did not want any direct involvement in Indo-China's internal affairs, and China foresaw the danger of the Viet Minh taking control of what was to become South Vietnam. Together they pressed Ho to conclude the Geneva Conference, which divided Vietnam into North and South.

Pham Van Dong unhappily signed the agreement on 20 July 1954 to assume control of North Vietnam. There was a provision in the agreement for national elections to take place and possibly to unify the country, depending on how the people voted. It was suspected that the Viet Minh intended to fight for a total victory, unifying South and North Vietnam, dominating Laos and Cambodia, and ultimately controlling all of Southeast Asia. Such an outcome would also have blocked any southern expansion by China.

The elections to unify the North and the South never took place. South Vietnamese Prime Minister, later President, Ngo Dinh Diem distrusted the communists' fairness in an open election, and he never agreed to hold it. At that point, there was also fear from the American side that Ho Chi Minh's party might have won the election.

Problems for the North

According to the Geneva Accords, the French Expeditionary Force and the Vietnamese nationalists had three hundred days to withdraw south of the seventeenth parallel, turning over the northern sector of Vietnam to the Viet Minh.

In Hanoi, the North Vietnamese temporarily cleared their forces from the vicinity of Hanoi, evacuating the cities of Haiphong and Hai Duong to make way for the French to move to South Vietnam within one hundred days. In the southern part of the northern sector, above the seventeenth parallel, the Viet Minh concentrated their units in Dong Thap, Xuyen Moc, and Ham Tan areas to move to what was now to be North Vietnam. In Central Vietnam, the French left Quang Tri, Quang Ngai, and Binh Dinh Provinces to make way for the Viet Minh's movement to the North.

The number of people who moved from North Vietnam to South Vietnam was 887,000, excluding the French Expeditionary Force and the ethnic Chinese who were moved by the Chinese Consulate. The total count approached one million people. After eight years of war, the French gave the Viet Minh the most devastated part of the land, with its people left in desperation, hunger, and bewilderment over the division of the country. These people neither wished to leave their ancestral land nor wanted to live under the hand of the communists.

Ngo Dinh Diem, Future President of the South

Much of what happened in South Vietnam between 1954 and 1963 revolved around the first president of South Vietnam, Ngo Dinh Diem, and his family.

The following background material is provided to help the reader better understand Diem and his effect on developments in South Vietnam.

Ngo Dinh Diem, a fervent Catholic in a Buddhist country, was born on 3 January 1901 in Hue, Central Vietnam. He graduated from the Administration School in 1922, began his career as a district chief, and later was promoted to province chief. In 1933, Emperor of Vietnam Bao Dai appointed Diem minister of administration. Diem held this position for only two months and resigned, citing that the representatives from Central Vietnam were not given enough authority.

During the August Revolution in 1945, the communists from the north assassinated Ngo Dinh Khoi, Diem's older brother and chief of Quang Nam Province, and Khoi's only son, Ngo Dinh Huan. Diem was arrested and taken to the northern sector of Vietnam.

Respecting Diem as a popular nationalist who had Japan's attention during its occupation of Indo-China (1940–1945), Ho Chi Minh invited Diem to come to the Presidential Palace in Hanoi, hoping for his support of the Democratic Republic of Vietnam (North Vietnam). Ho argued that Diem should join in rebuilding the country and rationalized that the murder of his brother and nephew was an error of the lower-level staff that had become known to Ho only after the fact. Diem emphatically refused to cooperate with the Viet Minh because they took the life of his brother and other nationalists. Shortly afterward, Diem managed to escape and flee the north of Vietnam. After Diem's inauguration as president of South Vietnam in 1955, Truong Chinh and Le Duan, two communist politburo members, without criticizing Chairman Ho, the godfather, made the observation that the early decision not to permanently eliminate Diem was a big mistake.

Diem in America—Getting Ready for the Call

In 1950, Diem went to Japan for a visit with Ky Ngoai Hau (a well-known Vietnamese nationalist in exile), who was then incapacitated because of old age. In Japan, Diem also met with Wesley Fishel, a lecturer from Michigan State University, who persuaded Diem to visit America. In the United States, Diem boarded at Maryknoll Mission of Lakewood, New Jersey, where he cleaned house and washed dishes in exchange for food and lodging.

During his stay in America (1950–1953), Diem received Cardinal Francis Spellman's wholehearted assistance. Through Spellman's introduction, Diem became acquainted with Senators William Knowland, Mike Mansfield, and John F. Kennedy, Supreme Court Justice William O. Douglas, and the Dulles brothers (John Foster, secretary of state, and Allen, director of the CIA), who influenced Diem's rise to power in South Vietnam in 1954.

Back at his home base in Hue, Central Vietnam, Diem had a lot of comrades and popular support across the three regions of Vietnam, especially in the central region.

In May 1953, Diem went to Belgium and then France and stayed in Europe until Emperor Bao Dai invited him to return to South Vietnam to become the prime minister on 16 June 1954. Although Bao Dai disliked Diem and felt his family was rather overrated and sometimes conniving, Bao Dai allowed Diem to assume the prime minister's post with full administrative and military authority. When Diem accepted the post, in the presence of Nguyen De, director of cabinet, and Dinh Xuan Quang, director of protocol, Diem knelt down in front of Emperor Bao Dai and Queen Nam Phuong to take his oath of allegiance and pledge his loyalty to the Nguyen Dynasty and Prince Bao Long.

Diem's First-Term Accomplishments

After a fierce and successful struggle to preserve his administration against an array of internal enemies, Diem dethroned Bao Dai in October 1955 and declared the Republic of Vietnam under a temporary constitution. Diem then became president of the republic as his reputation grew steadily and his power firmly solidified.

The three-year period of 1957, 1958, and 1959 could be considered the golden age of Diem's government. After restoring public security and social order and establishing the upper governmental structure (1955–1956), Diem concentrated the country's resources in the construction of a society with justice and compassion and the development of an efficient industrial base to promote and use the national potential.

The primary goals of Diem's administration were to serve the interests of the population and to counter the communist threat. His administration's accomplishments were partially due to vigorous American support to help relocate and settle almost one million people in the exodus from north of the seventeenth parallel to the southern part, now called South Vietnam. He was also instrumental in the formation of a modern military force capable of fighting the communists and the importation of practical and needed commodities for the population to control inflation and prevent hoarding.

Militarily, Diem's main task was to reorganize the old French colonial system. Diem, with the advice of Gen. Samuel T. Williams, head of the U.S. Military Assistance Advisory Group (MAAG), created major military units such as divisions and military regions and armed them with modern weapons and American military techniques. General Williams was very knowledgeable in conventional warfare, yet he paid little attention to unconventional tactics.

He assumed, with the view of a World War II general, that the communists would launch an attack across the seventeenth parallel via lower Laos or would land on the coast of Central Vietnam. To counter these possible assaults, the South Vietnamese would need seven military divisions at strategic locations. The military organization (divisions and military regions) was thus established with this faulty assumption, which would prove fatal to South Vietnam in the long term.

Meanwhile, the Viet Minh from the North focused on forming secret bases and transporting weapons and ammunition to the military units of the fifth column they had implanted in the South (those left behind who would carry on the cause for the communist North).

Diem's administration, in the first Five Year Plan (1957–1961), increased agricultural production by 25 percent. This plan was used as the standard for other economic, social, public, and private investment programs. Transportation routes were improved, and the highway from Saigon to Bien Hoa and new roads to the Highlands were constructed. A railroad, connecting the entire length of South Vietnam, was built. Significant accomplishments were also achieved in improving and opening new waterways. Dong Tien Canal (twenty-six miles in length) and Don Giong (twenty-five miles long) were completed.

Diem concentrated efforts on large-scale agricultural improvements, such as land-use reform and agricultural pacification programs to capture the "hearts and minds" of village farmers. With the land-use reform, Diem promoted privatization of land ownership by farmers. The land-reform program in the South was initiated by Wolf Ladejinsky, an American and a very close friend and adviser to Diem. This program was carried out in a civilized and humanitarian manner, in contrast to the brutal treatment of landowners in the North by the communists (according to the teachings of Mao Tse-tung). Diem's main goal was to reduce the size of individual landownership and sell the excess land to small farmers who could pay for the land in installments. The maximum landownership limit was established at one hundred acres for agricultural use and fifteen acres for cultural beliefs of Buddhist ancestor worship. According to government reports, more than 170,000 farm families had become landowners who received low-interest loans from the agricultural credit offices.

In reality, Diem's land-use reform did not bring all the expected results. In some areas previously controlled by the communists, whenever landowners felt unsafe or insecure, they did not dare to farm the land. Earlier during the war against the French, the communists took over the land and gave it to the peasants without any obligations to pay. Diem's land-reform policy allowed the original owners to repossess their land from the squatters farming it but not owning it. The real owners would then be forced to sell their excess land to the government, which then resold the land back to the settlers who had been farming it. These squatter farmers suddenly had to make payment to the government for the land they had been farming for years and thought they owned. With very limited understanding, the farmers felt that they were getting cheated. Consequently they became unhappy with the South Vietnamese government.

Overall, Diem's agricultural policy was considered successful. Along with the goal of popularizing landownership, Diem's agricultural plan aimed to farm undeveloped land in the Central Highlands and the undeveloped areas in the southwest part of the country.

Total farming areas increased with more agricultural development. They later became effective forefront battlefields against the communists. The industrial-development plan included the construction of fabric and paper factories, a sugar-manufacturing plant, Da Nhim hydroelectric dam, Nong Son coal mine, and Ha Tien cement plant, along with other lesser developments. They were designed to solve unemployment problems, and the program was celebrated with great success.

Diem's Daunting Task

In the beginning, the then Prime Minister Diem faced powerful opposition in South Vietnam. However, with valuable assistance from U.S. advisers (which is described in detail in Maj. Gen. Edward Lansdale's book, *In the Midst of Wars*), as well as the support of the majority of the population and the military, Diem overcame all major obstacles.

During a trip to the United States (early May 1957) in response to President Eisenhower's invitation, President Diem was greeted as a major head of state in New York City and Washington, D.C. He was also invited to address a joint session of the U.S. Congress, a special honor given to few foreign leaders. Returning to South Vietnam after the two-week trip, Diem understood that he was in a better position to govern his country than ever before. First, he knew he must find the means to counteract Ho Chi Minh, a skilled opponent heading North Vietnam, and the powerful Indo-China Communist Party, which received strong support from both the Soviet Union and China.

Diem Family's Abuse of Power

Meanwhile, South Vietnam was divided by many separate political groups that constantly competed against one another and that destabilized its internal politics. President Diem realized that the most important thing for him to do was to continue to solidify his power. Diem issued Executive Order 57A to broaden the authority of the province chiefs appointed by the president. The province chiefs were the only local officials with full power to govern both civilian and military units. Furthermore, citing the necessity for maintaining national security under the threat of communism, the province chiefs were empowered to appoint village chiefs. Thus, the political infrastructure was straying away from the principles of democracy and against Vietnam's ancient custom of self-governing at the village levels.

It was a life and death struggle for both Ho in the North and Diem in the South to quickly grasp tight control over the village governing system, thus consolidating their positions in their struggle against each other. In that process, both in their own way, they would greatly diminish the Vietnamese ancient village custom, the centuries-old democratic foundation of Vietnam society.

With flagrant nepotism and cronyism, President Diem appointed members of his family and their loyal followers to key government positions. This short-sighted political decision was among his greatest mistakes, and it promoted corruption and abundant abuse of power by his brothers.

In Central Vietnam, Diem's younger brother, Ngo Dinh Can, considered himself akin to a regional king. Praised by his cronies as an adviser to Diem and leader in the central region and Highlands of South Vietnam, Can was an unreasonable, self-centered individual and the least educated of the brothers. However, he was well liked by the first family because he spent much of his time caring for their ninety-year-old invalid mother.

Every day, dozens of high-level officials waited in turn to offer their respects and their personal services to him. Can pretended that he was only a peasant at heart and that he had little authority and little status in society. Quite often, he pretended that he wanted only to be left alone so that he would have time to care for his elderly mother.

Diem became unhappy with the constant abuse of power by Can. Diem was unable to find an effective way of dealing with the younger brother who had cared for his mother and was responsible for destroying powerful opposition to him in Central Vietnam. Most of all, Diem was indebted to Can and felt obligated to him for his effective handling of the election campaign and the national referendum to depose Emperor Bao Dai.

In the western part of South Vietnam, Senior Archbishop Ngo Dinh Thuc, the head bishop of South Vietnam and Diem's older brother, used his family influence to promote Catholicism. Many incompetent and unqualified individuals came to Thuc for baptism and for assistance in finding employment or business contracts. During special holidays such as Christmas or New Year's, special events such as Thuc's sixtieth birthday, or the ceremonies to open new religious establishments presided over by President Diem, large crowds of high-level officials gathered around Thuc, ready to do anything to please him. President Diem was sometimes uncomfortable with such activities, but he was not displeased with all the royal respect given to his family.

Diem's brother and national adviser, Ngo Dinh Nhu, was also displeased with the exposure of the Catholic Church and had once questioned Truong Vinh Le, president of the National Assembly, and Bui Van Luong, minister of interior, on why the National Assembly and the cabinet should go to Vinh Long to meet with the bishop so frequently. Government officials, through the Diem "brotherhood," were exposed to, and entertained, intolerable political opportunism and social corruption.

During the early years of the Ngo Dinh Diem administration, Thuc was successful in mobilizing Catholics in support of President Diem. This caused Thuc to gain excessive confidence in Catholicism and in himself as a religious leader to the point that he was unable to tolerate the growth and expansion of any other religion. It was his intolerance of religious freedom that led to the serious conflict between Thuc and the Buddhist organization in Hue when he was transferred to this stronghold of Buddhism.

Meanwhile, the youngest Ngo brother, Ngo Dinh Luyen, kept a low profile. He graduated from the École Central des Mines, a well-known French university. With a degree in mineral engineering, Luyen was later appointed ambassador to the United Kingdom, a position that kept him away from the power struggles of his brothers. He visited South Vietnam only a couple of times each year to report on the political development of the European community.

Ngo Dinh Nhu and Madame Nhu

On the opposite side of the spectrum, Ngo Dinh Nhu, the other brother, held a key role in establishing and organizing Diem's regime. Nhu and his wife, Madame Nhu, were primarily responsible for the destruction of the first Republic of Vietnam (South Vietnam).

Nhu was a thoughtful scholar with a progressive mind. He had a bachelor's degree in literature from Sorbonne University in France and later graduated from École National des Chartes and worked for the French Archive Department. He was known by his associates as unassuming and quiet, and he rarely expressed his feelings. He was also unemotional, cold natured, self-confident, and lonely. In President Diem's first term, his influence was well hidden from the public. After the coup attempt on 11 November 1960, Nhu found it necessary to step out of his brother's shadow to run key governmental programs. That was when I got to know Nhu personally. By 1961, Nhu directed the implementation of the Strategic Hamlet Program and became the powerhouse behind the presidency.

Ngo Dinh Nhu's wife's maiden name was Tran Le Xuan. Madame Nhu, who was known by the general public as the Female Tiger and by the U.S. media as the Dragon Lady, would become a victim of her own ambitions. She wanted to become a contemporary female leader of South Vietnam, like previous national heroines such as the Trung sisters of ancient history. She was a progressive, attractive, extremely ambitious, self-confident, intelligent, and courageous woman. During the 1960 coup attempt, while President Diem and his brother Nhu sat for hours in a bunker in the Gia Long Presidential Palace in Saigon pondering a solution, Madame Nhu contacted the Military Region V commander, Col. Tran Thien Khiem, from the west and Gen. Le Van Nghiem from the east and arranged for the rescue of the president and his staff.

To establish a public position of her own, Madame Nhu ran for congressional representative for Duc Hoa and Duc Hue Districts in Long An Province (later changed to Hau Nghia Province). After being elected, she used the power of her brother-in-law, the president, to pass the first family law of South Vietnam (prohibiting polygamy and divorce), a law on social ethics (prohibiting society's evils such as gambling and prostitution), and a law on equality (prohibiting sex discrimination).

In addition, Madame Nhu created the Women's Coalition and the Women's Republic Force, which trained women for military service. She also built a national monument exhibiting the statues of Trung Trac and Trung Nhi, the legendary sister heroines universally known in Vietnamese history as Hai Ba Trung, or the Two Trung Sisters. (The facial resemblance of Madame Nhu and her daughter to the statues raised suspicions among Vietnamese that Madame Nhu had built a monument to herself.)

The Strategic Hamlet Program

In 1961, Great Britain sent a delegation, led by Sir Robert Thompson, to visit South Vietnam. The group recommended that President Diem formulate a plan similar to the one carried out by members of the British Advisory Mission (BRIAM) in Malaya. The delegation recommended that Diem concentrate resources and target the first eleven townships around Saigon to issue identification cards to control the population, establish curfews, and limit the movement of material. In Binh Duong Province, Maj. Gen. Van Thanh Cao, government delegate in the east of South Vietnam, along with Col. Nguyen Duc Thang, the Fifth Infantry Division commander, launched Operation Sunrise after the BRIAM format and failed miserably. Operation Sunrise could not withstand the communist concentrated attacks, which lasted several months.

The concept of a special commissioner for security of Military Region III had been developed at that time, and the position was assigned to me. Upon receiving the order to return to Saigon for this position, I placed it just slightly below the rank of a cabinet member and a step higher than the four-star general, chief of the Joint General Staff (JGS). I was taken aback and felt quite lonely in this new and tough assignment.

One day while I was waiting for an audience with President Diem, Nhu, the president's brother, passed by, and I greeted him. Until then, I had met Nhu only once. I accompanied Nhu to the balcony of the Presidential Palace, when he asked, "The old man gave you a task only an angel could accomplish; how do you plan to manage it?" I explained the troubling situation to him. Nhu replied that as an administrator, Diem just signs an executive order and then expects the situation to take care of itself. The project was huge and needed much manpower and effort to show accomplishments. Nhu advised me to propose that Diem form an interministerial committee, chaired by Diem, and that I be the standing member. Before leaving, Nhu carefully reminded me to present that idea to Diem as my own and promised that he would lend a hand to run the committee if Diem was too busy.

Birth of the Strategic Hamlet Program

After meeting with Diem to discuss the plan, Diem asked me to meet with his chief of staff, Quach Tong Duc, to compose the executive order to form the Inter-Ministerial Committee of the Strategic Hamlet Program. When Duc and I presented the document for signature, Diem asked whether the plan had been reviewed with Nhu. I replied that I had already talked with Nhu about it. When the Strategic Hamlet Council was formed, new programs were introduced, and Nhu practically ran the council, although Diem was supposed to be the chairman.

Before sending me to work for Nhu, Diem had said repeatedly that "Mr. Nhu is a well-educated and knowledgeable person, especially in international affairs." Diem delegated many of the important national tasks to Nhu. However, Nhu was an impractical person with a strong anticommunist attitude.

Nhu learned a great deal after taking administrative command of the Strategic Hamlet Program. At the first meeting, I asked Diem to be the chairman. The president instead told me to ask Nhu to sit in his place. In meetings, Nhu used most of the time giving lengthy speeches in his boring, broken tone of voice. Yet when my meeting minutes were completed, they were recomposed into clearly defined and well-organized subject matter. I asked Nhu for approval to have the materials translated into English and copies sent to MACV and AID (Agency for International Development). Nhu emphasized the need to explain any ambiguity to U.S. officials and obtain their consensus for the Vietnamese to reach their own goals.

Nhu once told me, "To fight against the communists is tough, but to deal with the U.S. as an ally is even tougher. The U.S. policy changes constantly with changing objectives. The superpowers like the U.S. capitalists, as well as the USSR communists, do not have permanent friends or permanent enemies, they both have only permanent interests." Only after 1975, when South Vietnam was lost to Hanoi and I was a refugee in America, did I fully understand Nhu's statement.

U.S. support was very necessary, but the Vietnamese could not rely forever on the assistance of a friendly nation. U.S. advisers helped South Vietnam to solve various technical problems and established accurate statistical reports, but they could not guide or replace the people needed to carry out a Vietnamese revolution.

The Strategic Hamlet Concept

The concept for the Strategic Hamlet Program was based on the real situation in South Vietnam at that time. This situation included the following important characteristics: the underdevelopment of a traditionally agricultural economy; the social contradictions and instability of a country recently ridding itself of colonialism; and the persistent aggression and subversion by North Vietnam communists, supported by the Communist International movement. This program was to create a true revolution, not the sort of temporary and superficial reforms that were done in the past. This revolution was to go all-out and to include various programs and changes in rural areas where social justice and democracy needed to be established. These were the preliminary conditions to restore the national ideology damaged by foreign cultures and by the war, to revive the village traditions, to carry out local policies, and to modernize rural life for the protection of South Vietnam's cultural values.

Militarily speaking, the Strategic Hamlet Program was intended to reverse the deteriorating situation with a new revolutionary concept instead of reorganize the military according to an outmoded conventional plan. Strategically, the concept was to separate the communists from the people, physically and morally, and transform the support-and-supply forces of the enemy into effective sources of intelligence (popular) and local anticommunist support. Once expelled from their guerrilla bases, the communists would no longer be able to exploit the people, and then they would completely lose their position of a frontless and rearless army, mingling with the peasants. The guerrillas would be forced to accept the frontal war that they had tried to avoid for fear of destruction.

The main mission of our army would be to carry out operations to support the construction of hamlets and to build our own guerrilla infrastructure in the villages and hamlets. Simultaneously with the construction of strategic hamlets, the Chieu Hoi (Open Arms) program was also an avenue we left open for the Viet Cong who wanted to defect.

The Strategic Hamlet Council met with Nhu every Friday to receive orders and discuss problems. The province chiefs wanted to please Nhu as they did Diem, by forcing poor peasants to build defensive moats and walls like a fort, sometimes kilometers in length. These took away the peasants' time for tilling the fields. In Vinh Long Province, Rufus Phillips had taken pictures of such hardships in one hamlet and intervened. I reported this to Nhu, who issued an order to stop this practice.

From the American Side, the Office of Rural Affairs

On the U.S. side, to support the Strategic Hamlet Program, a special committee was established and chaired by William Trueheart, the U.S. deputy chief of mission. Trueheart opposed Diem, disliked Nhu, and openly expressed his resentment when I met with him at his office. MACV established a task group led by Col. Carl Schaad, a very brilliant and professional officer.

The U.S. Operations Mission (USOM) created a position to head Rural Affairs (associate director of the USOM and director of Rural Affairs), which was filled by Phillips, a young idealist with an open mind. The Office of Rural Affairs was to be the heart and soul of the American efforts to win the hearts and minds of the Vietnamese peasants. The Rural Affairs Program had channeled about ten million dollars in cash to South Vietnam to purchase local currency, the piaster. To quickly take care of local expenditures and streamline the program, the purchase of piasters was a much-needed action. Otherwise, trying to expediently initiate programs and the accompanying paperwork through normal channels would have been impossible.

General Weyland and General Lac at MACV headquarters in Saigon, 1971

This local-currency transfer was administered with simple procedures by the Strategic Hamlet Council. It was divided into several categories and paid out based on the accomplishments of the various provinces.

At the theoretical level, the Strategic Hamlet Program was a political as well as social and military revolution that marked the beginning of a decisive period. It was a courageous effort to build up an underdeveloped country simultaneously facing two enemies—division and communism. On the practical level, although the Strategic Hamlet Program had somewhat reduced the strength of the communists in the countryside and had received strong support from the United States, many major problems persisted. Nhu practiced favoritism in assigning his loyal followers to key positions, although they were not qualified or capable. The practice of forced labor to accelerate the construction of the hamlets was done just to please the central government. Nhu's followers created deep resentment among the peasants, the people the hamlets were intended to protect against the communists.

The most serious problem for the Strategic Hamlet Program was the unrealistic and impractical timetable for completing the establishment of new hamlets throughout the country. The entire program was to be completed by the end of 1963, and two-thirds of the population of South Vietnam was to be located within the boundaries of these hamlets. Obviously, this task was impossible to accomplish and caused deep resentment among the peasants.

Buddhist Fiasco—A Major Blunder

Nhu's political and military fronts began to lose ground rapidly during 1963. The Viet Cong launched offensives in all remote locations in South Vietnam. Opposition parties were openly opposed to the administration, internal problems grew, and the United States began to insist that matters be conducted in the American way. Then came the reverberating explosion of the conflict with Buddhism, Vietnam's major religion. The Diem administration had begun its final days.

The first Buddhist incident began twenty-four hours before Lord Buddha's birthday celebration (8 May 1963). It started with a complaint that too many Buddhist flags were being displayed in Hue in Central Vietnam. President Diem asked his chief of staff, Quach Tong Duc, to issue a national executive order regulating where and how the Buddhist flags should be displayed. The order also applied to all Buddhist temples and pagodas. Buddhists in Hue demonstrated in protest of the tyrannical order with the conviction that a religious discrimination policy was being implemented by President Diem, a Catholic. Masses of people gathered at the local radio station to have their complaints broadcast. Fearing that there might be some complaints that would criticize the government, the station's manager refused and requested that the city intervene for protection.

Mayor Nguyen Van Dang and Maj. Dang Si, commander of Thua Thien Military Sector, ordered the regional and police forces to intervene, which resulted in the death of eight civilians and injury to an unknown number. Dr. Le Khac Quyen, the dean of the medical school and leader of the Buddhist community in Thua Thien, commented upon examining the bodies that the victims had been "killed by high explosive plastics."

The Buddhist antigovernment movement expanded rapidly while gaining strength. The Diem administration became more concerned and more brutal in dealing with the demonstrators. On 11 June 1963, Venerable Thich Quang Duc, a ranking Buddhist monk, publicly had himself burned to death in protest in downtown Saigon across from the Cambodian embassy. The incident was well organized and well publicized, with international news correspondents present. When the national police arrived, sixty Buddhist monks wearing traditional yellow robes were walking in a circle and surrounding Quang Duc, who sat in the center meditating as he was preparing himself to die in the flames.

A commoner named Nguyen Cong Hoan (who after the communist takeover of South Vietnam in 1975 became a congressional representative from the province of Phu Yen) poured gasoline over Quang Duc's shoulders and set him afire, turning the monk into a human torch. Photographs of this well-staged drama were taken by the international media and put on the first page of newspapers and magazines around the world. As a congresswoman, Madame Nhu announced that the incident was considered the "barbecuing of a Buddhist monk."

American Ambassador Frederick Nolting and Gen. Paul Harkins, commander of MACV, announced their support for Diem. Nhu showed his appreciation by naming a strategic hamlet near Nha Trang as Don Tin, in honor of the ambassador, and Nolting attended the opening ceremony of this hamlet.

Nolting left Saigon on 15 August 1963, and CIA Station Chief John Richardson was called back to the United States on 5 October 1963. Diem, Nhu, and other knowledgeable people suspected that this was an important turning point in Kennedy's policy toward Diem's regime. During this stormy period, President Diem faced many crises that caused him to become exhausted and mentally drained; he began to rely heavily on Nhu.

In August, September, and October, during every Strategic Hamlet Program meeting on Fridays, I recognized that Nhu's appearance was on the downside, that his face was gaunt, that he was not as talkative as before, and that he immediately left after the meetings. I had to summarize the weekly notes by myself to forward to the military regions, divisions, and provinces to keep them informed of the fluid situation.

Despite my obvious dedication to the program, Nhu once asked me, "Lac, what do you think of the current situation?" I promptly replied, "As Mr. Presidential Adviser is well aware, the situation is a critical and dangerous one; there's talk everywhere about overthrowing the government. I don't know about politics, but militarily speaking, we can't at the same time be fighting two powerful opponents."

Nhu did not say anything; he just walked away. Realizing that American–Vietnamese relations were in disrepair over the handling of the Buddhist situation, Nhu had ideas of making concessions and taking his family abroad for a period of time. His brother, Senior Archbishop Thuc, urged Nhu not to leave. The rumors of Nhu's planned departure, abandoning Diem, flamed high in Saigon, but in the end, he did not go.

America's Policy Change in Support of Diem

During this period, the United States also became very active in communicating with Gens. Tran Van Don and Ton That Dinh in Saigon. Rufus Phillips flew to Can Tho twice but could not meet with General Cao. In the early days of August 1963, Cao flew to Saigon for a meeting at the Joint General Staff of ARVN. Phillips invited him to his residence on Cong Ly street and asked Cao whether the government had any intention of clearing out the temples and arresting more Buddhist monks. Cao replied, "I don't think so; as for myself, I do not agree with the solution because it will bring down President Diem."

On 16 August 1963, Henry Cabot Lodge received authorization to become U.S. ambassador to South Vietnam. In his first meeting with Diem to present his credentials, Lodge attempted to open up the Buddhist topic, but Diem beat around the bush with old stories of past successes. Before leaving, however, Lodge raised two issues—a recommendation to send the Nhus abroad and make peace with the Buddhists. Diem avoided answering and cited the construction of new Buddhist temples and his past support for the Buddhists.

Beginning of the End—Countdown to a Coup

Believing that the time was right, quite a few opposition groups decided to move against President Diem and his brother Nhu. There were three major rebel groups that were composed of the following people:

- Gens. Duong Van Minh, Tran Van Don, Le Van Kim, Mai Huu Xuan, and Ton That Dinh
- Col. Do Mau and a coalition of many political groups, including the Personalist Labor Party of which he was a member. Later, Mau joined with General Minh's group through arrangements made by General Don.
- Dr. Tran Kim Tuyen and a coalition of other political parties, including the Vietnam Nationalist Party and Lt. Col. Pham Ngoc Thao (former communist and political commissar of the 410th VC Battalion)

In brief, all those who were closest to Diem had turned against him and were now conspiring to overthrow him.

In observing the revolutionary groups, it appeared that General Minh, or "Big Minh" as he was affectionately called, was elected leader because of his down-to-earth personality that gained the support of many people. Col. Nguyen Van Quan, former province chief of Phuoc Tuy, a peaceful and honest person, was assisting Big Minh.

General Don was acting chairman of the Joint General Staff and also was an army commander, replacing Gen. Le Van Ty who had gone to the United States for treatment of cancer. General Don had a close working relationship with retired Lt. Col. Lou Conein of the CIA. Both were born in France. Don was born in Bordeaux and carried French citizenship but later changed it to Vietnamese. Conein grew up in Paris and became a naturalized U.S. citizen and then a CIA operative. Don was also involved in French intelligence because he was a second lieutenant in the French military infantry in 1944.

General Kim was Don's brother-in-law. At Lansdale's recommendation, Kim and Don were utilized by Diem. A hard worker, Kim gained the confidence of President Diem. Big Minh had high regard for Kim's talents and liked his hardworking attitude as well as his honesty. It was Kim who helped Minh decide to sever the relationship with Diem.

General Xuan was a secret police officer for the French Federation for many years, beginning in 1940. Although he was still employed by Diem to head the Quang Trung National Military Training Center, Xuan wanted instead to head the national police because he thought he was the most capable person for this position.

General Dinh had gained the nickname "ba," or goat, when he was a captain in 1953 (a goat can have strong sexual connotations in Vietnamese lore). This is when he headed the Sixth Battalion in North Vietnam. He was a heavy drinker and indulged in profanity with everyone he worked with. All he cared about were money and women. However, he displayed a two-faced, shameful attitude in trying to please President Diem. When dealing with Nhu and Can (the president's brothers) and Madame Nhu, Dinh always behaved like an obedient servant.

Most important for the group's success was the support or lack of opposition from Gen. Tran Thien Khiem, chief of staff of ARVN. While the commander of Military Region V, he had brought troops back to Saigon to defeat the rebellion and rescued President Diem during the 1960 coup attempt. Although Minh and Don did not trust Khiem, they knew they must have his support because of the key position Khiem held. They threatened to eliminate Khiem if he opposed them.

President Diem Suspects a Coup

During this time, Diem was not totally blind to the political forces that were moving against him, and he became very concerned. He was not sure how much support his opposing generals had attained from his opposition, nor was he sure who his opponents were. A few weeks before the Vietnamese Independence Day celebration, Diem made a personal call and summoned me to the Presidential Palace at 9:00 P.M. to be the "special aide to the president" during the ceremony of Independence Day on 26 October 1963.

Diem asked me about the recent developments and advised me to take all precautions against a possible coup, especially during the ceremony. What could I say to Diem when deep down I knew his days were numbered? The wheel of history was turning against the president. His closest followers were ganging up against him. I alone had no power to stage a rescue if the coup was to occur. And one could no longer tell friend from foe in the heavy, political atmosphere of Saigon.

One time while riding in the back of Col. Do Mau's Peugeot 203 automobile, I whispered to him, "You do what you wish so long as it is good for the country. I will not participate in this, but I promise not to disclose the matter to anyone else. Trust my words, we have worked a long way back together. You talked me into serving Diem. Other people can do this but me, count me out."

Ngo Dinh Nhu frequently visited the Joint General Staff headquarters to gather information and to boost the loyalty of the officers. One time, in a conversation with me, Nhu lit a cigarette, looked at the generals, and said casually, "A general told me that the CIA had contacted him. If he agreed to overthrow the administration, he would be rewarded with a large amount of money in U.S. currency. I told him to accept the offer, take the advance money, and inform President Diem. That money could be put to better use in tasks which would benefit our country." He paused, then continued, "There have been a lot of rumors about a possible coup. I believe that there are two ways to deal with the situation, either destroy the conspiracy early or pretend as if you would support the coup to obtain information."

In the United States, President Kennedy had decided to cut assistance to the Vietnamese Special Forces and reduce economic aid as leverage to increase American pressure. On 29 August 1963, in a National Security Council meeting in Washington, President Kennedy agreed that Diem must be overthrown in order to be successful in the conflict with the communists.

In Saigon, John Richardson, the CIA station chief, who knew more about South Vietnam than any other American, agreed with General Harkins in opposing the removal of Diem, and he was called back to the CIA headquarters in Langley at Lodge's request. When Richardson packed up and left in October, Ngo Dinh Nhu understood he could no longer go back to the way things were before. Lodge had decided to burn the bridge behind him.

On the morning of 26 October 1963, at 9:45, I invited President Diem to preside over the national Independence Day ceremony, which was organized on Thong Nhat street, but Diem sat quietly and did not reply. Ten minutes later, I returned to repeat my invitation. Diem looked very tired. He stood up to walk to the door, and his foot hit a porcelain pot, causing him to fall toward the right, but he regained his composure and went on his way. (Diem, although small in stature at approximately five feet, three inches, always walked in fast strides.)

Colonel Lac with President
Ngo Dinh Diem, 26 October
1963, just days before Diem's
assassination

The ceremony went on for almost three hours, and then I accompanied
Diem back to the Presidential Palace. Upon returning to the palace, Diem
turned around, thanked me, and vaguely mumbled to himself that the day
had turned out to be beautiful. I then saluted the president and returned to
my office.

Generals Solidify Support for the Coup

At a meeting of the coup plotters, Big Minh took Gen. Nguyen Van La to a
secluded place and said, "I am going to overthrow the administration, are you
with me?"

La answered, "If you are saying to overthrow President Diem, the answer
is no."

Big Minh continued, "Thao [Pham Ngoc Thao] and Tuyen [Tran Kim
Tuyen] are totally committed. I will overthrow Nhu and his wife, are you
with us?"

General La then said, "Okay."

Big Minh had been La's friend for many years, since the time they conducted
military operations in Dong Thap and western South Vietnam. They were as
close as blood brothers.

After first learning of the group's plan to overthrow the president, Col. Le
Quang Tung, commander of Special Forces, raised his voice to curse the group,

"You despicable officers, you wear military uniforms, get handsome pay, kiss the president's ass to gain his trust, and now you want to turn against him?" Tung was immediately taken out of the room, and Capt. Le Minh Dao, aide to Gen. Le Van Kim, brought him to the guard tower of the JGS headquarters and shot him to death that night.

Tung's brother, Maj. Le Quang Trieu, operations chief of Special Forces, went to the JGS after receiving the news and was also killed. Navy Capt. Ho Tan Quyen, chief of naval operations of the South Vietnamese navy, escaped but was later shot by his aide, Navy Lt. Nguyen Van Luc, as he rode with him in a black Citroen sedan to Thu Duc Reserve Officers Training Center.

Twenty-four Hours Leading Up to the Death of a President

In the early morning of 1 November 1963, American Ambassador Lodge and Admiral Felt, U.S. commander in chief of Pacific Forces, met with President Diem to discuss a U.S. request to send his brother Nhu and Madame Nhu out of the country. The visit was also to review the status of military operations as well as the civilian unrest in South Vietnam. (Later, many people believed that Ambassador Lodge's purpose was to keep Diem occupied to allow time for the revolutionary forces to make more adequate preparations.)

When the American delegation left, Diem personally walked them to the front steps of the Presidential Palace. He told Admiral Felt that he would fully comply with the other U.S. requests except for sending Nhu into exile. This statement was probably directed at Lodge rather than at Admiral Felt.

About 1:00 P.M. on 1 November 1963, there was a series of loud automatic gunfire heard at the Hoa Lu stadium on Dinh Tien Hoang street.

At 1:30 P.M., Radio Saigon played military music and announced that the military was launching a coup to overthrow Ngo Dinh Diem's regime and his family dictatorship.

At 2:00 P.M., a fighter plane appeared and dropped a bomb on Cong Hoa (Presidential Brigade Headquarters), wounding three soldiers; Saigon Radio announced the formation of the Military Revolutionary Council to overthrow the administration. All participating members came to the microphone one by one to announce their names and ranks.

At 2:30 P.M., Major Due sent Lieutenant Bao, assistant chief of staff (J5) of the Presidential Brigade, to the Presidential Palace to tape President Diem's message and ordered Capt. Tran Thanh Xuan to lead an armored column to take back the radio station. One hour later, Xuan reported he had taken the station. In fact, he had reached only the ground floor and lost communications from then on.

At 4:00 P.M., President Diem telephoned Ambassador Lodge to inquire about the coup. The president said, "Some units are in rebellion, and I want to know, what is the attitude of the U.S.?"

Ambassador Lodge: "I do not feel well informed enough to be able to tell you at this time. I have heard the shooting, but I am not acquainted with all the facts. Also, it is 4:00 A.M. in Washington, and the U.S. government cannot possibly have a view."

President Diem: "But you must have some general ideas. After all, I am a chief of state. I have tried to do my duty. I want to now do what duty and good sense require. I believe in duty above all."

Ambassador Lodge: "You have certainly done your duty. As I told you this morning, I admire your courage and your great contributions to your country. No one can take away from you the credit for all you have done. Now I am worried about your physical safety. I have a report that those in charge of the current activity offer you and your brother safe conduct out of the country if you resign. Had you heard this?"

President Diem: "No (then after a pause). You have my telephone number, yes?"

Ambassador Lodge: "If I can do anything for your physical safety, please call me."

President Diem: "I am trying to reestablish order." Then President Diem hung up.

At 4:15 P.M., President Diem called General Don, agreeing to satisfy all demands of the generals involved in the coup; Don rejected his offer, requesting that the president leave the country. Diem did not agree.

At 4:30 P.M., Lt. Col. Vinh Loc, commander of Van Kiep Training Center, led an armored column to Phan Thanh Gian bridge and was stopped by the Presidential Brigade force. Vinh Loc's force was allowed to pass after some discussion.

At 8:00 P.M., Vinh Loc broke the main gate of the Presidential Brigade Headquarters on Thong Nhat street with an armored vehicle.

At 9:00 P.M., Diem left the palace. Before leaving, Diem gathered the officers and staff together to say good-bye.

Nhu seemed unafraid and was determined to continue to fight, organizing a countercoup. But, in the end, he wanted to please his brother and so went with him to Cholon. Diem knew his time was over but still believed that the generals would not have the heart to kill him. Diem tried to avoid any further bloodshed, which would benefit only the communists, and his pride would not let him seek Ambassador Lodge's help.

At 4:00 A.M., on 2 November 1963, Diem telephoned Maj. Huynh Van Lac, his security guard company commander, and informed him that he was safe. Diem thanked Van Lac and the guard for being loyal to him. Diem then asked them to surrender to avoid being massacred.

At 8:00 A.M., Diem and Nhu attended mass at Cha Tam Catholic Cathedral in Cholon, the Chinese section of Saigon.

President Diem gave General Khiem his location. General Minh called a meeting of all the rebelling generals to find a way to react. While waiting for the meeting to begin, General La privately suggested to Minh, "We should approach this as in the case of Syngman Rhee (the former Korean president), and send Mr. Diem into exile. We should not kill him because we will need the support of Catholic organizations, which are strongly anticommunist." Minh replied, "Good idea, Vietnamese should be more civilized than Koreans, but let me ask the opinions of our other colleagues." At the meeting room, three-quarters of the officers wanted to let Diem go abroad. Several wanted him assassinated.

After the meeting, General Minh decided to let Gen. Mai Huu Xuan head the group, assisted by Cols. Nguyen Van Quan and Duong Ngoc Lam, that would abduct President Diem. In addition, General Minh also sent Captain Nhung, his longtime bodyguard; Maj. Duong Hieu Nghia, commander of an armor squadron; and Maj. Nguyen Van Day to join the group. After they left, General Don asked Lt. Col. Le Soan, chief officer of the JGS headquarters, to prepare a lodging room for Diem. Don told Soan not to install a telephone line in the room to prevent Diem from making outside calls.

Upon arrival at Cha Tam Catholic Cathedral, Xuan and Quan waited outside. Colonel Lam, wearing black beret armor military gear, went inside the church alone to meet with Diem. Lam was formerly the armored commander who had received help from Diem and was promoted to the position of director general of the National Militia.

Trusting Lam, Diem and Nhu agreed to leave with him. An M 113 military vehicle waited outside the cathedral to pick up the president. When asked to get into the vehicle, Nhu became angry at the lack of respect shown in the use of the transportation means for the president. An argument erupted, and Captain Nhung pushed both Nhu and Diem into the armored car with vehicle number 80989. He then tied their hands behind their backs. Major Day and Captain Nhung yanked a briefcase and a walking cane from Diem and brought them to Gen. Mai Huu Xuan.

After the back door of the vehicle was closed and locked, Nghia and Nhung sat on top of the vehicle. On the way back to headquarters, they stopped at railroad crossing number six. Taking advantage of the train noise, Nhung jumped down to open the back of the vehicle. He then shot Nhu and Diem with his Colt .45 pistol. Major Nghia used the Thompson submachine gun to end their lives, calling it a mercy killing. With his anger not fully vented, Nhung stabbed them repeatedly. Diem was dead. On his body, they found a pack of Blue Bastos (Vietnamese cigarettes) and a rosary.

The Briefcase with Six Million Piasters

While the murder of the president was taking place, the rebelling generals gathered in the office of Gen. Le Van Ty. Lou Conein from the CIA sat in Ty's armchair, his feet on the desk next to a magnum pistol. Below the desk was a briefcase with six million piasters (worth $80,000 to $150,000, depending on whether the official or black market rate was used). Half of this amount was given to Don; the remainder was distributed among the officers.

The picture of Vietnamese military leaders surrounding Conein and his money made Big Minh feel uneasy. He walked onto the balcony to watch the dawning sky.

The news that Diem and Nhu had committed suicide reached the officers during this happy moment. Everyone was in disbelief. Conein's face turned pale. He stood up and cursed the operation. He did not believe that Diem, a fervent Catholic, would end his own life. Before leaving the building, Lou said, "All of you will be fully responsible for the death of Mr. Diem."

The rumor was that Big Minh had decided to kill Diem instead of sending him into exile. The excuse was that the U.S. ambassador had implied to Minh, "If Mr. Diem was forced to go abroad, any colonel could initiate a coup and bring him back." Because Minh was worried about his future and his life, he wanted Diem killed. Later on, General Don revealed that Big Minh himself had ordered Nhung to kill President Diem.

The Inevitable and Fatally Crippling Power Struggle

The military coup started a new chapter in Vietnamese history. President Diem no longer was alive. All the earlier losses on the battlefield were blamed on Diem and his nepotism and dictatorship. Now that the coup was a success, the gambling casinos, nightclubs, and bars were wide open to celebrate the newly found freedom. The first action of the Military Revolutionary Council was to reward, monetarily and through promotions, the high-ranking officers and their families for a job well done. Also, those who did not support the revolution were fired regardless of their accomplishments and skills in their technical areas.

In Big Minh's eyes, every policy initiated by Diem was wrong and useless. After 2 November 1963, many people were happy and believed in the military, hoping that it had the ability to strengthen the nation and defeat communism.

This hope soon turned to disappointment when the people witnessed Gen. Nguyen Khanh, with the cooperation and support of Gen. Tran Thien Khiem and Col. Cao Van Vien, complete a quick Military Correction operation early on 30 January 1964. In the name of revolution, Khanh seized Generals Don, Kim, Xuan, Dinh, and Vy. He accused them of collaboration with the French colonialists and communists to neutralize South Vietnam (i.e., to turn South Vietnam into a nonaligned country). Major Nhung was captured, tortured, and killed by Khanh's paratroopers.

On 23 June 1964, Ambassador Lodge announced his resignation. Several days later, Lodge told the press before boarding his plane, "When I leave Vietnam, my only regret is that I could not save Mr. Diem's life."

Gen. Maxwell Taylor was appointed American ambassador to South Vietnam.

U.S. Conventionalism versus Viet Minh Unconventionalism

As a powerful country, the United States entered the Vietnam War with an overconfident attitude fueled by its experience of winning (or at least not losing) every war it had ever fought. The Pentagon itself, also overconfident and subjective in its military philosophy, did not take care to understand the causes and effects of the 1946–1954 war between France and the Viet Minh. In addition, the United States did not understand the true face of communism, particularly the North Vietnamese communists. As a result, the United States held to a defensive policy in South Vietnam while North Vietnam took the offense and made known its intent to expand socialism in Indo-China, solidify controls in the North, and liberate the South. Such intentions were expressed through North Vietnam's establishment of military bases in south Laos and on the Ho Chi Minh Trail, the military buildup in east Cambodia, and infiltration of South Vietnamese waters (South China Sea). And last but not least was an organized campaign of terrorism in South Vietnam.

The military forces of South Vietnam were structured and trained for conventional warfare following the standards set during the Korean War of 1950–1953. The army included seven divisions, equipped with M1 and carbine rifles, which were used in World War II. The navy and the air force were organized to provide tactical support for ground troops, which were limited to movement only in South Vietnam. Clearly, it was a defensive policy that provided no threat to North Vietnam. For that reason, Hanoi felt safe to focus all its forces on invading the South.

Communist hardware captured by the South Vietnamese army in Military Region I. Mai Hoang, wife of General Lac *(left)*, Hoang Lac *(center)*, and Hoang Long, eldest son *(right)*

When the Republic of (South) Vietnam was pushed into a defensive mode, the situation deteriorated. Instead of American and Vietnamese representatives discussing possible strategies of mutual interest, the United States faulted the Diem administration for the South's military and political deficiencies. The death of President Diem and the political chaos that followed required deeper U.S. military involvement in South Vietnam to prevent its total collapse.

Some Final Thoughts

In our book, *Blind Design,* we have tried to show that both U.S. and South Vietnamese soldiers heroically fought the communists, but it was the politicians, playing field marshal, who directed the war and constantly stepped on their feet. In his book, *In Retrospect: The Tragedy and Lessons of Vietnam,* former Secretary of Defense Robert McNamara, the chief U.S. architect of the war, blames himself and his government colleagues, including President Johnson, for a series of blunders that led to tragedy. Mr. McNamara initiated the wrong policy (limited war, limited targets, lack of determination) and the unwinnable strategy (defensive in an attrition war, gradual escalated retaliation). McNamara lacked an understanding of the nature of guerrilla warfare. How could he win the war? At the fiercest moments, he confused himself while conduct-ing the war. He did not understand the North Vietnamese communists, he did not understand South Vietnam, he did not know what should be done, and finally, he did not even know how to effectively use his forces. The "best and the brightest," as reporter David Halberstam called McNamara and other U.S. leaders, played no-win poker with the lives of fifty-eight thousand American patriots and three hundred thousand loyal wounded. Almost three decades later, McNamara regrets misjudging the war.

Blind Design offers future generations the truth of a betrayal that the war was never fought to be won. The war effort was led by a group of people who initiated a wrong policy, an unwinnable strategy, and wrong tactics.

Learning from all that has happened, we want succeeding generations of Vietnamese to never again let a friend, no matter how big, powerful, and resourceful, seize their destiny from them. To our American friends, we want them to never again fight in a foreign land, no matter how small, without the determination to win and a complete knowledge of the enemy. In any fight, in your heart, if you do not want to beat the enemy, get out early. If you stay inside the ring, sooner or later the enemy will surely knock you out.

Counterinsurgency in South Vietnam

The Real Story

Bert Fraleigh

As one of the few Americans who played a key role in the development of South Vietnam's counterinsurgency efforts from 1962 through 1964, I am appalled by the superficialities and misinformation contained in former U.S. Defense Secretary Robert McNamara's book *In Retrospect: The Tragedy and Lessons of Vietnam*. This feeling is shared by most of us who worked at the grassroots level in our part of this program. Together, we were responsible for helping the Vietnamese with their social, political, and economic components administered under American aid by the U.S. Operations Mission (USOM) and its Office of Rural Affairs (RA). The program's major security component was the responsibility of the Vietnamese military and its American military advisers, known as the U.S. Military Assistance Advisory Group (MAAG) and later U.S. Military Assistance Command, Vietnam (MACV). I feel compelled to set the record straight by telling my own story of what we really did in South Vietnam and why we did it so that the truth may prevail in the public domain.

In writing this story, forty years after the experience, I have spent several months reading through two trunks of my own files, as well as many official government records and more than a dozen books on South Vietnam written at the time and since. This research has reinforced the accuracy of my memory and, unexpectedly, strengthened my conclusion, then and now, of why we lost in South Vietnam. Scores of reasons and excuses have been advanced for America's failure, some with varying degrees of validity. But going through my memory, the records, and the literature from the earliest days of communist insurgency in Vietnam in 1945 to the end in South Vietnam in 1975 is the fact of the persistent unwillingness of American military leadership to recognize that this was a different kind of war. Put simply, it was unconventional, and it demanded a thoroughly unconventional response.

History shows that for the thirty years leading up to 1975, the political and military leaders fighting the insurgency, though giving lip service to the nature of its unconventionality, refused to fight it unconventionally, with only two major exceptions. First was in 1954, when America's leading unconventional warfare expert, Col. Edward G. Lansdale, outwitted the conventional American bureaucracy that had written off South Vietnam to communism. By working behind the scenes with a handful of Americans, he helped President Ngo Dinh Diem defeat several armed groups of opposition and stabilize South Vietnam for another six years.

The second exception was when John F. Kennedy and his brother Robert, believing in the necessity of an unconventional response in South Vietnam, pushed both civilian and military conventionalists to develop one. It was their efforts that brought the contributing writers of this book to the forefront in South Vietnam. We were well along in the job when President Kennedy was assassinated. After the assassination, the conventional approach was then resumed by the American leadership responsible for our South Vietnam policy.

The unconventional program developed with the Vietnamese and other allied aid donors decentralized the Vietnamese government and foreign aid to the provinces and hamlets and brought rapid political, social, and economic progress throughout the rural areas of South Vietnam by early 1963. This is a fact never reported very well by the news media, which preferred more sensational war stories. This program depended on the Vietnamese military and its American advisers to provide a security response for the rural people when attacked by the communists. Although always promised, this security was seldom provided. This failure is the theme of many famous books on the Vietnam conflict. Responsibility for it must be placed squarely at the feet of unbending, conventional military thinking. Had this security been provided and the counterinsurgency program gone forward, South Vietnam might have become one of the prosperous Asian Tigers in the 1970s, given its similarities to Taiwan, Malaysia, and the Philippines, where counterinsurgency programs worked and communism withered on the vine.

In his book, *In Retrospect,* Secretary McNamara often states, "I was wrong." I agree. It was the highest-level military and political leaders in the United States and South Vietnam who, because of arrogance, stubbornness, and ignorance, followed conventionality to certain defeat and profoundly damaged both South Vietnam and America for many years.

Our Credentials

McNamara asserts in *In Retrospect* that America simply lacked experts on Vietnam and Asian communism and could not come to grips with South Vietnam's insurgency nor develop a winning strategy against it. To refute this perspective, I must outline my own experience as well as the credentials of many who worked with me in South Vietnam. McNamara made no effort to seek out or try to use America's counterinsurgency expertise. That's the bottom line.

I supervised airfield and wharf construction in the Yukon River valley in 1942 and in the Aleutian Islands in 1943 and then served three years as a pharmacist mate in the U.S. Navy in the Pacific at Saipan and Okinawa. Experience with the Alaskan Natives and with the local people in Saipan and Okinawa convinced me that world peace could best be achieved by helping equalize opportunities and living conditions among all peoples. My Navy ship, the USS *Snowbell* (AN 52), was sunk in the October 1945 typhoon at Okinawa, and I washed up on a tiny islet and lived with the impoverished people there for a few weeks.

Later I read in *Time* magazine about plans for United Nations Relief and Rehabilitation Administration (UNRRA) programs in Japan and China. I wrote a letter to the United Nations, applying to join this organization in Japan. To my surprise, I received a reply and was offered a job in China as an engineer repairing dikes on the Yellow (Huang) River. I was then sent to Shanghai in June 1946. Instead of going to the Yellow River, I was detailed to supervise construction of a special wharf and supply yard in Shanghai. Soon I was unloading scores of ships that had been waiting for months in the congested port to unload relief supplies. My entire staff, clerks and laborers, was Chinese. Together we set up Shanghai's largest supply depot in a rapid and orderly fashion and broke the port congestion in less than three months.

During this period I became a close friend of Chou En-lai, later to become premier of China, who represented the Chinese communists for the receipt of UNRRA supplies. UNRRA supplies were allocated to both the nationalist government of China and the communists according to the percentage of population each controlled. It was my friendship with Chou that later enabled me to leave China at the end of 1950 after being detained by the Chinese communists for eighteen months.

In late 1947, the U.S. government decided to set up, under the Truman Doctrine, aid to Turkey, Greece, and China, with its own assistance mission in China under the State Department. I was chosen as one of seven Americans to organize this mission and became its supply and operations officer for the $450 million program. It was a hectic time, with the communist armies advancing from the north and infiltrating the cities. America was trying to halt or slow their advance with economic and military help to the nationalists while holding the door open for negotiations with the communists.

In just one of our major unpublicized efforts, we maintained an airlift of more than two hundred flights per day by civilian aircraft of foodstuffs and medicines from northern Chinese cities into surrounded Mukden, Manchuria, during August and September 1948. Mukden, with nearly two million civilians and 150,000 of nationalist China's best troops, had fought the Japanese with U.S. Gen. "Vinegar" Joe Stilwell in India and Burma. This city had been under starvation siege by communist China's largest army of half a million men under Lin Piao. In effect, these nationalists were keeping Lin Piao's elite force tied down. America's airlift solved the food and medicine problems and broke the siege, and the nationalist troops drove Lin's army back more than fifty miles. A few months later, nationalist leader Chiang Kai-shek ordered his Mukden army to withdraw to central China to help defend the Nanking capital. This opened the door for Lin Piao's troops to march into Tientsin and Peking (Beijing) and then, in rapid order, the center and the south.

In April and May 1949, as the Chinese communists' Fourth Field Army was descending on Shanghai, I was made responsible for evacuating U.S. government supplies for all American agencies in Shanghai and Nanking. The exception was to hold back a three-month reserve of aid materials such as food, cotton, medicines, and oil to forestall civil breakdown in China's major cities. This reserve was also to show good faith to the communists for our forthcoming negotiations with them to continue U.S. aid if they agreed to recognize the Four Freedoms (freedom of speech and worship, freedom from want and fear), which was the major U.S. foreign policy tenet of the day.

More than two hundred thousand tons of excess supplies were then shipped from Shanghai and other Chinese ports to Hong Kong, Japan, Korea, and Taiwan. The last ship sailed the morning of the same day in 1949 that the communists entered Shanghai. It was the fortuitous large shipments of supplies to Taiwan and the assignment of my staff there to receive them that started America's assistance program in Taiwan and protected that island from U.S. abandonment.

Three other American aid personnel and I were detailed to stay behind in the Shanghai office to continue our assistance program and to negotiate with the communists.

The Communists Take Over China

After early hopes and some local signals to us of a cooperative relationship, Mao Tse-tung announced on 1 October 1949, the day of the formation of the People's Republic of China, his "Lean to One Side" policy, saying China had chosen to bend to the "socialist camp." This halted our aid distributions and most negotiations. Then began our real difficulties. As the main contact person for the U.S. assistance program and the American consulate in Shanghai, I was frequently summoned by the Communist Foreign Affairs and Public Security Bureaus for questioning. They asked for long explanations of America's activities and for confessions of alleged affronts to Chinese sovereignty and policies.

Fortunately, my interrogators always prefaced our meetings with the statement that because China and America had no diplomatic relations, they recognized me only as an American citizen and not as a government representative. In turn, I would always reiterate this to them and use evasiveness to avoid replies to their questions of a sensitive nature. This visibly frustrated them, and they would try to wait me out, sometimes holding me in their office for several days while rotating interrogators. Several times they made me stand in a corner for half a day at a time.

Finally, when my answers were not forthcoming, they would smile and say, "The People's government is very magnanimous, so we will allow you to go to your comfortable home and think things over. You must give us a written report of self-criticism within five days." I would comply but never wrote what I knew they wanted to hear. They would then move on to another topic.

Although I filed many applications to leave China for over a year, I was unable to obtain an exit visa until late November 1950, and then only from Tientsin by ship. By that time, of thirty-two hundred Americans who had stayed behind in Shanghai, only some thirty were still there, and most of them by their own choice. The communists were holding me under many pretexts. As a last resort, in October 1950, I sent a registered letter to Chou En-lai, by now the government's foreign minister in Beijing. Enclosed was a photograph taken of us in UNRRA days in Shanghai. I asked him for help on my exit visa to leave China.

There was no direct reply, but within a few days my name appeared in the Shanghai *Liberation Daily* newspaper as being considered for an exit visa. The same day I was called to the Public Security Bureau and shown a copy of my letter to comrade Chou. The officials there were furious and told me I had no right to contact him. I argued this point, referring to one of Mao's earlier eight guarantees to foreigners in China. They said, "You are a hopeless reactionary and cannot leave China until you have written an acceptable analysis and confession of your reactionary actions and an apology for them to the Chinese people. This must be submitted to us within one week, together with one hundred handwritten copies." After three days I telephoned them and said I had studied the matter closely and could find no mistake on my part and that I had telegraphed the whole story to Chou En-lai. Within an hour, a police detail came to my house and escorted me to the Public Security Bureau.

As I was standing at attention in front of the senior officer's desk, an aide came in with a telegram. The chief opened it, and as he read it, his face changed from a wolf's scowl to that of a smiling sheep. He said, "We know you very well, and we know you are a friend of China and have always loved and tried to help the Chinese people. You really don't have to leave China, you can stay and work with us as long as you like. You can be one of us." I thanked him and assured him I would always love the Chinese people and wished them well, but I had to go home because my mother had recently passed away and there was much to be done there. It was obvious Chou En-lai had rescued me.

Just at that time, an old friend who was leader of one of the minority parties in the Communist National Front returned from a Party Congress in Beijing where he had roomed with Communist Party leader Li Li-san. He told me that the party had decided to send the People's Liberation Army into North Korea in force as soon as troops and materials could be moved to Manchuria in support and that "you must let the Americans know." On my way north by rail to Tientsin to leave China, I saw train after train of trucks, tanks, and artillery destined for use against America in Korea. With thankful relief, I said a prayer as our tiny British freighter left Tientsin for Hong Kong that gray and cold November twilight. The American consulate in Hong Kong was duly warned of the coming Chinese invasion of Korea.

On my return to America, I worked for a year with the Asia Foundation in San Francisco before rejoining the State Department's Taiwan foreign assistance mission in 1952. Altogether I served ten years in Taiwan, the last six as personal adviser to Chiang Ching-kuo (son of President Chiang Kai-shek), who later became the distinguished president of the Republic of China. In Taiwan, I helped set up and manage the Chinese Veteran's Program, funded by direct order from President Eisenhower with fifty-two million dollars originally intended for assisting French forces in Vietnam. I also supervised Chinese refugee programs in Hong Kong and defense and relief programs on Quemoy and Matsu.

Before his departure from Taiwan, Bert Fraleigh shakes hands with the defense minister, Gen. Chiang Ching-kuo, with whom Fraleigh had worked in economic development programs. Fraleigh left Taiwan in 1962. General Chiang would later serve as president of Taiwan for six years.

One of my most cogent observations was that when I first arrived in Taiwan, almost all the forty Americans then serving in our aid mission felt economic development in Taiwan was hopeless because of presupposed Chinese ineptitude and corruption. Only a few of us had a positive attitude about the potential of the Chinese people and saw great promise in them. We realized that one needed to thoroughly analyze and try to understand the ordinary people, mix with them, exercise great patience, gain their confidence, and, in turn, give them confidence in their own future. I was to later find this same negative attitude toward locals among most of the 110 American aid colleagues in South Vietnam when I joined the aid mission there in 1962.

Requested by the CIA for Laos in 1959

In early 1959, the CIA sent a request to the Agency for International Development (AID), America's umbrella organization for our assistance programs abroad, to send an experienced rural development manager to help in a special counterinsurgency effort in Laos. My name was suggested. The CIA felt, probably from investigations, that unlike many State Department aid officials, I would cooperate with their own local activities and not be jealous or prejudiced against them. I was transferred to the USOM in Vientiane, Laos, with my new Chinese bride, on a few days' notice. My new title was assistant director for Rural Affairs for the USOM.

It took less than a week to find out I was not welcomed at USOM, the in-country designation for our AID office in Laos. USOM had neither requested nor wanted me. The USOM there had very weak leadership and direction and was unwilling to make changes. Thus, the good intentions of the American ambassador to Laos, the CIA, and our military advisers to have USOM/Laos reach out to rural Laotians as part of the U.S.–Lao government counterinsurgency effort were thwarted by those idealists in the USOM who viewed counterinsurgency as somehow being sinister and dirty.

The structure of the foreign assistance agency in Washington is paralleled in its field missions. AID/Washington is an independent agency within the State Department and has its own administrators (called directors in its overseas missions), administrative and technical bureaus (divisions in the missions), and regional and country overseers. The administrative side includes personnel, finance, audit, security, and general services. The technical arm includes services for field projects in agriculture, industry, public administration, health, education, family planning, and training. There are also program offices with economists, planners, procurement specialists, and others to coordinate field programs and provide support to them.

AID and USOM are used interchangeably in this book for America's overseas assistance program, although the name changed several times during its fifty-year existence. AID/Washington backstops each field mission with a country desk officer. In the early years of AID, 1947 through about 1956, its Washington offices were frugally staffed and quite efficient, and the bulk of AID's personnel worked, planned, and managed programs in the field. Then Parkinson's Law kicked in, and in recent decades, the great majority of AID personnel have become Washington paper shufflers and generalists second-guessing its field missions and quite divorced from field realities.

AID Technical Personnel Lack Vision and Imagination
Most of AID's technicians who are sent as advisers to developing countries have been selected in midcareer in their respective fields from other U.S. government agencies, such as Agriculture or Interior, and from America's colleges and

universities. Their cultural shock is often traumatic, and their advice to host ministry counterparts bewildering. Half their advice is dead wrong and inapplicable to local practices and conditions. Former Peace Corps and other volunteers usually make better AID advisers.

AID's traditional field technicians are almost always comfortably quartered in host country capitals. Their counterparts are officials in the local ministries. Both advisers and counterparts spend very little time in the rural areas. Both are frustrated when little assistance trickles down to the countryside. AID technicians tend to consider themselves as advisers only. A joke that made its rounds in South Vietnam told of a famous and expensive Santa Gertrudis bull brought in by AID for stud purposes. The story goes that he refused to perform because he was there as an adviser only. AID advisers seldom assume responsibilities for their projects, and those projects often become only paper tigers. These advisers are quite prone to criticizing the host government for its shortcomings instead of offering positive solutions.

Many of these technicians, however well intentioned, feel severely threatened by AID's small number of experienced boondocks specialists, who often are younger, former Peace Corps or volunteer-agency people. Frequently, older AID advisers try to stop the outreach of these younger people to the rural areas, terming it "out of ministry" channels; such channels, at best, barely exist in many developing countries.

This is the perennial AID conflict I was confronted with in Laos, where a number of AID "desk theorists" were inherently opposed to the CIA and to me. The American ambassador and other American agency heads in Laos (the country team) called the counterinsurgency effort America's most important effort there. The Lao government agreed, but no one would face down the AID mission director and his technical division heads; AID/Laos withheld its full economic support.

On the other hand, I was warmly welcomed by Henry Hecksher, the CIA station chief, and his staff, and through my own contacts in Taiwan secured donations of seeds, small farm machinery, and grassroots technicians with dramatic results on a demonstration basis. I also made close and lasting friendships with Laotians throughout the country.

Rufus Phillips, My Future Boss in South Vietnam

Most important, I soon became a close friend of a very remarkable, young CIA worker, Rufus Phillips. Rufe, a Yale graduate and football star, spoke French well. He had worked with Col. Edward Lansdale in Saigon in 1954 and 1955. Lansdale's small American advisory team, overcoming huge odds, helped Ngo

Dinh Diem put down all internal resistance and become president of South Vietnam. The U.S. State and Defense Departments had already conceded South Vietnam to the communist Viet Minh. Many State and Defense leaders were never happy with Lansdale's unconventional success, which proved them wrong. They were to hold this grudge against him in later years, which would bring tragic results in South Vietnam.

Rufe Phillips, only twenty-five in 1954, was one of the "Quiet Americans" in Graham Greene's book of that era. Rufe helped negotiate the surrender of the Hoa Hao and Cao Dai opposition sects to Diem in South Vietnam and the removal of the Viet Minh, or North Vietnam communists, from the deep southern Delta.

Counterinsurgency in South Vietnam

When Washington officialdom realized that AID/Laos had clipped my wings, the U.S. National Security Council adhered to the request of Taiwan's Gen. Chiang Ching-kuo that I return to Taiwan in early 1960. By 1962 it had become apparent that America's economic and military assistance programs in Taiwan for more than twelve years, always closely coordinated on the American side with patiently developed Chinese inputs, were an immense success. Taiwan was denied to Chinese communism and was well on its way to becoming a worldwide social and economic miracle and model.

I had always believed this would happen and had worked tirelessly for it. From my earliest days in China, I had believed that if communist military power, guerrilla and conventional, could be held at bay long enough for real market-based economic growth to take hold in rural areas, communism would have no appeal. I still believe to this day that, had we had another three years to carry out Jimmy Yen's Program for Joint Rural Reconstruction, with its land reform in south China as envisioned by Supreme Court Justice William O. Douglas and Eleanor Roosevelt in 1947, that part of China might not have fallen to communism.

Back in Taiwan in 1962, I remained a regular reader of the Shanghai *Liberation Daily* and was astounded one day in May to see a front-page article stating that "famous and vicious U.S. spy Fraleigh is being sent by the U.S. government to Saigon to help the puppet South Vietnam government develop an antipeople's program." I had no clue what the article was talking about until four days later when I received a top-secret cable directing me to meet Phillips in Saigon in forty-eight hours. (I mention this to illustrate that Chinese communist intelligence was apparently better than ours.)

Concurrently came a secret message from Phillips saying that as a result of the Taylor Mission (a fact-finding visit by Maxwell Taylor, Walt Rostow, and Ed

Lansdale to Saigon in October 1961), he had been asked by AID/Washington to go to Saigon. He was to determine how the AID mission there (known as USOM) could best use its resources to support the newly contemplated counterinsurgency effort. Phillips had asked that I be detailed to help him. AID/Washington agreed. He told me that he knew this would be very disruptive to me but that he felt I was AID's most experienced person in civic action, rural development, and Asian communism and that it was my patriotic duty to join him.

The next day, 11 May 1962, I flew the fifteen hundred miles to Saigon to find Phillips already there, living in a small bedroom with a tiny desk, two beds, mosquito nets, a creaky old ceiling fan, and an attached shower. This was our billet for the next twenty-three days, used only for sleeping and washing because we were extremely busy on the outside twelve to fourteen hours a day, seven days a week.

Our assignment from Washington's highest levels was to ascertain how USOM could best support South Vietnam and America's counterinsurgency efforts and ensure their outreach to the rural areas, where the great majority of South Vietnam's people lived and most Viet Cong activity was located. The Taylor Mission had reported to President Kennedy that USOM was not particularly responsive to what was happening in the countryside. It was suggested that America should be helping South Vietnam's government to decentralize and become responsive to the needs of its people in the 38 provinces (the number would increase with province divisions), 212 districts, and some 15,000 hamlets.

We found on our first day in Saigon that USOM had about 110 Americans on its rolls. Only three were stationed outside this appealing city famed as the *Pearl of the Orient*. It was pretty much a comfortable, business-as-usual AID operation. We were delighted to find that my good and old friend Bill Fippin, an agriculturist from the Joint Commission for Rural Reconstruction (JCRR), AID/Taiwan, was serving as USOM's acting director in the absence of the regular director and deputy director. Both were away on leave. I found out many years later that both of these men had been withdrawn by AID/Washington because of their basic opposition to counterinsurgency.

Fippin could not have been more accommodating to Rufe and me. He did everything possible to help us and eagerly solicited our opinions. Had we gone into a completely alien situation, it is doubtful we could have done as much. He gave us the director's office waiting room as an office and provided us with the use of his one American secretary. He offered his own office if we preferred. Of course we refused.

On our first afternoon in Saigon, Fippin called together all his American staff members and introduced us to them. He told them we had been sent to

Saigon to review South Vietnam's counterinsurgency effort and to propose a coordinated program of American assistance. He said that the whole thrust of USOM's aid should be integrated to support this activity. He instructed all USOM staffers to work with Rufe and me in every possible way and, if requested, give us priority over their regular work. We had not expected, nor could we have asked for, a more sincere, positive leadership response.

Interestingly, Rufe and I had sensed some hostility toward us and our presumed ideas for decentralizing America's assistance program. This came from some of USOM's old-line technical types who thought American economic aid should not become deeply involved in counterinsurgency activities. However, with the warm reception we received from Bill Fippin, Ambassador Nolting, and John Richardson, the CIA chief of station, there was little interference from the typical USOM technician during our first few weeks. In fact, rumors, untrue of course, quickly spread that Rufe and I were CIA employees about to be appointed the new USOM director and deputy.

From our first hour in South Vietnam, Rufe and I agreed to split responsibilities, share information, and make joint plans and decisions if we felt the need. Rufe decided to concentrate on Vietnamese government, U.S. military relations, and CIA liaison. He told me to concentrate on USOM work and its counterinsurgency program development. In deference to the mentality of old USOM types, we decided to call our potential program Rural Affairs rather than the more arousing Counterinsurgency.

We found that Fippin had recently organized a committee within USOM to study how the agency might support a counterinsurgency effort. Each technical division had designated a low-ranking representative, and these representatives would meet weekly. We met with them immediately and asked them to hold meetings within their divisions to get all their people involved and thinking on how to orient their work and that of their Vietnamese counterparts toward a rapid, expanded rural effort countrywide. I asked to sit in on each of their initial meetings. We also asked all divisions for copies of their current projects and for their evaluation of how they were progressing, as well as their opinions of rural impact and how their efforts might be enhanced. We requested lists of their Vietnamese counterparts and evaluations of their effectiveness, and we asked for informal opportunities for me to meet those who were most effective. This was our introduction to USOM in South Vietnam.

Working with President Diem

Phillips, though young, had a superb entrée with the Vietnamese, both civil and military, stemming from his work with them in the mid-1950s. President

Ngo Dinh Diem treated him like his own son. As soon as we arrived in Saigon, Diem started calling Rufe to his residence for long talks day and night. He told Rufe his feelings of growing cleavage between the Vietnamese and Americans, of his fervent hope that Colonel Lansdale could return to Saigon to help him, and of his happiness, at least, that Rufe was back. He said he was sure that Rufe would work in the best interest of South Vietnam and that he would give his full, prompt support for any ideas and plans that Rufe might have.

Diem explained in great detail his plan for the Strategic Hamlet Program, developed with his brother Ngo Dinh Nhu, which was based largely on an earlier Malayan program that overcame the communist insurgency there. Wisely, Phillips saw this as a program in which the Vietnamese were genuinely interested in reaching their people nationwide politically, economically, and militarily. It was probably the only program capable of becoming the vehicle for an effective, quick counterinsurgency response. Diem asked Phillips for American support for this program and to help develop political, social, and economic inputs for it.

We had to deal with the Vietnamese government administration. This consisted of the Office of the President, a prime minister, and a cabinet of ministers. There was also a National Legislature. There were thirty-eight provinces at that time and three special cities. Each province had a province chief, usually a middle-rank military officer selected by the president. Each province had from four to ten (or more in some cases) districts governed by district chiefs, again headed by military men of about captain's rank. Each district had from five to twelve villages with locally appointed village chiefs, and each village had a number of hamlets, the smallest division of human settlement without formal government structure.

We studied the Strategic Hamlet Program in-depth and visited a few pilot hamlets the Vietnamese had established in different parts of the country. Apart from several minor, easily corrected shortcomings, the basic program, if effectively implemented, was very solid. Most important, it represented a firm Vietnamese central leadership commitment to reach all its people, and it was a program developed and being implemented by the Vietnamese.

Fundamentally, the Strategic Hamlet Program aspired to separate the people from the communists, provide them security, put in place democratic processes, and bring to them government services such as land reform, health, education, and rapid economic development. This would be done by focusing on the rural population and working to change the traditional thinking of Vietnamese bureaucrats, civil and military. There had been neglect and contempt for the peasantry and little concern for its well-being and protection, including provisions of justice.

Phillips and I were confident that if we could use expedited and unconventional methods and work with the Vietnamese whose support Diem had pledged, USOM and America's allies could deliver on all but the security aspects of the program. Security would depend on the effectiveness of the Vietnamese military and its American advisers in MAAG. If the military failed to provide security, we envisioned that the program would probably collapse.

Diem was determined to proceed with the program, regardless of the depth of American support. It was obvious that the strategic hamlet concept presented the best available opportunity for a combined, successful Vietnamese–American counterinsurgency effort. MAAG, at least at the top level, was confident it could work with the Army of the Republic of Vietnam (ARVN) through MAAG's sector advisers to the Vietnamese province chiefs at provincial levels and through the Civil Guard (security forces assigned to province chiefs) to guarantee security inputs.

Based on earlier observations of inadequate and inappropriate conventional American training of the Vietnamese armed forces, Phillips and I were highly skeptical of MAAG's assurances, and we were very unsure of the vital security component. This security element was crucial for the rural population to have faith that the government would protect it from the insurgents. We knew that commencing as early as 1951, American military inspectors had pointed out repeatedly that the military answer to communism in South Vietnam would have to be unconventional, as would our training for the Vietnamese military. Yet, here in 1962, except for limited action by U.S. Special Forces in the Vietnamese Central Highlands, there was almost nothing unconventional in MAAG or in its thinking.

The threat to South Vietnam's security in the very early 1960s was from guerrilla insurgents, who operated without armored vehicles, tanks, and helicopters. The insurgents, the Viet Cong (Vietnamese name for the South Vietnam communists), relied on ambushes, surprise attacks, and above all, political indoctrination of the rural population. This indoctrination was to try to coerce and convince the people that they were being exploited by local officials. And, at the least, the population was often ignored by these officials.

Phillips knew many of the province chiefs from his earlier days, and they liked and trusted him and were quick to confide in him about their problems. Phillips's character projected simplicity, friendship, confidence, strength, and action. He and his staff were better liked by the Vietnamese than were their more prosaic American peers.

My character seemed also to appeal to Asians, and, likely because of lifelong participation in sports, I am teamwork and action oriented and appreciated by younger people. In fact, because of earlier work in China with young American farm boys attached to the Brethren Service, I helped develop with one of them, Frank Wallick, the Peace Corps concept, which we sold to Congressman Clement Zablocki and then President Kennedy.

Rufe and I decided to talk to as many American staff members of various American agencies in South Vietnam as we could and then to visit all the provinces and many of the districts. In the provinces, we met with MAAG's sector advisers and U.S. Special Forces but spent most of our time with the province chiefs and their staffs, often overnighting with them. We also sought out local sect leaders, Catholic priests, and Chinese businesspeople for their viewpoints.

Vietnamese government services from the technical ministries usually ended at the province level in the person of a service chief with a small staff; positions were often unfilled because of constant staff escape to Saigon. These French-educated functionaires on a constant move to Saigon were called the *lycée mandarin* (the French established *lycées*, or schools, in the larger towns and cities of South Vietnam, which were equivalent to a good U.S. high school). Many graduates became civil servants. Proud of their French education, many were arrogant and disdained the local people. Lycée mandarin was hardly a complimentary term.

At best, ministry outreach, even to the provinces, was unpredictable and untimely. Supplies were frequently skimmed off or arrived spoiled or too late for use. These included those from USOM, which were always turned over to the ministries on the wharves in Saigon. Just as in our experiences with UNRRA in China, interpreted by the local Chinese as "you never really receive anything," we found that South Vietnam's rural folks never expected to receive anything either. Rufe and I spent a good twelve hours daily talking to people at every level everywhere in South Vietnam. We soon had a very good feel for what was happening and even more so for what was not happening, though usually reported otherwise to Saigon through Vietnamese and MAAG military channels.

We found that insecurity in the provinces was generally overstated and that we could travel quite safely by road in most provinces except An Xuyen, Binh Dinh, Quang Ngai, Binh Duong, and southern Quang Nam. We confirmed that the most serious flaw in solving the security problem was the failure of ARVN and the province and district Civil Guard to move out of their bases, particularly at night, to respond to Viet Cong infiltration and attacks on hamlets.

We noted that the Viet Cong tended to attack those areas weakest in religious, political, and economic organization. For example, the Hoa Hao sect inhabited almost all of An Giang Province in the deep Delta of South Vietnam. The Hoa Hao were strongly anticommunist and well organized, and the Viet Cong made no serious attacks on them during the entire Vietnam conflict. Later, a comprehensive economic development project created by the South Vietnam government and USOM transformed this bleakest of areas into one of South Vietnam's richest provinces in just three years.

We learned much from the MAAG sector advisers billeted in the provincial capitals with their seven- or eight-man teams. We were deeply moved by their dedication and high quality and more so by their frustration over the lack of action from MAAG headquarters in Saigon to their suggestions and needs. MAAG/Saigon (later to become MACV) was particularly unresponsive to their complaints about ARVN and Civil Guard reluctance to engage the Viet Cong except with random, noisy, usually undirected artillery fire from miles away. This went on from sunset to dawn, and it terrified the hamlet people.

MAAG also had field advisers attached to major ARVN field units who usually, and parochially, rationalized ARVN's performance. This was similar to the way most USOM technical advisers were covering up the failure of their ministry counterparts to reach the field. This spurred Rufe and me to look for ways to help them directly from Saigon.

Joint Counterinsurgency Program Is Developed

After a review of USOM's resources and actions and those of other U.S. agencies, as well as other country aid donors and volunteer agencies, we began to devise a program to aid the rural areas. After three weeks in South Vietnam, we spent a Sunday around a Vietnamese friend's dinner table drafting a proposed "Office of Rural Affairs Program" and an organizational structure to implement it.

Before Rufe left AID/Washington, he had been told that the White House had authorized a special fund of ten million dollars to be used to buy piasters (Vietnamese currency) in Saigon. These piasters would be used to finance USOM inputs toward a decentralization of its program to support the counterinsurgency effort. This funding was contingent on the development of an effective plan and Vietnamese government concurrence. We drafted our plan accordingly.

We suggested creation of a special Office of Rural Affairs within USOM to be headed by an assistant director with a deputy. We called for assigning one USOM American provincial representative in each province. These would be back-stopped by three regional representatives paralleling South Vietnam's three (later expanded to four) military regions. Each representative, regional and provincial, would have one locally hired Vietnamese area specialist plus one clerk-typist.

Each USOM technical division would detail one technician to backstop provincial projects and focus regular USOM projects into the provinces where possible. We called for a Rural Affairs Program officer for planning and project processing and monitoring, and for our own administrative officer to service our field personnel.

Having noted that USOM and, in fact, the whole American effort in South Vietnam lacked an efficient local procurement and provincial transportation capacity, we requested two American and eight Filipino personnel to set up a logistic section to receive, store, and move aid supplies to the provinces. I had won AID awards in China for logistics and truly knew how to handle large amounts of incoming aid in Asia. I found that the American Catholic Relief Services in South Vietnam had an excellent system for moving commodities without pilferage through Vietnamese and Chinese contractors. It gladly let us use its system and large Saigon warehouses.

The proposed Rural Affairs Logistics Section was approved, and it was so efficient that it took over from MAAG and ARVN the movement of nearly one hundred thousand tons of barbed wire, surplus French rifles, and other defense materials to the strategic hamlets. MAAG and ARVN's logistics commands simply couldn't do the job. The key was fair and prompt payment to the contractors. We also called for a Command Center with around-the-clock radio and telephone contact to the provincial representatives (prov reps) and progress reporting controls for all projects.

Finally, we proposed jobs for roving special-project managers for hamlet self-help activities, Asian methods of manual water well drilling, hamlet pig raising and composting, Viet Cong analyses and surrender programs, and hamlet women's work. In total, we asked for fewer than seventy Americans in Rural Affairs for the whole country.

After laying out the organization, we finished the Rural Affairs Program proposal. It called for decentralizing aid directly to the provinces, with discretion for framing projects locally in several broad categories. First priority was to support the Strategic Hamlet Program, itself designed to bring security and economic development to the villages and hamlets. Program projects were designed to induce local cooperation for constructing and establishing hamlet security and local, democratic institutions.

A hamlet was considered strategic and complete after it had erected an exterior, double barbed-wire fence with moats or mounds in between and built pillboxes and command posts. It also had a trained and armed twenty-four-hour self-defense force and a wind-powered two-way radio link with the Civil Guard in the province or district capital and the closest ARVN unit. In addition, it had to elect a hamlet council and chief—the first time hamlet leaders were selected by ballot in most of South Vietnam. The program was coordinated with the Education Ministry, and for the first year we funded teachers' salaries for new hamlet schools. Classes were set up at district and village levels to train new village and hamlet leaders in basic administration.

Once the hamlet was completed and the council in place, residents would meet to consider and select a self-help project for which we provided, from the province level, immediate cash, tools, construction materials, and small machinery such as pumps and generators. They could choose to build school-houses, clinics, temples, bridges, or wells. As soon as one self-help project was finished, working, and inspected, the hamlet people could vote and start the next.

We cleared the program with USOM's newly energized Counterinsurgency Committee and with Acting Director Bill Fippin. Rufe then obtained approval from the U.S. embassy and MAAG and secured a general go-ahead from the CIA station chief. He then cleared it with President Diem, all in just one day. Rufe then returned to Washington with the proposal in mid-June 1962, where it was promptly approved. I returned to Taiwan.

AID/Washington requested that Rufe give up his private business and return to South Vietnam to head the Rural Affairs Program. I was directed to Saigon to be his deputy. Reluctantly we agreed, and I arrived in Saigon on 20 September, several days ahead of Rufe. USOM was ready for us and had prepared two small offices directly opposite Bill Fippin's office. We were provided one American and one Vietnamese secretary and were authorized to supervise and use the members of USOM's Counterinsurgency Committee. Meanwhile, the U.S. embassy had set up a Counterinsurgency Coordination Committee under William (Bill) Trueheart, the deputy ambassador, made up of representatives from the U.S. agencies in South Vietnam; it met weekly at the American embassy.

I had arrived in Saigon ahead of Rufe, so I was first on board with author-ity to implement the Rural Affairs Program as we had devised it. Rufe telegraphed that he would be several days late because he was recruiting peo-ple to be prov reps. I cabled back that I would also search for some people who were already in-country.

I asked Bill Fippin to call a USOM meeting of all American personnel and requested his permission to ask for volunteers to become prov reps. He did so that very afternoon, and we all lined up in the parking lot behind the USOM office building. I was looking for, primarily, younger men and women who could be Rural Affairs "tigers"—sincere go-getters who could run a program outside the business-as-usual bureaucracy. Fippin and I explained the program and the challenging responsibility of being a Rural Affairs prov rep, as well as the great opportunities of the job. But when I asked for volunteers from the hundred or so assembled, only two men and one woman stepped forward, the latter a nurse already in the field much of the time.

In our earlier study visit, Rufe and I had been very impressed by the work of the young men and women in International Voluntary Services (IVS), an American voluntary agency partially funded by USOM that was doing Peace Corps–like work (before there was a Peace Corps). All IVS activities were in rural areas of South Vietnam. Many of the IVS volunteers were Vietnamese language speakers with several years' experience in the countryside. Fippin's own nephew was an IVS volunteer. I thought of deputizing some of them to be USOM Rural Affairs prov reps, and Fippin agreed, so I called on their team chief, Don Luce (who later would publicize the infamous Tiger Cage political prison). He said that it was an interesting idea and that he would let me know later. To my delight, he called me the next evening and said that he had clearance from his U.S. headquarters and that he could give me the names of ten prospective volunteers. I asked to meet with them the next morning.

It was heartwarming to talk with the IVS people and to observe their maturity, enthusiasm, intelligence, and knowledge of South Vietnam. They convinced me that they were just right for the type of work we had in mind. I spent the next several evenings at the IVS office and house in Saigon discussing the Rural Affairs Program with these volunteers and laying out their jobs. Although their IVS pay was only eighty dollars per month (about one-tenth of the salary for an American in USOM), they seemed much more interested in and motivated for the job ahead.

Rufe arrived in Saigon, and we prepared job descriptions, a work manual, and letters of introduction to various province chiefs. We also had Vietnamese letters from the Interior Ministry authorized from President Diem's office. We accompanied our first prov rep, Bob McNeff, from IVS, to his new post in Tuy Hoa in Phu Yen Province in Central Vietnam on 28 September 1962. We had found our first "Tiger" for Rural Affairs.

We decided that we would pay our prov reps a standard per diem of nine dollars and provide them with a jeep-type vehicle and gasoline. They were told to hire their own Vietnamese area specialists and clerk-typists as their assistants. The per diem was to cover meals and rent of very modest accommodations, preferably a shop front with rooms upstairs. The shop space could serve as office space and storage.

During our provincial visits, Rufe and I had found that costs in the provinces were very low and that the nine dollars would be adequate for the lifestyle we wanted our prov reps to project. We expected them to live with the people at the people's level. Particularly, we wanted to avoid the huge administrative and logistic burdens that would accrue if we tried to manage their living arrangements and offices from Saigon. We told them that if they rented big houses and looked even a little bit like Ugly Americans, we would return them to Saigon. The book *The Ugly American* had just been published, depicting the lavish lifestyle of most American government officials abroad. Amazingly, our system, so totally foreign to USOM, worked beautifully, and we had to recall only one person in the first year of the program. We showed the Vietnamese in the provinces that we were totally unlike old French officialdom and that we were all dedicated to working with them.

Rural Affairs Goes to the Provinces—Full Steam Ahead
Rufe reported that he had recruited some twenty-five people in Washington from many sources. Some he had worked with earlier in South Vietnam and Laos, others were new State Department Foreign Service inductees. Among them was Richard Holbrooke, who would later become a high-level official in the State Department and U.S. ambassador to the United Nations. Meanwhile, we started contacting former associates worldwide that we felt would be suitable. About fifteen responded favorably.

As fast as they came in, we indoctrinated them and assigned them to the provinces according to Strategic Hamlet Program priorities. We constantly encouraged and reminded them as they came and went on Rural Affairs business to "be a Tiger!" which became the Rural Affairs motto and rallying cry. Although it must have sounded strange to the Vietnamese secretaries and older USOM-types in the halls of USOM/Saigon, it surely won the hearts and minds of our men and women and our Vietnamese staff. Our only prayer was that the old-line bureaucratic system would give the Tigers enough time to get the job done.

We told the prov reps to work with their respective province chiefs and the MAAG sector advisers to develop provincial pacification and development plans. These plans would be based on ongoing ministry projects and actual needs in the various provinces and, more important, the progress and needs of the Strategic Hamlet Program. All were to be measured against local appraisals of the actual security situation within each province. Most of our prov reps had several years of Southeast Asian experience, so their assignments were hardly foreign to them.

We quickly built the Rural Affairs Saigon staff and put Rural Affairs regional representatives to work coordinating provincial plans in the three military regions. While still developing their provincial plans, the prov reps were already helping the Vietnamese start development projects in completed strategic hamlets, such as leadership training, elections, self-help, and Viet Cong surrenders (Chieu Hoi).

To finance these activities, we sent out amounts of five hundred thousand piasters (thirty-five piasters to one U.S. dollar was the official rate, and about seventy piasters to one U.S. dollar was the unofficial, black market rate) in cash to each prov rep to be receipted by his province chief. This cash had to be carried to the provinces by hand because there was no system for telegraphic remittances nor local banks. There were only three banks outside of Saigon, in Da Nang, Hue, and Can Tho. This fact alone is a sad indication of South Vietnam's backwardness and an indictment of USOM's failure in helping the country develop economically during the 1954 to 1962 period of peace.

Projects framed locally within program guidelines were reviewed in almost daily meetings of the prov reps, their counterparts, and the province chief, with the MAAG sector adviser often sitting in. There had to be complete agreement for each project between the prov rep and the province chief before supplies or funding were allocated. The prov rep and the province chief kept joint books on the cash flow, and I know of no instance of any misuse of these funds.

By the end of October 1962, we were getting a very solid feeling about what was happening in many provinces. But we were also getting endless reports of shortcomings in regular Vietnamese governmental ministerial programs because of bureaucratic breakdowns, poor logistics, and inadequate or nonexistent follow-through from Saigon. More disturbing were the mounting reports of ARVN failure on its commitment to use its logistic commands to deliver strategic hamlet defense supplies, as well as to respond to small-scale attacks on the hamlets by the Viet Cong. We did troubleshooting on many of the complaints about ministerial projects, working directly with the ministries in Saigon when USOM technical advisers were unwilling to intervene. We used Rural Affairs' own resources and logistic system when the ministries demonstrated a lack of funding. Finally, at the weekly USOM-Trueheart meeting, when MAAG was unable to prod ARVN to deliver the strategic hamlet defense supplies that had been piling up, we took over the job and moved one hundred thousand tons of materials to the provinces in forty-five days.

Three of USOM's technical divisions, Health, Education, and Public Administration, backed Rural Affairs wholeheartedly and energized their counterpart ministries as well. Hundreds of thousands of elementary-level textbooks were

Bert Fraleigh (center) with Joseph Brent (left), AID mission director, Saigon, 1963

printed and distributed; medical kits for clinics were developed; and teachers, barefoot village doctors, and local-level leaders were trained. Rural Affairs gladly funded these activities when regular ministerial budgets were unavailable. The USOM Program Office, which detailed very competent staff to Rural Affairs, was most cooperative. Above all, Acting Director Bill Fippin and his successor, Director Joseph Brent, whom I had served under in Taiwan, were totally supportive.

Rural Affair's main problem was the USOM Agricultural Division, whose leaders failed us constantly, although some of its section chiefs were helpful. Because improving agriculture in the rural areas was the major counterinsurgency economic objective and because I had been deeply involved in Taiwan's incredibly successful agricultural development, I turned to the Chinese in Taiwan to support us in South Vietnam.

Taiwan provided us with a Chinese Agricultural Technical Mission of about twenty-five men, many from the JCRR and local Taiwan extension agencies. These specialists went into selected areas throughout South Vietnam, worked directly with Vietnamese farmers, and achieved a number of farming miracles. Taiwan backed them with tons of improved seeds, chemicals, and equipment, and Rural Affairs funded their local expenses. They introduced dry season crops such as soybeans, muskmelons and watermelons, pole beans, bok choy cabbage, high-yield sweet potatoes, and rice, along with Chinese vegetables. Composting techniques that Vietnamese farmers had never used before were also implemented. Soon these farmers were making many times their normal income, and new farmhouses were popping up like mushrooms wherever the Chinese lived and worked.

Fertilizer for Rural Areas

Chemical fertilizer was rarely used in Central Vietnam, which was largely a rice-producing area, with less than one-half acre of tillable land per family. We decided, over the bitter objections of the USOM Agricultural Division, to send twenty thousand tons of triple-sixteen rice fertilizer to strategic hamlet farmers who had worked on building their hamlets and defended them. We imported this directly from the United States and shipped it to Rural Affairs prov reps who helped their province chiefs move it to their provincial hamlets and who instructed the farmers in its use. For the first time in many years, South Vietnam produced a surplus of rice in 1963 and was able to export nearly two hundred thousand metric tons.

Improved Pigs for the Rural Areas

Many Americans know about the scrawny, swaybacked, black Vietnamese pigs that became popular as pets. In our experiences, we saw that these pigs, running around unpenned as wild stock, were all the farmers had in Central Vietnam. When we talked with the farmers about the pigs, they told us that these sixty-pound grubbers took about two years to mature and provided them very little meat or manure for fertilizer. We discussed this situation with Harvey Neese, an IVS animal husbandry graduate from Idaho. He said he could do something about it, and we hired him knowing how successful and vital hog production was in other Asian countries such as Taiwan and Hong Kong. Harvey (later to be dubbed *Ong Heo,* or Mr. Pig, by the Vietnamese) went to work with Dr. Vu Thien Thai, a former Viet Minh leader and head of animal husbandry in Vietnam; Earl Brockman, a USOM cooperative adviser; Nguyen Qui Dinh, a recent Arkansas livestock nutrition graduate; and Nguyen Quang Luu, head of South Vietnam's national cooperative agency. We then drew up plans for the Pig Corn Program.

Under the Pig Corn Program, Rural Affairs provided each farm family who applied, in completed strategic hamlets, with bags of cement and corrugated roofing sheets. Each participating farmer would receive on credit three Yorkshire piglets (about twenty pounds each) and two hundred pounds of U.S. surplus corn on credit. The piglets were bought from Vietnamese producers in the south near My Tho, the center of pig raising in South Vietnam.

Technical advice in the provinces was given by local Vietnamese animal husbandry agents on building a standard, sanitary pigpen and compost pit and on caring for the piglets (one male and two females). Neese and Dinh traveled the countryside continually offering assistance. In less than two years, fifteen thousand farmers had joined the program and repaid their loans. White, improved hogs weighing up to three hundred pounds could be seen everywhere, descendants of the twenty-five thousand handled under the Pig Corn Program. The program must have impressed the North Vietnamese along the Ben Hai River north of the seventeenth parallel because they started a similar program there, even copying the cartoon characters Dinh and Neese had used in their extension pamphlets.

MAAG Sector Advisers Join Rural Affairs

By mid-November 1962, prov reps were reporting major progress and receiving encouraging news from the economic and political inputs, though we only had enough prov reps for about half the thirty-eight provinces. Phillips argued that it was all right to go slow in adding the remaining half. I argued that it was imperative that we fill in the blanks because strategic hamlets were being built in all provinces and the Viet Cong were out there as well. After long discussions, we suddenly got a bright idea. Because MAAG sector advisers (military personnel) were in all the provinces, why not appoint them as acting prov reps in the unstaffed provinces and as members of the provincial Rural Affair Program committees in all provinces? Phillips took this idea to Gen. Paul Harkins, the MAAG and MACV chief, who agreed immediately, as did his Saigon chief coordinator for sector advisers, Col. Carl Schaad.

Letters went out from USOM and MAAG to the MAAG sector advisers in the unstaffed provinces appointing them as prov reps. They also received prov rep manuals and visits from Rural Affairs regional representatives. The advisers were delighted with this new assignment because the requirement for joint project review with the Vietnamese province chief and sign-off gave them much closer contact with him and his district chiefs. We followed up by putting the sector advisers in all provinces on the local provincial program committees and expanding the sign-off to include them in a procedure that was promptly called "troika." Any of the three signers (prov rep, province chief, sector adviser) had the right of veto, but they hardly ever used it.

The idea for the three-party sign-off came to me from my work with JCRR in Taiwan, where American aid was given to the rural areas through a five-person commission. There were three Chinese and two Americans, with all projects requiring unanimous approval and each commissioner retaining the right of veto. That system worked very well and involved all the signers and their respective countries in taking responsibility for each project's success. In Vietnam, this veto and sign-off system protected Vietnamese sovereignty. In fact, from my years of observation, relationships between the prov reps, the sector advisers, and their province chiefs were remarkably warm, and they worked like a team. The relationships between most ARVN commanders and their MAAG and MACV advisers did not seem to be nearly as close.

Early on, with the fervent desire to get the U.S. and Vietnamese governments in Saigon planning and working together on the rural and strategic hamlet efforts, particularly the Vietnamese ministries and USOM technical divisions, I proposed to Acting Director Fippin, with Rufe's approval, that we form a JCRR-like organization for the task. We called it VARDO (Vietnamese/American Rural Development Organization). Rufe obtained Trueheart's and the Vietnamese presidential office's approval, and the idea was sent to AID/Washington for final approval. Several months elapsed before we learned that the U.S. Department of Agriculture objected vehemently, claiming it would surrender American sovereignty over U.S. agricultural aid in foreign countries. This was just one more example of the unwillingness of top-level American officialdom to use unconventional organizations and methods in South Vietnam that had proved successful in defeating Asian communism elsewhere.

About the same time, the Vietnamese government decided to establish its own small office in Saigon to oversee the Strategic Hamlet Program under Col. Hoang Lac. This office soon became the Ministry of Revolutionary Development (MORD) and was a most congenial counterpart for the Office of Rural Affairs. By early 1963, we were fully staffed in Rural Affairs, with 80 Americans and 120 Vietnamese. The program was very efficiently fulfilling Rural Affairs' portion of the Strategic Hamlet Program and delivering ministry technical support and our special development projects to the countryside.

Our reporting system from the provinces consisted of comprehensive Friday afternoon submissions augmented by reports from our traveling Rural Affairs regional representatives and special projects implementers. Rufe and I also made several field visits each week, especially on Sundays. MAAG's sector advisers submitted their own reports according to a very rigid format prescribed by MAAG and MACV in Saigon, as did MAAG field advisers to ARVN units. Although our prov reps usually showed their reports to sector advisers in their respective provinces, we told our people to report the situation exactly as they themselves saw it. Most of them were on the road every day in their provinces (a province being about the size of an American county) and little escaped their attention.

Security Not Provided for Strategic Hamlet Program

Prov rep reports from November and December 1962 on, particularly from the Mekong Delta provinces east and south of Saigon, told of increasing Viet Cong activity and a general failure of the Civil Guard and ARVN to respond to radio calls for promised backup support. Prov reps also reported that in many cases the local hamlet militia and self-defense forces were fighting off these attacks with bravery but that their morale was slipping because the Civil Guard–ARVN backup failed to appear or was too late to help. MAAG's sanitized reports hardly reflected these growing problems and erroneously reported a much more positive situation.

Each week the Trueheart Counterinsurgency Coordination Committee would review one or two province plans as they were completed, with the individual prov rep and sector adviser present to explain them. It was obvious that most of the prov reps and sector advisers got along very well, cooperated closely, and gave similar verbal reports. When asked why their written reports submitted through their respective channels varied widely, the sector advisers said they made their reports through MAAG/soliders Saigon guidelines, which called for a positive picture, whether warranted or not. MAAG/soliders Saigon was anxious that they corroborate ARVN's notoriously specious field reporting.

We in Rural Affairs, together with concerned civilians in other U.S. agencies in Saigon and with Vietnamese governmental counterpart Hoang Lac, had many discussions with MAAG leaders and with the ARVN about improving security response for the hamlets. We made many suggestions, the final being to integrate small numbers of American Special Forces into the Vietnamese response units to ensure improved communications, logistics, and an immediate response. Integrating the response units would also ensure regular rations and pay for these local Vietnamese soldiers, who were frequently months behind in both. Although similar arrangements had proved to be a major incentive for South Korean troops to fight in the early days of the Korean War, MAAG rejected the idea.

The Special Forces solution had been implemented earlier in certain areas of the Vietnamese Highlands within the Montagnard Program Civilian Irregular Defense Group (CIDG) and along the Cambodian border with outstanding success, but it was never seriously expanded. It was common knowledge that the U.S. conventional military had little use for the Green Berets and was reluctant to recognize them as a special force. This attitude extended to the whole concept of unconventional warfare and counterinsurgency.

Despite glowing promises made by MAAG and ARVN, there was little action. The Chinese and Vietnamese have a cogent saying for this: "Dragon head, snake tail." We felt that most top U.S. and Vietnamese military leaders understood very little about unconventional warfare and fighting a communist insurgency. Their arrogance and ignorance frightened us and frustrated our prov reps, many MAAG sector and field advisers, and the province chiefs. The bottom line was this: if security could not be provided to the villagers, then the Strategic Hamlets Program and its counterinsurgency connotations were not going to work.

Viet Cong Attacks Increase in Mekong Delta

Late 1962 saw a quickening series of larger-unit Viet Cong attacks, and where the Civil Guard and ARVN were drawn or chased into a fight, they often were badly beaten. Although MAAG knew about these losses and finally admitted to some of them, it still tried to put a positive spin on these engagements. Instead of opting for an unconventional response, however, MAAG turned to training more Vietnamese troops conventionally and adding more equipment and American military advisers. Slowly, in many provinces, as new strategic hamlets were completed, increasing numbers were undermined by the absence of military response to the calls from their beleaguered hamlet militias.

Also, in 1962 world attention was turning to Saigon, and more news correspondents were pouring in. They soon unmasked MAAG's and ARVN's conventional war syndromes, the cover-ups, and the threats these problems posed to the strategic hamlet solution. Their criticisms were particularly demoralizing to President Diem and his leadership and frustrating to President Kennedy and his staff in Washington. The Saigon press picked up this pessimistic reporting, which was also damaging the morale of the local populace.

Although economic activities blossomed in the countryside, there was little change in Vietnamese military tactics or performance, and security deteriorated, as did hope in the cities. The U.S. reaction, strongly opposed by Rural Affairs and by other unconventionalists, was to add more military personnel and more money. MAAG changed to a supreme command, the U.S. Military Assistance Command, Vietnam (MACV), and enlarged quickly, adding mostly Saigon staff in huge administrative sections. Superficially, this encouraged the Saigonese who saw the Americans as taking over the war. Some Vietnamese saw this as a golden opportunity to make a lot of money—fast.

The U.S. government–supported Rural Affairs Program was intended as a long-term, nation-building effort, carried out by a very, very few experienced, dedicated, and humble Americans, in cooperation with Vietnamese counterparts. These dedicated people were willing to put in the years that might be required for success. We knew that more than ten years of quiet, thorough grassroots work was required to defeat insurgency in Malaya (later Malaysia) in the 1950s, and we were prepared for a similar effort in South Vietnam. We even brought in Sir Robert Thompson, architect of the Malayan counterin-

Bert Fraleigh (*right, with glasses*) talking to An Giang Province Chief Col. Ly Ba Pham (*left*) in Long Xuyen, An Giang Province, 1965

surgency effort, to advise us. This is why we abhorred a huge American buildup and takeover of the Vietnam conflict. We knew that sending more men and more money was a conventional American response that would doom counterinsurgency in South Vietnam.

Assassinations Threaten Counterinsurgency

In 1963, South Vietnam's Buddhist monks were becoming very restless, feeling that Diem and his influential family members were giving too many favors to Catholics. Diem, his brother and closest adviser Ngo Dinh Nhu, Nhu's wife, Madame Nhu, and yet another Diem brother, Ngo Dinh Thuc, the Catholic senior archbishop of South Vietnam in Hue, were suspicious of Buddhist motives. A severe crackdown on Buddhists followed, and the war seemed to turn inward, away from the communists to a confrontation between the government and Buddhism. This finally led to the 1 November 1963 military coup and the assassination of President Diem and his brother. A few weeks later, John F. Kennedy was tragically assassinated. With these epochal losses, the situation in South Vietnam irrevocably changed for the worse. There was no South Vietnamese leader who suddenly appeared to assume Diem's steadfast role, and, with Kennedy gone, the U.S. Department of Defense and MACV no longer had to give even lip service to unconventional warfare. Coincidentally, Rufe Phillips's father was terminally ill in Virginia, and Rufe had to resign from his job in South Vietnam and go home to take over the family business.

The passing of Diem, and especially his brother Nhu, was greeted with jubilance in South Vietnam, as predominantly Buddhist crowds cheered the ARVN everywhere. There were great expectations from the southern-born Gen. Duong Van Minh, whose physical countenance and six-foot stature earned him the nickname "Big Minh." He radiated a charisma never to be confirmed by his leadership.

I knew him quite well as a jovial and fairly regular tennis partner. About a week after the coup, I was surprised to see him at the tennis court. I congratulated him and told him that the rural program was continuing with good progress. I also said that our prov reps were reporting that there was euphoria in the rural areas, along with high expectations for the new government. I offered him our full support and said I hoped that he could improve the local military response for hamlet security. He turned serious and said that the new government depended very much on the rural work and that he was determined to make the Strategic Hamlets Program successful. He said he wanted to strengthen Col. Hoang Lac's office so that it could bring the civil government in Saigon fully behind the program. He asked Rural Affairs to work hand in glove with his administration and to let him know of any problems or new ideas. That was the last time I ever saw him at the tennis court.

There was no hiatus in the progress of our work in the provinces, but we soon began to notice an aimless drift developing on the Vietnamese government side in Saigon and a growing erosion of popular confidence. There seemed to be no new initiatives or programs, and no one seemed to be leading. On the American side, there was no Ed Lansdale, who had helped Diem solidify his position as president, helping the new leadership make things happen and creating positive images.

Thus, a great political opportunity, and an even greater opportunity to wrest the military initiative from the Viet Cong, was lost almost by default. It was not because we in Rural Affairs did not sense the situation and pass ideas to the new leadership through an equally frustrated Colonel Lac. One initiative called for a national "People's Prosperity Program," with accompanying political reforms to be announced by Big Minh and supported by multidonor assistance, public and private. The leadership must have been too busy with internal squabbles, for nothing was ever heard of this and other submissions. Shortly thereafter, new coups became fairly regular events. I was stricken with hepatitis at the end of November 1963 and benched for about ten weeks. Len Maynard, Rural Affairs' I Corps regional adviser, filled in for me.

When I returned to work, I found that political pressures were building in Washington over South Vietnam and that President Johnson was pushing for a bigger light at the end of the tunnel. This pressure seemed to be caused by the increased, high-level attention being given to our prov reps, weekly reports of deteriorating security, and poor military performance. MACV was continuing to demand optimism from its sources (even if there were no reasons to be optimistic), but journalists were exposing the real situation. I was under constant pressure from Saigon to have Rural Affairs reports sanitized. MACV officers asked me to write my own briefings in advance for their comments and to rehearse them in their frequent briefing rehearsals for censorship. Of course I refused. This hardly endeared me to them.

Accurate Reporting Incurs Military Hostility

I had a number of talks with MACV field advisers such as Cols. John Paul Vann, Dan Porter, and Fred Ladd, and many of lower rank. These colonels were reporting to MACV quite accurately but were generating great hostility from General Harkins. They were the exceptions, and MACV moved quickly to silence them. Vann was even considered for court-martial for failing to toe the party line and soon resigned his military commission. All of us in Rural Affairs greatly admired these honest officers, and we tried to support them as best we could.

Several months after Vann retired, he applied to AID/Washington for a job in South Vietnam. Walter Stoneman, AID/Washington's Vietnam backstop officer, called me in Saigon, asking if we could use Vann. I told him "by all means" but to give me time to let me clear it with MACV because adding Vann to our staff could be very delicate for USOM. I went to see Gen. Richard Stilwell, my usual MACV liaison officer. To my surprise he said, "It's your business, you'll find him hard to handle, and we won't be too happy, but we won't hold it against you." I called Stoneman and okayed Vann, saying that we could only make him a prov rep in a tough province. We assigned him to the newly created no-man's-land of Hau Nghia Province, just west of Saigon.

Although I did not attend, I was told that at a presidential conference in Manila about this time, Lyndon Johnson showed his frustration with South Vietnam pacification progress and continuing MACV requests for more military advisers. He purportedly said, "I thought this was a war to win the hearts and the minds; how many civilian advisers do we have out there?" Someone said, "Three hundred." Johnson said, "God damn it, I want one thousand civilian advisers out there in sixty days. I want those coonskins tacked on the wall."

This apparently reflected his belief that any problem could be solved with more people, more money, and bigger programs. It also showed his ignorance of counterinsurgency.

U.S. Military Moves to Take Over Rural Affairs

MACV apparently had an idea, supposedly generated by Gen. Victor Krulak and Robert Komer of the National Security Council in Washington, to take over control of Rural Affairs. We were told about this plan in Saigon and informed that AID/Washington was starting a large recruitment campaign. USOM Director Brent, the Trueheart Counterinsurgency Coordination Committee, and I protested vigorously to AID/Washington, particularly over adding American civilian personnel in the provinces. We pointed out that it was totally against counterinsurgency principles, wholly counterproductive, and bureaucratically stifling. Our opposition was to no avail.

To my thinking, it was the beginning of the end of a meaningful, unconventional, civilian counterinsurgency response. I recalled my first few days in Saigon, telling Rufe that from my experience, we would have to do a damn good job in the first year because after that the bureaucrats would move in and we would be the victims of Parkinson's Law. If only John Kennedy had lived, we would have had much more time to prove that America's counterinsurgency program could follow in the footsteps of similar winning programs in Malaysia and the Philippines.

Destruction of the Rural Affairs Concept

As part of this new buildup, AID/Washington decided to send out a tough new USOM director, "Big" Jim Killen. Uncertainty about my recovery from hepatitis led to the recruitment of George Tanham, a RAND Corporation vice-president, to head Rural Affairs, with Col. (later Lt. Gen.) Sam Wilson, detailed from the U.S. Army, as a new deputy. AID/Washington also decided to change the Rural Affairs office name to Provincial Operations.

Killen arrived, together with his personal, female secretary, about the middle of 1964. A former AID director in several countries, he was a chain-smoking, large, craggy man who prided himself on having been a labor-union agitator and organizer from the pulp mills of Washington State. He acted like he had little formal education and seemed to regard college graduates as management types who needed to be taught lessons in humility. He tried to look tough, act tough, and used frequent profanity to sound tough. He was a very insecure man and the poorest executive selection that I ever saw in thirty years of government service and twenty years of private enterprise. Yet here he was with unbridled power in a very key position at a very critical time in American history. I was not told until 1995 that Killen was selected for Saigon by Rutherford Poats, a former newsman who had met Killen in Korea and thought him strong, decisive, and suitable for South Vietnam. Poats, at the time, was heading South Vietnam affairs in AID/Washington under overall AID administrator David Bell.

One of Killen's first actions on arrival in Saigon was to have the U.S. government spend thirty-five thousand dollars installing an elevator in his residence for the first and second floors. This caused immediate, widespread gossip and set the tone for his administration. Meanwhile, South Vietnam was deteriorating politically and militarily.

In addition to his secretary, Killen brought with him his executive and administrative officers and two security investigators. When he arrived, he convened no general staff introductory meeting. He simply holed himself up in his office and seemed to talk only with his own newcomers. After a few days, he started calling each office and technical division chief, one-by-one, to his office for about an hour's conference. That is, everyone except me. I went to his office and asked his secretary if I could brief him. She replied curtly, "He'll get to you last, you can bet on that."

Although my office was just across the hall from his and Provincial Operations was USOM's largest program, and Tanham and Wilson, assigned to this program, had not yet reached Saigon, Killen never spoke or even nodded to me once in three months. When telegrams, correspondence, or problems required joint action, he would call one of my lowest-ranked program people and give him his orders for Provincial Operations. This young man would then sheepishly come to me. He said that Killen told him our office was corrupt, unprofessional, not worthy of being in AID, and full of homosexuals. He said he was "sure as hell going to clean it up." He also said that our prov reps were incompetent, that such important jobs should be filled by experienced AID men who had been former mission and deputy mission directors, and that he was in the process of recruiting them. How Poats and Administrator Bell in AID/Washington could believe in, and tolerate, this type of person, I could not understand. And I never will.

One day Killen told his emissary that he was canceling the troika provincial sign-off agreement because it was an affront to Vietnamese sovereignty and against standard AID procedures. Actually, troika was the keystone of our provincial operations; it ensured constant consultation and cooperation among the prov reps, the sector advisers, and province chiefs, responsible use of funds and supplies, and project monitoring. I told the emissary to tell Killen that I opposed canceling the sign-off agreement and wanted to discuss it with him personally. Killen said he wouldn't see me and that he would write his own order to the prov reps. I took the problem to the Trueheart committee, reporting Killen's attitude toward me and our office. Sadly, at this very same time, the Trueheart committee itself suddenly escalated its membership to the heads of agency level, virtually the country team. They let Killen's disastrous whims stand.

George Tanham and Sam Wilson arrived about this time. Killen treated Tanham just as he did me but cultivated Wilson, who quickly became his man. Wilson explained this to Tanham and me saying, "I have to be Killen's buddy so that Provincial Operations can continue to be effective." USOM Deputy Director Al Hurt had been in place for nearly a year when Killen arrived. Killen also ignored him and froze him out. Hurt, Tanham, and I became close friends; we were fellow pariahs.

Killen Declares War on Rural Affairs
About a month after his arrival in Saigon, Killen ordered his new security men to conduct investigations on Rural Affairs prov reps and some of the special project leaders for the Pig Corn Program, well drilling, windmills and irrigation, and

Bert Fraleigh (*center*) with a hamlet militia in Chao Duc Province, South Vietnam, 1966

other areas. Soon these investigators were making accusations of petty violations of standard AID regulations, particularly the practice of having our field people manage their own living arrangements and office rent out of their paltry nine dollars per diem. The investigators claimed that often the prov reps were driving into Saigon and spending more hours that day in Saigon than in their provinces and therefore were not eligible for per diem even though their trips were on official business. They also hinted that at least ten of our Americans were homosexuals, some involved with their Vietnamese area specialists. They spread these allegations widely about Saigon without ever confirming even one.

They recommended changing the per diem system so as to have Saigon administrators go to the provinces to rent houses and offices for USOM personnel. They advocated buying mobile homes from the United States and installing them for living quarters. Killen, and apparently AID/Washington, agreed.

I was furious and defended our Rural Affairs personnel most vigorously and brought their cases to AID's regional investigators from Tokyo, but they would not intervene in the charade. All were simply buffaloed by Killen, including the U.S. embassy security in Saigon. In the end, these goons refused to show me their reports, and I was dropped from the loop and unable to provide further defense. Hurt, Tanham, and I even accosted Killen on the subject in the hallway one day. He spun on his heel, cursing, and refused to talk.

I spent the last few months of 1964 preparing the Provincial Operations (Rural Affairs) 1965 Annual Program Proposal, which involved detailed descriptions of all our projects, commodity and budget requirements, personnel staffing (American, Vietnamese, and third country personnel from Taiwan, Philippines, and other countries), and administration. The procedure required that each operating office and technical division prepare its Annual Program Proposal and present it to a review board consisting of an economist, the USOM program officer, the financial controller, and the USOM deputy director or director in the USOM's main conference room on a scheduled date. The whole USOM was aware of Killen's vendetta against the old Rural Affairs people, so nearly sixty people crowded into the conference room to witness my presentation of the 1965 Program Proposal. A number of us had worked hard on this, and we were ready with handouts, charts, and other graphic support. Each of our project men and women was present to answer questions.

The program officer opened the meeting about 1:30 P.M. and asked me to begin. Suddenly, the door behind me opened, and to everybody's amazement, Killen sauntered in. The program officer jumped up and showed him his seat. With a slight grunt, Killen slumped into the seat. He pushed his chair back and allowed his long legs to thrust out, fumbled for a cigarette, assumed a slouch, lit up, and hung his head in a sideways position. Although his face was expressionless, his body language gave him away. He was there to end it all. I thought to myself, at last I get to see Killen, and he gets to hear about our program straight from the devils' mouths.

The start of my presentation, I thought, was smooth, lively, and well prepared from decades of experience. After about an hour of presenting activity after activity and answering occasional questions, with no comment from Killen except for voluminous tobacco smoke, I started to present our well-drilling activity. Killen suddenly straightened up and shouted, "Stop, I've heard enough about your corrupt, half-baked projects." I then answered, "I don't know anything about your allegations, but I agree that if they are true, they cannot be condoned; but what we are doing here is measured by the number of new holes that are in the ground from which good water is coming out for the people in South Vietnam who need it. I am measuring by results and the very low cost of this project."

He jumped to his feet, beating on the conference table, and screamed, "God damn it," along with a stream of other violent oaths, "I'm going to clean it all up. The first thing I'm going to do, to get this under control, is to appoint regional directors who have been former AID mission directors who will report directly to me. Every prov rep will have to be at least an FSR-3 (GS 16 or 17 Civil Service rating) and thirty-six years of age and an experienced AID professional. I'll set these people up in the field with decent offices and houses where everybody will respect the way they live, and I'll give them all kinds of support."

I answered, "You realize that many of the province chiefs and almost all the district chiefs are under thirty-six" and could not resist adding, "By your standards, Bobby Kennedy cannot qualify."

Amid the twitters, he stalked out. I mustered a smile and finished my presentation.

During that time, Killen, through one of his former staff members in AID/Washington's MIS (Mission Internal Security), launched a worldwide investigation of me, which turned up empty.

Killen Gives Me Seventy-two Hours to Depart

Killen's tactics soon caused Tanham to resign and forced Al Hurt to transfer to another AID mission. Then, just at the end of 1964, Killen sent an urgent secret cable to AID/soliders Washington, requesting that it order my immediate removal from Saigon. It responded by ordering me to report to AID/Washington within seventy-two hours. Knowing that I would not be returning to Saigon, I asked for an extra seventy-two hours to allow my wife to leave with me. We had to pack our belongings, which could not be done easily during the New Year's holidays. Jim Killen and Sam Wilson refused this courtesy. I departed, leaving my wife alone to do the job of packing and moving our possessions out of Saigon.

Altogether, Killen succeeded in removing thirty-two of our original Rural Affairs people, locally known as the "Tigers," plus Hurt and Tanham. I believe these were the finest civilians America ever had in South Vietnam. Many of them had Vietnamese language capabilities and long years of experience in Asia, plus a motivation, dedication, and patriotism most uncommon in bureaucratic circles. They were the catalysts who quick-started the counterinsurgency effort. Probably no other group of young American civilians has ever been given positions of greater responsibility and performed so magnificently.

USOM Rural Affairs and other organizations affiliated with the counterinsurgency program were the training grounds for some Americans who later became famous. Among them were Richard Holbrooke, Frank Wisner, Anthony Lake, Hamilton Jordan, Vincent Puritano, John Negroponte, and more than ten other future ambassadors, as well as a number of extremely successful businesspeople.

Then there were the quiet ones who were effective in their preferred, silent ways. They never made the headlines because they lived and worked in sometimes dangerous situations. Some of them were most disillusioned by Killen's sabotage tactics and a government that allowed him to run amok in such a crucial situation. Some of them vowed never to work for AID again.

But we from Rural Affairs will always be grateful for the support we received from many at the lower levels in AID/Washington and especially from Walter Stoneman, who always responded to our needs with great alacrity, despite the bureaucracy. He really was a man of granite when we needed one. At the same time we will never forgive Rutherford Poats or David Bell for failing to stand up against Killen or for allowing him to carry out his program against us, their finest AID employees, and for never apologizing for their despicable performance.

I had been reporting by personal letter to a number of friends in AID/Washington what was happening in USOM/South Vietnam. They replied that they knew about the deplorable situation but were powerless to help because of the confusion and personalities involved in the rapid buildup in South Vietnam. They bent with the gale that was blowing South Vietnam into the communist camp.

My Friendship with Sen. Hubert Humphrey

From my days in Taiwan and work with Chinese refugees in Hong Kong in 1960, I had become a close friend of Sen. Hubert Humphrey and his staff. He always asked me to keep him informed on my observations of events in Asia. I believe I was instrumental in changing his views on Taiwan from the liberal doubts of the Kuomintang Party to the positive realities of the rapid social and economic progress that was being made there and the erosion of communism that resulted. He became Taiwan's strong supporter thereafter.

After my first temporary duty in Saigon in 1962, I went to Washington and had a two-hour visit with Humphrey. He was not particularly conversant on South Vietnam and was surprised when I told him that I felt the Vietnam problem would likely become very serious for America. In fact, I said it might be the biggest problem we had ever encountered in Asia, bigger than China and Korea. This would happen, I continued, unless we did things carefully, unconventionally, and quickly. I repeated this in writing to him two days after he was sworn in as vice-president, outlining what the dangers were, what was happening, and the issues at stake.

I repeated my thoughts on South Vietnam during an afternoon visit with Vice-President Humphrey in February 1964. He was visibly moved and called in Senators Fulbright and Sparkman. My thirty-minute appointment turned into a six-hour meeting with no supper for the four of us. Senator Sparkman dozed off, but the vice-president and Senator Fulbright were totally engrossed. I told them about what was happening in South Vietnam in infinite detail and answered as best I could their scores of questions. I emphasized the security and military failures and the denial of the unconventional approach. At one point Fulbright said, "This all reflects the inherent arrogance of the military and its high commanders." I have often wondered if this was the genesis of his book title, *The Arrogance of Power.* We all agreed that America would be much better off if we could substitute elected politicians for military leaders in South Vietnam because "they know their jobs depend on appealing to the people." I told them about Ed Lansdale and his unconventional successes in the Philippines and later in South Vietnam in 1954. They seemed to know little about him, and so they invited Lansdale, Rufe Phillips, and me to meet with them the next afternoon.

The vice-president told us the lament of the seemingly powerful in the American government, "My title sounds like the second most powerful man in government, but it doesn't work that way. I'm that emperor with no clothes. The president hardly listens to me and tells me little. But I am going to talk to him about Vietnam because I've found he really knows very little about it and certainly doesn't understand it. Of all I've heard and read, you men make the most sense to me and to Senator Fulbright. We'll try to back you and your message."

From then on, Humphrey's senior aide, Bill Connell, and Humphrey himself maintained close contact with Rufe Phillips. All this occurred before Killen's posting to Saigon.

Much later, when AID/Washington recalled me at the end of 1964, Phillips told the vice-president, and a staff person from his office intercepted me at the Los Angeles Airport as I entered the United States. I was told to proceed directly to Humphrey's office in Washington.

As I walked into Humphrey's office, he greeted me by saying, "Don't tell me about Killen, I know all about that wild man, and we're taking care of him. There will be no beltway around Saigon." Somehow he had heard of one of Killen's favorite projects—to have USOM build a beltway around Saigon. We then discussed South Vietnam for about two hours, and Humphrey said he was sick over what was happening but that President Johnson was more confused than ever. Nevertheless, he was still doing everything in his power to improve the situation and to reintroduce the unconventional approach and the direct involvement of Ed Lansdale.

My sudden recall from Saigon was front page news in the *New York Times* and in other newspapers around the country. U.S. government sources provided no explanation, and eager American reporters from South Vietnam

Bert Fraleigh (*right*) receives the highest award for foreigners serving South Vietnam through the brother of President Nguyen Van Thieu (*left*) in Taiwan, 1970.

seized on this as yet another example of American policy confusion and direction reversal.

Officials in AID/Washington seemed embarrassed to see me and assigned me to roam the halls of the State Department for a while and then to a midcareer training course in the U.S. Foreign Service Institute for three months in Rosslyn, Virginia. The institute was a traditional holding area for Foreign Service officers who were surplus and outcasts. No AID leaders made any attempt to debrief me, although Walter Stoneman was most friendly and helpful in keeping me professionally alive. My wife was sent to a safe haven in Taiwan. During this period, I saw the vice-president and his staff a few times. He told me they were still working for changes in AID's South Vietnam office.

One day a friend introduced me to Supreme Court Justice William O. Douglas. He wanted to hear about South Vietnam. We walked along the ship canal in Washington for four hours, and he invited me to dinner at his home, cooked by his delightful, young bride. Over a nightcap, he said, "Lyndon has to know all this; he has to be made to understand. I want you to tell him your story next week." He was never able to arrange that, but he remained interested in me and extremely concerned about South Vietnam. What made us closer was that Justice Douglas truly understood Asia and had been one of the midwives of the JCRR program in China and Taiwan.

After my training course, AID sent me on a three-month temporary duty assignment to Laos to help on food aid projects there.

Humphrey Directs Me to Return to Saigon

About two months into the Laos assignment, an urgent telegram arrived from Humphrey asking me to proceed to Saigon immediately to head up USOM's new refugee program. It also said General Lansdale was forming a team and would be arriving in Saigon shortly. This was followed by a cable from AID/Washington, ordering me back to Saigon and addressing me by my old title of deputy assistant director for Provincial Operations.

The need for a major refugee program arose from the new U.S. military policy in Central Vietnam of direct search-and-destroy operations against hamlets, which caused millions of civilians to flee their homes to the towns and cities—an often counterproductive form of conventional warfare.

I was quite reluctant to return to Saigon, although Killen, fortunately, had been removed. I did not agree with the huge American buildup and the increasing conventionality of the war effort, both military and civilian. But I felt I had to support the vice-president after his valiant effort to change things, so I was on the plane the next day for the two-hour hop to Saigon.

Upon my arrival in Saigon, my worst fears were confirmed when I saw the tremendous Killen-inspired buildup in USOM with its overloaded administration. I also discovered that USOM had already brought in an expert from some American voluntary agency in New York to head its new refugee program. He had never seen Asia before. I was assigned by Charlie Mann, the new USOM director, to be the new man's deputy. I could see that Mann was nervous because he kept shuffling the Humphrey cables, copied to him. I told him I was supposed to head the program as his cables showed, but I would be willing to help this person for a while to break him in to AID and Asia. He said, "Please."

I found my own billet and an extra bed in the apartment of a friend from our old Rural Affairs logistics office when USOM's administration could find no other space.

American Military Overwhelms Saigon

After several weeks, I moved in with two other USOM officials to a lovely, small apartment on the sixth floor of a grand old French building with a cage elevator and with porch verandas open to the huge trees lining Yen Do street. This was still part of the lovely old Saigon that I had known. But I was appalled by what the precipitous and inconsiderate U.S. military buildup had done to the *Paris of the Orient* since the last time I saw Saigon.

Thousands of American noncoms and officers, each seeming to have his own jeep or personnel carrier, had been crammed into Saigon's yellow stucco houses and hotels, leased for them at exorbitant rates. (Our military and USOM had to buy local piasters with dollars to pay for them.) They were mostly support troops who were there at an approximate seven-to-one ratio to combat troops. Contrary to what most Americans may believe, only one in seven of our military personnel in South Vietnam ever saw combat.

Because Saigon could be hot and sticky, each room was provided with an air conditioner, and each billet had a refrigerator. Soon the energy demand far exceeded the capacity of the city's old French power plant, even augmented with U.S. military generator barges. Constant brownouts followed new troop arrivals. Not to worry. MACV responded by flying in thousands of small generators, which were installed one-by-one outside each billet. Within a few weeks, the quiet old city was filled around-the-clock with a strong, low-pitched hum from these generators, and the previously clear, perfumed, tropical air became a brown, diesel-fumed miasma, which curiously seemed to cling about forty feet off the ground.

The jeeps, with GI drivers often the only occupants, in best American freeway tradition clogged the streets going both directions from dawn till dusk. Not to worry. MACV acted—"Let's widen the streets"—and proceeded to cut down many hundreds of Saigon's famous, grand old trees as sacrifices for their blasphemous convenience. This statistic must have made Secretary of Defense McNamara's day.

This astonishing lack of American leadership and overall mismanagement were also evident in rumors about the operation of the PX (U.S. Navy Post Exchange) in Saigon. All American dependents had left Saigon, and perhaps fewer than three hundred American women remained in various assignments. Yet the PX reportedly stocked two hundred thousand cans of hairspray destined for GI girlfriends and the black market. At that time, bouffant hairdos were the rage among Vietnamese girls, and hairspray was liquid gold. The chief of the PX quickly earned the name "Captain Hairspray," and as such he was known derisively all over South Vietnam.

I shall never cease to be astonished at how top American leaders in our embassy and military in South Vietnam, as well as back in Washington, could have been so arrogant, callous, and stupid as to permit this desecration of Saigon, ruining the American image while playing into the communists' hands. I know that they also lost the respect of thousands of Americans in South Vietnam and our hope for an eventual victory.

I still clung to the hope that the arrival of Lansdale and his team might turn things around through yet another of his miracles. He arrived to an impossible assignment with clipped wings and unclear authority and was effectively caged. The Saigon bureaucracy, feeling somewhat threatened, belittled him and his theories and said he was burned out. But that is another story. I worked a bit with him and his team and then was asked by Ambassador William Porter, who was overseeing pacification for the Saigon embassy, to undertake a special project in peaceful An Giang Province to demonstrate what successful economic and political development could do in pacified areas. It was a huge success, though vigorously attacked by the diehard conventionalists imported by Jim Killen and still lounging in Saigon and the region.

After nearly six years in South Vietnam with only one home leave, I returned to AID/Washington in 1966 and was assigned, with another AID veteran from South Vietnam, to set up a training program and Vietnam Training Center at the Foreign Service Institute in Virginia. Nearly two thousand people from various government agencies went through this demanding course, where we were able to inculcate an appreciation for an unconventional approach and an understanding for their work ahead. I resigned from AID in 1967 and entered private business in Taiwan.

Until my last breath, I will continue to salute and be inspired by the thousands of dedicated and brave Americans and our allies, military and civilian, who gave their unconventional best for South Vietnam, America, and all humanity in our failed effort in that faraway country. But I will also hold responsible for our failure the many-times-larger number of Americans, leaders and otherwise, who, through ignorance and arrogance, denied counterinsurgency for South Vietnam and led America and South Vietnam to ignominious defeat.

Some Final Thoughts on Rural Affairs

The first major Vietnamese–American counterinsurgency effort of what has come to be known as the Vietnam War is scarcely mentioned in the many books and histories that have been written about this dismal conflict. When USOM Rural Affairs is described, it is usually called a CIA program, which it was not; or it is termed a sort of minimal, do-gooder exercise with little forethought or impact, awaiting the arrival and shaping by the true American unconventional gurus, the William Colbys and Robert Komers and their legions of pseudoexperts. These experts would swarm the countryside with more organizational acronyms than Rural Affairs had people.

The criticism is made that Rural Affairs had little political acumen or feel and that the strategic hamlets swept the countryside of farmers, concentrating them in lightly fortified enclosures with no effort to ferret out the Viet Cong sympathizers and infrastructure. But anyone who knows the geography of South Vietnam realizes that the rural population lived in clusters of houses called hamlets. The Strategic Hamlet Program helped these hamlet dwellers build defenses for their enclaves while training them to better govern themselves and defend against guerrilla attacks and providing them with radios to call for formal military assistance if needed. Quick-impact social and various economic activities were also implemented. The program moved out from secured areas to extend them through a process called "oilspot." It was not until the U.S. military buildup in 1966, under the ignorant and mistaken policies of Gen. William Westmoreland of "search-and-destroy" fame, that Vietnamese hamlets were routinely shelled and burned and their people uprooted, resulting in millions of refugees who were forced to escape and squat in the cities.

From its very inception, Rural Affairs developed Chieu Hoi, a successful Viet Cong surrender and weapons-turn-in program. We also worked with USOM's police advisers and Vietnamese counterparts, at all levels, doing a thorough census in each strategic hamlet to identify the political leanings of each family and the whereabouts of absent family members.

That Rural Affairs and the Strategic Hamlet Program drew such minimal media notice shows the lack of understanding of unconventional warfare on the part of the many young American correspondents covering South Vietnam at that time. There was nothing secret about what we were doing, and it could have been thoroughly analyzed and reported. This might have given some comfort to the bewildered American public that something was going right in a program tailored on one that had been successful in Malaya (later Malaysia) and in the Philippines. Reporters could have explained how this quiet effort needed a lengthy commitment and a patience unusual in frenetic America. They could also have reported that ultimate success was dependent on a sophisticated military backup to reinforce hamlet self-defenders under attack from larger guerrilla Viet Cong units. Although such military backup was planned and promised by the U.S. and Vietnamese military, it seldom arrived.

Further, the fact that the Strategic Hamlet Program was inadequately reported and badly misunderstood in Saigon and abroad is a tribute to those few Vietnamese and Rural Affairs men and women who quietly helped spread it in the provinces. This was real counterinsurgency at work because the Americans in the program were hardly noticed. It was succeeding in just the way it was planned.

It should also have been reported that this program did not require, and in fact would be hindered by, large amounts of money and civilians and hordes of troops in brigades and divisions with their overloaded and complex administrations. When Lyndon Johnson's buildup did start, at the insistence of Secretary of Defense Robert McNamara and the military, MACV co-opted the old Rural Affairs Program but not its counterinsurgency methods. The result was a plodding monster with an insatiable appetite for more money and men. It also sucked in the Vietnamese military and economy to its maw and eroded their self-reliance. The Vietnamese military, nearly always unwilling to fight the Viet Cong on the hamlet perimeters or their jungle trails, was a huge and inviting target in the large base areas.

The media did report this evolution in-depth and ad nauseam, and America's involvement in the Vietnam War became a national embarrassment and politically unacceptable. This led to America's withdrawal and total communist victory in 1975.

The People's War or War on the People?

Lu Lan

Yes, I, too, have my part of the Vietnam story to share, but I wanted to do it when passions had subsided and when strongly held personal beliefs had given way to a genuine consciousness of what really happened in what now is called the Vietnam War. By weighing objectively all the facts, at all levels, from all angles, I can confidently and unequivocally state that America and South Vietnam could and should have won the Vietnam War and that Southeast Asia was and is a place worthy of America's playing an important role, in war as in peace.

To better understand the background of that era, we should let the words of President John F. Kennedy resound once more in our minds:

> Today no war has been declared—and however fierce the struggle may be, it may never be declared in the traditional fashion. Our way of life is under attack. Those who make themselves our enemies are advancing around the globe. The survival of our friends is in danger. And yet no war has been declared, no borders have been crossed by marching troops, no missiles have been fired.
>
> If the press is waiting for a declaration of war before it imposes the self-discipline of combat conditions, then I can only say that no war ever posed a greater threat to our security. If you are awaiting a finding of "clear and present danger," then I can only say that the danger has never been more clear and its presence has never been more imminent.
>
> It requires a change in outlook, a change in tactics, a change in missions—by the government, by the people, by every businessman or labor leader, and by every newspaper. For we are opposed around the world by a monolithic and ruthless conspiracy that relies primarily on covert means of expanding its sphere of influence—on infiltration instead of elections, on intimidation instead of free choice, on guerrillas by night instead of armies by day . . . .

Its preparations are concealed, not published. Its mistakes are buried, not headlined. Its dissenters are silenced, not praised. No expenditures are questioned, no rumor is printed, no secret is revealed. It conducts the Cold War, in short, with a war-time discipline no democracy would ever hope or wish to match.[1]

These words by President Kennedy, more than thirty-five years ago, were both sound and clear. However, the members of Kennedy's cabinet, consisting of the "best and the brightest" (as described by David Halberstam in his book of the same name) were not able to bring about "a change in outlook, a change in tactics, a change in missions." They failed to meet the need for a new U.S. global response to an enemy whose strategy was to infiltrate Western nations and their allies by exploiting their differences with respect to race, culture, wealth, and aspirations. By undermining Western societies and their allies from within, the enemy hoped to divide our nations and disrupt our will to resist.

In furtherance of this objective, the Viet Minh, or North Vietnam communists, forced entire generations of Vietnamese to renounce their traditional Confucian way of life in favor of Marxism-Leninism, which ended up being nothing more than pure Stalinism.

In this account, I would like to acquaint Western readers with that strange happening, the Vietnam War, through facts and events that I personally witnessed and experienced. It began on 20 December 1946, when the People's Army of Vo Nguyen Giap (military commander of the communist Vietnamese forces) launched an all-out war of resistance against the French Expeditionary Force in Indo-China. It would last until 30 April 1975, when North Vietnamese tanks crashed through the gates of Independence Palace in Saigon and raised the communist flag on its roof.

In this narrative, I will pay particular attention to the period leading up to the introduction of U.S. combat troops in 1965 and to the events that set the stage for the final ten years of the struggle against the communists, which ended in humiliating defeat for South Vietnam and the United States. I want to give special emphasis to explaining how the communists work and the importance that must be placed on winning the hearts and minds of the people in a war such as that in South Vietnam. Our inability to understand the importance of the political and psychological aspects of the struggle forced us (the governments of America and South Vietnam) to resort principally to military force, which many of us knew could not be successful, by itself, against the communists.

This will not be a critique of strategies, tactics, or techniques. I will instead describe how the communists were able to manipulate and transform peasants and students, much like myself, into a formidable fighting force, happy and willing to do anything for the communists' cause, including giving up their lives. Under this scenario of a people's army fighting a people's war, the communists' manipulation of mass psychology and their astute handling of the news media became their most effective weapons.

How It All Began for Me with the Viet Minh

In August 1945, I joined the Viet Minh (translated into English, the League for the Independence of Vietnam). This was a revolutionary movement that promised thirty million Vietnamese with an extreme hunger for independence that it would lead the whole nation to the goals of independence, liberty, and happiness. Thoroughly aware of Vietnamese grassroots indignation against Marxist-Leninist immoral concepts and ruthless practices, Ho Chi Minh and his accomplices used deceptive propaganda to hide from the masses their goal of putting the entire nation at the disposal of the world communism doctrine. The Viet Minh cadres insisted that they were not communists and that the people would decide their own political regime for the country. As part of his duplicity, Ho Chi Minh never hesitated to collaborate on several occasions during the 1930s and 1940s with imperialist or colonialist governments to eliminate Vietnamese patriots like Phan Boi Chau and the founders of the Vietnam Nationalist Democratic Party and the Great Viet Revolutionary Party.

In those early days, the whole population participated in the activities proposed by the movement with enthusiasm but also with inner concern. No one knew toward what end the Viet Minh would lead the country, but people knew that changes were necessary and that they might be painful.

In October 1945, the Vietnamese people were stunned by the sight of hundreds of thousands of Chinese troops marching into Vietnam between the sixteenth parallel and the Chinese border. Activities in the southern half of the country were supposed to be the responsibility of British troops, who were to disarm the occupying Japanese, but in fact, this disarmament came to be handled by the hated French colonial forces.

The French carried out a twin-pronged approach to assure their return to Indo-China. On one hand, they negotiated an agreement with Chinese leader Chiang Kai-shek to replace the Chinese in disarming the Japanese north of the sixteenth parallel. In another move, on 14 September 1946, they signed an agreement that granted Ho Chi Minh and the Viet Minh special status as an autonomous government within the French Union. With this agreement, Ho

Chi Minh allowed the French to disembark their troops at Haiphong and Da Nang cities. The return of the French colonial troops caused great concern and consternation among the Vietnamese.

On 20 December 1946, after months of provocation, harassment, and skirmishes between French troops and Viet Minh militia in Hanoi and Haiphong, Ho Chi Minh declared the unavoidable war by calling on Radio Hanoi for the entire nation to stand up for a protracted war of resistance against the French colonialists. His government had quietly left Hanoi the night before to join his guerrilla bases in the mountainous jungle near the Chinese border.

Self-defense instincts ran strong through every Vietnamese citizens' veins. In every town, every village, every hamlet, the Vietnamese hastily organized their armed units and devoted themselves to military training. Their arms were kitchen knives, farmer's machetes, and crude hand grenades made by technical-school students. There was a competitive effort by different groups to produce these weapons—any kind of weapons.

French Attack My Hometown

At the age of twenty, I lived in my native town of Quang Tri. I served as the leader of a militia platoon, which was to conduct guerrilla actions in case of enemy aggression against the town. The Viet Minh regular force defending Quang Tri consisted of one infantry regiment. Civilian inhabitants of the town were ordered to implement the tactics of leveling houses and emptying gardens— the same tactics applied by Russia during the German invasion in World War II. To move around town without exposing ourselves to the French, we had to make holes in the walls between houses.

Our enemy consisted of two columns of the French army, one maneuvering eastward from Laos along Colonial Route 9 roadway and another from Hue heading north on National Route 1 Highway. When French troops were about ten kilometers from Dong Ha, a town some ten kilometers from Quang Tri, the Resistance Committee ordered the residents of Dong Ha to burn down the entire town. That night we were positioned at La Vang on a bare hill on the outskirts of Quang Tri. Watching the huge wave of flames sweeping the horizon at Dong Ha, some twelve kilometers away, my heart felt an intense sadness as I thought that things would never be the same again.

The ordinarily peaceful scene around me had abruptly changed to a disaster. That afternoon, while marching with the battalion to which we were assigned, I saw a lot of dead dogs here and there on the ground. The citizens of Quang Tri Province received the order to slaughter all their dogs to assure the secrecy of our future night maneuvers and operations. The atrocity and cruelty of war caused a severe shock to the young, school-aged men. At that time, I had no knowledge of the whereabouts of my parents and my seven younger brothers and sisters.

On 6 January 1947, two French legionnaire battalions began an assault on the town of Quang Tri (in Quang Tri Province) from the south and the west. The Resistance Committee decided that it could not defend the town. The aim of our fighters, rather, was to inflict as many casualties as possible on the enemy. It was also our objective to grab their weapons and flee, because weapons were the most precious possessions of the Resistance. Only one-third of the men of our main-force regiment were equipped with French 1914 muskets.

My platoon had only one shotgun, which my father gave me, and one rifle, carried by my senior squad leader. The rest of my men carried only machetes and homemade grenades. We later found out the hard way that these home-made grenades were not reliable when thirteen of our twenty-eight-man platoon were killed playing hide-and-seek in the marketplace buildings with French legionnaires. Our tactic was to throw grenades at an enemy patrol to create chaos, and then rob the legionnaires of their weapons and run. The results were catastrophic, as half the homemade grenades failed to explode. We could not even recover the corpses of our brave men. At dark, we withdrew to a village near the sea. The regular Viet Minh battalion suffered only light casualties and faded away in the forest, west of town.

This was the first battle of my life and for the large majority of my fellow countrymen of Quang Tri Province. It was filled with maladroitness and naïveté—novice militia against French legionnaires. However, such a battle was not peculiar to my native town only, for there were hundreds of similar encounters throughout the country. What was unique about these encounters was the strong motivation and sky-high morale of the Resistance forces and a genuine willingness to sacrifice, even one's life, for our cause.

I Leave the Viet Minh

The next morning, on receiving word that the Quang Tri Resistance Committee had withdrawn to Bich La village, we reported there and received orders to work on fortifications for the next line of resistance. I noticed a wealth of communist training materials in the village headquarters. The library was filled with educational materials about Marxism and Leninism, hammer-and-sickle banners, and slogans such as "Advance to proletariat dictatorship." My platoon was renamed Labor Hero No. 1, with replacements recruited at this village.

That night the political commissar summoned me to his desk to have a talk. He praised our gallantry for the way we handled the fight at Quang Tri and asked me the whereabouts of my family. He then stated that with my background (being educated and from a mandarin family), I should consider joining the provincial armed-propaganda task force. He then said that I could not stay with my former platoon because serving in that platoon was a high honor reserved for the proletariat. It became clear to me that the commissar wanted me out of the platoon because of my mandarin background but didn't want to hurt my feelings because of my good showing against the French. This was my first encounter with the concept of the proletariat and class struggle. I later learned that Bich La was the native village of Le Duan, who eventually became the successor to Ho Chi Minh. So my decision was to depart from the Viet Minh.

Reunited with My Family

The commissar provided me with a safe-conduct pass and wished me well. I surrendered my shotgun to him and bid him farewell. Wandering from hamlet to hamlet along the seashore, I finally found my parents and my seven brothers and sisters in a fisherman's hut in the village of Gia Lang. I reconciled with my father, who had opposed me joining the Viet Minh. He had been a district chief under the Bao Dai government and believed the Viet Minh to be communists intent on establishing dictatorship over the proletariat, rather than the Vietnamese nationalists that they claimed to be. My experience in Bich La village had opened my eyes to the communists' intent, and I recognized that my father had been right.

To get away from the combat zone, we hired a boat and sailed north to Vinh Linh District where the French campaign had not yet reached. We stayed in Vinh Linh for several days, seeking news about what was happening in Quang Tri and Hue, the capital of Central Vietnam. While in Vinh Linh, we met a group of old friends, teachers, and court clerks who were preparing to move south to Hue. They had received word of a nationalist government that had recently reached a compromise with France to establish a sovereign Vietnam within the French Union, while other rumors told of another negotiation under way between France and Emperor Bao Dai. That night, we embarked in a sampan (small boat) and sailed south, using the same route we had used to come north. The safe-conduct pass that the commissar had given me was a lifesaver because it allowed us to pass through the many checkpoints on our hazardous journey to the south.

Ho Chi Minh Seizes Leadership

Every Vietnamese aspired toward an independent Vietnam. Struggles and sacrifices had been going on since 1884, when French colonialism imposed a protectorate over Vietnam. With the end of World War II, opportunities arose for the Vietnamese people to take their fate into their own hands. The French government of Indo-China was knocked out by the Japanese coup d'état of 9 March 1945. French authorities were still in Japanese hands while the Japanese were waiting for Allied authorities represented by the Chinese army of Chiang Kai-shek to accept their surrender. Ho Chi Minh and an operative of the American Office of Strategic Services (OSS), Maj. Archimedes Patti, who had been working together in counter-Japanese guerrilla operations on the Chinese border, made their way to Hanoi. At this time, Ho Chi Minh installed the provisional government of Vietnam and proclaimed its independence on 2 September 1945.

This spectacular fait accompli secured a fundamental foothold for the independence movement of Vietnam. Unfortunately, by an ironic twist of fate, Ho Chi Minh, the man who claimed to struggle for the independence of his country, had offered his motherland a dictatorship of the universal proletariat. In other words, he submitted Vietnam to another colonization, the worst known to humankind. Stalinism and Maoism surpassed Hitler's Nazism by silently exterminating tens of millions of people who happened to have possessions or an education. Ho was trying to establish the same type of system in Vietnam.

After half a century of actions and declarations, including the text of his *Will of the People's Leader,* in which Ho expressed his desire to be reunited after death with Marx and Lenin instead of with his own ancestors, Ho Chi Minh would demonstrate to the Vietnamese, in the three generations since 1945, that he was one of the most fervent, fully dedicated communists who made Lenin and Stalin the new gods of universal laborers. These were gods that he ordered all Vietnamese to place on the altars in each household under his regime and to pay homage to whether they were Communist Party members or not. Conspicuously, pictures of Ho Chi Minh and Mao Tse-tung superseded those of Buddha and Jesus Christ in all pagodas and churches. Yet, in his book *In Retrospect: The Tragedy and Lessons of Vietnam,* Robert McNamara, former secretary of defense, asserted once more in 1995 that Ho Chi Minh was a nationalist. One wonders what Hanoi did to obtain that piece of propaganda.

Joining the Nationalist Vietnamese Forces

Vietnam found itself divided between those who wanted a dictatorship of the proletariat on one side and those who wanted to have a democracy for everyone. Nationalist Vietnamese faced hard choices as they foresaw a two-phase struggle: first, to rally with former colonialists to defeat the communists, and then second, to engage in international diplomacy to gain full independence from the former French colonialists. It was clear in the minds of many Vietnamese that such an approach would be easier to achieve within the atmosphere of the New World Order after World War II, one in which colonialism was finally receding as a force in world politics.

After returning to Hue, I continued my studies and worked in the nationalist government set up by the French in 1948. In 1950, I went to the Vietnamese National Military Academy at Dalat. I was in the class that formed the first contingent of army officers of the newly independent country. By mid-1951, 134 second lieutenants (including my friend Tran Ngoc Chau, a contributing writer of this book) graduated and were dispatched to field units. Half of the first class were killed during twenty-five years of war, and a dozen of us reached the rank of general.

First Counterinsurgency Campaign

I was assigned as commander of a reinforced Vietnamese military company, responsible for the subsector of Bao An holding a fortified line of nine outposts overlooking the Viet Minh Interzone V in Dien Ban and Ai Nghia Districts of Quang Nam Province in Central Vietnam. This line had been held by a French infantry battalion of legionnaires and was a continual showcase of atrocities by both sides. During the night, the Viet Minh conducted propaganda, kidnapping, and harassment and forced civilians to sabotage the roads. In the daytime, French troops would gather the villagers to repair the damage. The French military believed that in order to cause the local inhabitants to blame the communists for their troubles, they should have to tear down roofs and walls of their houses, as well as fill the holes dug during the night.

French troops applied an entire array of reprisal techniques that seemed to have been learned from the Nazis in occupied France during World War II. For each Vietnamese mine exploding on the road, five civilian heads were cut off and displayed at the site of the mining. One round of small-arms fire directed at an outpost was answered by five mortar rounds into the village. The number of innocent victims reached into the hundreds. The rural people abandoned their homes en masse, and many moved to join the Viet Minh. Waves of youths went to enlist in the Viet Minh armed forces, more to seek vengeance against the French than to help the communists.

The territory in our area of operations was partitioned into three different categories: the nationalist government's control zone, the Viet Minh control zone, and the disputed zone. French authorities pursued a policy of local economic siege by burning down farmers' homes, killing their water buffaloes, and destroying irrigation systems. All this destruction was done in the hope of denying supplies to the Viet Minh.

As soon as I was put in charge of the area, I proposed to the Vietnamese province chief and the French military sector commander that my troops conduct a pacification program, and I explained this concept to each soldier of my company. It was simply aimed at winning over the hearts and minds of the people. While doubling our vigilance against the Viet Minh armed units and subversive agents, we considered the civilian population to be our friends who needed our help and protection. The results were nothing short of magical.

Day by day, the people in the area recovered their former sense of peace and prosperity. The elderly came to see me at my post to have friendly conversations. Mutual trust reached the point in which one of them disclosed to me that the Viet Minh Resistance Committee had warned the civilian population that my subsector would be liberated. The village representative then strongly suggested that the Viet Minh delay the campaign until the villagers had at least harvested all their crops. They also warned that if the nationalist Vietnamese

Prime Minister Huong (left) and President Thieu (center) are briefed by Gen. Lu Lan (right) in 1969 on the pacification program in South Vietnam's Central Highlands.

army outpost was decimated, French artillery would resume its harassment fire into the village, hampering the economic growth of the entire area. These arguments caused the Interzone Communist Committee to reconsider its plan.

One day I asked the elderly villagers what the government could do to help them. "Leave us alone," they replied adamantly. I realized that it was extremely important to let the peasants live and work in peace, with security provided by the government but with minimal government harassment and interference. In line with this way of thinking, the central nationalist government took over administration of the area and named it Ky Lam District. I was then assigned to another battalion, conducting pacification programs farther south in the Vietnamese Interzone V territory of Quang Nam Province.

Importance of the People in Revolutionary Warfare

In October 1953, I was selected to attend the Senior Staff Course at the Hanoi Military Studies Center organized by the French Expeditionary Force in Indo-China. Experienced field grade officers, from various French units fighting in Tonkin (northern sector), lectured the students about tactics and techniques they encountered while engaging Gen. Vo Nguyen Giap's divisions in the Red River Delta in the north.

The instructors endlessly stressed the many characteristics of guerrilla tactics, typified by the enemy making its presence felt everywhere but never getting pinned down in a fight. The enemy's preferred form of engagement was ambush, where it enjoyed the advantages of terrain, surprise, initiative, and momentary superiority. It also forced the civilians to remain in the battle area and to go about their lives normally, which hid the Viet Minh presence and enticed government troops to enter the area without proper deployment. The Viet Minh would jump from their hiding places and engage our troops in close combat. Although government forces tried to avoid hurting civilians, the Viet Minh used them as shields.

Instruction manuals about guerrilla war and the People's War of Mao Tse-tung dictate that a guerrilla war should not remain as it begins. Rather, it should mature into conventional warfare, maneuvering personnel to defeat the enemy's regular forces in the field to achieve final victory. Giap also warned his divisions to always keep in mind the intelligence of combining their efforts with those of other regional forces such as self-defense units and village peasants, even at the stage of conducting a war of movement. This was because, as he said, "Never isolate yourself from the masses." He was not afraid to keep repeating the word "people" and the need to motivate the people, because without the people we will become a machine without fuel.

In a theater of war without fronts, where opposing forces are widely dispersed in search-and-destroy or hit-and-run operations, the role of the population and auto-defense militia is of utmost importance. It forms an infrastructure serving as eyes and ears for the friendly forces. Once the enemy ventures into unfriendly terrain, it will be overwhelmed by a sense of pervasive danger. Mines and booby traps are everywhere, not to mention enemy troops without uniforms, who are virtually indistinguishable from the local civilians. If an innocent person is killed by mistake, the standing of the government forces vis-à-vis the population is greatly compromised. At the very least, the victim's family is likely to join the opponent's camp, and the enemy's propaganda machine gets a big boost.

Giap's military used hundreds, even thousands, of civilian porters throughout its area of passage. Civilian porters evacuated the wounded and buried the dead. They also cleaned the battle sites and recovered the spoils of war. The Viet Minh always compared their relationship with the masses to that of a fish in water.

During our journey to North Vietnam, we made field visits to observe programs to involve the local population as promoted by the respective governments. We were introduced to residents of a former Viet Minh fortified village that had just rallied to our side. It was a typical hamlet, with fortifications on its border. First was a bamboo fence, strongly reinforced and anchored to the ground. A trench line also fortified the border, along with several trails that led to dead ends or to traps. Several sites were prepared for use of machine guns. The hamlet was partitioned into sections, and only the hamlet inhabitants knew which trails were safe or open to traffic.

One of our officer-guides told us of his experience with Giap's resistance villages. His regiment had just finished engaging a Viet Minh stronghold on a mountain side and, upon returning from the battle area to his base, had the misfortune of crossing a defensive line of a fortified village. Cornered in hellish terrain full of traps, holes, and fences, his company was delayed for more than an hour before fighting its way out and having five soldiers wounded by steel spikes at the bottom of the camouflaged foxholes.

In contrast, we saw how the nationalist side protected the rich and populous Red River Delta in Tonkin (later to become part of North Vietnam). French troops built a belt of heavy concrete bunkers along the border of the Delta facing the contested zone. By coordinating fire and patrols day and night, they prevented Giap's troops from maneuvering through those lines without being detected, resulting in their encirclement by French reserve units. Viet Minh–infiltrated guerrillas were handled by the provincial guard and militia.

Villages inside DeLattre's Fortifications Belt (a line of reinforced bunkers named after Gen. Jean DeLattre de Tassigny, commander of the French Expeditionary Force and civilian high commissioner in Indo-China, 1950–51) were also fenced and patrolled by nationalist self-defense militia. This denied a considerable amount of supplies badly needed by Giap's troops who lived in mountainous areas where the local crops were scarce because most food supply lines evolved from the Plain of Thanh Hoa.

The organized civil auto-defense in the special sector of Bui Chu and Phat Diem was particularly effective. This sector consisted of a group of Catholic monasteries southeast of the Tonkin Basin that successfully isolated itself from the Viet Minh. Bui Chu and Phat Diem auto-defense groups were reportedly the most fervent anticommunists and defended themselves with unequaled fanaticism.

Viet Minh Defeat the French, Gain Half a Country

In retrospect, 1954 was a most sensational year when the (French) Vietnam War moved to such a large scale that it could attract the powers from both sides of the Iron Curtain to conduct political maneuvers aimed at furthering their interests in an eventual settlement for Vietnam and Indo-China.

The year 1954 saw Giap's People's Army gain a net superiority in troop numbers compared with the French Expeditionary Force in Indo-China. The local French commander, Gen. Henri Navarre, kept demanding that the French government reinforce his campaign with more troops. Meanwhile, Giap conducted a series of strategic provocations. Some were spectacular, unexpected appearances of large units at vital areas. These large-scale raids and swift withdrawals into the jungle demonstrated his ability to take the initiative throughout the Indo-China theater of operations. This tactic generated many headlines in the Western media, which called Giap's troops the Phantom Army.

To counter Giap's initiatives, General Navarre schemed to lure Giap into a large-scale engagement at a battlefield selected by the French, with the hope of decimating Giap's divisions with tremendous firepower from the air. Navarre, well known in the French army for his astute analysis of intelligence, picked a strategic site on the line of communication to Giap's principal logistical base in northern Vietnam. The site was called Dien Bien Phu. Here is where fifteen thousand of Navarre's men were deployed in a group of fortified positions. Giap accepted the duel by moving in fifty thousand of his men, reinforced with another twenty thousand civilian porters, who worked for one hundred days to transform the surrounding mountains into strategic positions for troops and artillery and filled them with supplies.

The battle started on 7 March 1954 and ended on 7 May and cost Giap the loss of eight thousand men. Navarre lost three thousand lives, plus another four thousand who perished in captivity.

During the agony of this Western garrison, and in response to pressure from the French government, Adm. Arthur Radford, chairman of the U.S. Joint Chiefs of Staff, and other U.S. military leaders wanted to relieve the French with heavy bombing of Giap's positions. While sympathetic to the French problem, President Eisenhower was opposed to such a move unless it was supported by the U.S. Congress and U.S. allies, principally Great Britain.[2] Such support was not forthcoming. The young senator from Massachusetts, John F. Kennedy, stated that no amount of American military assistance in Indo-China can conquer an enemy that is everywhere and at the same time nowhere—an enemy of the people that has the sympathy and covert support of the people.[3]

In this very remark, there is already a key word of new strategic value—the role of the people. I firmly believe that the role of the people, as well as the goal of winning over the hearts and minds of the people, is a thousand times more valuable than material assistance or charitable donations. We must demonstrate that we are defending a just cause and preserving justice, freedom, and democracy, and we must rally the grass roots to our side.

1954: Creation of South Vietnam

With the fall of Dien Bien Phu, the belligerents and their allies met in Geneva to negotiate the terms for an eventual cease-fire. Vietnam was partitioned into two parts, with the communists taking the north and the nationalists moving south of the seventeenth parallel. Two countries, North and South Vietnam, were then born.

This was a good break for the people of the southern half of Vietnam to reflect on the lessons of the struggle from 1945 to 1954 and to prepare themselves to resume fighting against international communist expansion. This goal was never hidden by Ho Chi Minh, who claimed that he wanted not only to liberate South Vietnam but also to carry out the international mission of the proletariat dictatorship in all of Indo-China.

Another event of great significance for the Vietnamese nationalists was the withdrawal of the French Expeditionary Force and the commissariat general from Vietnam. It was a mark of full independence for South Vietnam. Even though the move deprived Vietnam of a large contingent of allied forces, it gave a tremendous boost to the morale and prestige of the nationalists who, until then, had reluctantly accepted fighting side by side with the former French colonialists. For a century, in the eyes of the people at the grass roots, those who collaborated with the foreign invaders were traitors to the people.

July 1954 brought another event of historic significance, as Ngo Dinh Diem was appointed by Emperor Bao Dai to head the government of free South Vietnam. Its principal mission was to consolidate its independence and establish the foundation for building a nation. Recognized by the whole nation for his patriotism and integrity and for opposing the French repression of its Vietnamese protectorate, Ngo Dinh Diem also enjoyed the respect of the neighboring chiefs of state.

The 1954 turning point presented both new hopes and new challenges. The communist subversive networks remained in place after the Viet Minh regular forces moved to the North. They continued to control the rural grass roots by intimidation and clandestine terrorism. As more American advisers traveled around the country, the communists' propaganda theme was that U.S. imperialists had replaced French colonialists, and hence the mission of the communist revolution was to continue its war of liberation to rid the country of the new aggressors.

In an effort to gain the support of the masses, the Diem government proceeded to call a referendum that resulted in the proclamation of a republic, and by universal suffrage Ngo Dinh Diem became the first president of the Republic of Vietnam.

As the dark days receded, the government of the new republic had to look at its grassroots infrastructure and deal with any vestiges of the colonial and communist eras. The government had to carry out a delicate evaluation to determine the supporters and detractors of the new order and to eliminate all criminals, profiteers, and extortionists who exploited innocent rural farmers and corrupted the village and provincial public servants. This was necessary to build a new democratic structure from the bottom up.

Shaping the Armed Forces

To make public administration and the national army more effective, the government sent hundreds of public servants and army officers to the United States to be trained in various disciplines. I was among the first officers of the ARVN (Army of the Republic of Vietnam) to attend the Command and General Staff College at Fort Leavenworth, Kansas, in 1957. Upon my return to South Vietnam in 1958, I was appointed deputy chief of staff for operations and training for the Joint General Staff (JGS). It was at this time that the JGS drafted a doctrine for the ARVN and elaborated the basis of organization and equipment for the twelve infantry divisions and two airborne and marine divisions. The U.S. Military Assistance Advisory Group (MAAG) and JGS joint effort on this endeavor was the first major collaboration between ARVN and its American advisers. There were plenty of discussions, arguments, and sometimes intrigues.

The Vietnamese still retained vivid memories of their experiences engaging Giap's army, side by side with the French military in Vietnam. We strongly believed that when hostilities resumed in the field, they would be under exactly the same scenario we had witnessed nine years earlier. Thus, we wanted to emphasize the importance of a tight relationship between the three categories of forces involved in the struggle, namely, the regular forces, the regional forces, and the village militia. The militia also served as the bridge between the regular army and the rural populace we were protecting.

We wanted to be equipped with weapons suitable for both close combat and large-scale, human-wave assaults. We wanted to have a light and flexible force structure, with great mobility and tremendous firepower. We needed a replacement system that would recruit young men to start serving in the village militia, then elevating the most promising to regional forces and eventually integrating them into the regular main forces.

American Advisers Push U.S. Military Model
Even though American officers reputedly had open minds, they could not help but think of themselves as the heroes of World War II, victors in all the great battles of Normandy, Guadalcanal, and Okinawa, which still echoed in the minds of the people around the entire world. Moreover, many American officers held various degrees from prestigious universities such as Harvard, Cambridge, and Columbia. Thus, they believed that they had come to South Vietnam to teach the young ARVN soldiers how to do things the American way and not to listen to Vietnamese officers who, with their broken English, tried to relate their recent military experiences that ended in the disaster at Dien Bien Phu. Very proud of America's illustrious war record, they did not care to study their new enemy's modus operandi. The Americans also vastly underestimated the Viet Cong (the communists in South Vietnam) because of their lack of polished military uniforms and their antiquated, homemade equipment.

During a nearly five-year period serving as deputy chief of staff for operations and training, I put all my mind and soul into how to best structure, equip, and train a new generation of Vietnamese officers and fighting men capable of facing a new type of war that the world was just coming to know as a people's war by a people's army. It was a war to liberate not only a country from foreign domination but also the poor from exploitation by the rich. Finally, it was a revolutionary war to transform our Confucian kingdom into a labor force at the disposal of the world communists in their supreme task of achieving world dictatorship for the proletariat, the revolutionaries' term for world hegemony.

I wanted to train our officers and troops on how to wage a war of self-defense against a large-scale subversion that manifested itself in all fields—military, psychological, economic, political, cultural, and sociological. It was not a war in which objectives were defined as locations on a map or in which victory was achieved by the side with superior troop strength, firepower, or tactical skills. The objective of this new kind of war was not to seize a location or to destroy an enemy but to win over the hearts and minds of a mass of people upon whom the enemy forces depended for their existence.

The governmental system in Vietnam before 1945 was not democratic. It was a product of colonialism and an oligarchy. After 1945, when the Viet Minh seized power, it became a chaotic anarchy that the Viet Minh were able to control by dictatorship through methodical application of coordinated terrorism and propaganda.

The provincial revolutionary committees were authorized by Ho Chi Minh to execute by decapitation anyone who disobeyed the rules of the revolution. Abuses were menu du jour. One of my uncles obtained an audience with Ho Chi Minh through a close friend who was a member of the Hanoi Central Politburo. He reported to Ho the alarming extent of abuse by the provincial revolutionary committees, which had executed by mistake, among others, one of his cousins. Ho Chi Minh listened and tactfully comforted my uncle, explaining that accidents were unavoidable in chaotic situations. It was revealed later that the basic policy of the Viet Minh, supported by Ho Chi Minh, was that killing by mistake was wiser than overlooking a potential opponent of the party.

From the late 1940s to the early 1960s, particularly in 1963 when President Diem sought to introduce a higher degree of democracy into the rural areas, the predominant Vietnamese government attitude was to establish a parent-child relationship with the people, with the government as the parent. The armed forces' role was to act as the government's enforcer. There was a popular saying at the time that the "Rural peasants had their necks in two leashes—one from the communists and the other by the South Vietnam government."

Under those circumstances, I had a prioritized ambition to make the ARVN soldier a government representative to the population in areas where he was called upon for protection. It became essential to me that the ARVN soldier cease to appear as an enforcer for the government and that he conduct himself

General Westmoreland, U.S. military commander in South Vietnam, visits Gen. Lu Lan in the Central Highlands after the communist Tet Offensive in 1968.

as a servant of the people, staying close to them and not becoming isolated from them. That should not have been a difficult task, for all soldiers were recruited from the people. Furthermore, nothing is more demoralizing to a soldier than being rejected and resented by his own people.

When this concept was presented to my American advisers, they said that they shared my concern. However, they were also concerned that my concept would have burdened our soldiers with politics, and that was something against the constitution of a democracy. I was told that an American general in the Korean War had been removed from his post as division commander for distributing leaflets on communism to his soldiers. One of his enlisted men had written to his congressman, complaining that the commander practiced brainwashing.

Our U.S. counterparts' recommendations followed this line of reasoning: the U.S. military, since its formation two hundred years before, had never lost a war, implying that the strategies and tactics that it used were mostly always correct. Military leaders believed that the structure and equipment of a U.S. infantry division fit perfectly with all conditions of weather, terrain, and enemies and that with proper training, American soldiers could carry out any mission given them. As for weapons, they said that the Garand, or M1, rifle was the best rifle of World War II and that the Thompson submachine gun that I had requested was no longer manufactured (an improved version of the Thompson submachine gun was later issued to the American

Special Forces and the Montagnard Program Civilian Irregular Defense Group, or CIDG).

My American military advisers went on to say that they strongly believed that it would be best for the ARVN to copy the American infantry division model with lighter mechanized equipment, artillery, and engineering support. The ARVN soldier would be retrained in basic training like the American infantry soldier. What was said was done. Year after year, the U.S. Army rotated its senior advisers, serving a one- or two-year tour of duty, pushing the same line of reasoning. Although many of us in ARVN did not agree with the U.S. concept for structuring our forces, we did not get far in persuading our American advisers to our point of view and had to adjust our ideas to fit the circumstances.

Counterinsurgency Campaign in Quang Ngai

From 1960 on, North Vietnam launched its second war of liberation for South Vietnam, under a new name, the Front for the Liberation of South Vietnam. Whether known as guerrilla, revolutionary, or people's war, campaigns such as these were all implemented with the very same concepts and tactics—the control of the masses as their main objective.

In 1962, I was appointed commanding officer of the Twenty-fifth ARVN Infantry Division stationed in Quang Ngai Province. Quang Ngai was a very rich, populous province, with its citizens having a strong background in political struggle. For nine years, from 1945 to 1954, Quang Ngai was the capital of the Viet Minh's strongest guerrilla base, covering four large provinces. By virtue of the Geneva Accords, Quang Ngai was transferred to the control of South Vietnam in 1955. Quang Ngai reportedly produced the best hard-core cadres and the most fanatical partisans for the communists. Ironically, Quang Ngai also produced the strongest anticommunists, drawn from the families of the victims of the communists' repression of landowners from 1946 to 1952.

President Diem, who assigned me to the Twenty-fifth Division with the mission of pacifying Quang Ngai, made clear to me that he wanted to carry out a test, using an infantry division in direct support of civilian and paramilitary groups in a common effort to pacify a heavily contested area.

I immediately rallied all governmental agencies in the province and explained our goal, and together we set up a program. The results were more than satisfactory. The American advisory group at the ARVN Twenty-fifth Division, as well as AID (Agency for International Development), supported our program 100 percent. Our joint efforts brought significant change to the entire rural area. Life was prosperous and peaceful inside the strategic hamlet system under the protection of the hamlets' self-defense militias. They set up reconnaissance patrols, warning systems, and intelligence agents. With such vigilance, many communist infiltrations were detected, and most rebel movements were identified. The captured diary of an infiltrated communist cadre contained his own evaluation of the situation: "The chances of liberating South Vietnam are a frail five percent."

The first counterinsurgency campaign in Quang Ngai Province from mid-April until early June 1963 is still fresh in my mind. The consolidation of the Strategic Hamlet Program and the success of the counterinsurgency efforts in Quang Ngai Province during 1961 and 1962 resulted in a sound defeat for the Viet Cong, who always considered Quang Ngai their utmost exemplary revolutionary apparatus under temporary nationalist occupation.

Viet Cong Strike Back and Sustain Major Losses

As a general rule, the Viet Cong had a guerrilla base in each province, usually in a remote, almost inaccessible area, serving as a refuge for the provincial revolutionary committee and at least one Viet Cong main-force battalion. Each district had one main-force company and several guerrilla sections or squads to protect the local liberation committee. All these units were mobile within the borders of their district, making their presence known to the populace to show their power, collect taxes, and carry out other liberation interventions.

The South Vietnamese government pacification program of Quang Ngai Province reached such a degree of success that local Viet Cong companies felt unsafe being near populated areas. They had to seek refuge in the foothills of the Annamite Range, along the border with the Central Highland provinces of Kontum and Pleiku.

In 1963, the Central Viet Cong Committee, meeting in its guerrilla base in Do Xa, voted for a face-saving campaign to disrupt the Quang Ngai Strategic Hamlet Program. Mobilizing all their nine companies and reinforced by one main-force battalion and several demolition squads, the Viet Cong tried to mount a spectacular counteroffensive. This was an attempt to defeat or disrupt the pacification program and, at the same time, to intimidate the peasants who more and more sympathized with the South Vietnam government.

On the evening of 7 April 1963, the Quang Ngai Operations Center was alerted, almost simultaneously, by all nine district intelligence officers when several Viet Cong suspects were arrested by village militia patrols. The provincial security officer and the military sector S2 alerted the Twenty-fifth Infantry

Division duty officer, who, in turn, alerted me as the division commanding officer (CO). I called a meeting of the entire divisional staff in the operations center at 1:00 A.M. 8 April, with the province chief, the Fiftieth Infantry Regiment commanding officer, and the Reconnaissance Company commanding officer in attendance.

At 3:00 A.M., a plastic charge was detonated near the side window of the provincial police headquarters. One Viet Cong sapper was captured by the police, and another was killed by the explosion. This was followed by several gunshots aimed at the division CO's private quarters and the province chief's house and by several explosions at the marketplace.

No casualties or significant destruction on the civilian or government side was reported at that time. All the Viet Cong wanted to achieve was to show that they could penetrate beyond our fences and cause some panic among the civilians.

At 5:00 A.M., the two districts of Mo Duc and Duc Pho reported several encounters with Viet Cong platoon-size groups and two clashes with Viet Cong company-size groups east of National Route 1 Highway. I immediately ordered the Fiftieth Infantry Regiment to surround the two Viet Cong companies and dispatched another battalion to screen along the western borders, thus blocking their withdrawal to the jungle.

In extremely disadvantageous circumstances like these, the Viet Cong had been able to disperse and hide among the civilians. This time, their locations and whereabouts were reported to the government troops by fleeing peasants when the Viet Cong showed up in their villages. The Viet Cong were then forced to regroup at a large swamp area near the seashore. We surrounded this area, and our M 113 armored personnel carriers were used to penetrate the swamp to root out the hiding Viet Cong. Within five days, the entire enemy force in Quang Ngai was annihilated. I could imagine this as their first nightmare campaign. According to their own accounts of the failed campaign, two unexpected factors were responsible for their heavy losses: one was the negative attitude of the peasants toward them, and the other was the use of amphibious tanks (the Viet Cong's term for armored personnel carriers, or APCs) in the battle.

This campaign, code-named Dan Thang 106, was also the first inspiring victory for the government of South Vietnam. We fully enjoyed the support of the populace, which both sides needed to win the battle—the Viet Cong, to hide and avoid a direct face-off with our forces and to get resupplied away from their bases, and the ARVN, to locate and destroy the enemy. Although the first appearance of our armored personnel carriers was a tactical surprise to the Viet Cong in 1963, the real turning point was the support of the mass of the people for the government troops. It then became clear that winning the hearts and minds of the people was the most important mission of any government facing a guerrilla war of subversion. I can state this without equivocation because memories of my visit to the APC squadron on the afternoon of 11 April 1963 are still vivid in my mind. Mothers in hamlets surrounding the swamp were carrying food and goodies to our soldiers whose resupplies were late. The next day, when truckloads of C rations arrived, the soldiers gave chocolate and candy to the children in the villages as they passed through. Nothing convinced me more that the support of the mass of the people is essential for victory over guerrilla warfare.

A wise, elderly villager came to us with the statement that this was all the people had wanted for years—just to be left alone to cultivate their land and to live in peace. They did not expect charity from the government.

Impact of Buddhist Disturbances on Military Operations

While everything seemed to be going for the better, an incident occurred in the city of Hue at the ancient Royal Citadel. This involved removal of Buddhist banners or flags by some provincial public servants. This was an act that stirred a chain of demonstrations against the government for its religious repression. The movement kept expanding in magnitude and severity and soon reached all populous towns and cities. It triggered an enormous civil disturbance that was further exploited by rival political groups and the communists to create a national crisis.

A concerned U.S. government sent a fact-finding group to South Vietnam in September 1963. Maj. Gen. Victor Krulak of the U.S. Marine Corps, coleader of the group, visited the Quang Ngai area, meeting separately with the province chief and then with me at division headquarters so that he could assess the situation for himself. In response to his questions about the impact of the Buddhist situation on our efforts, I told Krulak that I was disturbed by the event because it threatened the stability of the government. But, I said, it had not yet hampered military efforts in the area because of our close working relationships at all levels. This assessment was separately supported by the province chief, confirming that there was no sign of dissidence between the Catholic province chief and the Buddhist division commander.

During a later meeting at the White House on 12 September 1963, Krulak said that the military aspects was going ahead at an impressive pace, and although military operations had been affected adversely by the political crisis, the impact was not great. This was an accurate reflection of part of my comments but did not convey my concern with the effect of the political maneuvering on the stability of the government. If allowed to continue, this would eventually have serious consequences on the military's ability to conduct its activities, as was demonstrated forcefully after the overthrow of President Diem.

A Downward Spiral Begins

At the central government level in Saigon, authorities inside and outside the government, as well as different political groups, played their part in the Buddhist turmoil, paying no heed to whether it hurt the national security or hampered the war effort. Then Diem was murdered after a coup in November, followed by the assassination of President Kennedy weeks later.

I was not approached to join the coup plotters and did not throw my support their way once the coup started. I firmly believed that the nation's best interests required the strong central direction provided by President Diem, although I had doubts about his brother Ngo Dinh Nhu and Madame Nhu, who said and did things to make a difficult situation even worse. Even though my support for President Diem was well known, I was surprised that I was the only one of nine division commanders who was not replaced after the coup.

The pacification program, after the overthrow of Diem, came to a crashing halt. Viet Cong cadres returned to the villages and retaliated against people who cooperated with the government. These attacks caused an exodus of loyal

Gen. Lu Lan *(center with hat)*, commanding general of the ARVN's Tenth Division in 1965 and 1966, visits the militia in Binh Gia.

civilians to little towns and district capitals, allowing the Viet Cong to rebuild their infrastructure and thus forcing the government's main forces to once again conduct costly search-and-destroy operations. Even though Viet Cong units were not present in some villages, it did not mean that they did not have control of those villages. Taking advantage of the situation, the communists delivered a fatal blow to the pacification program.

The Saigon media, infiltrated by Viet Cong spies and collaborators, sided with the military junta after the coup to criticize the government Strategic Hamlet Program. They even went so far as to compare the strategic hamlets with concentration camps, which they were not. Meanwhile, over the rural areas of South Vietnam, the Viet Cong launched a new slogan, calling for the leveling of the strategic hamlets, removing the permanent siege of the people, etc. To make matters worse, a general of the military junta, aiming to gain popularity with the press, declared during an interview that the Strategic Hamlet Program killed people. That was one of the many stupidities that eventually led to the fall of South Vietnam in 1975. Hanoi had succeeded, indeed, just by means of the news media, in destroying the credibility of the pacification program. The rural area became a sort of no-man's-land where belligerents on both sides conducted hit-and-run and search-and-destroy operations. Taking advantage of a year full of political turmoil, Ho Chi Minh found the situation ripe for an all-out offensive. Ho hastily boosted his insurgency campaign in South Vietnam to the largest scale and highest level. At the same time, Giap's divisions commenced to march to the South one after another.

The new American president, Lyndon Johnson, was faced with a pressing demand to pull South Vietnam out of chaos and danger. He responded to the political instability with American military power. Hundreds of thousands of American forces landed at Da Nang, Cam Ranh, and Saigon and began to engage in search-and-destroy operations at the very remote bases of the communists' main forces in South Vietnam. The slide down the slippery slope to final, humiliating defeat had begun.

The Communist Lions

Under the communist regime, the government does everything in the name of the people, on behalf of the people, for the people, by the people. But the people are really a possession of the Communist Party and owe their very lives to the party. The communists made a grassroots inventory by age and sex and enrolled everyone in cells of three, squads of one dozen, or sections of three squads. These were given names such as the Squad of Minor Patriot

Infants, the Squad of Teenage Youths, the Squad of Patriot Youths, the Squad of Patriotic Farmers, the Squad of Patriot Workers, the Squad of Patriot Women, the Squad of Patriot Elders, and so on. The specialists, professionals, machinists, farmers, and others were enrolled in groups or syndicates. They were all under the scrutiny of political commissars. This system of control was called the "parallel hierarchy." No action, statement, or attitude of any person could escape the scrutiny of the party during weekly or semi-weekly sessions of self-criticism.

From this human factory, the party and the administration mass-produced soldiers, managers, militias, farmers, porters, propagandists, and machinists. The communist soldier who served at the battlefront had his wife and children taken care of by the party. For a soldier who committed an act of gallantry, his wife or parents or both received compensation and commendations from the political commissar in the name of the party. If the soldier defected to the enemy, the whole family was exiled to an agricultural development center, another name for a forced labor camp. If an officer committed a grave fault, his whole village was reprimanded.

So, the whole society became the hostage of the Communist Party. This is what made the communist soldiers into lions. Each soldier was aware that his family's well-being depended on his attitude, which was always closely monitored by his comrades. A soldier was often designated by his superior to volunteer to sacrifice for the good of the cause.

That was the difference between the two systems. We, in the name of democracy, justice, and humanitarianism, could not afford to treat our soldiers the way the communists treated theirs. We could not brainwash, blackmail, and intimidate our soldiers to achieve our objectives. Instead, we led by motivation and by exemplary actions rather than by propaganda.

Psychology is an array of extremely complex phenomena. Our communist adversaries incited hatred of the enemy in their soldiers and maintained this hatred by showing the barbarism and arrogance of the enemy they faced. Or else they just invented instances of these negative connotations. Ever since the nineteenth century, Western foreigners have frequently been harsh with the Vietnamese people. French troops, for example, committed many atrocities against our civilian population between 1946 and 1954. These atrocities contributed a great deal to strengthening the will of General Giap's troops and their willingness to sacrifice, even their lives, for their cause.

As for us, we also sought independence, democracy, freedom, and justice. We didn't want to hurt our own country and our peaceful peasants. How embarrassing it was for us to fight side by side with an allied foreign force that was not able to distinguish a communist enemy from a loyal citizen.

United States, France Do Not Understand Vietnam

Many books have been written by foreign authors about the Vietnam War, but very few reflect the deep truths of the struggle. It was just too difficult for outsiders to penetrate the depth of the Vietnamese culture and the psychology of the Vietnamese peasant. Westerners tried to analyze the Vietnamese mind the way they did their own.

Vietnamese communists, writing about their war, always made extravagant propaganda claims, depicting themselves as supernatural, as superheroes, and hiding their real concerns, fears, and despair. Therefore, genuine truths were not readily revealed.

As a soldier, beginning my military career with the Viet Minh, then fighting side by side with the French army from 1950 to 1954, and later serving side by side with the U.S. Army from 1964 to 1973, I found a curious similarity in the attitudes of the French and American leaders. That is, they underestimated the Viet Cong's capability in the beginning and overestimated it at the end.

Some Final Thoughts

After five days crossing the South China Sea aboard the USS *Sergeant Miller,* I made my way to Subic Bay in the Philippines and was then flown to Guam and California. The morning of 6 May 1975, I arrived at El Toro Air Base in California. While disembarking from the plane and setting foot on the tarmac, I was struck by strongly mixed emotions, happy to be free but very sad about the fate of my country. Although enjoying a grant of safety on the soil of freedom, I know that the chance of returning to my motherland is very unlikely. I have no doubt in my mind that America will be where I spend the rest of my life, and America will be where my children and my grandchildren will learn to love, to build, and to defend our adopted country.

Since we arrived in America, I have had the opportunity to study American history and have found to my surprise that America is not what much of the world thinks it is—a blessed land where Mother Nature has provided a natural abundance for all to enjoy. Rather, the history of the United States is full of crises and challenges, hard work, determination, devotion, chivalry, and brilliance. Yes, but other nations on earth have experienced many of the same things as they developed.

What helped America survive and triumph? I believe that it is the indomitable spirit of America's founders. This spirit has reigned in the hearts and minds of America's silent majority—not necessarily those people with advanced degrees or business success, but the ordinary American people—ever since the early days of the republic. I read the 390 pages of McNamara's book, *In Retrospect,* and sadly could find no evidence of this spirit. Because McNamara was president of a famous automobile company, he certainly could help to make America rich. But without an understanding of the spirit of the nation's founders and why men and women are willing to commit their lives and their honor to a cause larger than themselves, he could never make America great.

Notes

1. From an address by President John F. Kennedy before the American Newspaper Publishers Association at the Waldorf-Astoria Hotel, New York City, 27 April 1961.
2. Stanley Karnow, *Vietnam: A History,* 197–98.
3. Arthur Schlesinger, *A Thousand Days: John F. Kennedy in the White House* (Boston: Houghton Mifflin, 1965), 322.

Defeating Insurgency in South Vietnam

My Early Efforts

George K. Tanham

In 1953, before the fall of Dien Bien Phu a year later, some researchers at RAND Corporation saw that the French were likely to lose in Vietnam and that the United States might become involved in future conflicts in Southeast Asia.[1] A series of war games called Project Sierra was undertaken. These war games looked at all sorts of conflicts, from nuclear to guerrilla warfare in Vietnam, Thailand, Burma, and Malaya, which was beginning to conclude successfully its own insurgency problem. I was asked to become a consultant at RAND, and when I started work in early 1954, it was just beginning to play a guerrilla-level war game on Vietnam. After becoming involved and observing for several months, I thought that RAND was "playing" the communist red forces, the guerrillas, in almost exactly the same way that it played the blue forces, the Americans. This did not seem correct to me because I had been following the war in Indo-China and noticed that guerrillas seemed to behave quite differently from conventional soldiers. I had done my doctoral dissertation on the Belgian resistance against the Germans in World War II. Although the Belgians didn't have big guerrilla units, they had a few small ones, and they were much like the communist red side. In fact, many were communists. So, with my background of information on the Belgian resistance, I knew a little about guerrilla warfare and subversion but not much about Asia or communist revolutionary warfare.

One day while talking with the director of the war games, Ed Paxson, I mentioned what seemed to me to be the unrealistic aspect of the games, namely, that guerrillas were behaving like regular armies. He said that he agreed with me and that we needed to learn more about how they actually behaved—how they fought, what their tactics were, for example. He admitted that this lack of knowledge was a real problem. By this time, Dien Bien Phu had fallen, and the United States was becoming more involved in Vietnam. I suggested that I write a handbook for the red forces, or a manual on how the Viet Minh had fought against the French in Indo-China, and he agreed to this.

I then proceeded to study everything I could find on Vietnam and communist revolutionary warfare available in the United States and talked with a number of knowledgeable people. Joseph Buttinger, who was working on his history of Vietnam, later to be entitled *The Smaller Dragon,* had a fantastic private library on Vietnam in New York and was extremely helpful. Bernard Fall, who lived near Washington and was researching and writing on Vietnam, was also very knowledgeable and helpful. John Donnell, a political analyst, and Gerry Hickey, an anthropologist, were both knowledgeable on Vietnam. Virginia Thompson at Stanford had written a book on Vietnam, and Ellen Hammer was finishing her classic, *The Struggle for Vietnam.* Several Americans had written about the war in Indo-China, and of course, many French had written about Vietnam and the war there.

My broader studies of insurgency indicated that the communist insurgencies could be defeated. The British were demonstrating this in Malaya, and President Magsaysay, with Ed Lansdale at his side, had also shown this in the Philippines. However, we simply did not seem to want to learn from their successful experiences.

Studying in Paris

All this research provided a good base and led to an opportunity to learn more about Vietnam as U.S. interest in Indo-China continued following the departure of the French. As I had planned to go to Oxford to give some lectures in fall 1956, I suggested to Ed Paxson that I go from there to Paris to study French documents and interview French officers who had fought in Indo-China. Ed readily agreed to this. It was fortuitous that General Ely, then the French equivalent of our chairman of the Joint Chiefs of Staff, had visited RAND and liked what RAND did. Upon receiving RAND's request for my visit, he approved it and agreed to open almost all the French classified archives for my use. This turned out to be of enormous benefit because, from November 1956 to September 1957, I was able to immerse myself totally in an enormous quantity of captured Viet Minh documents. This included their intelligence evaluation of the French, their plans for military actions of different sorts, their guides for logistic support, and their general doctrine of warfare. I was also allowed to see classified French materials, which included intelligence estimates at various levels, French operational plans, and after-action reports. Also included were many analyses of the war that the French had written during the conflict. I studied the documents intensively and dined and talked for long periods with French officers who had served in Indo-China.

The French military was also conducting some serious soul-searching about the war in Indo-China, analyzing very carefully communist strategy and tactics, critiquing its own actions and operations, and trying to assess how to do it better next time. French officers were extremely helpful in sharing their thoughts and informal writings based on their experiences in Vietnam. Some of them, including Captain Prestat, who later became one of France's four-star generals, were extremely helpful in meeting with me and locating documents. Col. Andre Lalande, who commanded Fort Isabel, the last fortress to surrender at Dien Bien Phu, was extremely helpful, as was Col. Charles Lacheroy, who wrote a considerable amount on psychological operations. The French thought that psychological operations were an important ingredient in the communist doctrine and therefore should be addressed in counterinsurgency programs.

I was particularly fortunate in getting to know Colonel Boussarie, who was a key intelligence officer in Vietnam. All these officers became friends and were extraordinarily helpful. At times I began to think like a Viet Minh, which of course was what I was trying to do in order to write a more realistic handbook on their modus operandi.

Military Aspects of the Struggle in South Vietnam

My lectures at the U.S. Army War College in 1957 highlight my findings about the Viet Minh and reveal what was known to the military at that time. The lectures naturally explained the military side but necessarily touched also on the nonmilitary aspects of the war. I also produced, at the Air University, a three-hour film on communist revolutionary warfare, which was distributed to many of the Air Force bases and was widely viewed.

The following material is taken directly from these lectures. This information was made available to the services, orally, in writing, and visually, well *before* America became heavily involved in South Vietnam. Despite President Kennedy's interest in the early 1960s, no one paid much real attention to communist revolutionary warfare. Superficial changes were made in the names of courses, for example, but the message was not taken to heart by the U.S. Army. Military leaders did not like this kind of warfare and felt that their primary mission was to fight a conventional war in Europe. (The big problem was that the U.S. Army was preparing for World War III, which was indeed its first priority, and didn't want to become involved in another war in Asia, even a semiconventional one like Korea. The "never-again club" [never fight again in Asia after Korea] included most of the top military brass.)[2] Some of the highlights of the talk that I gave at the Army War College, which should have alerted the military to the nature of communist revolutionary warfare in Indo-China, are paraphrased here.

In my lectures, I mentioned some of the military aspects of the war, as these are the ones Secretary of Defense Robert McNamara and the military should have understood because they had responsibility for countering them. From a couple of conversations with McNamara and those around him, I came to the conclusion that he never bothered to study the enemy and how to fight it. He seemed to see the American effort as a production problem to overwhelm the enemy with firepower. But the enemy was a fleeting and elusive target against which massive firepower had little effect.

The communists saw the war quite differently. I described the Mao Theory of the three stages of revolutionary warfare ("defense, transition, and general offensive"), which the Vietnamese adapted to their own circumstances. In this kind of war, it cannot be overemphasized that political and military measures go hand in hand.

The next point was that this was a total war, with the troops of the revolutionary armies used broadly, not just in the military sense. Gen. Vo Nguyen Giap wrote in 1951, and I am quoting this because it is quite an important point: "Some cadres possess a prejudice that armed deeds constitute the only mission of armed forces, they do not focus attention on serving the plan of total conflict, and especially propaganda."[3] There is thus clear subordination of the means to an end. The ends are political, and they may be attained by military, political, propaganda, and economic actions. Soldiers are considered as active political agents to spread propaganda, to win people over to the cause, not just to fight in the strict military sense. The communists emphasize that the soldiers and population are one. There is no distinction; they are all comrades—they just happen to be doing different things at different times. The Viet Minh had lists of rules on how the soldiers should treat the population. This was not always done. In fact, both kindness and force were used to gain the support of the population.

Parallel with the political side, which was part of the governmental organization, there was a clandestine party organization that existed alongside the political structure. In other words, there was a military hierarchy plus a political hierarchy and a party hierarchy, which was less well known. These elements provided the political guidance for military operations and also assured adherence to communist doctrine.

There were three major types of military organizations. One type was the "popular force," which included the everyday person in the village who was tapped to participate in communist activities such as learning to handle a rifle or use a dynamite charge. These villagers were poorly organized and not active, full-time combatants. They were supposed to convince their neighbors and friends of the value of the communist movement. They also gathered intelligence and sometimes participated in very small guerrilla actions. This was the grass roots, so to speak, of the organization of the communists.

Above the popular troops in the hierarchy were what were called "regional troops"—these were the "middle group," with more organization. They were not fully skilled troops, but they had some training in unit activities. They were the "local defense" forces. If the French or the opposing side entered their area, they were supposed to delay the advance and make their movement as difficult as possible. Their second duty was to cover the retreat of the "regular forces" whenever defensive actions were taken. The Viet Minh didn't waste their regular forces in defensive actions, so these regional troops came in for delaying actions. A very important mission of these regional troops was, in effect, to protect the regular forces. They also carried out rather large-scale guerrilla actions and ambushes. They helped train the popular forces, prepared the battlefields, and acted as a reserve for the regular army. After a regional troop unit was fully trained, it was integrated into the regular army, the top echelon military organization in the Viet Minh.

The Viet Minh, regular fighting units, did not normally engage in long, sustained operations because their weak logistic system couldn't support them. They were able to get around this, to some extent, by careful "preaction" preparation of the battlefield. First, this meant a complete intelligence study of the area. They knew well the terrain, weather, and people, as well as how much support they could expect and who would oppose them. The second important element in preparing the battlefield was the positioning of supplies. The Viet Minh didn't need much positioning of supplies, but they did need food and ammunition, and they organized the labor force so that resupplying could be handled quickly in an organized manner. Another aspect of communist warfare was extremely close observation of the enemy. The Viet Minh would sit for weeks and even months to observe French posts to see when there were changes of the guard, who went on leave, who got drunk after dinner, and such things. They also practiced infiltration brilliantly.

One of the Viet Minh's most important tactics was the ambush, which most guerrillas used but which the Viet Minh perfected. The French never really were able to solve the ambush problem. Revolutionary war is not "position warfare"—a war of lines where the opposing sides face each other for long periods. It is instead a very fluid form of warfare. Speed and surprise are emphasized again and again. Hit the enemy and move away. In every offensive action planned, there was also a plan for retreat because enemy forces did not wish to lose any more of their trained fighters than they had to, especially in a hopeless battle.

Finally, the Viet Minh had to make preparations to defend themselves against artillery and air attacks. In direct air attacks, they used the classical means of dispersion, camouflage, clinging tactics (staying close to the civilian population for protection), digging in, and mingling with the population.

George Tanham stands at the marker on Route 13, the northern-most road running east to west from Laos to South Vietnam, 1961.

These worked quite well. This review of some of the high points of Viet Minh tactics shows how carefully they prepared for battle, how patient they were, how they tried to reduce any casualties with their regular forces, how they tried to counter the French (and American) advantages of artillery and air power, and how very dedicated they were to their cause.

As is fairly well known, Mao Tse-tung's little book on protracted war outlined his principles on what came to be known as "communist revolutionary warfare." The Viet Minh studied this, particularly General Giap, who adapted it for use in Vietnam. There were some differences. Vietnam did not have the enormous space for long retreats to avoid the enemy, nor did it have the experience of fighting the Japanese and in-country nationalists as Mao had for many years. Nevertheless, General Giap accepted the general outline of a protracted war in three now-familiar phases.

The first phase is often referred to as passive resistance, or strategic defense. The second phase is active resistance and preparation for the counteroffensive, and the third phase is the general counteroffensive (for example, the Tet Offensive). It was a sensible approach for largely unorganized and untrained revolutionaries to develop their military forces, hopefully to the point that they could take on Western-type military forces.

Nonmilitary Aspects of Communist Revolution

The goal of the Viet Minh was a political one—independence from the French—and for their successors, the Viet Cong, the independence of South Vietnam. This would be similar to how the North had gained its independence after the battle of Dien Bien Phu when Vietnam was divided into the North and South in July 1954.

The communists' goal also included establishing a communist state, although this was not always emphasized. This meant that the communist cadres at all levels had an important, if not final, word in many military operations and activities. The clear political goal was constantly emphasized to remind the troops of why they were fighting and to motivate them. The political nature of the war and the intense motivation that the Viet Minh, and later the Viet Cong, leadership instilled in their people and their troops simply cannot be overemphasized. Theirs was a strong cause that eventually led to victory.

Fortunately for the North Vietnamese, they had a very charismatic, nationally recognized communist leader in Ho Chi Minh. They also had an extremely able military leader in General Giap. Sadly, for America, the South was never able to match this leadership or the dedication of either the Viet Cong segment of the population or the communist military forces. Once the United States became the dominant military force in the South, the Vietnam War became another nationalist war—this time against the Americans, and the South Vietnamese never were able to overcome this handicap.

My original plan had been to study only the military aspects of the Viet Minh struggle in Indo-China. However, as I did my research, I quickly realized that the military aspects were only a part of communist revolutionary warfare. I learned that revolutionary warfare was a concept of total conflict with revolutionary objectives. It was much more than simple guerrilla warfare; it was broader and more sophisticated. The communists put enormous emphasis on the political and socioeconomic aspects of this warfare. The French realized this, too, and had analyzed their experience and written a number of studies on the subject of these political and socioeconomic aspects. Some of the officers foresaw the next conflict in Algeria. These studies were thoughtful and pragmatic. The French army did not want to lose again.

I can remember how dedicated some of these French officers were in trying to make sure that the French army, at least, would do its part in any future conflict and that their role would be a broad one. They not only studied the communist military tactics and techniques, trying to analyze the weaknesses and strengths, but also began to think seriously about countering them. They particularly focused on the psychological aspects of the communist efforts and how the communists attempted to win over or coerce the people to support them. Even more important to them was how to undermine the will of the enemy's forces. Some of the same officers who were in Vietnam rebelled in Algeria when President Charles De Gaulle wanted to retreat. I can remember hearing Colonel Lacheroy on the radio explaining why they were revolting.

The more the French studied their war and the more I analyzed it, we came to the same conclusion that the communists were an extremely dedicated, imaginative, and creative enemy and much more flexible than we had thought. They developed their cause and their dedicated cadre, and they were extremely ingenious in their efforts to gain victory.

Later the Viet Cong demonstrated the same devotion, dedication, patience, and energy to nonmilitary affairs. Their agents in the villages quietly and cleverly worked to undermine not only the morale of the people in the villages but also any efforts of the government to help the villagers. The few capable local leaders were singled out for assassination or kidnapping. Government programs for education or health were deliberately sabotaged. Every effort was made to counter government programs or any initiatives to help the people improve their lives. The Viet Cong infiltrated the higher echelons of government, where similar counterefforts were made. Subtle and covert actions were taken to scuttle any potentially useful program, to assure that it never got off the ground, or to make sure it didn't work. The Viet Minh were a part of the people, and although in the short term they had retarded development, in the long term they felt that they were contributing to the freedom and benefit of all the people.

Communism in South Vietnam was a sophisticated doctrine that concentrated on creating the image that the Viet Minh were the good guys and that the South Vietnamese government and later the Americans were the bad ones. With the introduction of American troops and particularly aircraft, this message seemed all too true. Bombs and shells did not always distinguish between friendly and unfriendly Vietnamese.

The Viet Minh and later the Viet Cong also took measures that they knew would very likely lead the government to undertake countermeasures that would be brutal or be against the welfare of the people. This alienated the people. The communists used women and children as agents, as they knew the government and later the Americans would be reluctant to take action against them. Americans would not suspect that an innocent-looking little boy would sometimes quietly roll a few grenades that would blow them up. Women were used to undermine the enemy, uncover secrets, and generally assist the war effort. Every effort was made, often using the most simplistic methods, to make the South Vietnamese government, the French, or the Americans look bad and turn the people against them.

Activities Resulting from My Research

Upon returning to RAND in fall 1957, I wrote the promised manual, but by then the war games were about winding up. I was a little late. My classified report was published by RAND but largely forgotten. The French thought it was pretty good, but no one in the United States really expressed much interest. However, in 1958, it was decided that Ed Paxson would go to the Far East to brief the study to the commander in chief, Pacific Command (CINCPAC) in Hawaii and the Air Force commanders in Japan and the Philippines. I went along, and when I suggested that I should visit South Vietnam, which I had studied so long, Ed agreed. I spent several weeks wandering around South Vietnam, seeing as much of the country as I could and talking to U.S. embassy people and to as many Vietnamese as possible. This put some real flavor into what I had been studying and gave me a better feel about South Vietnam. I can still remember taking a "shortcut" to the coastal resort town of Vung Tau from Nha Trang, which was north of Vung Tau. The driver was a little skeptical because he thought it was an almost impassable back road. He was right. We got stuck several times and passed through several villages where I saw flattering pictures of Ho Chi Minh, which did not make me feel too comfortable. But this back-road drive gave me a feel for the nature of the terrain and the conditions for combat in South Vietnam.

When John Kennedy became president in 1961 and showed great interest in guerrilla warfare, a friend said to me, "George, why don't you dust off that 'bomb' you wrote on the Viet Minh, get it declassified, and make it into a book. You will be an instant expert." I requested permission from French government officials to publish the report, and to my delight, they requested only one thing: that I leave out the highly classified French sources in the bibliography that was in the classified RAND report. Otherwise they requested no changes and thanked me profusely for asking. Fred Praeger quickly printed the manuscript into a book and had it on the streets in mid-1961.[4] It became one of RAND's early best-selling books and was displayed in the front windows of many of the largest bookstores. I was, as my friend had predicted, at least a perceived expert on Vietnam.

In spring 1961, I was asked by the Department of Defense to make a trip to South Vietnam to assess the situation there. I stayed about a month, and some of the Americans whom I had seen in 1958 were still there, so I had a good start from the beginning. I traveled more widely, visiting the mountainous areas and the Demilitarized Zone (DMZ), the dividing line between North and South Vietnam. My firsthand knowledge increased and became broader.

Representative to SEATO Study Group

In late summer 1961, the U.S. State Department asked me to be the official U.S. representative on the Southeast Asia Treaty Organization (SEATO) Expert Study Group on Counterinsurgency. The group had representatives from almost all the SEATO countries and met regularly in Bangkok over two months. The SEATO study group included the following officials: Ron Richards, deputy director of the Australian Security Intelligence Organization; Capt. Charlie Albertt, a Filipino naval intelligence officer; Dick Noone, a British anthropologist and intelligence officer who had participated in the Malayan Emergency and was beginning to work in South Vietnam; General Chamras, deputy director of the Thai National Police; and a distinguished diplomat, Mr. Iqbal, from Pakistan. It was a diverse group, but all members were interested in insurgency, although from slightly different angles. Ron Richards was selected chairman, and we became a very close-knit group, spending seven days a week working, traveling, and hold-

George Tanham inspecting a rudimentary fort on the Lao–South Vietnam border near Route 13, 1961

ing discussions, finally preparing a report on our findings and conclusions for SEATO.

The Australians initially complained that the United States was not taking this exercise seriously because it had sent a private citizen rather than a high-level official, as the other countries had done. However, a couple of weeks later, they were kind enough to withdraw their objection to my presence, saying that they thought I knew a great deal about the subject. Because the group felt I seemed to know the most about South Vietnam, I was selected to visit that country for several days and to report back on the situation there. Another member went to Malaysia, but the focus was mainly on the incipient insurgency in northeast Thailand, which the U.S. ambassador had begun reporting on to Washington. We also made a fascinating trip to both West and East Pakistan at the invitation of the Pakistani government.

To South Vietnam with AID

By 1964, I had made several trips to South Vietnam and followed the conflict closely from Washington. In early 1964, I was asked by Rutherford Poats and Walter (Stoney) Stoneman, high-level officials in AID (Agency for International Development), to be associate director of the AID mission in South Vietnam, or USOM as it was called there. I would be in charge of the Rural Affairs Program, which had been started by Rufus Phillips and Bert Fraleigh. My friend marine Maj. Joe Taylor, who was on loan to AID at the time, urged me to go. We had been on several trips to South Vietnam together, and Joe saw it as a challenge for me to actually get involved in counterinsurgency, which I had been researching and reading and talking about for years. Furthermore, I was only too aware that South Vietnam was much more than a military problem, and therefore I was eager to try to help with the civilian effort.

Before departing for Saigon, I made calls on Secretary of State Dean Rusk and Secretary of Defense McNamara. I had an interesting discussion with Secretary Rusk, and I will never forget his parting remark, as he knew I had been at RAND. He said, "Mr. Tanham, if we had dropped all the studies we have done on North Vietnam, we would have won a long time ago." We both laughed, and I departed his office. I then called on Secretary McNamara. My most vivid recollection of that meeting was that he kindly offered to provide additional supplies such as cement and small machinery if I needed more than AID provided. All I had to do was ask General Westmoreland, and he would provide it. I thanked him but replied that I didn't feel the war required more materiel but that finding, training, and motivating qualified Vietnamese was the real problem. He said, "Yes, but if you need more supplies, do let me know." I appreciated his offer of help but was deeply upset by his apparent lack of interest in developing good people on the Vietnamese side. I was assured of high-level support, although I wasn't sure that top-level officials understood what was required. The American approach seemed to be one of what I called "more money, men, and materiel" with almost no attention to the vital job of educating and training the Vietnamese to govern their own country.

This was particularly important because in my study of French Indo-China, it had become clear that the French had in no way prepared the Vietnamese for any self-government at any level and, indeed, had not even provided basic education to many of them. The French had not developed a motivated and trained civil service corps to the extent the British had in India. The Vietnamese had no political experience and very little training of working in a bureaucracy and were generally employed at the lowest levels of government. Leadership was lacking, and they were in no way prepared to govern themselves, which I thought was key to success. The United States did little to improve this situation. America did provide some technical assistance, but it provided very little administrative training and certainly no training in how to develop and run a democracy, or any kind of government for that matter. This to me remained a critical failure of ours during the Vietnam War. A number of people laughed at Ambassador Henry Cabot Lodge, but he once made a remark that I thought showed a keen insight into the situation when he said he "needed some precinct workers from Massachusetts to work at the grassroots level to help train the Vietnamese on political development." I do not know how the ward and precinct workers from Massachusetts would have worked out in South Vietnam, but he had identified a serious and largely ignored problem that few Americans recognized.

"Winning the hearts and minds" became a popular American slogan but was not really understood. This was not just an idealistic goal but a practical one. If the people support the government, they will provide intelligence and information and refuse to give it to the communists. They can also provide cover for government operations, as well as labor and logistic support. I can remember one time that my life was saved by a friendly villager telling me not to take a certain route because there was an ambush set for the party. This was practical help, not theoretical.

What We Are Trying to Do

The name of the USOM Office of Rural Affairs was changed to the Office of Provincial Operations while I was there. The office had been established to encourage, advise, and assist the government of South Vietnam to deal with some of the nonmilitary aspects of revolutionary war to counter the Viet Cong efforts among the civilian population. It was a very sound idea. My own view was that in no way should the Americans do it for the Vietnamese but that we should help them. Part of the effort, seldom made explicit, was to help the government gain the confidence and support of people in rural areas by improving their way of life. To some extent this was a new concept for the Vietnamese, and a fair amount of encouragement was needed to get it going, but at least a few Americans realized that it was essential for a successful counterinsurgency effort.

There were a number of serious problems that surfaced from the beginning that hampered the effort. First, the Viet Cong's military successes tended to reduce the areas in which the programs could be administered or undid the efforts that were already undertaken. The Viet Cong would destroy school buildings and small health centers or sometimes induct or subvert the teachers.

A second major problem was the political instability in Saigon after November 1963. Leadership at the top changed fairly frequently, which had a direct and important impact on the leadership at the local levels. Provincial officials were changed frequently or given conflicting instructions. The government

seemed to have no consistent policies or programs, and therefore it was difficult to implement assistance programs for the people.

A third problem was a terrible dearth of trained and honest personnel.
Training people for some of these jobs could not be done in a few weeks, and
developing honesty among underpaid officials was almost impossible. Often
they robbed the people, and the assistance never reached the villages. There
were good provincial leaders as well as bad ones, but the latter seemed to out-
number the former.

These problems were very difficult for Americans at the provincial level to
correct. One of my criticisms of American operations was that we spent more
time building things, concentrating on the material aspects of the effort, than
we did on training and motivating officials to honestly serve the people. In fact,
in my judgment, this problem was never overcome.

Some of the programs worked reasonably well in some provinces. I quote
from a book I wrote with some of my provincial reps in 1965: "Progress has
been made in improving the material situation in certain social and economic
fields and in many places. Numerous small public buildings have been constructed, more pure water has been made available, local transportation facilities have been improved, and more and better food has been provided. There
is the beginning of a national and elementary education system, improvement
has been made in the public health and medical fields. These are rather impressive achievements given the underdeveloped nature of South Vietnam and the
rising Viet Cong threat."[5]

The actual impact of these efforts was almost impossible to determine, especially in the short term, despite Washington's demand for immediate results.
Did they really improve the welfare of the people, did they develop a more
favorable attitude toward the government, and did they contribute to a successful counterinsurgency effort? When I departed South Vietnam at the end
of 1964, I was afraid that much of the population no longer had a free choice.
Even if these programs had been partially successful, the gains had been more
than offset by Viet Cong military successes and their use of propaganda and
terrorism to gain popular support. I must confess that in the time when I was
there, we were not winning this battle.

Unfortunately, our side did not learn all the lessons, as the Army of the
Republic of Vietnam (ARVN) in 1964 misbehaved rather badly. Vietnamese
troops would come in to save villages but would take what they wanted, dis-
honor the women, and in general behave rather brutally toward the people. I
can recall arguing hard in Saigon with top American officials that we could not
build enough schools or medical facilities or other good things to compensate

for a raped, or sometimes killed, wife. There was no way on earth that material things could make up for this kind of behavior. I was often told that this was rare, but I saw enough of it to realize that it happened much more frequently than we liked to admit, sometimes with disastrous consequences. Our rural development efforts simply could not compensate for the human pain and misery inflicted by some of the ARVN forces. It is sometimes true that the Viet Cong carried out similar activities, but they would blame the government, and more times than not, they got away with it.

Not understanding how important the support of the people was to the overall effort, we didn't take these actions as seriously as we should have. This is a part of communist revolutionary warfare that was not often projected in the American press, which was much more concerned with the military aspects. I can recall Stan Karnow, who was then with the *Saturday Evening Post*, stating that he would like to do a story on the USOM Rural Affairs effort in South Vietnam. I said fine, and he wrote a good short summary for his editor in the United States. Much to his chagrin and mine, he received a prompt reply that essentially said, no one is getting killed; who is interested in that effort? And no story was written.

Killen's Impact on the Counterinsurgency Effort

Before going to South Vietnam in 1964, I became acquainted with Stuart Van Dyke, who was designated the new director of USOM in Saigon. We got along quite well, sharing ideas on what AID should be doing in an insurgency situation, and he was supportive of the Rural Affairs effort in South Vietnam. Unfortunately, he was transferred to Brazil before he ever reached South Vietnam. Shortly after I arrived in Saigon, James Killen took over as the new director of USOM in South Vietnam. Killen was a holdover political appointee from the Eisenhower administration and had been AID director in Pakistan. His reputation as an overbearing, bureaucratic bully preceded him because Deputy Director Al Hurt had known him in Pakistan. However, I didn't realize the situation could get as bad as it was to become. Killen knew nothing about South Vietnam and even less about counterinsurgency. He arrived with a closed mind and, as far as I could tell, made no effort whatsoever to learn about the situation or even about insurgency.

One of Killen's first acts was to invite a friend of his, a Greek city planner named Doxiades, to come and develop a plan for redoing Saigon as a city. This was hardly the top priority in the deteriorating situation in the country. To the best of my knowledge, while I was in South Vietnam, Killen never left Saigon. When U.S. ambassador Gen. Maxwell Taylor took trips, he invited Barry

Zorthian, the public affairs officer, and me to go along as his companions. I think Killen simply refused to go.[6] His knowledge of South Vietnam consisted mainly of going from his rather palatial, air-conditioned home to his large air-conditioned office in a large air-conditioned car with a guard. I don't think he ever knew, or understood how, the USOM Rural Affairs officers lived in tiny Vietnamese houses, often in small villages, some with only one light bulb, poor-quality water, and precarious security provisions. These officers were able to visit their families in Saigon about one day a week. While the American civilian advisers lived essentially with the Vietnamese, the U.S. military advisers lived in small forts, well guarded and lighted, protected against Viet Cong attack, and with many of the amenities of modern life—refrigeration, good beds, and movies. Killen never seemed to be interested in learning about what was going on in the countryside or with the insurgency raging there. I believe he thought he was in France. He once tried to take away the extra small per diem of nine dollars that the Rural Affairs officers received for their very primitive living conditions. I fought this, but I think he won after I left.

In fall 1964, I made a lengthy trip to I Corps in the extreme north of South Vietnam because the prov reps had given reports of the deteriorating situation there. I conferred with the military, the Rural Affairs people, and other civilians. I was careful not to base my findings on what the military told me, as that was really not my business, and even more important, I thought there was a need for a nonmilitary inspection of how counterinsurgency was doing in this sector. I learned that many families were sending their children out of the region and even out of the country, where it was safer. They were also sending much of their money abroad. The small shopkeepers were minimally restocking their stores to avoid large losses if the worst happened. And some of the children were spitting at U.S. soldiers, something I had not seen before. The atmosphere was one of defeat and pessimism. I carefully wrote a report, which I circulated to the ambassador, General Westmoreland, and others.

The situation was taken fairly seriously because General Westmoreland visited I Corps to check on the military situation, and he came back with the same impressions I had, that things were not going well.

I Throw in the Towel in Disgust

I became increasingly disillusioned by USOM Director Killen's lack of understanding and interest in the insurgency, his total ignorance of what had to be done, and his lack of enthusiasm for the U.S.-supported counterinsurgency program. And, I found that I was unable to influence or make any progress with him because he basically refused to discuss anything with me as he took

George Tanham visiting Montagnard children near Pleiku in the Highlands, 1964

aggressive steps to undermine the Rural Affairs Program. I knew Ambassador Taylor and Deputy Ambassador Alexis Johnson and discussed the problem with them. Neither seemed to be willing to take on Killen, although there may have been political pressures from Washington that he not be removed. I decided after about six months that I was wasting my time completely. I had discussed the problem with Dave Bell, administrator of AID, when I was on a recruiting trip to Washington in September, and he said that I could come home if I continued to be dissatisfied. I was, and I did. I then wrote Killen a short note saying that I was resigning and going home. He in his petty way said that because I hadn't been out for a year, I would have to pay my own way back to the United States. I was happily able to tell him that I had discussed the situation with Dave Bell, who said that under the circumstances he would reimburse my airfare back to Washington. I left in December 1964, very disappointed and very discouraged, as I saw absolutely no future for development in the rural areas of South Vietnam as long as Killen remained.

When Lodge returned for his second term as ambassador, he asked me to accompany him back to South Vietnam, but I declined, saying that I was not going back as long as Killen was there.[7] But I also have to admit that I had had a very serious heart attack in late 1965, at least partially attributable to stress, and was not in any condition to go back to Saigon. Lodge intimated that he planned to get rid of Killen. Eventually this was done, as Bert Fraleigh has described in his chapter.

After My South Vietnam Tour

My interest in South Vietnam did not disappear after I left Saigon. I continued to follow the conflict carefully and to try to stay on top of the situation there. I was invited to serve on several committees sponsored by the Department of Defense, including psychological warfare committees, research and development committees, and several others, which had built-in, long trips to South Vietnam.[8]

By 1967, it was more than clear to me that the war was being lost and that the United States had tried to make it into a conventional war; at that point I really gave up trying to help. South Vietnam had become a more or less conventional conflict with full American military divisions and air power playing a key role in the fighting. This was despite some efforts to develop ARVN into a more effective fighting force. A huge effort was made with the CORDS (Civil Operations Revolutionary Development Support) program to bring about change in the rural areas, but neither CORDS nor the American military, in my opinion, was succeeding in a real sense and would not do so if the Vietnamese did not play a greater role.

In 1965, after my tour of South Vietnam, I was asked by the U.S. State Department to speak at various universities about the war. I often started my lectures by stating the obvious, that we had made a number of mistakes in South Vietnam or we would have won, and we were not doing very well. It surprised many in the audience that someone from Washington would admit this. The tension in the largely anti-Vietnam audiences was reduced considerably, and I was able to explain what I thought was going wrong and what I had hoped to accomplish personally when I went to South Vietnam in 1964. Inasmuch as I advocated working to help the rural Vietnamese in a peaceful manner, the audiences at least listened, even if they did not agree with my support of the war. I still recall one lecture, I think it was at the University of Michigan, where the audience, mostly students but also many faculty members, relaxed somewhat after my usual opening remarks and asked some good questions in a not-too-antagonistic manner. But the highlight for me came after the question period when a professor approached me, wagged his finger in my face, saying, "You SOB, you nearly convinced me I was wrong tonight." I feel that if the war had been presented more honestly and explained more carefully, and our goals more clearly enunciated, the American public might have been more understanding and tolerant of the difficult task we were attempting in South Vietnam. However, I must confess that I don't think the U.S. State Department approved of my approach because I soon ceased to receive invitations to speak on the subject. Washington just did not want to admit it had a problem.

On what I thought was to be my last visit to Southeast Asia in 1967, Ambassador Leonard Unger invited me to come to Thailand as his special assistant for counterinsurgency. I arrived in April 1968. He gave me free rein to lay down policies and programs, at least as much as I could, given my limited authority and the conflicting views of the various agencies in Thailand. I was to develop an effective counterinsurgency effort. The cornerstone of this policy was that the Thais should do their own counterinsurgency program and that we should advise and help train them. My staff developed the motto, "Train the Thai trainers." Thailand also had the enormous advantage of being a more or less independent country during the time of colonialism and had a functioning governing apparatus. Furthermore, most of the communist leaders were Sino-Thai, not full-blooded Thai. After two years, by May 1970, I felt that I had done all I could in Thailand. The Thai had managed to develop some counterinsurgency ideas and were helped by the Chinese cutting off aid to the insurgents in 1969. They managed to contain the insurgency, which never became as strong as in South Vietnam.

Some Dilemmas of Counterinsurgency

The USOM support program for Provincial Operations did raise some basic dilemmas of counterinsurgency. One was how much decentralization of power should be undertaken. The Vietnamese government was patterned after the French, a highly centralized one, with all officials reporting directly to Saigon. This meant that province chiefs had little control over officials of other agencies, and indeed they may not have had very much power, a point often missed. Many of us thought that greater decentralization would have given local officials more flexibility to deal with their provinces, some of which were quite different from others. On the other hand, centralization tried to provide overall leadership and uniformity of policies and procedures and sometimes tried to counteract weak leadership in a given province.

Another dilemma was whether the government should build all the small schools and health centers or whether villagers should pitch in and build them themselves with materials provided by the government. In the former approach, the government at least got credit for doing something good for the people; in the latter approach, the people became involved in their own welfare and had a much greater interest in what they had built than in what the government provided.

There were also dilemmas over how small or large projects should be and which should be undertaken first—pure water, for example, or schools. Another dilemma was whether to impose controls on foods and other key items. The people would resent this restriction, but many of these items, particularly those in excess, were going to the Viet Cong. Tight controls would prevent this. We didn't really resolve these problems, and it is likely that they are best resolved on a case-by-case basis. But the problems had to be considered, although we didn't always face them.

From my extensive studies and observations on South Vietnam, I had come to the strong conclusion that unless the Vietnamese did it themselves, the war could not be won. It is true that Ho Chi Minh was a longtime communist, but he was primarily seen by the Vietnamese as a nationalist leader capable of unifying Vietnam and moving it into the future. The communists had cleverly gained the strongest possible motivation, nationalism, for their cause. If the South Vietnamese government did not develop better leadership, better government, and motivation for the people, then we simply could not win the war for them. I thought it best for us to help train the trainers and let the Vietnamese do the job and get credit and support from their own people. The more the Americans became involved, the more the Viet Cong argued that the war was against American imperialism, and the presence of hundreds of thousands of American soldiers with some civilians seemed to give credence to that contention. The only hope was for the South Vietnamese to win the civil war and prove that the democratic way was better than communism. Even if we won militarily for a time, it was my view that the communists would take to the hills again and recommence guerrilla warfare, just as they had done with the French. Once we took over, I could not envisage victory for our side. This does not mean that the Americans were necessarily incompetent, but rather that they did not really understand the war and that they could never replace the Vietnamese as leaders of South Vietnam.

Conclusions

I have drawn several conclusions from my observations and experiences in Vietnam. There was material on Vietnam available to American scholars and officials, as well as a large French literature collection on the subject. Almost none of this, as far as I can determine, was tapped. My own efforts to share the knowledge and understanding that I had gained were largely ignored, both in Washington and in the field, as were those of other knowledgeable Americans. The U.S. government didn't even try to take advantage of what the French had learned, and they had studied hard the lessons of Vietnam. In fact, the U.S. military looked down on the French, and when I suggested that we employ a few French advisers, one senior officer said, "Why George, they haven't won a war since Napoleon." Nor did we learn from the successful British counterinsurgency campaign in Malaya, although a five-man British advisory commission under the leadership of Sir Robert Thompson was assigned to Saigon from 1961 to 1965. We tried to create the Vietnamese government army and other institutions in our own image, often without regard for, or understanding of, how the Vietnamese operated.

Besides having an at least adequate knowledge of Vietnam available, considerable knowledge of communist revolutionary warfare was also available. The French and the British wrote a number of good works on the subject. Most of the top American leadership ignored this information, particularly the experience of the Filipinos, who had waged a successful campaign against the Huks. There was no need to turn the entire U.S. Army into a counterinsurgency organization; it didn't really require that many people. If we had started early, training lower-level cadres who were highly motivated and knowledgeable, we perhaps could have helped the Vietnamese turn the situation around. And until the Vietnamese did turn it around themselves, the struggle was almost hopeless. The South never developed the leadership, the will, the determination, and the skills to deal with an enemy that was patiently trained and motivated and that fought hard and well for what it saw as its cause.

The tragedy is that there was much material available on Vietnam and communist revolutionary warfare to be had from the experiences of both the French in Indo-China and the British in Malaya. The American government did not seem to want to learn from these experiences and was determined to fight the war its own way. The communists also prepared to move from guerrilla to conventional warfare, thus playing into American hands. In the last phases, the American army claimed it never lost a battle, but the war was lost for other reasons. One could argue that America and the American military did not lose on the battlefields of South Vietnam but in the battle for public opinion in America. As I used to say, the war was lost over the heads of the combatants. That was part of the communist strategy—it wasn't just a military affair.

Remembering that communist revolutionary warfare is total war and a revolution, there are both the military and the civilian sides to evaluate, and both are important. Without security, the civilians can't do much, so the military or

George Tanham joins a Montagnard ritual for VIPs by removing one sock and gorging on rice wine by sipping through a straw, 1964.

security aspects are very critical. But the American military had some serious problems in evaluating how the war was progressing. This was because, at least in the early stages that we are concerned with, the situation was very different from the war the military was trained to fight. There were no front lines, no key terrain features, no critical cities or communication points, and almost no familiar indicators of progress. How could the commander tell Washington about the war's progress? And, indeed, Washington wanted to know every day. This created real problems. The Air Force started counting numbers of sorties, bombs dropped, and targets attacked. These were activities, but they did not really tell much about the progress of the war, although they helped keep Washington reasonably happy. The U.S. Army was in an even worse situation, so it developed the body-count system. It couldn't claim key places captured because they rarely mattered; bodies could be counted and reported, which presumably indicated success against the enemy. A high proportion of casualties most often reduces the capabilities of a military unit. The trouble was that the body count became almost the sole indicator of progress, and this dubious system was even misused. Some officers, and Washington also, insisted on high body counts, whether they were real or not. One corps commander allegedly gave his subordinate units weekly quotas that they had to meet if they wanted good ratings. Although it may have made the commander look good, it didn't give any indication of how the war was really going in his area.

I once gave a lecture at the CIA's school and pointed out that, according to official U.S. reports, every Viet Cong soldier had been either killed or wounded in one year. With fifty thousand reported killed, and with a five- or six-to-one ratio of killed to wounded, that meant another two hundred thousand to three hundred thousand were wounded and several thousand more captured and missing. This would represent more Viet Cong soldiers than were estimated to be in South Vietnam. The audience didn't believe me and said something was wrong with the figures, but I pointed out that these were the official figures reported to the Department of Defense. No army can take such casualties for long, but the Viet Cong kept on going. Something was clearly wrong.

The civilians in the U.S. government–supported programs faced somewhat similar, if not even more difficult, problems of determining how the war was progressing from their point of view. As in the case of the military, there was enormous pressure from Washington to report weekly—I think they really would have liked daily reports. USOM resorted to reporting techniques that were similar to those used by the military—how many kilometers of roads were built; how many strategic hamlets were completed; how many wells were dug; and how many schools, health centers, and bridges were constructed. As in the case of the military, these were activities, and it was seldom reported how many teachers or nurses were recruited and trained for these installations, much less their effect on the population. In addition, the Viet Cong destroyed many of the schools and health centers, demonstrating the weakness of the government to protect its own installations and erasing any value they might have had. I don't recall any serious reporting on increased literacy rates or reduction in disease rates to suggest any notion of progress in these fields. Again, in the area of psychological operations, the numbers of leaflets distributed and the number of broadcasts made were reported. What their impact was, nobody seemed to know. Few seemed to care, as it was activities that were counted, and ascertaining their effect was very difficult. I can't even remember attempts to evaluate what any of these activities contributed to winning the war. Then again, my memory may have failed me.

Admittedly, effects or results of activities or actions, military or civilian, are extremely difficult to evaluate in this sort of struggle. Assessments tended to be very subjective and not totally reliable. Sometimes there are no real effects, other times there are, but it takes an awful lot of effort to find out what they were. On the military side, forcing the enemy to travel off the roads, or at night, could have some effect on the enemy's war effort. How much, it would be difficult to say, and opinions would differ. This sort of warfare, with no front lines and few visible targets on the military side, and attempts to assess the mindset and actions of a civilian population raise very difficult and complex problems not easily resolved.

In closing this chapter, I would like to say with some sadness that the tragedy of South Vietnam was that we settled for activities, actions, and numbers, not on their impact on the war.

Notes

1. RAND Corporation is a nonprofit research organization started by the U.S. Air Force after World War II. Over time, it has expanded from defense analysis to policy analysis in many domestic areas.
2. Fairly early during President Kennedy's administration, Walt Rostow asked me what I would do about Vietnam, particularly the military aspects. I thought about it and came back and suggested that it might be a good idea to pick out a young and very bright lieutenant colonel to lead a team. I would have him pick some of the best and brightest lieutenants and captains in the U.S. Army, send them out to Vietnam for six months, and then ask for a report. Walt asked me why I had hit upon this, and I replied that I thought it was a young man's war and that new, imaginative, and unconventional ideas were needed. Younger officers usually had less set and institutionalized minds than even first-rate superior officers. Walt didn't commit himself, and obviously my idea was never acted upon.
3. Vo Nguyen Giap, *People's War, People's Army: The Viet Cong Insurrection Manual for Underdeveloped Countries* (New York: Frederick A. Praeger, 1964).
4. George K. Tanham, *Communist Revolutionary Warfare: The Vietminh in Indochina* (New York: Frederick A. Praeger, 1961).
5. Tanham, *War without Guns: American Civilians in Rural Vietnam* (New York: Frederick A. Praeger, 1966), 126.
6. In fairness to Killen, he did have an invalid wife and perhaps felt he could not leave her for the dangers of the countryside.
7. Ed Lansdale, whom I had known well and who had been so successful in helping Magsaysay beat the Huks in the Philippines, also asked me to join his team going out under Lodge in 1966. In addition to my reasons for not going with Lodge, I was fearful that the military had taken over and that Ed would be left out of the main action, which turned out to be the case.

8. One time I visited Vietnam at the same time as Secretary of Defense McNamara. Upon my return, I met with one of the assistant secretaries of defense who was a good friend of mine. I gave him a fairly pessimistic report that was quite different from what McNamara was saying. He used President Kennedy's question, "Did you two gentlemen go to the same country?" I said, "Yes, but we talked to different people and saw different things." My friend then said, "You don't seem to realize, George, that Bob McNamara is personally taking on General Giap." I smiled and said, "Okay, but I know where I'm putting my money."

My War Story

From Ho Chi Minh to Ngo Dinh Diem

Tran Ngoc Chau, with Tom Sturdevant

Before the arrival of the Japanese at the beginning of World War II, we in Vietnam knew very little about the communists, except what we learned from French propaganda, namely, that they were violent radicals who denied the existence of family, nation, and religion. We did not take this completely at face value, however, because, as students, we were becoming increasingly aware of the hypocrisy of French policy: democratic and freedom loving at home, undemocratic and oppressive in faraway places like Vietnam. We were also beginning to appreciate Vietnam's long history of resistance to outside domination and to regard the Vietnamese peasants who were revolting against the French as part of an honorable Vietnamese tradition.

Although the French discriminated openly against the Vietnamese at large, Vietnamese of our social class were treated the same as French boys and girls, in and out of school. We loved almost everything French: literature, philosophy, movies, and sweets. We also had a longing for British- and American-made goods that, for some reason, we thought were superior to those made in France. And we had a keen interest in the American way of life, which

---

Much has been written about Tran Ngoc Chau's role in the Vietnam War, including the following: *The Chau Trial* by Elizabeth Pond, 1970; *Fire in the Lake* by Frances Fitzgerald, 1972; *Papers on the War* by Daniel Ellsberg, 1972; *A Bright Shining Lie* by Neil Sheehan, 1988; and *Facing the Phoenix* by Zalin Grant, 1991. And in the archives of Congress, see: Senate Committee on Foreign Relations, *Hearings before the Committee on Foreign Relations,* April, May, June, and August 1970; and *Congressional Record,* U.S. Senate, March 1970.

seemed the most modern and progressive. There was, in fact, a growing interest in the English-speaking world. My elder brother, Tran Van Chuong, was one of the first students in our school to excel in the study of the English language. Chuong went on to join the Viet Minh and stayed with them until he died in 1986.

World War II humiliated the French both in France and in Indo-China. We were shocked that not only the French but also the Americans and the British had suffered serious defeats at the hands of the Japanese. Of course, we were also somewhat pleased that the Japanese, another Asiatic race, had demonstrated that they were not inferior to the white European race. And even though we were occupied by the Japanese against our will, we were, at least, glad to be independent of France.

During the Japanese occupation, Vietnamese nationalism, and the determination to be free of foreign domination, increased manyfold. Patriotic organizations gained considerable popular support and intensified their activities. The Viet Minh in particular became very popular.

The support for the Viet Minh was due in part to the tens of thousands of political prisoners set free by the Japanese. Most of these prisoners had been converted to the communist cause by a small cadre of Viet Minh working inside the prisons. They promised a new Vietnam free of foreigners and exploitative Vietnamese landowners. Of course, prisoners were not the only ones attracted to Vietnamese nationalism. Many members of our Boy Scout organization also heeded the call and became the driving force behind the National Salvation Youth, a Viet Minh organization.

Nationalism after World War II

In August 1945, when the Japanese surrendered to the Allies, it appeared that Vietnam was about to become a free and independent state. It was less clear, however, who would govern this state because there was considerable conflict among the competing nationalist groups. The support of some of these groups was badly shaken, however, when their leaders returned to Hanoi accompanied by the Chinese nationalists, who had come in to accept Japan's surrender. Many Vietnamese were disillusioned by this apparent collusion with foreign soldiers.

In the coming weeks, we learned more about the disputes between Ho Chi Minh and the other nationalist leaders. Obviously, the Chinese were under orders to do whatever they could to keep Ho Chi Minh from taking a leadership position. The result was heavy fighting, assassinations, and kidnappings.

But the Chinese attempt to thwart Ho Chi Minh failed. He emerged from the jungle with the heroic guerrilla fighters who had fought so valiantly against the Japanese, declared the establishment of the Democratic Republic of Vietnam, and rallied the majority of Vietnamese patriots to his cause. Although some Vietnamese were wary of Ho's communist ideology, they were more wary of Vietnamese who would align themselves with foreigners, in this case the nationalist Chinese, in order to move ahead.

As mentioned earlier, I joined the Viet Minh as a Boy Scout. We sometimes engaged in minor clandestine activities against the Japanese. At that time, the national organization was led by three foreign-educated Vietnamese. Ta Quang Buu was educated in Britain; Ton That Tung and Hoang Dao Thuy were educated in France. All three went on to have very successful careers.

Ta Quang Buu held numerous cabinet-level positions in Ho Chi Minh's government and signed the Geneva Accords in 1954. Dr. Ton That Tung became an international figure in medicine. Curiously, Hoang Dao Thuy, a secondary education teacher with no military training or experience, became the first commandant of the National Military Academy at Son Tay. The officers trained there went on to fight against the French, the South Vietnamese, and the Americans, and many distinguished themselves on the battlefield.

In 1945, about two-thirds of the military officers and political commissars in the Liberation Army of Ho Chi Minh had been recruited from the Boy Scouts and the Avant Guard Youth, another youth organization in the southern part of Vietnam. As a result, all the secondary schools and colleges were closed because there were virtually no students. Young women joined the effort as well and volunteered to assist local defense forces to serve the population as nurses, teachers, and social workers.

Even Vietnamese expatriates joined the war. We would listen to radio broadcasts from Hanoi, the capital, to keep informed about prominent Vietnamese who were leaving their French wives and children, and prestigious positions in France, to return to Vietnam to participate in the revolution. It was the bourgeoisie, the mandarins, and the aristocrats of Vietnamese society that formed the backbone of Ho Chi Minh's Democratic Republic of Vietnam in 1945. They were all dedicated to an independent Vietnam free of the French.

I fought as a volunteer with Ho Chi Minh's forces for five years. Like thousands of others, I received no pay, not even a uniform during the first two years. We had one rifle for every three soldiers, a submachine gun for every twelve soldiers, and a light machine gun for every platoon, usually about forty men. We had no artillery, no tanks, and no air support, and most of us had less than a month of training. But in every village, we were given water, food, and shelter. Even in the French-controlled cities, people took great risks to support us and give us medicine, gifts, and admiration.

Our guerrilla units moved out of hiding to attack the French at locations of our choosing. We then retreated quickly back to another hiding area, usually with the assistance of the local population. To avoid being detected, we kept on the move, walking from one remote village to another, barefoot or in sandals. Officers and soldiers lived together, shared the same frugal food, and fought side by side.

Fighting the French

In mid-1946, I was a company commander in a special Viet Minh regiment operating in military Interzone V. The regiment, known as Trung Doan Doc Lap, or Independent Regiment, was commanded by Vi Dan, who was only twenty-five years old. One night we attacked several French positions in the Highlands. The political commissar told us our attacks were designed to support President Ho Chi Minh who, at that time, was in Paris negotiating with the French. On that night, we were badly beaten by the French and Vi Dan was killed, as was much of the regiment. My company lost more than half of its 140 men. Both my political commissar and deputy company commander were also killed. It took us several weeks to recuperate and reorganize.

The survivors of that debacle were reassigned to Regiment Seventy-nine, which was operating in a mountainous area that would later be called Phu Bon Province. It was between Pleiku and Phu Yen Provinces. Once again we engaged the enemy, and we were beaten. We withdrew to a safe area and spent several weeks in training and self-examination. We were then sent south to take part in a multibattalion ambush of a French military convoy traveling from the city of Nha Trang on the coast to Ban Me Thuot in the Highlands. As in the previous battles, we were very poorly armed and short of ammunition. We had single-shot rifles, three or four light machine guns, and two 60-mm mortars. But this time we won the battle. The French fled in their trucks, leaving behind their dead and wounded and lots of rifles, machine guns, and ammunition.

After the battle, we cleaned up the field, and someone in the regiment made a sign that he placed near the bodies of the French soldiers. The sign read: "We are a country with twenty-five million people determined to fight and win this war and get you out of this nation. How can your small army of 120,000 stand against us? Therefore, you better get out of our country before it is too late."

The next day, after the French had retrieved their dead, I went back to the site of the battle. The French had modified the text on our sign with their own words: "It is true that we are only 120,000 troops, but we are well-trained and equipped to beat you because your twenty-five million people are sick, under-fed, undertrained, and underequipped. How could you possibly defeat us? Lay down your arms and surrender. We are generous."

After all these years, I am struck more than ever by these two simple state-ments and what they revealed. The statement by the French soldiers emanated from a kind of quantitative logic and suggested that because of their appar-ent material superiority, victory would surely be theirs. The Viet Minh, on the other hand, focused on the power of an idea, the liberation of their country, and suggested that the Vietnamese people were determined to fight for this idea until they were victorious. What is incredible is that these crude state-ments, written on the battlefield in 1946, continued to reflect the fundamen-tal thinking of the two warring parties for the next thirty years.

The Communist Party: To Join or Not to Join

In early 1949, after I had recovered from a severe injury and was appointed head of the training section for the Eighty-third Regiment, my good friend Ho Ba, head of our political affairs section, tried to recruit me into the Commu-nist Party. It was then that I decided to leave the Viet Minh. I was still deter-mined to liberate Vietnam from the French and to bring social justice to the countryside, but I was not comfortable with the idea of becoming a commu-nist myself. At that time, I knew only two Communist Party members: Ho Ba and Nguyen Duong, the political commissar of our regiment. Both were entirely devoted to the revolution. Their dedication, frugality, and bravery were beyond reproach.

So resolute was their determination to serve the party wholeheartedly that they refused to meet their fiancées until the war was over. As for me, I knew I could continue to be as good a soldier as I had been for the past five years, on and off the battlefield. I also knew that I would never be capable of giving myself entirely to the party as Ba and Duong were doing.

I also had grave doubts about the ability of the Viet Minh to defeat the pow-erful French military, and I believed that a compromise would eventually be reached between Ho Chi Minh, Emperor Bao Dai, and the other nationalist fac-tions and that a truly independent noncommunist Vietnam would result. Con-sidering all these factors, I decided to leave the Viet Minh. The decision was made more difficult by the fact that my sister, her husband, and my two broth-ers were still serving with the Viet Minh. I decided not to tell them of my deci-sion. I simply walked into the office of the province chief in Quang Nam, who was an old friend of my father's, and announced my defection.

After leaving the Viet Minh, I underwent ten days of interrogation by the French. I tried to be forthright with my answers to their queries, but I also did not want to betray my friends and family on the other side, so I didn't always tell them everything I knew. After they were satisfied that my defection was in fact sincere, they sent me home to Hue where my father was a retired judge. I was ordered to report to the police once a week.

Oddly enough, it was after my defection that I began to become more familiar with Ho Chi Minh's communist ideology, something I had not had time to do when I was fighting in the jungle. I did a lot of reading and also discussed these matters with others, including some who had also defected from the Viet Minh. I came to the conclusion that the communist ideology was fundamentally inconsistent with my own values.

I also decided communism was not compatible with the Confucianist traditions of Vietnam, and I joined the newly established State of Vietnam under the leadership of Bao Dai. I then volunteered to join the first class at the newly created military academy in Dalat. After graduating a year later, I was asked to stay on as an instructor. It was during this period that I became a good friend of another instructor. He later became president of the Republic of Vietnam—his name was Nguyen Van Thieu.

After teaching in Dalat for a year, I volunteered to serve with combat units. In addition to a dozen medals and citations for merit and bravery, I was awarded the nation's highest honor, the National Order, and was promoted first to captain, then to major, all within a year's time. After the war ended with the Geneva Accords, I became the first Vietnamese commandant of the Cadet Corps at the National Military Academy at Dalat.

Despite the Viet Minh's victory over the French, I felt optimistic about the future in 1954. The end of the fighting was a welcome relief, and at last we had a truly independent noncommunist country: the Republic of Vietnam, or South Vietnam. The temporary division of Vietnam into North and South at the seventeenth parallel meant that my hometown of Hue was part of the South, for which I was grateful. I also felt I was well on my way toward a successful career in the Vietnamese army. In addition, of course, I was happily married and had three beautiful children. My feelings about the Americans, however, were somewhat ambivalent. We knew they were coming to help us, but it was difficult thinking about welcoming more foreigners so soon after the departure of the French.

Visiting America for the First Time

When I was asked to be part of the first group of twenty-five Vietnamese officers to go to the United States for ten months of advanced infantry training,

I was eager to go. We were first flown from Saigon to Guam, then to Hawaii, and finally to San Francisco. We were then taken to nearby Fort Mason. Going from South Vietnam to the world's most powerful and developed country was an unforgettable and somewhat bewildering experience. We really didn't know what to expect. The fact is, at that time, we knew very little about the Americans. We were aware of the language barrier, though, as the following story illustrates.

On the day before our scheduled departure from San Francisco to Fort Benning, Georgia, an American captain came to inform us that we were to take Yellow Cabs to the train station the next day. We Vietnamese were caught completely off guard by this statement. Were we being put in Yellow Cabs because we were yellow Asian people? Were the Americans really racists as we had been told in the past? Emotions were running high as we Vietnamese discussed the situation among ourselves. We were divided as to what course we should take. Some thought we should just say nothing and take the humiliating cab ride to the station. Others thought we should voice our protest and ask to be flown back home immediately. Personally, I was disappointed and hurt that our American hosts were treating us this way.

Finally, I gathered up my courage and spoke to the American commanding officer. Somehow I got my point across, even with my broken English. He threw his head back and started to laugh. He explained that there were only two major cab companies in San Francisco: Yellow Cab and Blue Ribbon Cab. He said that telling us to take Yellow Cabs had no derogatory meaning but that if we didn't want to ride in them, he would make sure we rode in the Blue Ribbon Cabs. When I told the other Vietnamese officers what had happened, there was little we could do but laugh.

It was a small incident, but nevertheless it revealed how insecure we were with the Americans at that time. We knew that there were racial inequalities in America, but we didn't know if they would affect us. Perhaps we expected the worst. Anyway, after the incident was resolved, we all breathed a heavy sigh of relief. And after ten months of training, I became very comfortable with Americans and receptive to the idea of working with them. In addition, I was very impressed with the military weaponry and firepower we saw demonstrated at Fort Benning. Although I had some doubts about how effective all the technology would be in South Vietnam, I was glad to have such a powerful ally.

No Opposition to American Military Proposals

After graduating from the Fort Benning course in September 1956, I returned to the National Military Academy in Dalat as director of instruction. The first thing I did was set up a committee to look into various military instructional programs around the world, such as the British Sandhurst, the French Saint-Cyr, and the Taiwan Chinese Academy, to determine which components of each we could incorporate into our training program. I envisioned a training program that combined modern technology with Vietnamese culture and traditions and that was taught by highly qualified Vietnamese officers. My counterpart, a highly educated West Pointer, Major Butterfield, made a recommendation that we should adopt the four-year program that had been put in place by the Americans in the Philippines. We would borrow instructors from there to train our cadets, in addition to our own instructors.

I did not agree with this approach, so I went to the Vietnamese superintendent for a decision. The colonel said that the Americans are going to pour in millions of dollars to expand and modernize the academy, and their West Point is regarded as the best in the world, so just listen to them. The colonel had never been to the United States and was one of many Vietnamese at that time who thought the Americans were much superior to the French.

In the following weeks, Major Butterfield and the staff of the U.S. Training Mission presented to the senior Vietnamese officers their plans for the future of the National Military Academy, which focused on conventional warfare tactics. Not one objection was made to any of their proposals. In talking with fellow Vietnamese officers working with the general staff, infantry units, and provincial forces, I found out the same thing was happening throughout the army. In general, the Vietnamese were totally intimidated by their American counterparts.

This was a serious problem—a noticeable lack of true cooperation and communication between the Americans and the Vietnamese. I blame both sides: the Americans for their natural superiority complex and the Vietnamese for their natural inferiority complex, a result of so many years serving under the French. The result was, of course, disastrous. The American concepts of warfare and how a war in South Vietnam should be fought were never seriously challenged by the Vietnamese. This meant that the Americans were never able to learn what the Vietnamese knew about South Vietnam, which was considerably more than what the Americans knew. This was particularly true when it came to knowing the enemy, the communists, whom we all expected to face some time in the future.

The people who knew the most about Ho Chi Minh's military forces were those who had fought with them or against them or, in some cases such as mine, both. Sadly, the Americans seemed not to be very interested in what we

Vietnamese knew about the communists, and we were not confident enough to make sure we were listened to.

And so, the American military essentially took charge of designing the Vietnamese armed forces. From the beginning, the emphasis was on conventional warfare. In addition to the officer training program, I was involved in the transformation of what had been the French Seventh Division into the Americanized Fourth Infantry Division. And I will admit it was exhilarating to watch the emergence of a modern Vietnamese army equipped with tanks, artillery, automatic weapons, and even airplanes. I even felt confident South Vietnam would be able to defeat the communists should they invade from the North.

But I wasn't so sure how these conventional forces would do against the hit-and-run tactics of small guerrilla units like the ones I had commanded when I was with the Viet Minh. But during this period, before 1960, there was very little trouble in the countryside and very little guerrilla activity. And so the Americans and the South Vietnamese congratulated themselves on the fine work they had done.

A New Job at the Palace: Seeds Planted for War

In late l959, I was transferred by President Ngo Dinh Diem from the regular army to a job as inspector of the Civil Guard and Self-Defense Corps forces. Unlike the regular army units, these soldiers worked locally to protect the people at the village, district, and provincial levels. My first task was to visit all forty of the country's provinces to evaluate the local military forces and to learn how they were interacting with the population. At the end of my three-month trip, I prepared a long report to the president. I reported that the Civil Guard and Self-Defense Corps forces were poorly paid, poorly armed, and poorly trained. In fact, they had no political education whatsoever and were therefore unmotivated and unable to foster good relations with the local population.

I learned something else that impressed (or depressed) me even more. Almost all the government employees, even those working in the intelligence service or for military security and the police, were the same people who had performed those jobs when the French were in power.

It was bewildering. At one level, it seemed that profound change had come to the southern part of former Vietnam. After almost one hundred years of colonial rule, the French had gone home. The new, independent Republic of Vietnam had been created with Ngo Dinh Diem as president. The Americans had come in to help create a democratic nation and a modern army. But in the countryside, nothing much had changed.

As I started to look around, I realized the lack of change wasn't just in the countryside. It was prevalent everywhere. Even President Diem himself was served mainly by people who were previously in the French colonial system. For example, Minister of Interior Bui Van Luong, who supervised the administration nationwide, was himself an administrator under the French during the war. The same was true for the national police chief, many security personnel, and most of the leadership of the armed forces.

The consequence of this was obvious. The French were gone, but their policies and their attitudes, particularly toward the rural population, were still in place. As far as the Vietnamese peasant was concerned, it was business as usual. And that meant oppression, duplicity, and corruption. It also meant that anyone who had supported Ho Chi Minh's forces against the French was now suspected of communist sympathies. Essentially, this meant that anyone who had wanted the French out of Vietnam was put on the government's so called enemies hit list.

In a way, the arrival of the Americans put the icing on the cake, at least as far as the communist propagandists were concerned. For years they had described the local Vietnamese functionaries as lackeys of the French. Now they simply described them as lackeys of the Americans.

The seeds of the second Vietnam war were thus planted. And they were planted in the exact same place as in the first war, in the countryside. Looking back, it is obvious that President Diem missed a great opportunity to gain the support of the rural Vietnamese. He should have overhauled the way the government did business with the peasants who for the most part considered the government the enemy. Diem should also have implemented a policy of reconciliation to bring former Viet Minh to the side of his government. Instead, Diem's police persecuted them and drove them back into the arms of the communists. Underlying these terrible mistakes was a simple truth. Neither Diem nor most of his American advisers had much respect for rural South Vietnam and the people who lived there. It was his and the Americans' greatest miscalculation.

Assignment in the Mekong Delta: The Growth of Communism
In the late 1950s, I was assigned to the Civil Guard and Self-Defense Corps forces in the upper Mekong Delta, covering a vast area of seven provinces. My responsibility was mainly in the field of control and inspection; the province chiefs were the recruiters and actual commanders of the forces. The Viet Cong insurgency was just beginning. The Viet Cong worked peacefully in their rice fields during the day; at night they attended political meetings and participated

Tran Ngoc Chau, who was elected secretary general of the Lower House of the National Assembly, is wearing the highest medal of South Vietnam, the National Order, as he is arrested in 1970 for meeting with his communist brother.

in propaganda activities designed to create an atmosphere of uncertainty. Along with this, small units of armed Viet Cong began to terrorize the countryside by assassinating village officials and others suspected of cooperating with the Saigon government.

One day on a trip to the capital of Kien Hoa Province, I stopped my jeep at a gathering of people in front of a village headquarters. On display were a dozen Viet Cong corpses and four or five World War II vintage rifles. I was told that the dead had been killed by a unit of the Civil Guard in an ambush the night before, about two kilometers from the district headquarters. The ten men and two women were between fifteen and thirty-five years of age, and all were farmers.

I had seen hundreds of bodies throughout my years as a soldier. I always felt bad, hurt personally, and felt compassion for the dead and their surviving relatives. But I had always been somewhat consoled in understanding that death was one of the brutal facts of wartime. This was different. It was the first time I had seen the bodies of farmers who were somehow motivated to fight against the government that was trying to protect them. Yes, I felt compassion, but I was also very angry. None of the relatives cried, as all rural Vietnamese normally would under such circumstances. One woman of about thirty years of age looked at me in my uniform so intensely that I could feel her hatred.

My mind was deeply confused. Why did these people, farmers living in peaceful villages, choose to join insurgents who roamed from village to village creating problems? Why did they renounce their peaceful lives and take such risks? Why? Another question was: How could they, in most cases, remain undetected and even protected by the villagers in areas controlled by the South Vietnamese government?

I stayed in the village for three days talking to people, trying to find answers to all my questions. I learned that those killed were indeed connected with the communists, although it is doubtful they knew much about the communist movement. Some of the people in the rural areas still looked in awe at Ho Chi Minh. To them he was a hero, the mythical figure who had defeated the French. The cadre whom the communists had left behind in the South after the French Indo-China War were regarded as Ho's representatives. And so they were honored, protected, and listened to. This was in sharp contrast to the way the villagers felt about the local representatives of the Diem government who, as I said earlier, were the same people who had oppressed them during the French occupation.

I also gathered some background information about Kien Hoa Province, which was called Ben Tre by the communists. Kien Hoa consisted of three large islands between two branches of the Mekong River. The population was just under six hundred thousand, nearly half of which was Catholic. The other half was Buddhist or Cao Dai. Unlike the Cao Dais in Tay Ninh Province, these were politically neutral and did not have their own army. Kien Hoa was a relatively prosperous area because of its rich agricultural resources.

The last Frenchman to govern Kien Hoa was a man by the name of Colonel Leroy. He ruled the province with total authority. In French, "le roi" means "the king." So Colonel Leroy was widely known, by both the French and the Vietnamese, as the King of Ben Tre.

Colonel Leroy administered Kien Hoa Province as if he owned the territory. He had his own tax collection system and his protégés on the government payroll at every level. He even had his own military forces recruited mainly from the Catholics. Colonel Leroy left Vietnam in 1954, but his autocratic philosophy and institutions stayed behind. In fact, they were enthusiastically adopted by a succession of Vietnamese province chiefs, including the one in charge when I visited there for the first time.

It is probably safe to say that nowhere in South Vietnam was the rural population more oppressed than in Kien Hoa Province. It is no wonder then that the birth of the Viet Cong, officially called the National Liberation Front, took place in 1959 in this province. Ever since, Kien Hoa has been referred to as the "Cradle of the Revolution," or the "Cradle of Insurgency," depending on which side you were on.

There was something else I observed on my first trip to Kien Hoa in 1960. I learned that as antigovernment guerrilla activity increased, the government's counteraction and oppression also increased. A vicious cycle had been set in motion. The more oppressive the government became, the easier it was for the communists to recruit peasants to fight on their side. A few months later, I returned to the village to learn that most of the surviving relatives of those killed that night had been imprisoned by the South Vietnamese government, had joined the Viet Cong in the countryside, or had disappeared into the slums of some city.

The Decision of War: At the Village Level

I came to a powerful conclusion: the future of South Vietnam would not be decided by the regular armed forces of South Vietnam, even with all their modern weapons, technology, and American training. Instead, it would be decided at the hamlet and village levels by local officials, by police, and most important, by the Civil Guard and Self-Defense Corps. They were the ones in direct contact with the rural population. If we were going to win the allegiance of the rural Vietnamese, and if we were going to win against the communist insurgents, we had to have our own military and political cadre in the field. And they had to be well trained. I decided to set up a center near My Tho to train all the Civil Guard and Self-Defense Corps forces in the region, with special emphasis on the political and psychological elements of warfare.

I planned to train the Civil Guard along the same lines as the training I had received some fifteen years earlier from the Viet Minh. There were five main components to the training: First was how to protect the villagers from the enemy; second, how to gain the support and allegiance of the villagers; third, how to obtain intelligence from the villagers to complement intelligence from other conventional sources, paid informants, etc.; fourth, how to execute the basic military tactics needed to protect the population and make it impossible for the Viet Cong to take human and material resources from the villages; and fifth, how to improve the Civil Guard's overall behavior and performance by means of daily evaluations. To give our trainees practical experience, I incorporated the villages surrounding the training center into the training complex. These villages became our real-life laboratory. In fact, we took over the responsibility of administering these villages and reported directly to the province chief. This gave our trainees a place to apply all they had learned.

To accomplish the third component of our training, the gathering of intelligence, I set up a program called "Census Grievance." It was very simple. Every day a member of every household in each hamlet was required to meet with one of our cadre and to answer the same three basic questions:

What was the good news and the bad news in the hamlet over the past twenty-four hours?
Who do you think was responsible?
What do you want us to do to improve security in your hamlet?

Because everyone was asked the same questions, it was impossible for the Viet Cong to identify specific informants. As a result, most of the underground Viet Cong were gradually identified.

The Census Grievance program was quite successful in improving security in the villages. Unexpectedly, it also revealed many of the negative actions committed by our own side, particularly harassment and abuses from village chiefs and police agents. It became a major job to work with the province chief and other officials to correct these wrongdoings.

During this time, there were no American advisers assigned to my command. Lt. Col. Frank Clay, senior adviser to the Vietnamese Fourth Division, was nevertheless very interested in what we were doing. Later on, I was asked by the U.S. Military Assistance Advisory Group (MAAG) office in Saigon to brief some VIPs about my work, including Generals McGarr and Timmes and Sir Robert Thompson, the British mission chief for counterinsurgency of Malayan fame.

Although some Americans were interested in my work, my fellow Vietnamese officers were clearly not. For example, I knew the Vietnamese colonel who commanded the infantry division assigned to our area. In fact, I often met with him over meals. He never asked any questions about my work. Like most senior Vietnamese officers, he was more interested in the conventional warfare tactics he had learned from the Americans. He was fascinated with fire and mobility, artillery and tanks, and air and naval support.

Although the Civil Guard had been fighting the communist insurgents for almost two years, the regular army was still being retrained and reorganized into big divisions, American style. Officers and men serving in the Civil Guard and Self-Defense Corps were regarded as inferior and totally lacking in prestige. The proof of this was that no Civil Guard or Self-Defense Corps units had

American advisers. Very simply, the American military didn't think they were very important, and neither did their Vietnamese counterparts.

Training Session in Malaysia

As I mentioned, one of the people who knew about my work was Sir Robert Thompson, the man credited with Britain's successful counterinsurgency efforts in Malaya (later Malaysia) in the early 1950s. Apparently Thompson had suggested to President Diem that I go to Malaysia to see what I could learn. President Diem called me in one day and gave me the assignment. He told me to take as much time as I needed but to make sure my final report was no longer than a single page.

I went to Malaysia with a clear purpose—to bring back ideas on how we could improve our efforts to beat the communists in South Vietnam. To accomplish this, I talked to many people in many different fields: military, paramilitary, police, intelligence, civic action, information, and community development. I ended up with a lot of information. Fortunately, I had four days in a small hotel in Singapore to work on my report. It took me that long to reduce my original draft of twelve pages to the single page President Diem had requested. Here are the main points of that one-page report:

> The system of government, state and federal, is firmly established and trusted by the general population; cultural and religious traditions are respected by the government.
>
> Counterinsurgency is under civilian, not military, authority. At the state level, a prime minister is in charge. The second in command is the police chief. All counterinsurgency actions must comply with state and federal laws.
>
> Military commanders are given specific zones of operation with clearly defined objectives. A police officer is assigned to assist each military commander.
>
> The police are vital—they enforce the laws and collect intelligence.
>
> Information released to the public must be accurate. In some cases the government will withhold potentially harmful information, saying the matter is under investigation, but it will not release false information.

President Diem spent half a day going over my report. He then asked me to talk with his brother and chief counselor, Ngo Dinh Nhu. After listening to me for an hour, and without looking at my report, Nhu made the comment that it sounds convincing, but here we are facing a different kind of insurgency that requires different solutions and methods. I replied politely, "Mr. Counselor, I

thought the methods might be different, but the principles could be the same."
Nhu said he would think it over. He then opened a book and started reading.
President Diem was always cordial with me, but Nhu was always cool, very
cool. That was as far as my report from Malaysia ever went.

I should add here that in 1991, Thompson invited me to visit him in Eng-
land. While there, and after a dinner one evening, we reminisced far into the
night. He said that his experience with Nhu was much like my own and that
his suggestions about reforming the police and justice systems always fell on
deaf ears. He also said that in later years, he acted more as an observer for President Nixon in South Vietnam than as an adviser (he went to South Vietnam
at Nixon's request). He said the Americans were very smart but not willing to
learn anything new if they'd already made up their minds. He did say the
Americans treated him very well and listened to him politely, but more out of
courtesy than seriousness.

My New Role as Province Chief

In early 1962, President Diem called me to his office in the Presidential
Palace. The minister of interior was also there. The president asked me to
take over as province chief of Kien Hoa Province. I politely refused, saying
I did not have the training for such a position. "My decision has been made,"
he said, "with compassion you will learn and make an excellent province
chief, like your grandfather and father." His words touched my heart. Both
my father and my grandfather had been honored for their long service to
their people, and both had entered public service with only one qualifica-
tion—they were students and practitioners of the Confucian philosophy. I
decided then and there that perhaps President Diem knew more about what
I was qualified to do than I did.

I went to Kien Hoa Province knowing full well what the situation was. Of
the approximately six hundred thousand people in the province, only about
eighty thousand were firmly under government control. I set out to turn things
around by applying all that I had learned over the past twenty years. I approached the job with one simple idea in my mind, that the conflict with the
communists was primarily political, not military. The main goals, then, were
to pacify the rural population, gain the support of the people, and thereby
eliminate the enemy's support and, ultimately, the enemy itself. This did not
diminish the importance of the military forces, but it did mean that their main
job was to support the pacification process.

The first thing I did was put the Census Grievance program in place, beginning with the villages that were closest in proximity to our military forces. The

information gathered by the Census Grievance cadre was the foundation for our effort to pacify the countryside. Immediately, many Viet Cong working in these villages chose to leave rather than be apprehended. We also reduced the social and economic injustices committed against the villagers by our own government officials.

We instituted an Open Arms program (Chieu Hoi), which offered amnesty to communist insurgents. As I said earlier, one of the great mistakes made by the Diem government in its early days was its treatment of former Viet Minh followers. After the Geneva Accords, there should have been efforts at reconciliation to bring former Viet Minh to the side of the new Republic of Vietnam. Instead, they were humiliated, hunted, and often killed. With our Open Arms program, we tried to correct that mistake and give our enemies and former enemies a positive alternative to the communists.

We also helped the villagers with self-help projects that they thought were worthwhile. Finally, and perhaps most important, we invited all the villagers to participate in the election of their own administrators and security officers. We also asked all the villagers to volunteer to serve in their own self-defense organizations.

To shift the war to the village level in this manner required a complete revision of the way the provincial government worked. Instead of the usual top-down mentality, the new idea was that civilian administrators, the police, and the military would all respond to what was happening at the village level. For example, social and economic development projects were to be defined by the villagers through the Census Grievance program rather than come from a bureaucrat sitting in the provincial capital.

After one year, an official survey estimated that 220,000 people in Kien Hoa were now loyal to the government, an increase of some 140,000. This fundamental change in the political character of the province was not due to any dramatic military victories. Instead, it was due to a shift in the way people in the general population thought of themselves in relation to the government and its representatives. Rather than abusing them and taking their power from them, as governments had done for years, we were helping them to have more power over their lives, to defend themselves, to govern themselves, and to move ahead economically.

The Buddhist Affair: A Monumental Blunder

Early in 1963, the order went out from President Diem that the Buddhist flag could no longer be flown over Buddhist temples. As a Buddhist myself, I could not agree with such a policy. But even more important, I thought it was a serious political mistake for Diem, a Catholic, to make. I called him on the telephone and told him so. He asked me to come to Saigon to discuss the matter, which I did. It was clear that although he was reluctant to reverse his policy, he respected my views on the issue. In fact, he made it clear that he would not object if I let the Buddhist flags continue flying in Kien Hoa Province, which I did. Unfortunately, I was not able to persuade him to change his policy throughout South Vietnam, and the situation continued to deteriorate.

Some weeks passed, and President Diem called me again and told me that he wanted me to play an important role in solving the Buddhist crisis. He said he had originally intended that I go to Hue, the center of the crisis, but he feared I would get into a conflict with his brothers, Senior Archbishop Ngo Dinh Thuc and Counselor Ngo Dinh Can. So instead, he had decided to send me to Da Nang, sixty miles south of Hue, where I would become the mayor of Da Nang as well as governor of the Quang Nam Province–Da Nang city area. President Diem emphasized that I would be accountable only to him.

I then asked him a question. "I understand," I asked, "that my new assignment is to help solve the Buddhist crisis, so I want you to tell me precisely what is your attitude and policy toward Buddhism and the Buddhist community that has been revolting against you and the government?" The president seemed not to listen to me. Instead he played with the cigarette in his fingers for a minute or two. Then suddenly he looked at me very intensely and said, "Whatever you would do to help solve the crisis would be along the lines of your attitude and policy toward Buddhism and the Buddhists." I understood this to mean that he had confidence in me, as a Buddhist, to do the right thing. I also understood that he was giving me complete authority to do what I thought was right.

Diem Considers Sending His Brother Abroad

Early the next morning, President Diem's personal plane landed in Kien Hoa to take me to Da Nang. While there, I talked with the president almost daily on the phone and returned to Saigon to meet with him almost every week. On one occasion he greatly surprised me by asking what I would think if he dismissed his brother Ngo Dinh Nhu and sent him (and his wife, Madame Nhu) abroad for a time. Nhu was widely regarded as the architect of Diem's policy toward the Buddhists.

At that time, it was common knowledge that the Americans wanted Diem to remove Nhu from power. It was in all the newspapers. And Diem himself seemed to understand that Nhu was causing him great harm, but he was afraid that if he sent Nhu abroad, the Vietnamese people would think that the

Tran Ngoc Chau before a military tribunal that sentenced him to ten years in prison. He had served over four years when the communists overran South Vietnam; he was held in confinement for another three years.

Americans had made him do it. He did not want to be perceived as a puppet or lackey of the Americans. I told the president that it would be wrong to dismiss his brother for his own personal gain. But if dismissal was in the best interest of the country, then it would be a wise and correct decision. Diem suggested that perhaps Nhu could be reassigned to some official position outside the country.

One can only wonder what might have happened in South Vietnam and whether the assassination of President Diem might have been avoided if he had followed his political instincts and sent his brother and sister-in-law into exile.

The Death of President Diem

Unfortunately, Nhu was not removed from his position. The situation with the Buddhists became a national crisis. The whole world witnessed the fiery suicides of Buddhist monks and the attacks on the Buddhists by government forces. The Vietnamese military grew more and more impatient, as did the Americans, especially the new American ambassador, Henry Cabot Lodge. President Diem was overthrown in a coup that began on 1 November 1963, and the president and his brother Nhu were murdered the next day. The coup was carried out by a group of Vietnamese officers working closely with the U.S. government. Clearly, the Americans had decided that a change in the Vietnamese leadership was in their best interest.

The overthrow of President Diem was a great tragedy for South Vietnam and for me personally. I did not always agree with the Diem administration, but I respected President Diem and considered him a true Vietnamese patriot. Unfortunately, his brother Nhu influenced him too much, and his policies became oppressive. I do not know why Diem did not follow through with his idea of removing Nhu from power. Perhaps he had just grown too dependent on him or maybe he could not reject his own brother. Then again, perhaps, the Americans put too much pressure on him, so much that he had to maintain his loyalty to his brother, no matter at what cost. I have always wondered what might have happened if Gen. Edward Lansdale had been brought in as ambassador instead of Lodge. Lansdale and Diem had been almost inseparable during the early years of Diem's presidency, and they had developed a great friendship. It is possible that Lansdale could have helped Diem solve the Buddhist crisis (or even avoided it) and ease his brother out of power gracefully It is something we will never know.

Frustrating Conversation with Westmoreland

All our efforts toward pacification were thrown into serious trouble by the coup. The communists took advantage of the chaos in Saigon and increased their guerrilla activity everywhere. When I returned to Kien Hoa to resume my duties as province chief, I found that most of the progress we had made earlier had been lost. Fortunately, we were able to get our pacification efforts back on track, and by 1965 the situation was greatly improved. About that time, General Westmoreland, the commander of the American military forces in South Vietnam, came to visit me.

Westmoreland and his staff spent about two hours listening to my briefing about our efforts to pacify the countryside. The general then released his staff and talked with me privately. He invited my suggestions. I recommended that pacification be regarded as the prime national objective and that military and paramilitary forces be used to support that objective.

I went on to suggest that the Self-Defense Corps should be considered the frontline troops, supported by the Civil Guard. The regular army units should be broken up into smaller mobile brigades that could respond quickly and support the Civil Guard. Lastly, American troops should be stationed in strategic places such as the Demilitarized Zone and the Ho Chi Minh Trail and be used to support the Vietnamese army. I also recommended that Vietnamese

Special Forces and Ranger units be used to harass the enemy along the Ho Chi Minh Trail.

As I was about to continue with more suggestions, the general suddenly stood up, shook my hand, and departed. I guess he was tired of listening to the ideas of a Vietnamese lieutenant colonel, particularly because the ideas were so radically different from what he was hearing from the Vietnamese generals in Saigon. That night I could not sleep. I kept thinking about my conversation with Westmoreland. I wondered about this four-star general who had performed so successfully against the Germans in Europe and the Chinese in Korea but who seemed to lack a basic understanding of what the war in South Vietnam was all about, and he did not appear to be interested in learning. It was very frustrating for me because I felt I had learned a lot about fighting the communists, and I had developed strategies that were working, but no one at the top would listen.

Few American Officials Will Listen

The sad truth is that most of the high-ranking Vietnamese generals, the men whom Westmoreland naturally relied on, had little military experience and knew little about the Viet Cong and what was going on in the countryside. Most were given their positions because of their loyalty to those in power, not because of their success on the battlefield. So they did not have the knowledge or the confidence to make sound policy. The Vietnamese who understood the real situation were the younger officers in the field, but unfortunately they were often so browbeaten by their superiors that their voices were seldom heard. As a result, the American and Vietnamese generals were essentially directing a war effort without any real understanding of what the war was all about.

I had better luck getting my ideas across to the American civilians working in South Vietnam. The CIA particularly liked what I was doing, but so did representatives from AID (Agency for International Development) and the U.S. Information Agency. John Paul Vann, a former colonel working with AID, came by often and we talked about pacification. He brought along Daniel Ellsberg, who also became part of our little private think-tank. (Ellsberg would later be charged with unauthorized release of the *Pentagon Papers.*) John O'Donnell, a Rural Affairs prov rep in Kien Hoa (and a contributor to this book) was also quite understanding about the situation in the province. We all believed that the Vietnam War was fundamentally a political conflict that could be won only by political means, namely, a government that gained the respect and loyalty of the people, especially those in the countryside. The idea was quite simple. Without the support of the Vietnamese peasant, the communists could not continue their guerrilla activities. Therefore, they would have to fight a conventional war more along the lines of the Korean conflict, and we felt confident we could win such a war.

A New Position on the National Level

In late 1965, I was asked to help establish a nationwide pacification program similar to the one I had developed in Kien Hoa. It was supported primarily by the CIA. A new Ministry of Rural Development had been created in the Vietnamese government, with Gen. Nguyen Duc Thang at its head. I was named national director of the Revolutionary Development Cadres and director of the Training Center in Vung Tau. Our job was to train the cadre that would take the pacification program into the countryside. After a few months of working with the CIA, General Thang, and others, I realized that what they had in mind was really very different from my program in Kien Hoa. Superficially it looked similar, but the program was not built on a foundation of political and moral principles like my program. Very simply, the people at the top did not truly share the ideals that I knew were necessary for the program to work.

For example, it was all well and good to be anticommunist, but if we did not work to build a truly democratic system, what was the point? What did we have to offer the Vietnamese peasant if our system did not include democracy and the freedom to choose their own leaders? In addition, we needed to commit ourselves to establishing a fair and efficient system of justice. Our main goal in Kien Hoa had not been to kill our enemies but to use political and social action to bring them to our side. We always considered killing only as the last resort.

I decided that what they thought was a pacification program was essentially a sham. Vietnamese and Americans alike talked about winning the hearts and minds of the people, but what they really wanted to do was just kill communists. I became more and more disillusioned. One issue that bothered me deeply had to do with the visibility of the CIA. Time and time again, I tried to convince my colleagues, both Vietnamese and American, that the CIA's role should be kept behind the scenes and virtually invisible. As it was, CIA agents were actually out in the countryside directing the work of the Vietnamese cadre. To me, this was totally unacceptable. Such activity confirmed what communist propaganda had been saying all along, that we were lackeys of the Americans. Also, and even more important, it undermined the morale of our own cadre, young men and women, and made them feel like they were being paid by the CIA to be revolutionaries. My efforts to change this policy were greeted with suspicion by both the Vietnamese and the Americans. One American who agreed with me, John Paul Vann, put his career in serious jeopardy when he publicly supported my position.

Frustration and Resignation

So it was, out of frustration, that I left my job with the Ministry of Rural Development in 1966. I also resigned from the military. It was my way of stating my loyalty to my principles and to my country. I decided to write a book. I called it *From War to Peace: Renaissance of the Village*. It was another futile attempt to convince those in power that the rural population was the key to the war in South Vietnam and that to win its allegiance, we needed an all-out pacification effort founded on clear moral values and democratic ideals.

In 1967, I returned to Kien Hoa Province to run for a seat in the National Assembly. I reasoned that perhaps as a politician I would be more successful getting my message across. I was gratified when the population of Kien Hoa overwhelmingly voted for me, but even as a politician, I was unable to accomplish my objectives. The war effort was firmly in the hands of the militarists, as the introduction of half a million American soldiers proved. And although South Vietnam did have an elected president and an elected National Assembly, or congress, what it really had was a totalitarian military regime headed by President Nguyen Van Thieu, supported by the American government. The whole election process was essentially a farce carried out to quiet the voices of protest in America. Meanwhile in South Vietnam, a small minority of opportunistic Vietnamese profited from the war at the expense of the thousands of sincere Vietnamese patriots serving in the civil service and in the military.

After the communist-inspired Tet Offensive (Chinese and Vietnamese New Year) of 1968, it became clear to me that the American public would not support the war in South Vietnam indefinitely and that the withdrawal of American assistance was inevitable. And so I began to consider alternative ways to preserve the independence of South Vietnam. This search included the possibility of forming a coalition government with the National Liberation Front, the communist political organization in the South.

On several occasions, I met with my brother Tran Ngoc Hien, who was a high-ranking Viet Cong intelligence officer, to discuss these matters. Immediately after our first meeting in 1965, I reported the contact to John Paul Vann and the CIA, which eventually arrested Hien and used him to incriminate me as a communist sympathizer. As an assemblyman, I should have had immunity from such charges, but President Thieu, with the support of the United

States, made sure that didn't happen. In February 1970 I was arrested inside the National Assembly building. I spent the next four years in jail, watching South Vietnam fall to the communists.

Lessons and Observations of the War: Political Not Military

For the Vietnamese communists, the war against South Vietnam and the Americans was a continuation of the war against the French and had the same objectives: an independent Vietnam free of foreigners and a peasantry free of landowners and social injustice. Turning their ideological objectives into political promises, they waged a campaign of propaganda to mobilize the peasants to support their effort. For propaganda tools, they used the imagery of Ho Chi Minh and his victory over the French, of the Americans as successors to the colonialist French, and of former collaborators of the French as puppets of the Americans in Saigon. They also capitalized on the abuses of the South Vietnamese government toward the rural population and compared its attitude and tactics with those of the French. The communists then used sabotage, terror, and military action to create instability and insecurity, which they then could exploit politically.

In the South, the newly created Republic of Vietnam, headed by Ngo Dinh Diem, had been established as an independent, democratic state. It essentially owed its existence to the United States, whose main interest was stopping the spread of communism. The Americans saw South Vietnam as a piece in the global chess match between the communists and the free world. Unfortunately, this macroview meant that the Americans had difficulty appreciating, let alone comprehending, the reality of South Vietnam. For example, in 1955, 85 percent of the population of South Vietnam lived in the countryside, and the vast majority had supported the Viet Minh in the war against the French. The other 15 percent were city folks, bureaucrats, military officers, and businesspeople, the majority of whom had collaborated with the French.

When the French left Vietnam, the French collaborators became friends with the Americans. What the Americans knew about South Vietnam, they had learned mainly from these Vietnamese. It is not surprising, therefore, that these Vietnamese were also the ones to benefit the most from American aid, particularly the multimillion-dollar program to build up the South Vietnamese military forces. Meanwhile, in rural South Vietnam, nothing much changed. The peasants continued to be exploited and abused by those in power—the same people who had abused them under the French. And the communists continued to quietly exploit such abuses. Very simply, while the

Americans were naively preparing the South Vietnamese to fight a conventional war, the communists were recruiting South Vietnamese peasants to fight a guerrilla war.

Democracy as the Key to Victory

The great irony is that while the Americans brought their military know-how to help the Vietnamese fight the communists, they did not bring the democratic ideals and principles that had motivated them to fight their own wars. Their anticommunist fervor was so strong that they fell into an age-old trap: the ends justify the means. Their fear of communism was greater than their faith in freedom and democracy. And so they supported one authoritarian regime after another in Saigon, while at the same time they choreographed phony elections to convince the world of the rightness of their cause.

In one such election, while Diem was president, two very respectable Vietnamese, Dr. Phan Quang Dan and engineer Phan Khac Suu, were elected to the National Assembly. They were both intelligent men with their own ideas

Tran Ngoc Chau (*left*) and former President of South Vietnam Nguyen Van Thieu (*right*) with their wives at a reunion in 1997

about what was good for South Vietnam. Diem, however, didn't want competing ideas, so with the support of the Americans he forbade them from taking their seats in the Assembly. They were later sent to jail for plotting against the government.

In both of these cases, the illegal actions carried out by the Vietnamese government were supported by the U.S. government. The policymakers in Washington seemed to think that having a strong authoritarian leader was more important than having a leader who could gain the genuine support of the people.

By the time I retired from the military in 1967, I had figured out that democracy was the only thing that would save South Vietnam from the communists. That is why I decided to run for a seat in the National Assembly. I knew the communists were winning not because of their ideology, which to me was totally incompatible with Vietnamese traditions, but because they knew how to exploit the abusive policies of the Saigon government. There was only one thing to do—change those policies. What was needed was a complete overhaul of the system so that the administration, the Assembly, and the judiciary were responsible to the people. We needed the rule of law rather than the rule of strong-arm tactics.

But the forces opposing democratic reform were firmly entrenched and had the full support of the Americans. President Diem's most lasting and tragic legacy was a government run by people who had served the French. They were, almost by definition, not inclined toward democratic principles. Nor were they inclined to put South Vietnam's interests ahead of their own.

The Importance of Reconciliation

After the 1954 Geneva Accords, which temporarily divided the country at the seventeenth parallel, there were many former Viet Minh and their supporters living in rural South Vietnam. After all, the Viet Minh enjoyed as much support in the South as in the North during the war with the French. And although it is true that an estimated one hundred thousand Viet Minh went North after the partition, the vast majority remained in the South in the villages where they were born.

In 1956, President Diem, blinded by his anticommunist ideology and supported by his entourage and the Americans, launched a nationwide campaign of communist denunciation. It was carried out by the local police and other officials. The result was a campaign of terror and humiliation against former Viet Minh and their supporters. To the peasant farmers, and to many Vietnamese nationalists, it looked like the war with the French all over again because the Vietnamese carrying out these policies were former collaborators of the French. The effect was also the same; more people joined the communists, and more communists went underground, this time to prepare for resistance against Diem.

Diem missed a great opportunity. A campaign of reconciliation could have turned former enemies into allies and could have helped Diem consolidate the authority of his government throughout the country. Perhaps most important, it could have brought into Diem's government the Vietnamese nationalists who had supported the Viet Minh but who were really not communists and who were looking for an alternative to Ho Chi Minh. As a former Viet Minh myself, I knew there were many Vietnamese in such a position. Unfortunately, Diem could not or would not see it. He was a nationalist, no doubt, but his anticommunism blinded him to the fact that most of the true Vietnamese nationalists had at one time or another supported the Viet Minh. He needed those nationalists to build an independent, noncommunist South Vietnam. But he decided to build it with Vietnamese who had collaborated with the French in a war against their own people. It was a tragic decision.

Be Humble and Learn from the Past

The Americans came into South Vietnam full of confidence. "We've never lost a war," they'd say, "and we're not going to lose this one!" The French defeat seemed to be of little interest. "What do the French know about fighting a war?" they'd say. And the idea that Vietnamese history might in itself be something worth studying seemed far-fetched.

The Americans had a conception of how things would go, and that was all there was to it. Of course, things did not go that way. My own view is that it was impossible for most Americans to understand what was going on in a poor, undeveloped country like South Vietnam. Had Ho Chi Minh and his leadership been educated at Harvard, MIT, or West Point, they probably would have been easily defeated by the professional intellectuals and technologists of America. As it was, though, America's material and technological superiority was overshadowed by its ignorance about South Vietnam, its history, and its people. Essentially, the Americans were fighting blindfolded. I have always felt that the Americans' intentions in South Vietnam were honorable, even noble, but unfortunately they ignored rule Number One among military thinkers: Know Thy Enemy, which, in this case, might have been expanded to include a corollary, Know Thy Ally. There are two books that might have helped the Americans understand the situation better. These are *Vietnam: Sociology of War* by Paul Mus and *History of Vietnam* by Phillippe Devilliers. However, it is some four decades too late for them to learn.

The Importance of Image

One day in 1965, my American military adviser in Kien Hoa, Maj. Andrew Michael Simko (who subsequently was killed in a helicopter crash in Binh Dinh Province in April 1970), asked me why I rarely let him or other Americans accompany me when I went out to visit the villages. I told him I didn't want my people to think that the Americans had replaced the French and that we were working for them. At first, his feelings were hurt, but he came to understand the validity of what I said. Unfortunately, too many Americans, some in very high places, did not. The Americans actually seemed to think that the average Vietnamese would be impressed to see them in positions of authority over Vietnamese affairs. Whether it was President Johnson shaking hands with Gen. Nguyen Cao Ky (air force general and vice-president under Thieu) in Honolulu, CIA agents running around in the countryside, or William Colby (chief of the CIA Far East Division) proudly discussing the Vietnamese cabinet meetings he attended, the impression that emerged among the Vietnamese was that the Americans were running our country. And these images were exploited to the fullest by the communists. Then, of course, there was the horrific image created when five hundred thousand American soldiers arrived in South Vietnam.

The Power of Dedication

Let me share with you a story of something that happened in 1978. After officials in the now-installed communist government in Vietnam set me free, they invited me to work for their Social Sciences Institute in Saigon. I complied with their wishes mainly because I didn't want them to suspect that I was planning to escape the country. One day, a man approached me at the Institute. He was in his fifties and was ruggedly built. His ambitious eyes looked directly into mine, and he asked if I was Mr. Tran Ngoc Chau. As I nodded yes, he embraced me with one arm and cried softly. "Don't you remember me?" he asked. He said he had come all the way from Hanoi just to see me, and he said he was happy now. We then sat down and talked for several hours.

I had first met this man in 1946 when he was sixteen years of age. He and his older brother were from a family of uneducated peasants. When they joined the Viet Minh, both were assigned to my company. Soon afterward, the younger brother witnessed the death of the older brother in a fierce battle against a fortified French position. It was then that I took the surviving brother under my wing, so to speak, and made him my messenger. We had no radios in those days. In my spare time, I also taught him to read and write. I also taught him Vietnamese history and something about the politics of war. He was an intense and avid student. He was also one of the bravest soldiers I have ever encountered.

At one point I encouraged him to return to his village and join the local defense forces so he could be near his family. He felt, however, that he could better serve his parents and dead brother by fighting with a regular army battalion. Later, after I recovered from serious injuries and was assigned to regimental headquarters, I offered to take him with me, but he wanted to keep fighting in the jungle. My last contact with him had been in 1949. By then he had become a company commander as a result of heroism on the battlefield.

My old friend told me that he had gone on to become a highly decorated soldier and had retired as a colonel. He then became a lecturer of history and political science at one of North Vietnam's most outstanding graduate schools. In the midst of his recollections, he paused and looked at me intensely and related his story: "Almost thirty years ago, you used to tell us that President Ho Chi Minh gave us the opportunity to free the country and the peasantry from foreign colonialists, imperialists, and large landowners. We did just that. Moreover, without the direction of Bac [Uncle] Ho and the party, I would have remained a peasant, like my ancestors, working more for the benefit of the landowners and foreigners than for myself and my children. I am so proud and grateful to Uncle Ho."

As he said all this, he was in no way critical of me or the path I had taken. In fact, he told me that his respect and admiration for me were unchanged and that whatever I had done, he knew I had done it with the best of intentions. I was overwhelmed by his magnanimous spirit. I was also reminded of the powerful hold that Ho Chi Minh and his dreams for Vietnam had had on the Vietnamese peasants.

Some Final Thoughts

I will never forget the day in 1985 when my family and I became American citizens. It was a very proud day for all of us. For me, however, there was also an underlying sense of melancholy I could not shake off. I could not help thinking that I was forsaking my native Vietnam as well as my compatriots. And I could not help feeling sad that I had devoted the best thirty-five years of my life to a noble cause that had ultimately failed.

And like millions of other Vietnamese nationalists on both sides of the war, I felt betrayed. Betrayed by the South Vietnamese leaders who had viewed the war as a way to profit personally rather than as a nationalistic struggle against communist subversion. Betrayed also by the communists who used the war to consolidate their totalitarian hold on the Vietnamese. Following their military victory, they went on to impose a regime on South Vietnam that was so oppressive economically and politically that nearly two million people risked their lives to escape to other lands. Tragically, several hundred thousand died trying. In short, I mourn the passing of my own long-held dreams for Vietnam, dreams of an independent and prosperous nation whose democratic principles guaranteed social justice for all Vietnamese.

We are now in a new century, and much has happened in the years since the communists won the war and reunited Vietnam. Their strict policies during the first ten years proved disastrous. Vietnam, a country rich in natural and human resources, became one of the most impoverished nations in the world. In 1985, the leadership acknowledged its failure and decided to change direction. It instituted a program called Doi Moi, which gave the people more personal freedom to conduct their own lives and enterprises. The result has been dramatic. Finally, after all these years, the potential of Vietnam and the Vietnamese people is beginning to be realized. Not only is foreign investment coming to Vietnam but so are prosperity and self-sufficiency as well.

Unfortunately, Vietnam's increased prosperity has led to increased corruption, especially among government officials. It is everywhere and at all levels. Because it is a one-party state, there are no mechanisms to keep the corruption in check. It is running rampant and threatens to disrupt the entire nation and undermine all the progress that has been made. The only remedy is for the communist leadership to change its attitude toward criticism and opposing views. It should begin by listening to critics within the Communist Party itself. Then it should expand this policy to include people outside the party, even former enemies and supporters of the South Vietnamese government. Very simply, the future well-being of Vietnam depends on opening up the political process so all Vietnamese can participate.

I have now lived in the United States for about twenty years. My children have grown up here and have become trained and educated. They now have careers and families of their own. Our family has prospered way beyond what we expected when we landed here. And so, to my adopted country, I wish to express my gratitude for taking us in when we were the objects of humiliation and revenge by the new rulers of Vietnam and for letting us become a part of this great and generous country.

Life and Times of a USOM Prov Rep

John O'Donnell

In early 1962, I was twenty-six years old and working at Waialua Agricultural Company, a sugar plantation on the north shore of the island of Oahu in the Hawaiian Islands, where I had been born and raised. Little did I realize that by the end of that year, I would be deeply engaged in the most demanding assignment of my life, as a U.S. Agency for International Development (AID) provincial representative in South Vietnam.

The process that would lead me to South Vietnam started with a phone call from Washington in the middle of the night from Hank Miller, a senior officer with the U.S. Information Agency (USIA), asking if I would be interested in a job with USIA in Laos. I had known Hank when he was the U.S. Information Service (USIS) public affairs officer in Vientiane, Laos, in the late 1950s.

The call brought back a flood of memories of my assignment in Laos three years earlier as a young U.S. Army enlisted man. Bob Burns, a U.S. Army captain, and I had been sent to Laos in September 1958 by the U.S. Army/Pacific Psychological Warfare Unit on Okinawa. In Laos, we worked under the direction of the U.S. country team to assist the Royal Lao Army in developing its capacity to carry out political and psychological warfare activities. We worked in civilian clothes and reported to the deputy chief of mission at the American embassy in Vientiane.

Visit with Dr. Tom Dooley

When we arrived in Vientiane in 1958, we stayed at Hank Miller's house while he and his wife, Anne, were on home leave in the United States. Sharing the house with us was Dr. Tom Dooley, the American medical missionary who had been involved in the evacuation of refugees from North Vietnam to South Vietnam in 1954. Following the Vietnam experience, Dooley had established a medical post in Vang Vieng in central Laos and was planning to move his operations to Muong Sing on the Laos-China border.[1] We quickly became good friends with Tom, who took the time to teach me the basics of the Lao language, which proved extremely useful during my stay in that country.

My travels took me all over the country, including visits to Nam Tha and Muong Sing in the north and a drive by jeep from Vientiane through Savannakhet to Pakse in the south. My first visit to Muong Sing was a white-knuckle flight from Vientiane on an Air America C-54, piloted by a "Terry-and-the-Pirates" character named "Dutch" Schultz. After a prolonged period of flying above the clouds in northern Laos, Dutch announced that he thought Muong Sing was down there somewhere and that we would have to descend and take a look. Dense clouds were all around us, which made me extremely nervous. Frank Corrigan, my traveling companion who worked for the USIS and was subsequently killed in a plane crash in Laos, assured me that everything would be fine. We headed down through the clouds and couldn't see a thing for several minutes until we suddenly emerged in a narrow valley surrounded on all sides by jagged mountains, with Muong Sing dead ahead of us. I'm sure that we all had some special help from above that day in getting us safely to Muong Sing.

I stayed with Dooley at his Muong Sing Medical Center for several days. One day, I accompanied Chao Somsanith, a Vientiane-based politician, to visit some villages along the Lao-Chinese border. I remember going to sleep that night on the dirt floor of a small hut in one of the villages, hoping that we were really on the Lao side of the border and wouldn't have any unwelcome visits from Chinese military patrols.

Another day, Dooley asked me to help him and his assistants, Dwight Davis and Earl Rhine, while they operated on a ten-year-old boy to remove a volleyball-sized cyst under his right arm. My job was to hold the boy's right arm so that it would be out of the way during the operation.

The operation lasted for four hours, and I began to feel that I was holding the boy's life in my hands as Dooley worked on him. I was so relieved when he pulled through the operation successfully. So many memories—but I'm getting away from my story, which is about my work in South Vietnam in the early 1960s.

As many of these memories flooded back while talking with Hank Miller, I quickly decided that I did want to go back to Southeast Asia and agreed to take the assignment. Hank asked me to send in my papers, and he would start working on getting me into USIA. A few days later, Hank called to say that my processing for USIA would be delayed because I would have to take the Foreign

Service Exam, which was scheduled for later that year. However, he said that he had spoken that day with Rufe Phillips. Rufe was going to South Vietnam to head up the AID effort to support President Ngo Dinh Diem's Strategic Hamlet Program, and Rufe had said that he would like me to join his group.

Although we had never met, Rufe Phillips had worked in Laos before and after the time I was there, and we knew many people in common. He wanted to assemble a group of people with experience in Southeast Asia who had an understanding of, and empathy with, Asians. Growing up in Hawaii, I had lived, worked, and gone to school with Asians all my life and felt very much at home with them. Rather than waiting for USIA, I decided to accept the assignment with AID. So, on 14 October 1962, one day before my twenty-seventh birthday, my wife, Karol, my two young daughters, Allison, age three, and Shauna, age two, and I boarded a brand-new Pan American Boeing 707 jet for the long flight to Tokyo and on to Saigon.

October 1962—We Arrive in Saigon

As we approached Saigon, I could see the pattern of bright green rice paddies stretching in every direction. The first thing that hit us when we landed at Saigon's Tan Son Nhut airport was the blast of heat as we left the airplane. The next impression was the helter-skelter of people in the terminal, moving purposefully in many different directions, and the hubbub of many conversations with the sharp Vietnamese tones ringing in our ears. We were met by members of the USOM (the AID program in South Vietnam was known as the United States Operations Mission, or USOM) travel staff and whisked through Immigration and Customs to the welcome coolness of the air-conditioned USOM van. The roadway into Saigon was crowded with three-wheeled, human-powered and motorized rickshawlike contraptions called cyclos, as well as pedestrians, bicycles, and Renault sedans, weaving in and out of traffic. Peddlers were selling fruit, cigarettes, and other items along the sides of the road. We were careful to keep our windows rolled up because of stories that we'd heard about Viet Cong agents flipping hand grenades into open car windows.

Beginning My Work with USOM

Once Karol and the girls were settled in temporary quarters, I reported to the USOM headquarters on Ngo Thoi Nhiem street to start work. The newly created Office of Rural Affairs was the scene of intense activity, as Rufe Phillips, the newly appointed USOM assistant director for Rural Affairs was trying to put together a program to support the government of South Vietnam's Strategic Hamlet Program. Only a few staff members had already arrived—Bob Burns, my old friend from Laos who had resigned from the U.S. military to join AID, John Perry (a former Office of Strategic Services, or OSS, operative in France during World War II and longtime foreign-aid worker), Harvey Doughty, a former agricultural extension county agent from Maryland, and Dwight Davis and Earl Rhine, Dr. Tom Dooley's former medical assistants in Laos, who were in the central part of South Vietnam. Also, there was Len Maynard, who had served with the Michigan State University advisory team in South Vietnam in the 1950s, and Bill Nighswonger, a former university instructor. Len and Bill were in the northern part of South Vietnam; Dave Hudson, a former NBC News "stringer," was in the southern Mekong Delta.

At that time, Rufe Phillips was working closely with Col. Hoang Lac of the Strategic Hamlet Program office, Col. Carl Schaad of the U.S. military mission, and their staffs. They were developing plans and budgets for support of the Strategic Hamlet Program in the provinces of the upper Mekong Delta. Rufe asked me to travel with him as he visited Long An, Dinh Tuong, Kien Phong, Kien Tuong, Vinh Binh, and Vinh Long Provinces to negotiate strategic hamlet support agreements with the province chiefs. The province chiefs were all ARVN (Army of the Republic of Vietnam) officers at the major and lieutenant colonel levels, appointed by President Diem.

My Assignment in the Mekong Delta

After a few weeks of working directly with Rufe on the development of the Provincial Rehabilitation Plans, he called me to his office and told me that he wanted to assign me as the USOM provincial representative, or prov rep, for the seven provinces in the upper Mekong Delta area south of Saigon. He wanted me to pay special attention to the program in Kien Hoa Province where he thought Lt. Col. Tran Ngoc Chau (a contributor to this book) had some excellent ideas for combating the Viet Cong. When I asked him what he wanted me to do, he said, "You go out there and work with the province chiefs and the MAAG sector advisers to get the Strategic Hamlet Program going and then come back and tell us what we should do to support you."

With those instructions, I set off in late November 1962 on the most demanding and challenging year of my life. My usual routine during those first few months was to spend Monday in Saigon, making arrangements for shipments of supplies and visits of technical experts. I would also brief USOM, MAAG (U.S. Military Assistance Advisory Group), and Vietnamese government officials on developments and problems in the provinces in which I was working. Early Tuesday mornings, Le Ky Ngo, my Vietnamese assistant and interpreter, and I would go to Tan Son Nhut airport to board a Piper Apache or a

Dornier aircraft for the first of a series of flights to various provincial headquarters. We'd spend the morning and have lunch in one province, then be
picked up by an aircraft to spend the afternoon and the night at the next
province, leaving the next morning to repeat the pattern in two more provinces
the next day. This went on until we returned to Saigon on Friday night.

This routine required a lot of time aboard small airplanes and helicopters
in less than optimum conditions. One of the fields that we used was a short
strip outside of Cao Lanh in Kien Phong Province in the Plain of Reeds. The
Dornier pilot's standard procedure was to line the nose of the aircraft on the
strip. Then he would cut the engines and glide in with the nose up and tail
down like a big duck so the plane would lose speed quickly once it hit the
ground. One morning, we flew into Cao Lanh with some members of the Vietnamese government's Strategic Hamlet Program staff and the MAAG support
staff. The engines were droning comfortably as we approached the field and
then . . . silence as the motors were cut off; the strangled gasps of the first-time
visitors and the alarmed look in their widened eyes were priceless and stopped
only as we set down hard on the runway, giving way to relieved laughter as
they realized what had happened.

John O'Donnell visits an American-supported school in Long An Province, 1963.

Episodes like this provided welcome comic relief during those hectic and trying times. It also helps to illustrate some of the differences between those of us who lived and worked in the provinces and the Saigon warriors who made occasional trips to the field. Physical danger was a constant fact of life for us. At first, I was very concerned about the danger, but after a short while, and especially because we were extremely busy, I put it to the back of my mind. To those who made only occasional visits to the provinces, the sense of insecurity and danger was a fresh experience, keeping them more on edge.

The Strategic Hamlet Program Gets Under Way

My main task during those initial days was getting the various Provincial Rehabilitation Programs under way. Rufe Phillips and his deputy, Bert Fraleigh, believed strongly that a decentralized approach was needed to make an impact at the village level in the struggle against the Viet Cong. Provincial Rehabilitation Committees were established, consisting of the Vietnamese province chief, the MAAG sector adviser (usually a U.S. Army major), and the USOM provincial representative. This committee administered the Strategic Hamlet Program, and the signatures of all three members were needed to authorize expenditures from the Provincial Rehabilitation Budget.

The Strategic Hamlet Program was officially adopted by President Diem on 17 April 1962 as the principal vehicle for dealing with the growing Viet Cong threat. The objective of the program was to convince people in the rural areas that they should, and could successfully, oppose the Viet Cong. To do this, the program sought to create an environment in which rural peasants could hope for a reasonable degree of safety, a reasonable degree of opportunity for themselves and their families, and a just and responsive government. In essence, the government was competing with the Viet Cong for the loyalty and support of the rural population. The Viet Cong were intent on forcing the government to withdraw from rural areas to the larger towns and cities, where political subversion, economic strangulation, and increasing military pressure would lead to total collapse. The government was attempting to reverse this process and force the Viet Cong back to their base areas where they could be destroyed. In either effort, the support of the rural population was critical.

The counterinsurgency activities supported by the Provincial Rehabilitation Budget included the establishment of defensible population groupings (strategic hamlets), the training and arming of local defense forces (hamlet militia), and the temporary care of relocated families and refugees. Funds were provided for self-help projects, such as the construction and staffing of schools and dispensaries, and for the implementation of economic development programs such as the Pig Corn Program and the fertilizer program. Support was also provided for the development of democratic local governments through the election and training of village and hamlet officials. All these activities were designed to convince the rural population that its best hope for the future lay in actively supporting the government of South Vietnam in its efforts to eliminate the Viet Cong as a threat to peace and future prosperity in the countryside.

The Case of the Missing Cement

A major activity during the early days of the program was to make arrangements for the procurement and shipment of materials for construction of hamlet defenses and physical infrastructure and for temporary food supplies for resettled villagers. The movement of these materials provided me with two early lessons in the need to recognize and deal quickly with improper behavior.

In one case, USOM had a major shipment of cement to send to Kien Phong Province in the Plain of Reeds. The province chief offered to supply trucks to haul the cement. He borrowed the trucks from the Seventh ARVN Division headquarters in My Tho. Maj. John Norvell, the U.S. sector adviser for Kien Phong, was tipped off that two hundred sacks of cement destined for Kien Phong Province had been dropped off at Division headquarters in My Tho. Major Norvell and I discussed the problem and decided that we would need to talk with Colonel Phat, the Kien Phong province chief. Phat had the reputation of being quick-witted and sly (his nickname was the "Fox of the Plain of Reeds"), and Major Norvell and I agreed that we had to let him know that we knew what was going on to try to keep his wheeling and dealing within limits.

We decided that we should first verify the amount of the diversion. Major Norvell arranged for members of the U.S. military provincial advisory team to visit all storage locations in the province, ostensibly to check on storage conditions but in reality to make a bag count. The tip-off was verified—more than two hundred sacks were missing.

Then came the difficult part—to confront the province chief with this information. We requested a meeting for 9:00 P.M. at his home and covered a lot of different subjects, making a few minor concessions as we went along. About one o'clock in the morning, when the proper spirit of camaraderie had been established after a few cognacs, we dropped our bomb. We told the province chief that while checking storage conditions in the province warehouses, we had found that more than two hundred sacks of cement were missing and wondered if they had not yet been delivered or had already been distributed.

Phat became agitated and called for his supply officer. When he arrived, the province chief began to chew him out vigorously in Vietnamese. The supply officer, who was in his underwear after being rousted out of bed, was visibly frightened. After ten minutes of harsh tongue-lashing, Phat dismissed the shaken supply officer. Phat then told us that he had agreed to give the division commander fifty sacks of cement in return for the use of the trucks. He said that the supply officer had been weak and had given the division commander more than two hundred sacks.

Major Norvell and I said we understood that the province chief would make such a deal. However, we pointed out that the division commander had his own sources of cement, and we stressed the importance of not diverting supplies from the urgent needs of the Strategic Hamlet Program. Colonel Phat agreed completely, and the meeting ended on a friendly note. As a postscript to the story, the total amount of missing cement was returned the next day, and nothing of that nature ever happened again under Phat.

Price-Fixing and Collusion on Commodity Procurement

Another shady incident dealt with the procurement of foodstuffs, tools, and clothing for relocated families in Kien Tuong Province. It was our procedure to request bids and samples as part of the procurement process. Several weeks after the request for bids had been published, I received a set of bids and samples. I told the province chief about them and requested that he wait until we had a chance to evaluate the bids before purchasing the materials. The province chief, who had agreed to this procedure weeks before, said that he was sorry but that the commodities had already been purchased and delivered to the province. I told him that there should not have been any purchases before we had had a chance to review the bids. He sympathized with our concern but refused to cancel the purchase, and our meeting terminated on a tense note.

Le Ky Ngo, my Vietnamese assistant, and I then carefully reviewed the bids and found that the four firms that had submitted bids for all the commodities had each ended up as the supplier of one of the commodities. It was obvious that the four firms had colluded on setting the prices for the commodities and dividing the procurement among themselves. A visit to the local market disclosed that the wholesale prices submitted by the suppliers were substantially higher than the retail prices in the market. I believed that this was a clear case of collusion and corruption, and I reported it the next day to our headquarters in Saigon.

The following weekend, Rufe Phillips and Bert Fraleigh joined me for a trip to Kien Tuong. We had arranged a meeting with the province chief and the bidders. We brought along identical samples of the materials that we had purchased in the local market, without bargaining, for lower prices than the wholesale prices proposed by the bidders. After the initial amenities, we confronted the province chief directly and bluntly with the facts that we had uncovered.

The province chief became furious, turning several shades of red and talking in a very loud voice. We had made the decision to confront him bluntly because it was well known that he was a crook and a coward, owing his position to the fact that he was the godson of President Diem's brother. We wanted to make clear to him that we would not tolerate his taking advantage of the U.S. aid program to feather his own nest.

After considerable shouting and waving of arms on the part of the province chief, we addressed the bidders and requested that they lower their prices to conform with the going rate in the marketplace. They were obviously shaken and put up no fight, agreeing to the lower prices. We then left the sputtering province chief and the shaken merchants muttering to themselves as we boarded the small plane to return to Saigon. A little later, the province chief was reassigned to be the G-4, or supply officer, for the Twenty-first Division in Can Tho. This assignment unfortunately provided even greater potential for corruption. With large amounts of commodities and cash flowing into the provinces to support the Strategic Hamlet Program, there were many opportunities for corruption. As provincial representatives, we had to be constantly alert to the corruption scenario and collusion. We were the watchdogs for the American aid program.

Relationships with Vietnamese Officials and U.S. Military
Dealing with incidents such as these, in addition to trying to keep things going in seven provinces, kept me extremely busy during those initial months. Despite the incidents described, my relationships with Vietnamese officials were generally cooperative and cordial. The officials at the provincial level had not had much contact with American civilian or military personnel to that time, but we managed to adjust to one another, and they seemed to enjoy working with us.

Relations with the American military advisers at the province and division levels were close and productive. I was very impressed by the quality, motivation, and high morale of the U.S. military personnel in the provincial advisory detachments and at the Seventh Division headquarters. They were all volunteers with excellent records who wanted to be in South Vietnam and believed that what they were doing was important to both the United States and South Vietnam.

In those early days, I was a frequent visitor to the "Seminary," as the headquarters of the U.S. Army advisory team to the Seventh Division was called. The senior adviser was Lt. Col. John Paul Vann, an intense, sunburned dynamo from southern Virginia who was determined to help the Seventh Division become a mobile, aggressive, and powerful force to take on the Viet Cong main-force units operating in the area.

Vann thought he had been making some headway with Col. Huynh Van Cao, the Seventh Division commander, and was sorely disappointed by Cao's performance at the Battle of Ap Bac when Cao failed to aggressively engage the Viet Cong, allowing them to escape the battle scene. Vann was very vocal in his criticism of the performance of ARVN in general, and Cao in particular, and was not hesitant about making his feelings known to David Halberstam and the other correspondents who were covering the war in the Mekong Delta. This greatly upset Lieutenant Colonel Chau, the Kien Hoa province chief, who knew and liked Vann but thought that Vann and Cao should have locked themselves in a room after Ap Bac and not come out until they had settled their differences. Chau felt it was wrong to air these differences with the journalists, who then passed the reports of discord between the two allies on to the United States and the rest of the world.

Zeroing in on Kien Hoa Province

As additional people joined the Office of Rural Affairs, I turned the responsibility for managing USOM's involvement in the Strategic Hamlet Program in other provinces over to them. Rob Warne took over in Vinh Binh and Vinh Long in December 1962; Ron Davidson, an engaging young AID Foreign Service officer, took over in Kien Phong and Kien Tuong in February 1963; Hatcher James, a retired U.S. Army major, assumed responsibility for Dinh Tuong in May 1963; and Earl Young, a former employee of Air America in Laos, took over in Long An in June 1963. This left me with responsibility for only Kien Hoa Province. Lieutenant Colonel Chau had been assigned as province chief to Kien Hoa in May 1962.

Upon his arrival, Chau began an intensive study of the situation in the province. He visited every district town and most of the accessible villages, talking to government officials, paramilitary commanders and their troops, businessmen, money lenders, farmers, bus drivers, captured Viet Cong, women, and children. He read books on the history of Kien Hoa and its heroes.

Lt. Gordon Goff, John O'Donnell, and Richard Holbrooke *(left to right)* discuss the situation in Kien Hoa Province at a Rural Affairs get-together in Saigon, 1964.

He studied the flow of products and money between the towns and the countryside and reviewed past production figures for rice, copra, tobacco, fish, and duck feathers. He discussed the land-reform program with landowners and tenant farmers and the educational system with teachers, students, and parents and analyzed the reports of enemy activities, both military and the complex political-psychological-economic combination.

From May to October 1962, Chau studied the province from every angle. In early November, Chau presented his Provincial Rehabilitation Plan to the joint U.S.–Vietnamese government committee in Saigon. The plan was well-thought-out, daring in several respects, and included details that conveyed his deep understanding of Viet Cong strategy and tactics and what would be needed to cope with them.

Chau's request for resources seemed high to some members of the committee, so the whole group went to Kien Hoa to discuss the matter further. The committee was impressed with what Chau had been able to accomplish with the limited resources at his disposal and decided to go along with his plan. The provincial budget was negotiated and approved, and I was assigned to work with Chau as the USOM provincial representative in December 1962.

As a first step in carrying out the approved plan, Chau held a meeting of his district chiefs and instructed them to start recruiting candidates for the positions of hamlet construction cadre, which would be responsible for guiding the rural population in the establishment of strategic hamlets. While the district chiefs were recruiting people, Chau reorganized the provincial administration. The position of special assistant to the province chief for hamlet establishment was created. This position was at the same level as the deputy province chiefs for military affairs and for administration. A young ARVN major, Cao Minh Quan, who was born and raised in Kien Hoa, was appointed to fill the new position. When the hamlet construction cadre arrived in the province capital for training, Chau dropped his other duties for two days and personally interviewed all the candidates. The persons selected then underwent an intensive training program conducted by the province chief, his special assistant for hamlet establishment, and various other provincial officials. Chau's personal involvement in the recruitment and training of the cadre was critical to their future success in the field.

The hamlet establishment cadre were organized into eleven-person teams and divided into three sections. Three members of the team were responsible for gathering detailed information on all aspects of hamlet life (e.g., breakdown of the population by sex and age, agricultural and livestock production figures, names and attitudes of families with members in the Viet Cong, existence and condition of schools, dispensaries, temples, etc.). Three members of the team were responsible for organizing the hamlet residents into work groups and directing the construction of the hamlet defenses. The defenses usually consisted of a wide moat and a mud wall studded with bamboo spikes and topped by barbed wire, which followed the perimeter of the population groupings. In addition to the team leader, the remaining four members of the team were responsible for explaining the philosophy and objectives of the Strategic Hamlet Program, organizing the residents into social and economic action groups, developing a hamlet charter, and arranging for the election of hamlet officials by secret ballot.

A hamlet establishment team would generally stay in a hamlet from three to eight weeks, depending on the attitude of the population, the degree of Viet Cong penetration, and other factors. When all the basic steps had been accomplished to the satisfaction of the cadre, the village officials, and the district chief, a ceremony was held, usually presided over by the province chief, to inaugurate the new strategic hamlet.

In addition to these basic steps, there were several complementary programs. One was Chau's version of a complaints-and-action system employed by President Magsaysay in the Philippines during the Huk (communist) rebellion. Under this system, the hamlet deputy chief for security was responsible for setting up a regular interview schedule for all the adults in the hamlet. The interviews consisted of three basic questions related to complaints against the government, suggestions on what the government should do to improve conditions, and questions about Viet Cong activities.

The reports of the interviews were sent to the provincial complaints bureau, where they were consolidated and passed on to the province chief who read through them daily. This was a big aid to Chau in identifying and correcting government abuses and understanding the aspirations of the villagers. It was also very useful in providing information about Viet Cong activities and vulnerabilities.

To get his message out, Chau started a bimonthly provincial newspaper to acquaint the people of the province with the things that the government was doing to improve conditions and what the Viet Cong were doing to disrupt the peace. The provincial committee authorized the formation of a provincial theatrical team to carry the government's message to the villages. The provincial committee was successful in getting a five-hundred-watt radio transmitter assigned to the province. Chau commented at the time that having a radio transmitter would be as valuable to the Provincial Rehabilitation Program as one division of troops.

In the economic-development area, schools and health stations were constructed, improved rice seed, fertilizer, and pigs were distributed to farmers, concrete-lined wells were dug, and concrete-block cisterns were built for storing rainwater.

After many months of intense effort, Chau's approach to pacification was beginning to achieve results. The following excerpt is from my provincial report for June–July 1963:

> The Provincial Rehabilitation Program in Kien Hoa has reached a point during the past two months where encouraging indications of the progress of the program are reported daily. Hamlet militia and SDC [Self-Defense Corps—a village level fighting force] are working together to fight off Viet Cong attacks on strategic hamlets, increased intelligence from hamlet residents and defectors from the Viet Cong have resulted in inflicting damage against the Viet Cong, information on Viet Cong units have allowed provincial authorities to track and locate these units and launch successful operations against their bases, hamlet citizens are responding to ever-increasing security by building new homes, schools, hamlet offices, dispensaries, etc.

I have been able to make several field trips through the province and have been impressed by the progress which I have seen. Damaged roads are being repaired and new roads are being built; areas which were inaccessible except by helicopter six months ago can now be reached by jeep with relatively light escort.

The Viet Cong still control or dominate large areas of the province and the threat of Viet Cong attack is still ever present, yet it appears that strategic hamlet residents are gaining confidence in their ability to resist the VC. The effective use of artillery and mortars at night in support of hamlet defenses, increasing numbers of militia to supplement the SDC and Civil Guard troops in the area, provincial operations against Viet Cong safe areas—all of these factors are contributing to a growing willingness of the people to commit themselves to the government and against the Viet Cong.

Chau's approach was paying off. Captured Viet Cong documents reported that the Strategic Hamlet Program was hurting them badly in many ways—young men were defecting, intelligence agents were being arrested, tax collections were falling off, and travel from base area to base area was becoming more difficult.

The program was beginning to succeed, and not because a massive amount of resources had been provided to the province. The total value of USOM and military funds and materials allocated to Kien Hoa from December 1962 to May 1963 was approximately one million dollars, or two dollars per person. There is no doubt that these external resources helped a great deal, but the important thing was that the people were beginning to believe in the sincerity and honesty of their government and their own ability to resist the Viet Cong.

The progress in any area depended upon the ability, honesty, and sincerity of local officials such as the district chief, the village chief, and the commander of the local security forces. Chau's approach concentrated on selecting good people and supporting them and on establishing systems such as the complaints-and-action approach to identify and weed out government officials who did not treat the rural population with respect.

An outstanding example of a successful local leader was Capt. Huynh Anh Hoa, district chief in Binh Dai. Captain Hoa was a native of Kien Hoa and had been involved in the struggle against the Japanese, French, and Viet Minh. He was a short, slightly chubby, happy-looking man, who showed several teeth missing when he smiled. Riding with him in his battered jeep was an instructive experience in applied counterinsurgency techniques. Men, women, and children would smile and wave as he drove by. He would stop to chat respect-fully with a village elder, to speak seriously with a shabbily dressed hamlet militiaman, or to fire a few questions at a passing bus driver. Captain Hoa was a dedicated, capable, and brave man who understood the people of Binh Dai and how to lead them.

Trouble Mounts in Other Provinces

As progress was being made in Kien Hoa, conditions began to deteriorate in other provinces and at the national level. The Buddhists were unhappy with some of President Diem's actions and the favoritism he showed toward his fel-low Catholics. Conditions went from bad to worse as Buddhist monks burned themselves in protest and Diem's Special Forces raided the Xa Loi pagoda. To assist him in quelling the Buddhist uprising, President Diem asked Lieutenant Colonel Chau, a Buddhist, to leave Kien Hoa to go to Da Nang as mayor to try to calm the situation in that city. The move was good for Da Nang but bad for Kien Hoa because Chau's leadership had been a critical factor in carrying out the struggle against the Viet Cong.

In other provinces, the situation was worsening as the Strategic Hamlet Program was overextended, and the Viet Cong had regrouped to strike back. Chau had resisted government pressure to accelerate the Strategic Hamlet Pro-gram in Kien Hoa because of the dangers involved in overextension.

In Long An Province, directly south of Saigon where I also served as USOM provincial representative, the province chief was under great pressure to accel-erate the establishment of strategic hamlets. The province chief, Maj. Nguyen Viet Thanh, was a brave and dedicated officer who responded to the pressure from Saigon by working day and night and urging his provincial and district staffs to move ahead faster.

Standards were not observed as the teams moved rapidly from hamlet to ham-let. Masses of people were relocated, resulting in serious problems for the provin-cial government, and it soon became apparent that the program had been extended far beyond the capabilities of the province to sustain and defend it. The Viet Cong, who had been carefully plotting their response to the Strategic Ham-let Program, took advantage of this overextension and began an intensive mili-tary and psychological campaign against the government-controlled zones.

The following excerpt is taken from my provincial report on Long An province for June–July 1963:

The Provincial Rehabilitation Program in Long An Province suffered some severe setbacks during the past two months. Viet Cong activity

John O'Donnell at the inauguration of a radio station in Kien Hoa Province, 1964

has picked up considerably—concentrating on attacking strategic hamlets, tearing down walls and fences, kidnaping young men, assassinating hamlet officials and in general destroying the morale and will to resist of the rural population. The hamlet militia have not performed well; the Viet Cong have entered completed strategic hamlets with trained and armed militia squads and have encountered no resistance. Why aren't the hamlet militia standing up to the Viet Cong? There appear to be a number of reasons: 1) The militia do not seem to have confidence in their ability to resist the VC—rather than test their ability they are avoiding the enemy. 2) In many hamlets, the militia do patrol the defensive perimeter, lay ambushes and stand guard—but only until 2300 or 2400 hours at which time they all go to sleep, enabling the VC to penetrate with ease during the early morning hours. 3) Long An Province is suffering from a critical shortage of troops—the limited number of troops are committed in great part to static defense (district towns, bridges, posts and security for hamlets under construction). Offensive operations against VC safe areas have been curtailed, thus allowing the enemy a breathing spell to regroup and then strike at known government weak points. Because of the shortage of troops, few are available for reaction against VC attacks at night. The militia have come to realize that they will have to stand or fall alone, which has done nothing to improve their morale.

Essentially the same sequence of events took place in other areas of the Mekong Delta. American reporters covering the war, such as David Halberstam, Neil Sheehan, and Malcolm Browne, spent a lot of time in Long An and Dinh Tuong Provinces, which were immediately south of Saigon and just to the north of Kien Hoa. They saw and reported on the escalation of Viet Cong activity, the deterioration of the Strategic Hamlet Program, and the failures of the Vietnamese military.

We Can't Talk to You Anymore

One day in early October 1963, when I returned to Kien Hoa after a short vacation trip to Malaysia, Maj. John Ames, the military sector adviser, greeted me, saying, "Hey, you know we can't talk to you anymore!" As he noted my surprise at that greeting, he said that he had received instructions from MACV (U.S. Military Assistance Command, Vietnam) headquarters in Saigon that the members of the U.S. military detachments in the Seventh Division tactical area were not to share military and intelligence information with USOM prov reps. By way of explanation, he handed me copies of a couple of articles by David Halberstam of the *New York Times* on the deteriorating situation in the Mekong Delta. One of the articles had the notation in the margin, "Who talked? PDH." PDH were the initials of the MACV commanding officer, Gen. Paul D. Harkins.

Major Ames reported that the top military levels in Saigon were very upset about the American press reports on the deteriorating situation in the Delta and thought that the USOM prov reps were responsible for leaking information to American reporters.

I actually had not had much contact with journalists. I did meet and talk with Stanley Karnow in Saigon and Hong Kong and with Joseph Alsop, who was supportive of the American effort in South Vietnam. Alsop came down to Kien Hoa for a visit, accompanied by Lt. Col. (retired) Charles (Bo) Bohannan. Bo had been with General Lansdale in the Philippines and in Vietnam in 1954 and 1955 and was then serving as an adviser to Rufe Phillips. Other than that visit by Alsop and Bohannan, there was not much press contact with Kien Hoa Province in 1963. The American journalists tended to spend more time in Long An and Dinh Tuong, which were closer to Saigon and easily accessible by car. Lieutenant Colonel Vann and members of his staff were friendly with several of the correspondents. I suspect that most of the information on the deteriorating situation in the Delta came from these friendships and from the firsthand observations of reporters like Halberstam.

What Do You Mean, It's Not Going Well?

There was a tendency for the higher levels of the U.S. military in Saigon to want to report positively on what was happening in the rural areas. I remember very well an encounter with an American lieutenant colonel on the MACV staff who asked me how things were going in the upper Mekong Delta when I was in Saigon for a visit in early fall 1963. I told him that things were not going well and that the Strategic Hamlet Program was beginning to fall apart in many areas of the Delta.

"What do you mean, it's not going well?" he asked sharply, saying that the program could not be falling apart. He pointed at the chart behind his desk, which showed numbers of hamlets completed, numbers of rolls of barbed wire issued, and number of militia trained. He said that the numbers showed that things were going very well and that more numbers were coming in daily. This statistical self-delusion was practiced by many of the Saigon warriors who desperately wanted the war effort to go well.

The United States Decides to Oust Diem

Things were, in fact, going badly in the Delta in fall 1963. In addition, the political situation in Saigon was very tense, sending ripples through the entire country. As prov reps, we were asked by our superiors about the effect of the Buddhist agitation and other political developments on the pacification program and whether the program could be successfully carried out under President Diem.

We reported that the Buddhist agitation was beginning to have an impact at the provincial level. In response to a question on whether the counterinsurgency program could be successfully implemented under the Diem administration, the majority of my colleagues and I said that we had serious problems with President Diem's brother Ngo Dinh Nhu. We urged that he be eased out of his position of power as soon as possible. On the other hand, we were equally as convinced that President Diem should remain in power because allegiance to him was the glue that held the government together.

Unfortunately, our opinions did not carry much weight with American decision makers, as Ambassador Henry Cabot Lodge gave the go-ahead for the military coup against President Diem. I believe to this day that this decision was one of the two most serious mistakes that the United States made in South Vietnam. The other mistake was the introduction of American combat troops in 1965 and the subsequent Americanization of the war. I firmly believe that if President Diem had been able to ease his brother out and get some much-needed advice from a friendly source, such as Gen. Ed Lansdale, then he could have defused (or avoided) the Buddhist storm and set the country once again on a positive course. The complete political collapse and the strong Viet Cong campaign that followed the coup against Diem could have been avoided, and with them the need to bring in U.S. combat troops. The great tragedy is that the Vietnam War, as we came to know it, did not have to happen if Diem had been given some help in working his way through the Buddhist crisis. Unfortunately, President Kennedy's original intent to send General Lansdale to South Vietnam was blocked by highly placed officials in Washington.

The Coup d'État

On Thursday, 31 October 1963, I left Kien Hoa in the late afternoon for the drive back to Saigon because the next day was All Saint's Day, a Vietnamese holiday. After lunch at home in Saigon on Friday, my wife, Karol, was getting ready to go to her regular Friday afternoon French class. I had been hearing small-arms fire during lunch and told her that I didn't think it was a good idea for her to go out that afternoon. She said that such small-arms fire was commonplace in Saigon, and she had no intention of missing her class.

As we argued on the balcony of our house off Hai Ba Trung street, we noticed a Vietnamese fighter plane circling above us. As we watched, the plane suddenly dived right toward us, firing its machine guns down our driveway, and then launched a rocket that hit the U.S. Marine cookhouse directly behind our garage, destroying it in a blast of fire and smoke. Needless to say, we didn't argue any further but dived for cover. We rigged up a makeshift shelter from our beds and mattresses and crawled in with our two small children.

After a while, I left my family in the shelter to see what was going on and heard the sound of small-arms fire and tanks coming down Hai Ba Trung street. I cautiously went down the narrow alley to the street as the first tank rolled by; ARVN soldiers were following behind the tanks or maneuvering along the sides of the street. What I saw next is indelibly etched in my memory. There, walking a few paces behind the lead tank, was Drew Pearson, the nephew of the famous American columnist, with a television camera on his shoulder, recording the whole show for American television audiences.

The attack against the Presidential Palace continued all afternoon and through the night. Howitzers were lobbing shells at the palace from an ARVN training center on the outskirts of Saigon. The shells were going directly over our house toward the palace, which was a couple of blocks away. We spent a very uneasy night hoping that none of the artillery shells would fall short.

After the shameful murder of President Diem and his brother Nhu, a troika of generals, Duong Van Minh, Tran Van Don, and Le Van Kim, took over the government, and we all hoped that it could bring order to the chaotic situation. General Kim was a close friend of Rufe Phillips and the uncle of my assistant, Le Ky Ngo. We went back to the provinces to carry on with the pacification program.

Ambush

Three weeks after the coup, I accompanied Major Quan, deputy province chief for the Strategic Hamlet Program, on a visit to several strategic hamlets in Ba Tri and Thanh Phu Districts in Kien Hoa Province. These districts had been strongholds of the Viet Cong where Colonel Chau's program had made some real inroads. On our way back, we stopped at a Self-Defense Corps (SDC) guard post to see whether the road ahead was clear. The normal procedure was to

Maj. Gen. Nguyen Duc Thang, minister of revolutionary development, and John O'Donnell in a lighthearted sing-along session at General Lansdale's residence in Saigon, 1967

have the SDC troops walk through the rice paddies on either side of the raised road, dragging long poles with hooked tips to snag the wires that were used to set off command-detonated mines in the roadbed.

The SDC troops got about two hundred yards out, with us following on the road, when one of the men let out a shout and proudly displayed the long wire that he had snagged with his pole. He cut the wire as we looked on from the roadbed. There were four vehicles in our small convoy. This included a vehicle carrying an American military medical team that had been treating people in the hamlets we visited. I was riding with the Vietnamese USIS field representative and my assistant, Le Ky Ngo. Tom Ahern, a political officer from the embassy in Saigon, was riding with Major Quan. We all decided about the same time that it was pretty stupid to be standing there because command-detonated mines are usually covered by small-arms fire. We jumped into our vehicles and started toward the next SDC outpost, three kilometers away, hoping fervently that there were no more mines in our path. We were about one kilometer down the road when an ambush was sprung on us from the tree line about one hundred yards away, and bullets started whistling around us.

I yelled at the driver, the USIS representative, to "Go—Go—Go!" Amazingly, he stopped the car, looking very ashen. The gunfire was coming from the driver's side of the vehicle. I kept yelling at him and finally reached over and hit his shoulder. He looked over at me, startled, and said, "Oh! Yeah! Okay!" He put the jeep in gear and sped off. All this time there was rifle and automatic fire going on all around us. Although the jeep had been hit, none of us were injured. (When I later asked the USIS driver why he had stopped the jeep, he said that he thought I was yelling "Stop! Stop!" at him instead of "Go! Go!"— a dangerous breakdown in cross-cultural communication.)

We made it to the next SDC post, which was beside a river. As we arrived there, we saw bodies being lifted off an ARVN landing craft. The district chief had been on his way to resupply a post in a very difficult area. He had been warned by the soothsayer in that district not to go. But he had gone anyway, and the Viet Cong had ambushed him about a mile up the river with 75-mm recoilless rifles. The landing craft was hit directly five times. Of the one hundred people who were loaded on it, sixty-five were killed and most of the others were seriously wounded. The district chief was killed instantly. We saw the bodies being dragged out.

As we were watching, the commander of the SDC post, whose soldiers had been dragging the rice paddies for mines, came and reported that his men had driven off the Viet Cong who fired on us and that they had found another mine, which failed to detonate, at that spot. The next week, when Tom Ahern returned to Kien Hoa, he brought me an Uzi submachine gun, saying, "At least next time, you'll be able to shoot back."

Briefings for Secretary of Defense McNamara

When Secretary of Defense Robert McNamara came to South Vietnam in December 1963 and February 1964, the U.S. military sector advisers and the USOM prov reps from critical provinces were called to Saigon to brief him and other visitors from Washington. Kien Hoa was one of the critical provinces, so I had the opportunity to brief McNamara on two occasions.

The briefings were like mini-National Security Council meetings. For example, in the second briefing in February 1964, McNamara and Joint Chiefs of Staff Chairman Gen. Maxwell Taylor sat at the head of a U-shaped table facing the briefing stage, flanked by Ambassador Lodge, CIA Director John McCone, Assistant Secretary of State for Far Eastern Affairs William Bundy, Assistant Secretary of Defense for International Security Affairs John McNaughton, and director of the Vietnam Working Group, William Sullivan, on their right. Gen. Paul Harkins, Gen. William Westmoreland, and AID Administrator David Bell were on their left.

In each briefing, I tried to highlight the importance of providing security for the inhabitants of strategic hamlets, including rapid reaction by provincial and ARVN troops to Viet Cong attacks. I also stressed the importance of issues such as land tenure and the honesty and responsiveness of government officials. On both occasions, McNamara listened attentively and asked questions. But his questions were not about the attitudes of the strategic hamlet residents and what was important to them, the performance of the military or civilian officials, or the tactics of the Viet Cong, but they were all related to logistics—numbers of this and numbers of that and whether things were arriving on time and in good condition.

McNamara displayed absolutely no understanding of, or interest in, the political and psychological nature of the struggle or of what needed to be done to win the rural population over to the side of the government. I am firmly convinced that this inability to try to understand that what was going on in South Vietnam was much more than a military and logistical problem led McNamara and other high-level U.S. officials on a path to the militarization and Americanization of the war and the eventual defeat and abandonment of the Vietnamese people. If McNamara and other decision makers in Washington and Saigon had stood by President Diem, provided strong support to the pacification effort, and assisted the Vietnamese in restructuring and strengthening the military forces at the local, provincial, regional, and national levels to provide security for the strategic hamlets and to keep pressure on the Viet Cong during the critical period from 1962 to 1965, I believe that the Vietnam War as we came to know it might never have happened.

Rural Pacification Effort Undermined

The situation at the national level and in the provinces continued to deteriorate as Generals Minh, Don, and Kim failed to consolidate their position, and they were replaced by Gen. Nguyen Khanh. Instructions to the field were erratic and contradictory. About the same time, the leadership of the U.S. economic aid program changed when Jim Killen replaced Joe Brent as director of USOM, South Vietnam.

Killen was a tough, abrasive product of the American labor movement who had been an AID mission director in traditional economic development programs in Pakistan, Korea, and other countries. In a short time, it became clear that he intended to do everything he could to discredit and undermine the unconventional counterinsurgency program in the rural areas and to replace it with a more conventional AID economic development program run by more senior officers, experienced in AID's normal way of doing business (or some might say, trying to do business). Killen was an AID traditionalist who wanted to put his own imprint on the program, doing things that he had tried elsewhere. He and other AID traditionalists were uncomfortable with the dynamic, flexible, and, some might say, freewheeling programs of the Office of Rural Affairs and felt that they were completely wrong. His security investigators began to look for dirt and perceived wrongdoing on the people involved in the counterinsurgency effort. Some were accused of being homosexuals, others of falsifying their expense accounts or colluding with Vietnamese officials for their own profit.

One friend, who had decided to resign from AID and leave in mid-1964 before his two-year tour was up, was called in by Killen's security investigators. They told him that they were investigating the Office of Rural Affairs, especially Bert Fraleigh and Rufe Phillips, and urged him to give them any information that he had on misconduct by Fraleigh and Phillips or others in the counterinsurgency program.

This vendetta against the Office of Rural Affairs caught up with me a year after I had left South Vietnam and was working in an AID program in Peru. A security investigator presented me an internal AID/Vietnam memorandum that stated that I had been responsible for serious laxity in the administration and control of expenditure of U.S. funds in Kien Hoa Province. The memo went on to say that one of the factors responsible for this laxity was my acceptance of free meals from the province chief while I was visiting the province.

At first I was surprised that anyone would accuse me of any sort of misconduct, and then I became angry. I prepared a strongly worded response, stating that I had indeed frequently eaten lunch or dinner with the province chief, alone or with other Vietnamese and Americans, during which time we discussed the ongoing provincial counterinsurgency program. I believed that it was an important part of my job to work as closely as I could with the province chief, and this often involved having meals together. I couldn't believe that anyone would put a sinister cast on the fact that we frequently ate together. But that was typical of the type of charges that were made against Rural Affairs personnel in Killen's effort to discredit the counterinsurgency program. In my memorandum replying to the charges, I ended by requesting confirmation that my conduct was in accordance with the highest standards expected of U.S. government employees. I never received a reply but also heard nothing further about the charges.

The Viet Cong Hit Hard

With the breakdown of the Vietnamese government at the national level and the undermining of the U.S.-supported counterinsurgency program by Killen and his cohorts, activities in the provinces began to suffer. Road minings and ambushes increased throughout the rural areas. Many of the most effective Vietnamese officials lost their lives. Capt. Huynh Anh Hoa, the outstanding district chief of Binh Dai District, was one of them.

One day in March 1964, when Captain Hoa was returning from a trip to resupply the men in a post that had been attacked the night before by a band of Viet Cong, land mines in the roadbed erupted in back, under, and in front of the bus in which he and his men were riding. A murderous cross fire from the sides of the road poured into the bus. Hoa jumped out and began to rally his men for a counterattack when he was dropped by a bullet through his forehead. By that time, most of his soldiers were dead or badly wounded. The Viet Cong moved up to the bus and asked one of the wounded men to point out Hoa. They gave the dead body a kick, talked briefly among themselves, and then moved back into the coconut groves, their mission accomplished.

One afternoon, also in March 1964, Maj. Le Huu Duc, who had replaced Colonel Chau as province chief, and I decided to work out our stress on the tennis court on the grounds of the province chief's residence. We had been rallying for a few minutes when mortar rounds started exploding nearby and automatic-weapons fire opened up on the province chief's house from across

A strategic-hamlet defense mechanism using sharpened bamboo stakes to encircle and protect village homes

the river. We thought that the Viet Cong were going to storm into the town, and we went immediately to our defensive positions. After half an hour, the firing stopped as the Viet Cong pulled back. The next week, about the same time, mortar rounds once again pounded the town. One round almost got one of the U.S. military advisers as he was rushing to provincial headquarters.

An amusing sidelight at the time of the second attack was the reaction of a couple of USOM auditors who had come down from Saigon to check on the distribution and storage of commodities. When the attack started, they dived for cover under the dining room table in the MAAG detachment and didn't surface again until well after the attack had ended. They remained shaken and nervous through that evening. The next morning, when we were about to go by jeep to Binh Dai District to check on commodity receipts and storage, a USOM plane unexpectedly buzzed the MAAG house. When I told the auditors what it was, they said at once and in unison that they had to return to Saigon right away because of urgent business. When I asked them about checking on conditions in Binh Dai District, they replied that they were sure that everything was fine but that they really had to get back to Saigon immediately.

Reassignment to Saigon and Return to the United States

Not too long after these two attacks, my recently arrived assistant, Bob Mellen, took over as UOM prov rep for Kien Hoa Province, and I was called back to Saigon to work on some special studies related to the Strategic Hamlet Program and land-tenure issues. A few months later, I left Saigon for home leave in October 1964 with the intention of returning to South Vietnam for another tour. In February 1965, U.S. Marines were put ashore at Da Nang and American dependents were evacuated.

Because we had two small children (with the third arriving in late January 1965) and my family was not allowed to return to Saigon, I accepted an assignment with AID's Latin American Bureau. After one and a half years in Peru, I was recalled to the South Vietnam effort as AID officer in residence at the University of Hawaii's Asia Training Center in Honolulu. I spent the next two and a half years in Hawaii, training AID personnel, particularly field operations personnel, for assignments in South Vietnam and Laos.

Some Final Thoughts

My last visit to South Vietnam was in August 1967 to work for a month with the Lansdale team in preparation for the upcoming national elections. By that time, it was clear that the direction of the effort against the Viet Cong had been largely taken over by the Americans, with emphasis on the military aspects of the struggle rather than on the critical political, psychological, and economic dimensions.

One evening, I had dinner with Lieutenant Colonel Chau, who had resigned from the military and was running for the Vietnamese National Assembly from Kien Hoa Province. He told me how difficult it had become during his final years as Kien Hoa province chief when he was inundated with American advisers and advice. He was so overrun by Americans urging him to do one thing or another that he scarcely had time to do his own job. He said that many of his colleagues were experiencing the same problem. He was disturbed and disappointed that the Americans had changed their modus operandi from supporting a Vietnamese-led effort to taking over the effort as their own.

It was with a heavy heart that I left Saigon in 1967 for the last time with the nagging feeling that the critical mistakes that had been made during the 1963–1965 period, particularly the American support of the coup against

Diem, the failure of U.S. leaders to understand the political and psychological nature of the struggle against the Viet Cong, the undermining of the AID counterinsurgency program, the introduction of U.S. combat troops, and the Americanization of the conflict, had set the Vietnamese and Americans on a path toward failure. The tragedy was that the Vietnam War as we came to know it really didn't have to happen.

Notes

1. For more information on Dr. Tom Dooley, see: Dooley, *Deliver Us from Evil* (New York: Farrar, Straus & Cudahy, 1956); Dooley, *The Edge of Tomorrow* (New York: Farrar, Straus & Cudahy, 1958); and Dooley, *The Night They Burned the Mountain* (New York: Farrar, Straus & Cudahy, 1960).

Destination South Vietnam, 1959

Harvey Neese

My story is representative of the sorts of things that happened to several hundred other young Americans who grew up and matured in the rural areas of South Vietnam in the 1950s and 1960s, attached to a nonprofit organization, International Voluntary Services (IVS). A substantial number of other volunteers had similar experiences and, more important, learned a lot about what was happening in the rural areas where they were stationed, the same areas where villagers experienced continual problems with nature, the elements, and later the Viet Cong. These included crop damage by monkeys, wild pigs, grain-eating parrots, and livestock-eating tigers; debilitating diseases such as malaria, dengue fever, and amoebic dysentery; and harmful insects like scorpions and centipedes existing in an environment with large constrictor and poisonous snakes, including the python and cobra. It was this same environment in which the Vietnam War would later be fought.

Volunteers in IVS were mostly naive and idealistic during their initial years in what was a very strange setting for most of them. However, they learned the language, customs, and even some of the politics of their new adoptive country. Whatever the reader takes away from this chapter, and this point bears repetition, there were many young Americans who accumulated knowledge of the rural areas of South Vietnam and the villagers who lived and worked there. All of us had our unique situations, but we were all in the same country, dealing with the same people and involved in the same simmering conflict. It is sad to say that few, if any, of us were ever consulted by high-level American officials on our viewpoints about what was happening in the rural areas of South Vietnam before the decision to escalate the conflict was made. This tragic decision, to introduce American combat troops and to militarize and Americanize the conflict, led to America's first and only loss of a war in its history.

We experienced the ugly faces of politics and the bureaucracy and saw how good intentions and meaningful work could be wiped out without rational reasons. And we feared that policymakers in the bureaucracy were doing many things wrong as they tried to keep South Vietnam free from communism. We couldn't understand the reasons why these things were happening. We know now that our fears were well founded and were eventually confirmed vividly on television screens in 1975 as U.S. Marine helicopters could be seen lifting off the roof of the American embassy in Saigon with Vietnamese hanging on to the wheels in their desperation to escape.

The late 1950s and early 1960s in South Vietnam were a time of contentment, fun, surprises, idealism, anger, puzzlement, and sadness for the group of young American farm boys in IVS (later, joined by young women). At that point, we thought that South Vietnam could become one of the economic tigers of Southeast Asia in the 1960s and 1970s instead of being engulfed in a war that was destined to be won by the communists. We, the forerunners of the hundreds of thousands of Americans who were to serve in Vietnam, were politically naive with little knowledge of how the U.S. government conducted foreign policy. We were to be ingloriously initiated into this process as America became entangled in what turned out to be an unwinnable conflict.

After living and working in South Vietnam for several years, many of us felt that the slow-brewing conflict was being made worse by the blundering decisions of U.S. policymakers who were in over their heads because of their lack of knowledge of what made the Vietnamese and South Vietnam tick. And most important, they did not seem willing to learn or listen because of their belief that any given set of problems could be solved by American technical know-how. The United States arrogantly blundered into the Vietnam War without sufficient knowledge of the most critical element in warfare—that is, to know your enemy.

One wonders what would have been the outcome of the conflict if U.S. policymakers had gathered together a group of Americans and Vietnamese who had experience in the rural areas of South Vietnam in the 1950s and early 1960s and asked the following question: Should the United States militarily intervene in South Vietnam? And, what if the policymakers had actually listened to the views of these people? What might have been the outcome of the conflict that was destined to destroy countless villages and disrupt thousands upon thousands of people's lives, leaving an estimated three million Vietnamese and fifty-eight thousand American military dead?

Many of us in IVS have personal stories about our work on the village level throughout the rural areas of South Vietnam. In addition, there were people with the Mennonite Central Committee and some missionaries stationed throughout the country. Most of them learned to speak Vietnamese, and they would become very familiar with village life and rural areas in South Vietnam, where the war would be fought and won by the communists.

First Assignment in South Vietnam—1959

After I graduated from the University of Idaho, and without anything surfacing on the job front, I decided to begin work on a master's degree in livestock. However, I was getting tired of the monotonous routine of classroom studies, mixed with part-time work after class and on the weekends as I worked my way through school. So for a break, I decided to apply for a volunteer position with IVS, a little-known private organization that had an agricultural program in South Vietnam. To make a long story short, I was accepted by IVS for a post in South Vietnam, and I left the United States on 23 March 1959 for Honolulu, Tokyo, Hong Kong, and my home for the next two years, South Vietnam. This was my first commercial airline flight, although I had previously flown in small planes to some remote mountain lakes in Idaho. The Japan Airlines plane was propeller driven and must have traveled at less than half the speed of later jets.

I traveled to Saigon with Clyde Eastman from Iowa, Burr Frutchey from Colorado, and Neal Spencer from Florida, who had also been accepted by IVS. We had not known one another before meeting in San Francisco for the flight to Saigon.

First Night in Saigon

As we touched down at Tan Son Nhut airport in Saigon, a remark I made as we departed from the airplane would live with me and become the brunt of more than a few jokes. As I felt the searing heat on my first step down the rickety ladder, I wiped my brow and complained to Burr Frutchey, "The heat from those plane engines sure hits you, doesn't it?" Plane engines, hell! It was the middle of the dry season, and I was encountering, for the first time, the ambient temperature of that part of the world. Needless to say, my travel companions didn't let me forget the remark all the time I was with IVS.

Clyde Eastman and I got off on the wrong foot with the IVS acting director our first night in Saigon. After a meal at the Continental Hotel with the two acting co-chiefs of party of IVS/South Vietnam, Clyde and I decided to do the town. We were given explicit instructions on how to reach the IVS house after our night out. To find our way back, we were to say to the cab or cyclo driver in Vietnamese, "Hai muoi hai duong Le Qui Don," which translated to 22 Le Qui Don street. We practiced the strange words several times before the dinner party broke up. Needless to say, our pronunciation was a little on the atrocious side.

Clyde and I hit the tea houses and a nightclub or two (there weren't many nightclubs in Saigon in those days) till past midnight and then realized we didn't remember the street and number of the IVS house. Sometime after we closed a lot of tea houses (where young aspiring Vietnamese songstresses were on display), we engaged two cyclo drivers who took us for a ride (literally and figuratively) looking for the IVS house. Cyclos are three-wheeled, bicycle-type vehicles, a nonmotorized mode of transportation in which the driver sits behind on a bicycle seat and pedals, and the passenger sits down in a cubbyhole seat in front between the two front wheels.

In our fuzzy state of mind, we weren't thinking clearly, or the task of finding a house in the early hours of the morning in an unfamiliar city whose inhabitants speak a strange-sounding language would have seemed impossible. Because we were feeling no pain at that point, we weren't thinking of the odds of completing our task.

In our slightly inebriated state, we thought we could remember the street name, Le Qui Don, and maybe the number, but our pronunciation must have left something to be desired. As we toured the dark streets of Saigon, joking and laughing, we should have realized that the cyclo drivers were taking advantage of us. We couldn't figure out why these little guys refused to understand us. Cyclo drivers, we were to learn later, were famous for taking foreign passengers for long rides to increase the fares. We were getting the standard treatment for ignorant and inebriated foreigners.

About 2:00 A.M., the cyclo drivers became tired of the game and didn't want to pedal any farther. After some interesting negotiations, consisting of the two of us moving our hands up and down a lot, simulating a language we couldn't understand and demonstrating we knew how to pedal, we talked (hand motions would better describe the exchange) them into changing places. So Clyde and I got in the driver's seats, and away we went. The cyclo drivers probably thought this was the best thing that had happened to them since they had their first taste of sliced bread—two crazy and somewhat inebriated Americans who couldn't pass a sobriety test, agreeing to pedal them through the deserted streets of Saigon in the wee hours of the morning—and they were getting paid for it.

To make it an even more exciting evening (morning), the cyclo drivers began challenging other drivers to race. With some bets placed on the outcome, Clyde and I would head down a selected street, hell-bent for election, as our cyclo driver-passengers cheered us on with great exuberance. Somewhere in the midst of the shouting, laughing, and racing, we cruised past a house that had the number twenty-two on the outside wall. By some miracle (the Lord must take care of the genuinely helpless), in the metropolis of Saigon, we managed to end up on Le Qui Don street. "That's it," Clyde said, "that's the IVS house!" We climbed off the driver's seats and paid the cyclo drivers. They didn't act like they were happy to see us go. By that time, we had a large entourage of tagalong cyclos following and racing these crazy Americans who could actually pedal cyclos.

We attempted to enter the IVS house at that ungodly hour in the morning. The door was locked. After considerable pounding and shouting (we were still feeling no pain), one of the IVS acting party co-chiefs opened the door with a somewhat displeased look on his face. On a somewhat somber note, he asked where we had been and whether we had been lost. "Hell no," we replied, "we were racing," with a slight slur in our words. We got a jaundiced look from the acting co-chief of party, but he did let us in. Because Clyde already had a mark against him (he had been rolled of his wallet in Hong Kong), we were immediately suspect of being somewhat nontraditional IVSers.

Harvey Neese and a Montagnard tribal family with a twelve-foot python killed after the snake dropped from a tree onto their dog at Hung Loc agricultural station

IVS was, in those days, a quasi-religious organization, and all volunteers were expected to display at least some semblance of a religious background. Although none of our crew of four volunteers were out-and-out hell-raisers, to say we outwardly displayed many noticeable religious tendencies would be stretching the point somewhat.

In the Highlands, Studying Vietnamese

The four of us were sent to Ban Me Thuot in the Highlands for language study. I don't know if the instruction was originally planned to be at Ban Me Thuot or if the site was hastily selected to get us out of Saigon. Don Luce and Paul Worthington were old-timer IVSers at the Ea Kmat agricultural experiment station near Ban Me Thuot. They both could speak Vietnamese well, so the four of us had something to aim for in our language study.

During the month of language study, we heard some stories of previous IVS snafus that gave us a lot of laughs. However, we soon found that IVS members in South Vietnam were well respected and well qualified in their technical fields. IVSers on the fifteen- to twenty-person team in South Vietnam at that time (1959) were all agriculturists. They spoke Vietnamese, some of them quite well. Some had advanced degrees and were respected professionally by their Vietnamese counterparts. The IVSers made an effort to learn the customs and language that were somewhat strange to a bunch of recent graduates from American universities. We would soon learn that not all Americans in South Vietnam made the same effort.

Before leaving Ban Me Thuot, I was engaged in several, let's say, unfortunate incidents that made life increasingly interesting for me. But I chalked it up as part of the learning process in a strange land with strange people who spoke a strange-sounding language (monosyllables with a number of tones to distinguish between meanings).

One day, I wanted to take a bath in a more improved atmosphere than the muddy, red-water creek behind the IVS house. The monkeys had a curious habit of dropping huge jackfruit near us as we soaked in the reddish water. A makeshift shower was in the works after we four new team members took on a project to help lay some 650 feet of water pipe from the well to the IVS house area. Running water would be a real luxury, but it was still in the future.

Near the well, I had seen a fifty-five-gallon barrel of clear, clean water. So I sneaked out one afternoon in my swimming trunks, with my towel and soap in hand, and climbed into the barrel. I was able to soak in the first clean water in weeks. After soaping myself down, I began to hear female voices all around me jabbering in loud tones. Wiping the soap from my eyes and face, I could make out the blurred images of half a dozen Vietnamese women, who worked on the farm, pointing at me and talking in a not-too-friendly manner. I thought it better to quickly exit my "bathtub," because I didn't know, at that stage, what Vietnamese women could do to foreigners when they became angry. And these women appeared very angry. To make matters worse, I clumsily slipped on the soap getting out of the barrel and fell on my keister. So my plan to hurry back inconspicuously to the IVS house was foiled. I got back up as the women were looking in the soapy water barrel, gesturing angrily and pointing in my direction.

Back at the IVS house, I was told, between a lot of guffaws and snickering, that I had just taken a bath in the barrel containing the drinking and cooking water for the farm laborers and the IVS house. Talk about being embarrassed.

Another incident involved animals. Wild hogs were destroying an experimental manioc (tapioca) field. Burr Frutchey, Neal Spencer, and I volunteered to spend the night in the manioc patch to keep the wild hogs from eating the rest of the crop. As I had my .375 magnum rifle, I thought I could perhaps bag my first wild hog.

In the middle of the night, I dozed off and was dreaming deeply. Or so I thought. I heard the distinct sound of grinding and gnashing of teeth and an occasional snort. And it sounded very near. In the dream, the noises got louder and louder. Suddenly, I was wide awake. There, only a few feet from me, was the outline of a huge hog busily chomping on manioc roots. There were other outlines of the same animal species moving around near us. I was both scared and surprised at the closeness of the animals. I didn't dare awaken Burr and Neal because I would scare off the hogs, and I wouldn't get off a shot.

I waited till one big, dark shape was in the right position, away from the direction of Burr and Neal and the station buildings, and I slowly raised my rifle in the darkness, pointing at the darkened glob. I then squeezed the trigger, the sights more or less pointing, not aiming, at the outline of the animal. Wham! The .375 magnum sounded like a cannon. Dust flew several feet in the air, and the animal leaped four feet, straight up, and turned around, all in the same motion, but I missed him clean. Hogs were running in every direction.

The next morning, Neal, in his slow Southern drawl, complained that his ears "may never stop ringing" after the hog incident.

The last incident, before leaving Ban Me Thuot, involved a celebration of the anticipated coming of the rains by a Rhade Montagnard village near the IVS house. The Montagnards, as described in an earlier chapter, were indigenous tribal groups who lived mostly in the mountainous areas throughout much of South and North Vietnam.

The chief of the village invited all the IVSers to celebrate the end of the five-month-long dry season. I remember so well the red dust from the red soils in the Highlands. All white apparel turned a rusty red color after washing. It would be nice to see the rains for the first time in South Vietnam, my adopted country for the next two years.

On the last night of the several-night celebration, the chief went all out with a big meal and, of course, plenty of "zuom zuom" (crude rice wine) to drink. I sat next to the chief as he gave his chants and prayers to the gods, I supposed to hurry up and make it rain. In one final attack on the rice wine jug, he ordered a big gourd filled for each newcomer. I had had enough at that point and wondered if I could make it down the hand-carved ladder from the elevated longhouse porch if I drank any more.

With all the noises, chanting, drums, and Rhade music, I slowly set my container on the bamboo-stripped floor of the longhouse (a long, thatched dwelling for communal living). Then without being conspicuous, I reached down, without looking, and started pouring the zuom zuom through the slatted floor. Or so I thought. As I reached to retrieve my container to show I had finished my drink, I looked down, and there was a neat puddle of zuom zuom cupped on the chief's brightly colored robe. As my eyes moved up, the chief and I met in an awkward stare. He glanced down at his soaked robe and then at me. We both knew what he was thinking, even if he didn't express himself other than with eye contact.

Incidentally, before we left the longhouse that night, it began to rain, and it kept up the entire night. I have often wondered how they knew it was going to begin raining at the end of the celebration that night. Or was it just a coincidence?

Assignment to Hung Loc

IVS sent me to the Hung Loc agricultural station, which was some sixty miles north of Saigon on the road to Dalat, after a month of language study at Ban Me Thuot. The work there involved the development of an expanded agricultural and livestock experiment station. To create space for the station, stretches of the jungle were being cut down and cleared for planting of experimental crops.

Mr. Tuc was the Vietnamese station manager. We developed into a good working team, and we became good friends. Mr. Tuc was a veteran of the French Indo-China War, which had concluded some five years before. He was wise, experienced, and cheerful, with a good personality, and he was a gentleman. In later years, I have often wondered how Mr. Tuc must have felt, having to tolerate a young, inexperienced American who at the outset was about as ignorant of South

Vietnam, the customs, and its agriculture as anyone could be. Thinking back, I believe Mr. Tuc treated me more as a son whom he was teaching to survive in a strange world where I was obviously very unknowledgeable.

I was happy Mr. Tuc played along and began to teach me the things I needed to learn in order to be useful. Mr. Tuc was a dedicated manager. He would constantly pick my brain on my experiences with livestock and pastures in America. Perhaps he was trying to determine where a young American, fresh out of college, might fit into the whole scheme of things. In other words, how could I become useful?

My first contribution was an idea to build a trench silo to store silage for cattle feed. (A trench silo is cut into a hillside and filled with forage, enabling vehicles to back into the trench to unload and load.) The farm buildings were built under the French system. Traditional storage for silage consisted of concrete-walled, underground cylinders, six to eight feet in diameter and twelve feet deep. This meant that the silage had to be put in and removed by hand and manually lifted from the underground silos. Because the silos were under a roof, a truck couldn't even back up to them. It was a very awkward and unhandy way to handle anything, much less silage.

The first trench silo was designed by Mr. Tuc and me and was filled with grass silage. It was reportedly a first in South Vietnam, and Mr. Tuc was very proud of it. It enabled a tractor to back up a trailer full of silage grass and unload without manually removing it by hand. Perhaps Mr. Tuc had more positive thoughts on the usefulness of an American greenhorn on his station in South Vietnam. He did invite me to visit his home and wife in the beach area of Nha Trang on the next long weekend. And he even introduced me to some of the nurse helpers at his wife's midwifery clinic. I must have made some headway in meeting some of Mr. Tuc's expectations.

A small cafe in a small town
Maybe a pig and an old sick hound.
The animals with a barefoot cook
Gave the cafe an Oriental look.

    H. C. Neese, 1959, Hung Loc, South Vietnam

Mr. Tuc and I would go to the only cafe in Hung Loc each morning to develop the day's plans over a bowl of delicious pho, a Vietnamese soup that in popularity would be akin to a hamburger in the United States. Here is where I also began to get used to the sights and sounds of South Vietnam. A typical rural cafe at that time, with perhaps a dog or two on the dirt floor looking for a morsel of food, was one of my cultural classrooms. I gradually became accustomed to

A village blacksmith from the Ma Montagnard tribal group in a remote jungle area of South Vietnam

the smoky charcoal fire, the smells of Asian cooking, and the ability to ignore the sanitary shortcomings. I learned to look forward to each day because I was becoming used to my new, adopted land. And I liked it.

First Signs of the Simmering Conflict

On 8 July 1959, I was introduced to the then-silent war that was going on in South Vietnam and that would greatly intensify in the future.

Just beyond a charcoal production village, Thanh Hoa, on the road to Saigon was the town of Bien Hoa. It was about twenty to twenty-five miles from Hung

Loc. At Bien Hoa was the small U.S. Military Assistance Advisory Group, or MAAG. These were noncombat American military advisers. There were a few hundred throughout the country.

On this particular night, the military group was watching a movie at the MAAG headquarters. American movies were sent to the MAAG groups, through the military system, for in-house entertainment. As the showing of the movie finished, and the window shades were being raised, Viet Cong gunfire opened up on the occupants of the room from outside the window. When the smoke cleared, five people were dead, including two Americans. They were the first American military casualties of what was to become a prolonged war. IVS volunteers didn't know if this was the start of a policy to assassinate Americans or if the ambush was just directed at these particular American military personnel. I slept very uneasily the next few weeks because there was no protection from a repeat of such an incident at the somewhat remote jungle outpost of Hung Loc.

I kept trying to make myself useful at the Hung Loc station, as I always had that nagging self-doubt that I was ill prepared to teach the Vietnamese anything worthwhile. I was learning a lot, and somehow it didn't seem right because I was there to teach them something. One day, I suggested a way to plant corn using an old planter that was not made for seed as large as corn. At my suggestion, the Vietnamese mechanic removed the seeding plates, and I climbed on the planter. I told the tractor driver to drive slowly as I practiced manually dropping kernels of seed corn through where the plates were supposed to do it automatically. My demonstration worked. By substituting a farm laborer in my place, we were able to plant several acres of corn by this method. My knowledge quotient in the eyes of station personnel must have increased a slight bit.

One of the directors from the IVS board was in South Vietnam on a visit at the time of the corn-planter episode. He just happened to drop by the station as I was jury-rigging the simplified planting device. He gave me such a write-up in his report that I began to feel that I might just be learning to do something useful after all.

Taking the Bull by the Horns

Another incident gained me some fame with the farmworkers at the Hung Loc station. We were notified that Hung Loc was to receive half a dozen Santa Gertrudis bulls from Texas through the generosity of USOM. The bulls were on a boat in Saigon harbor and had been there for several days. As soon as the Livestock Directorate could get the animals loaded into trucks, they would be delivered to Hung Loc.

Mr. Tuc was happy to get the bulls, but he confessed to me that his workers had never handled such large animals before. He was concerned. So was I, because I had never handled such large mature bulls before either. And these had been on a boat for weeks and probably were in a cantankerous mood at being removed from the plains of Texas.

Our concerns were warranted. The bulls were very big and appeared to be very unhappy at being taken from their ranch home and shipped to South Vietnam. They were very cantankerous. The decision was made to back up the trucks to the large cattle shed at Hung Loc and unload them. This was accomplished after much coaxing and jabbing. The huge bulls bellowed and roared constantly.

Mr. Tuc wanted to transfer the bulls to an open corral that was somewhat secure, but he didn't want to risk his workers trying to drive them from the cattle shed. He was both afraid for his workers and worried that the bulls might make a run for the nearby jungle, where hungry tigers were poised for a tasty beef dish from Texas. So Mr. Tuc came up with a solution. He said I could rope the bulls by the horns in the cattle shed and then they would be tied up until they calmed down and could be led to the corral. Whoa, I thought, this is going to be a new experience for me. Mr. Tuc wasn't trying to embarrass me. He probably thought that because I was originally from Texas and that, of course, all Texans were cowboys, I damn well ought to know how to handle those big Texas bulls.

Well, I had to try, but to say I was nervous would be a gross understatement. I fixed the rope into a loop, and I leaned over the barred sides of the cattle shed to try to throw a rope over one of the bull's horns. Many of the workers on the farm thought they were watching a real Texas cowboy rope bulls. I was very nervous because I had never thrown a rope at an animal in my life. There was a lot of face to be saved or lost in the next few minutes. And it seemed a lifetime as the station workers stood around to watch me in action.

As the good Lord takes care of the down-and-out and the helpless, swish! the first throw of the rope actually landed over the horns of a bull. I couldn't believe it. The Vietnamese workers went wild. Then I got the hang of it and was surprised at my own dexterity. I commenced to put a rope over the horns of each of the other bulls with only a few misses. To this day, I don't know how I did it nor could I ever duplicate the feat again. We tied the bulls in the shed for a day or two until they had calmed down enough to move. During the moving process, two bulls broke loose and must have been heading toward Texas via the nearest jungle. Luckily the tigers weren't nearby because eventually the animals wandered back to be with the other bulls.

After the bull-roping incident, I was labeled a real cowboy by the workers. Several asked me to teach them how to rope, actually believing I was experienced in the art. I, of course, played up my newfound skill for all it was worth

A Ma Montagnard with elephant tusk ivory piercing his earlobes

and then some. I was King of the Hill from that day on with many of the farm-workers at the Hung Loc station. I could do little wrong. My crude and untrained voice must have even sounded like a real western singer at the local school function, where I was coerced into singing a western song. Yes, to the laborers on the farm, I was a Texas cowboy.

Changing Jobs and Moving Around Rural Areas

After my first year in South Vietnam with IVS, I was asked to take another position as assistant chief of party and to travel around to all the livestock stations. I was probably ready for a different activity, although I didn't ask for the change. Gordon (Brock) Brockmueller, a very able chief of party, asked me to take the post.

I traveled to Phan Rang, on the coast, M'Drak and Ban Me Thuot in the Highlands, and the Tan Son Nhut livestock station at the IVS headquarters compound in Saigon. I was also able to make a couple of trips into the deep jungles south of Bao Loc (Blao), an area that was dotted with large tea plantations. The purpose was to visit the mountain tribal group called Ma.

> On muddy rivers, through dense jungle growth
> Drifting along in dug-out boats.
> With two buffaloes, they buy their wife.
> The people called Ma, the primitive tribe.
>
> *H. C. Neese, 1960*

The Ma Montagnard tribal group lived on the Da Oai and Da Teh Rivers in the villages of Bla Da Trang, Kring, Bla Da Dung, Bla Da Kla, and Bla Da Ramit.

There were no roads or landing strips in those days in the area inhabited by the very primitive Ma Montagnards. We were the only outsiders having contact with these people, and we learned to become very protective of the Ma. They were so peaceful and friendly, and we very much took to this ethnic group that had its ancestors from Mon-Khmer stock.

We helped to start cacao nurseries to give the Ma a cash crop. We also introduced vegetables, mainly bean varieties, after we observed skin and eye diseases in many of the children, which could have been nutritional diseases to our untrained eyes. We would travel the rivers in dugout canoes (each made from a single log) and occasionally hike to other villages over narrow mountain trails.

The Ma, in each village where we spent the night, would usually have celebrations in our honor that consisted of drums and chanting songs, some food, and, most important, rice wine zuom zuom. I always felt they were looking for an excuse to celebrate. After all, they had not been introduced to radio, tape recorders, movies, or any of the other amenities of Western life. As a guest, I was required to drink sizable portions of the rice wine from crocks by sucking on long reeds that reached to the bottom of each two-and-a-half-foot-tall jug. I tried in many ways to forestall these celebrations, and the zuom zuom, but to no avail. In resignation, I had to give in because it went with the territory.

I learned, in our trips, how to flick off leeches from my ankles with a Ma "coup-coup" long-handle knife as I traversed the mountainous trails barefoot. I forced myself to eat the half-raw pork sliced from a whole pig that was roasted over a fire without being eviscerated or having the bristles removed. I found out that my aviator-style sunglasses were worth a skinny, little jungle chicken in a trade. And I learned that if I wanted to enter holy matrimony with a Ma young lady, it would probably cost me two buffaloes. I was slowly picking up the lay of the land in South Vietnam. My language proficiency was improving also. I felt more and more comfortable in the jungles and less and less out of place.

The Ineptitude of Some USOMers

Bob Falasca, an IVSer who lived and worked near the Ma area, ran the cacao program with the Ma tribal group in conjunction with Dan Levandowsky, an agronomist for USOM. Levandowsky (he was born in Russia and escaped during the 1918 Revolution) was perhaps USOM's best technical person in the Agricultural Division. He knew tropical agronomy, and he was in the field constantly. He was one of a few in USOM's Agricultural Division with whom IVS could work. Most of the rest were typical USOM advisers who sat and waited for the Vietnamese to come and ask for advice. Along with Levandowsky, Jack Dempsey, fiber expert, and Howard Harper, also an agronomist, had good programs in the field. Les Britton was active in insect-and-disease control in various crops.

Most of the other American foreign-assistance agricultural workers considered a field trip flying to Dalat, South Vietnam's Highland resort city, with a small dab of seeds to deliver. They didn't like to spend the night outside of their protective Saigon. Or, if they visited a station such as Hung Loc, and the Vietnamese station manager invited them out to lunch, which he inevitably did, they would go to the restaurant but eat bag lunches they had brought from Saigon. They never seemed to learn the customs or common courtesies expected in a country like South Vietnam. It was embarrassing to be around some of these so-called experts. One never knew what they would do next to violate a custom or show their ineptitude. They cut up and joked a lot, but seldom would they offer any advice worth listening to.

One USOM agriculturist came to the Hung Loc station and observed me in my bare feet helping the farm laborers plant corn. The ground was quite muddy, and traversing the mud was easier without shoes. His report later criticized an "IVSer at Hung Loc for going native!" Most of these so-called experts were noncontributors to South Vietnam's agricultural development in the 1950s and 1960s, which added to the problems America would find itself in during the next decade.

My job the second year with IVS, or rather what I took on as part of my job, was to locate equipment or machinery that USOM agriculturists had ordered for the Vietnamese but that was still stored in warehouses across South Vietnam. I found tons of it. Much of it was useless because there were no operating manuals or dealers in South Vietnam from whom to purchase spare parts or service. I was appalled at the amount of unused or little-used machinery. Meanwhile, the USOM agriculturists felt they were doing their job by just ordering the equipment with no follow-up after its arrival. I learned that machine shops in Saigon, with primitive equipment, could make an axle for a huge jungle-clearing Rhome disk at a fraction of the cost and time it took to order it from the United States. I learned that because there were no dealers and no spare parts, most of the agricultural equipment ordered for South Vietnam by USOM experts was useless when repairs were needed unless the spare part could be made in-country.

The IVS Years—The Good, Bad, and Uncomfortable

I've been asked many times about how it really was during my two years with IVS. This was a time before the war broke into the headlines, and South Vietnam did not have hundreds of thousands of U.S. military personnel and their mountains of equipment strewn everywhere with their vehicles clogging the roadways.

In considering this point, I must confess that the two years with IVS were two of the best years of my life. There was a vast new world to explore and many things to learn that I did not know existed. I found the Vietnamese people good to work with, and I often marveled at how they put up with us young, inexperienced Americans. This is not to say that all the Vietnamese worked smoothly with IVS at all times. Some were typical bureaucrats who would tell you one thing and then do another, and at times they could be exceptionally deceptive in their dealings.

One key official in the agricultural system seemed to take pride in not signing the paperwork required to pay the workers on time or to enable the Hung Loc station to purchase fuel for the fieldwork. With this Vietnamese official, I made a colossal mistake by causing him to lose face. This happened in front of his American USOM counterpart and the station manager as I confronted him with his deficiencies. When he began to chew out the station manager for not getting the crops planted on time, I told him that the reason was that he had not signed the papers to purchase fuel for the tractor. I learned my lesson on the loss of face after a fatherly lecture by Howard Harper, USOM's contract representative for IVS, who was the Vietnamese official's counterpart. He told me that what I had told the Vietnamese official was the truth but that it was an unforgivable error in South Vietnam to cause loss of face. After that cultural dressing-down, I never forgot my miscue.

The Vietnamese girls in their flowing "ao dais," or traditional female dress, were eye-openers to young American bachelors. The young ladies, as much as anything else, gave us the incentive to study more diligently the Vietnamese language than we might otherwise have done. I was constantly invited to school functions at Hung Loc by young, pretty Vietnamese schoolteachers. I handed out gifts at the end of school, watched school plays, and generally became close friends with the schoolteachers and other people in the village area. I was inevitably asked to sing a song for such groups. My musical talent was severely challenged (near nonexistent would be a better description), so it was not easy either to perform or to try to get out of it.

I believe one thing stood out, and that was that IVS volunteers weren't like other Americans who flaunted their citizenship in one of the most developed countries in the world and who thought they were in South Vietnam assisting an underdeveloped country. We made many friends and few enemies by treating the Vietnamese as equals. The Vietnamese must have had a lot of good laughs at our mistakes, but they seemed to overlook them because we were genuinely trying to be helpful and friendly. And I very much believe we made

An eighty-five-year-old farmer in Qui Nhon in Binh Dinh Province

a contribution in showing them that all people from the United States weren't "Ugly Americans."

I also began to learn what made the rural people tick. I saw that most things important to Vietnamese farmers were the same things that were important to Americans farmers—rainfall amounts, crop diseases, the price of crops, better housing, profits, education for the children, and access to doctors. Villagers in areas close to the jungle had problems saving their crops from animals, insects, and the elements. Wild pigs, parrots, monkeys, and tigers could devastate months of crop and livestock work in a single night. One night, I had a memorable forty-mile-an-hour ride in an old jeep as I chased wild hogs running full speed through a tree-stump-laden, half-cleared jungle. The pigs were destroying our meager hybrid seed corn crop, and with my shotgun pointed through the open windshield, the revenge factor really took hold. But then again, that's another story.

Then there were the four-inch-long dangerous scorpions and centipedes that left a reddish trail when they would cross human skin. The poisonous and constrictor snakes were always present to steal a chicken or sink their fangs into an unwary human leg.

Then there was the superstitious nature of rural folks in small villages in South Vietnam. The Vietnamese and the Montagnards were very superstitious about a lot of things that seemed to shape their lives. This beginning learning process would help me in my future work with rural people in the countryside.

The Ma and other Montagnard tribal groups were a real joy to work with. They seemed to have developed such a trust in us that we often became cautious in our advice because we knew they would do precisely what we asked. I was envious of where they lived, away from the traffic and noise and in the beautiful jungle areas. On the other hand, I felt sorry for them, for I knew that a troubled birth, a toothache, or appendicitis would mean terrible pain or even death because there were no medical facilities available to them.

My Most Memorable Moment in IVS

My most memorable experience as an IVSer had nothing to do with my work and took place on the back of an elephant. Burr Frutchey, another IVSer, Bob Tyson, a USOM health expert (Tyson was from Moscow, Idaho, where I came from, and we knew each other before he went to South Vietnam), and I decided to go tiger and guar hunting on elephant back. The guar, a wild-ox-type animal, had a reputation for being as mean as the Cape buffalo in Africa. Tigers were plentiful in those days in many jungle areas.

We contracted for three elephants from the Rhade Montagnard group, along with three drivers who sat on the necks of the beasts to guide them. The elephant grass was some six to seven feet in height on the way to our hunting area, so traversing it by elephant back was the most practical and safest means. Or so we thought.

All day, the first day of the hunt, we trudged over streams and through the grasslands. We sat partially on top of and partially inside a small, makeshift bamboo box on the backs of the elephants. Our elephant constantly sprayed Burr and me with water and saliva at each stream crossing (because we were the youngest, Burr and I were on the same elephant). The elephant either didn't like Americans or didn't like any humans, we didn't know which. Our pachyderm trumpeted constantly. If we had known more about elephants, we probably would have guessed there was something very wrong with the huge beast that we found ourselves holding on to for dear life. We would have known that he was still half-wild.

At one point, on the second day of the hunt, we had to slowly make our way through a thick patch of thorny bamboo on the backs of the elephants. The lead elephant, which was marvelously intelligent, pulled out of the way large bamboo logs, six inches in diameter, that had fallen in our path. He would respond to commands immediately. Meanwhile our bozo pachyderm kept trumpeting and seemed to give us the evil eye as he constantly twisted his head sideways to look at us with his large eyeballs. The thorns were numerous as we finally got through the bamboo patch in half an hour.

The next obstacle was a very steep hill that the elephants were expected to climb. The smart lead elephant started up the steep hill. The second elephant followed. Our elephant looked at the hill and started trumpeting loudly as if objecting to this most un-elephant-like stunt to make life more comfortable for the hated humans riding on top. He really didn't like what he was being guided to do as he continued trumpeting and flapping his ears back and forward. The crazed beast then whirled around, and the Rhade driver jumped off his neck in the same breath. He knew what we didn't know—that we were going for the ride of our lives.

The huge beast then started running back through the thorny bamboo jungle—full speed ahead. Burr and I had our legs locked in the box on the top. We couldn't have made a quick exodus if we had wanted to. This was one of the few times in my life that I was mortally afraid, afraid of having my eyes scratched out from the thorny bamboo in our path.

The thorns immediately began to tear off our clothes, and our skin was scratched unmercifully in the high-speed run through the thorny patch. We tried to shield our eyes with our arms as the bamboo logs across our path pounded into our arms and upper bodies relentlessly. The elephant traversed in less than a minute the thicket that had taken us a half-hour to thread through the first time.

I knew what I had to do, as all sorts of thoughts raced through my mind with uncharacteristic speed. I didn't have time to calculate how high up I was or what the consequences would be of the first known person from Idaho, in its entire history, to leap from atop a runaway elephant. I started working my legs free from the perch. Then, in front of us loomed an impenetrable mass of a bamboo thicket. The elephant was heading straight for it. The crazy beast was going to try to go through the bamboo mass, I thought to myself. I pulled my legs free and shouted, "Bail out, Burr," as I half-dived, half-jumped off the galloping pachyderm. Miraculously, I landed on my hands and feet on the left side of the elephant. I don't know what would have happened if the animal had turned to the left instead of to the right after my jump. Perhaps I would still be mired somewhere in the Highland soil of South Vietnam.

After the momentous leap, the elephant turned to the right and raced off into the distance with Burr, the cowboy from Colorado, yelling, "Whoa, whoa, you son of a bitch, whoa you cr-a-zy bastard!" The elephant ultimately sped through the rest of the bamboo and into a large savanna and eventually got tired and answered Burr's plea to stop. As it turned out, Burr was too scared to jump off, and I was too scared to stay on. We both survived, except for a lot of scratches and bruises and the loss of some of our clothes. To show our youthful and perhaps misguided tenacity in those days, we again climbed back onto the elephant after he had calmed down, to continue the hunt.

Oh yes, we didn't bag a tiger on the trip. One did stalk my bait, and I was caught in the middle of the night in a jungle fire—but that's another story.

There would be other thrills in my life in South Vietnam, like the time the Air Vietnam passenger plane landed at Saigon airport with a flat tire as Mike Chilton, another former IVSer, and I gripped our armrests for dear life. Then there was another C-47 airplane ride with Mike that ended up with only one engine operating *in the air.* We began throwing out cargo over the South China Sea like NFL linebackers grabbing and disposing of opposing linemen as we prepared for a bumpy landing (we hoped) at Nha Trang airport.

And then there was the day a Saigon policeman began shooting at two alleged Viet Cong terrorists going full speed on a motorbike down a Saigon street. I was walking gingerly down the sidewalk, wondering what all the ricocheting noises around me were. When I finally figured out what was happening, I dived for cover in a dirty sewage drain. These were exciting events, but none matched the ride on the half-wild elephant in the remote highlands of M'Drak.

Returning to South Vietnam—With My Feet to the Fire

I returned to Idaho from South Vietnam in 1961 and finished my master's degree at the University of Idaho in the livestock field in 1962. I contemplated a farming partnership with a high school mate in the southern part of Idaho. But when I left Saigon, I knew I was going to return in some capacity. The place had a way of growing on a person that has always been difficult to explain. I followed in the footsteps of others who had the calling to return to this troubled Southeast Asian country.

I was hired by a new division of USOM called the Office of Rural Affairs. Rural Affairs was created to implement a counterinsurgency or pacification program, which seemed to be the U.S. government's favorite buzzwords in those days. Many talked about it, I was to find out, but few knew what it really meant. Nor did many of the American traditional USOM types support the concept.

Rufe Phillips was the associate director of USOM and the director of the Office of Rural Affairs. Bert Fraleigh was the deputy director of Rural Affairs. I arrived in South Vietnam for my second tour in November 1962. Rural Affairs was still in an organizational mode. Fate then stepped in and guided me into a special program within Rural Affairs.

John O'Donnell, who had arrived in South Vietnam for Rural Affairs shortly before me, was the program's provincial representative, or prov rep, for a num-

A Vietnamese woman separates chaff from rice the old-fashioned way, using wind power.

ber of provinces directly south of Saigon. I was proposed as the person to take over one of the provinces from John. I made the trip down with him and was introduced to various provincial Vietnamese officials. I returned to Saigon to meet with Bert Fraleigh for the first time. He was one of my bosses. As I sat outside his office waiting for him to finish a meeting with someone with a loud, boisterous voice, I heard Bert say, "What about that new guy who just came in, isn't he a livestock specialist? Let's get him up to Phu Yen to see if he can find out why the pigs are dying." I was then introduced to Bob Burns, the Phu Yen prov rep, who was meeting with Bert. I was to find out that Burns was one of the real characters in Rural Affairs and was dedicated to helping the poor folk in South Vietnam.

In a day or so, I was sent on a trip to determine why one-third of the initial six hundred pigs shipped to Phu Yen Province, the pilot province in the fledgling Pig Corn Program, had died. Again the feeling of inadequacy began to creep into my psyche. I had raised a few pigs and worked with them in my animal husbandry curriculum at the University of Idaho. But I was no expert on pigs. I knew I had to display some confidence that I really knew what was going on. I was dealing with a prov rep and a boss who knew very little about raising this popular animal in South Vietnam, but they knew how to assess a person's skills. The Pig Corn Program, I was to learn, was high on the list of counterinsurgency activities to show that the Vietnamese government was interested in helping the rural people in the countryside.

A Close Call with the Viet Cong

While in Phu Yen visiting the villages where the pigs were dying, Bob Burns, the boisterous and heavy-drinking Irishman, and I decided to visit a village that requested pigs just west of Tuy Hoa, the province capital. I don't remember specifically why we planned to drive out to the rather remote village so early that Sunday morning. It was some distance from Tuy Hoa, and it was cool riding in Bob's open-air jeep. As we approached the village on the narrow dirt road through some rice fields, I noticed that no one was on the dirt roadway leading to the village. I remember commenting to Bob that perhaps these people didn't get up as early as most other Vietnamese.

We drove into the village yard and still nobody was visible. Finally, someone peeked his head out of one of the small houses. We asked him where the village chief was. He slowly approached us and nervously began telling us a scary story. The Viet Cong had ambushed a sizable contingent of Vietnamese military personnel bivouacked on a small hill beside the village. He pointed to the hill, just a few hundred yards away. He said all the Vietnamese soldiers had been killed in the attack. And after the attack, the scared and nervous Vietnamese informant told us, a group of Viet Cong had lain in ambush in the rice field we drove through to attack any Vietnamese troops that might come to help their comrades. Apparently the Vietnamese troops on the hill did not have time to make radio contact to ask for help. All the troops were dead on the hill, but the villagers had no way of notifying anyone of the massacre. The informant told us that we were lucky we didn't come half an hour earlier, or we would have also been ambushed by the Viet Cong. We felt we were indeed lucky as we raced back to Tuy Hoa to report the attack.

A Pacification Program with Dying Pigs

The initial driving force behind the Pig Corn Program was Bert Fraleigh and Earl Brockman, who was a cooperative adviser to USOM (oddly enough, Brockman also came from Idaho). Frank Tan, who worked with an American chemical firm out of Bangkok, also was instrumental in the initial concept.[1] Bert provided the main push to start a credit program with pigs and corn as a pacification or counterinsurgency effort within Rural Affairs. A credit program for purchasing improved pigs was very popular with the six hundred families in Phu Yen Province. And if it worked in this Central Vietnam province, it would be expanded. I was to find out later that villagers' being able to purchase improved Yorkshire pigs from the Mekong Delta was one of the most popular programs the Directorate of Animal Husbandry initiated in South Vietnam. The poor rural farmers loved the opportunity to own Yorkshire breed piglets.

After my initial observations, I returned to Saigon and approached the livestock and veterinarian adviser in the USOM Agricultural Division. I expected some cooperation in determining the illness that had killed about one-third of the initial shipments. What I received from the USOM veterinarian was just the opposite. He not only was unhelpful but also didn't seem to know much about the program. I was surprised to say the least. I talked to the chief of the Agricultural Division, who combatively commented, "What's Fraleigh up to now?" I began to realize that the Pig Corn Program was not nearly as popular with the sit-on-their-duffs USOM traditional personnel in the Agricultural Division as it was with rural villagers.

I met with Dr. Vu Thien Thai, the director of the National Directorate of Animal Husbandry, and Nguyen Quang Luu, director of the National Directorate of Cooperatives. Both were very helpful, and this program would be the beginning of a close two-year working relationship.

Dr. Thai assigned to work with me a recent Vietnamese master's degree graduate from the University of Arkansas in animal nutrition. Bob Burns had heard that the graduate was to be assigned to a remote province, and he brazenly asked for him to be seconded to the Pig Corn Program. It seems that some of the directorate people wanted to get the Arkansas graduate out of the national spotlight so his degrees from an American university wouldn't boost him in the ranks faster than others. His name was Nguyen Qui Dinh. Dinh went to Phu Yen Province with me on a second trip as we visited many of the villagers who had received pigs. We were told by Bob Burns that unless the death losses were solved and corrected, the program would not continue.

I found Dinh to be very active and intelligent and sometimes a bit too brash for some of the sensitive Americans. He would joke a lot about the razorback hogs at his alma mater.

We traveled to the villages in Phu Yen and found several possible reasons for the large death losses of the first shipments of pigs. They were transported as young weaner pigs in the middle of the typhoon and rainy season, and the wind and rains are quite cold in Central Vietnam in the coastal climate that time of year.

Another possible cause was that rural villagers were superstitious about the direction pigsties should face. The front of the sties had to face a certain direction, which turned out to be the direction from where the cold monsoon rains swooped in from the South China Sea. It was quite difficult to convince the villagers that the front, or high side, of the pigsties should be protected from the cold winds and rains.

Third, Dinh rode with a truckload of pigs destined for Phu Yen from its origin in the Mekong Delta south of Saigon, and he found the driver washed down the pigs with cold water in the two-tiered trucks every chance he got. Some of the pigs were constantly wet and cold during the two- to three-day trip to Phu Yen Province. The diagnosis of what was killing the pigs was pneumonia and some lungworms. Adequate treatment of the remaining pigs with antibiotics and other medicines, along with better management of transporting the animals, cut the death losses. The Truong Chinh Bap Heo, or Pig Corn Program, was still alive, and it would later be greatly expanded to other provinces thanks to Bert Fraleigh's driving force and the excellent cooperation with the Vietnamese agricultural ministry.

The Pig Corn Program was developed as a Vietnamese counterinsurgency or pacification program to raise the incomes of poor rural families. And, very important, because it was administered by the South Vietnam government, it would hopefully gain some support from the rural people for the government. I was basically the only American associated with the program in the field and was the lone American on the Central Committee of the National Pig Corn Program in Saigon.

I was surprised at the high level of interest that existed in the villages for this program. Weaner pigs were bought and quarantined in the Mekong Delta by the Directorates of Cooperatives and Animal Husbandry. Pigs would be vaccinated for prevalent diseases and fattened on nutritious rations near My Tho in the center of the largest pig-raising area in the Mekong Delta. In the provinces, Animal Husbandry and Cooperatives would select poor villagers who requested and were eligible for purchasing pigs. Loans were made to the poorer villagers for usually three pigs, two females and one boar. Loan recipients also could buy on credit a certain number of bags of U.S. PL480 surplus corn. Corn was given to the South Vietnamese government under the American assistance

A Vietnamese farmer plowing a rice paddy with water buffaloes

program. South Vietnam agencies were allowed to sell it to generate funds to support the Pig Corn Program.

Eight bags of cement were given free for the pigsty floor, along with a few sheets of metal roofing, if available, to be used for roofs for the sties. The Directorate of Cooperatives and the Farmers Associations provided loans to participating villagers. Vietnamese animal-husbandry technicians treated sick pigs and would replace sick or puny pigs and those that died within a three-month time period.

As stated, the significance of the Pig Corn Program was that it was implemented by the Vietnamese government with a minimum of observable American involvement, and it was very popular with poor, rural villagers. As one traveled farther from Saigon, the cost of improved Yorkshire pigs, as sold in the program, became very costly. In Central Vietnam, there were few improved Yorkshire hogs and hardly any raised by lower-income rural people. The high cost of the pigs was the main factor. Vietnamese pig dealers hadn't quite figured out how to move young piglets to Central Vietnam without high mortality along the way. It just wasn't a paying proposition. We were warned by local pig dealers that we couldn't ship pigs to the far northern reaches of South Vietnam without unacceptable losses. Because of the popularity of the program, we aimed to prove them wrong. And we did.

An American and a Vietnamese Roaming the Countryside

In 1963, the projection was to sell twenty-five thousand pigs on credit through the Pig Corn Program. Over 60 percent of the program was realized, or about fifteen thousand pigs were distributed. Many of these recipients were in provinces distant from Saigon, such as Quang Tri, Quang Nam, Thua Thien, and Quang Ngai, the provinces farthest north of the Mekong Delta where pigs were bought and quarantined.

Dinh and I were on the Central Committee of the Pig Corn Program, governing all decisions. We traveled constantly throughout South Vietnam in an old jeep, visiting villages that had received pigs with a loan or that were requesting to be in the program. The homemade, painted license plate of the jeep driven by Dinh was numbered "3535," which in Vietnamese has a double meaning with some jest.

We both wore "ao ba bas," the traditional pajamas-type clothes one would see in the rural areas of South Vietnam. Dinh also made me wear a conical hat "so the Viet Cong," he said, "couldn't readily see your gringo blond hair and bluish eyes." These disguises were done for security reasons because the Viet Cong were becoming increasingly brave in their attacks on government installations, programs, and people. About the same time, President Diem was assassinated, giving the Viet Cong an opportunity to take advantage of the unstable political conditions.

Dinh was superb in working with rural villagers in the countryside, even though he had a master's degree. I mention this because higher, formal degrees in South Vietnam usually meant a person didn't get his or her hands dirty. Dinh was different. He came from modest beginnings and understood how villagers thought and their many superstitions. I also grew up during this period, as far as learning about Vietnamese rural life. My Vietnamese language proficiency was continuing to improve, and I was becoming quite proficient in talking pig talk with the villagers.

Dinh and I would put on seminars to introduce the program in provinces. We would invite participants from the various Vietnamese and American organizations (usually one IVSer, a USOM prov rep, or both if in the province). Dinh would lead off in Vietnamese, and I would translate into English. Dinh was perfectly capable of presenting in both languages, but we thought we could be more effective (and less fatigued) if we split the talking chores. We traveled in the provinces between twenty and twenty-five days a month during the Pig Corn Program years.

Some Mishaps in the Pig Program

Dinh and I, to put it bluntly, screwed up at times as we traveled from province to province in the Pig Corn Program. One incident, I remember vividly, happened within sight of the Tuy Hoa airstrip in Phu Yen Province. I say airstrip, and not airport, because there wasn't even a building there at the time. Air Vietnam flew into Tuy Hoa airstrip once or twice a week, and arrivals and departures were rather erratic and unscheduled. Passengers had to be alert to be assured of boarding their plane.

There was a village within sight of the runway that we planned to visit as we waited to see if Air Vietnam would arrive. Our usual routine was to inquire if there were any sick pigs and then advise the farmers or treat the animals. One old farmer stepped forward and led us to his pigsty. He called us "bac si," or doctor, referring to us as veterinarians.

In his pigsty lay a very sickly looking animal with apparent digestive problems and diarrhea. As we began examining the pig, we heard the roar of the Air Vietnam flight overhead, and it was coming in for a landing. Dinh suggested we give the pig some sulfa medicine. I grabbed the squealing pig and held open its mouth so Dinh could drop in a sulfa pill. Dinh opened the medicine bottle and found only the large pills used for cattle. I told Dinh we should break the pills into several pieces. As we looked down the runway, passengers were already lined up to board the plane. We both agreed we had to hurry, so we poked one of the large, round sulfa pills down the pig's throat. As I held the animal, he rolled his eyes backward, coughed a couple of times, and succumbed. Right there. He had choked to death on the large pill. The Vietnamese farmer began to gasp, "Bac si, con heo co chet, khong?" or "Doctor, is the pig dead?" The old farmer almost had tears in his eyes as we affirmed his worst fears.

We apologized two or three times and promised the farmer that we would replace the pig in the next shipment, free. Then we raced for the airplane. Our "bac si" label suffered greatly in that village, I can attest to that.

Another incident involved feeding corn to the pigs. Now, all swine like corn, right? So I had the opportunity to prove it. I went into a village and asked a farmer what he fed his pigs. He told me what he was feeding, but he said the con heo My, or American pigs, wouldn't eat corn. I told a joke in Vietnamese about how every American pig eats corn, and lots of it. When he insisted the three improved pigs wouldn't eat corn, I asked him to bring me some corn. Most of the crowd were shaking their heads in the negative, backing the farmer's story.

I took a small pail of corn and emptied it into the feed trough. The three pigs raced for the trough as if they were ready to eat anything. The pigs suddenly stopped and sniffed the corn. Just sniffed; they never ate a single kernel. I stood there kind of dumbfounded and stupid at the same time. I left with my tail between my legs. I later found out the reason why the pigs didn't eat the dry corn. Vietnamese liked to cook their pig feed, although we sent out information telling the farmers to feed pigs the corn raw and uncooked. These pigs never had dry, uncooked food before and didn't know what to do with those hard kernels. So I learned another important lesson from a Vietnamese peasant farmer.

USOM *and the Pig Program*

In 1963, more than fifteen thousand pigs were sold on credit through the Pig Corn Program. In 1964, somewhere between thirty thousand and forty thou-

Vietnamese women in a rural area planting rice one plant at a time

sand pigs were distributed in the very popular program developed within the counterinsurgency concept.

It was somewhat puzzling as I was working on this important pacification effort to observe the inconsistencies in the technical people who should have been concerned with the program in the USOM Agricultural Division. In my two years with the program, only two USOM agricultural people displayed any interest in the Pig Corn Program. Earl Brockman and his successor, Henry Gerber, both co-op specialists, handled all the paperwork to transfer U.S. PL480 surplus corn to South Vietnam from the United States. The livestock people in USOM or the director of the USOM Agricultural Division didn't seem to want to become involved with the program. From what I learned, they had a vendetta going against Bert Fraleigh, my boss. It was awkward for me because I was assigned to the Rural Affairs Program but was working on an agricultural program with little interest displayed by the USOM technical agricultural people. I had expected more cooperation.

The Agricultural Division did try to take credit, when possible, without actually becoming involved. One example was when I met the USOM veterinarian escorting a half-dozen navy officers to the small snack bar in the main USOM building. The USOM veterinarian and livestock adviser bumped into me unexpectedly and awkwardly introduced me to the navy veterinarians. After the navy vets (mostly meat inspectors) learned I was involved with the Pig Corn Program, they began to grill me on all aspects of the operation. It must have become apparent that I knew much more about what was going on than the USOM veterinarian adviser did. The officers said they were going to take a trip and look at some pigs in the provinces and then meet with Dr. Thai of the Directorate of Animal Husbandry on a certain date. They asked me to attend.

After their trip was completed, I went to the meeting, and the leader of the navy veterinarian group started the conversation by saying, "I can tell you people that if we hadn't seen it with our own eyes, we wouldn't have believed it. That you can ship thousands of young pigs through several climatic changes, over mountain ranges, in monsoon and hot seasons, and do it with the small percentage of losses is simply amazing. We are impressed." After that introduction, we didn't know quite what to say because visiting firemen usually didn't learn enough about a program to give a fair assessment, or they spent most of their time in Saigon, afraid to visit the provinces. We were pleased with the assessment even though it didn't put any feathers in our hats with the USOM Agricultural Division.

The Pig Corn Program was a success to those who cared to look at it with an objective evaluation. We had our detractors in the traditionalism of the USOM Agricultural Division. You can feel it in your bones when you know you are involved with a program that is benefiting sizable numbers of people and that generates enthusiasm among the recipients. I wore my nickname of ong heo, or Mr. Pig, with pride throughout South Vietnam. As the program got larger, I was able to hire Jim Green, a former IVSer, to assist with the program. Jim spoke Vietnamese well and knew agriculture better than I did. He would travel to certain provinces with a Vietnamese associate and report on the status of the program in areas that Dinh and I couldn't visit. It gave us better control over how the program was going in far-flung provinces.

An unsung hero of the Pig Corn Program was Bob Burns in Phu Yen Province. Bob gave us lots of support in the early stages when the program could have been terminated if death losses weren't reduced. At one point, Bob was able to beg, borrow, or steal several thousand dollars to pay for a hog-cholera vaccination program because local pigs were dying, thereby infecting the improved pigs from the Pig Corn Program.

I remember well the C-46 cargo plane landing at the Tuy Hoa airstrip that brought Burns's piasters in a blue plastic bag. (The plane almost hit a farmer and his buffalo cart as they meandered across the runway.) Being somewhat naive in those days, I didn't know enough to figure out that it was the CIA that had dropped off the cash. Bob had lots of connections.

Bob had a way of getting a whole village of kids chanting slogans or about anything he decided to lead them in. His favorite was to start chanting, as he led the passel of kids down the narrow village trails, "Vietnam Cong Hoa Muon Nam" (Republic of Vietnam for Ten Thousand Years). At times, he would shout out my name and lead the kids in, "Harvey Neese, Harvey Neese, Har—vey Neese." There was no one in Rural Affairs who was as flamboyant or more dedicated to helping the Vietnamese than Bob Burns. And he was a real showman.

North Vietnamese Copycat Pig Program

The Ben Hai River separated Quang Tri, the northern-most province in South Vietnam, from North Vietnam. On one of my trips to Quang Tri, I walked onto the bridge separating the two countries to converse with the North Vietnamese guard who walked back and forth to the middle of the bridge. I told him I was a Nguoi Duc, or German, because I was afraid he wouldn't talk to me if he knew I was an American.

When he asked me what I was doing in Quang Tri, I told him I worked with the national Pig Corn Program. After explaining a bit about the program, the guard said that the North had a similar program in the provinces along the Ben Hai River. It sounded very similar to our Pig Corn Program. Afterward we would obtain a brochure the North Vietnamese had distributed to villagers.

It was a replica of a brochure with Disney-type cartoon characters that Dinh and I had made up, explaining the dos and don'ts of the program. We felt pretty good at the news that the North Vietnamese thought it such a good program that they were copying it.

Viet Cong Close By in Quang Ngai

Quang Ngai Province, in Central Vietnam, was a hotbed of Viet Cong activity. Dinh and I spent considerable time with the Pig Corn Program in Quang Ngai because of its popularity and counterinsurgency implications. On one visit, we had been invited to a particular village by the village chief because the people wanted to get in on the program.

We met the village chief outside the village, and he walked with us to meet some of the interested villagers. In the village yard was a flag pole with a flag emblem I couldn't recognize because it was kind of folded over. I asked the chief what kind of flag it was. He kind of pooh-poohed it and said something in Vietnamese to the effect, "That's political, our interest is pigs and the economic side—that's what's important to us."

Later I would see the Viet Cong flag emblem as the wind picked up. I began to suspect that many, if not most, of the villagers we worked with in the program felt the same way. They only wanted help in growing better pigs and rice and then to be left alone. This, I believe, was the desire of the majority of rural people we met. Somehow, the side we supported in the conflict never really understood this important part of rural South Vietnam life. This was especially true of the next director of the USOM economic assistance program in South Vietnam. His actions would lead to a low point in the counterinsurgency program and in many of our lives.

The Ballad of James Killen

His name was Mr. Killen
He was one of Taylor's lads
And he was faithfully promoted
By those statey petatey cats
   Statey petatey cats
   Statey petatey cats
And he was faithfully promoted
By those statey petatey cats.

   H. C. Neese, 1965, song lyrics

Little did I know that ominous political storm clouds were gathering on the horizon and would soon engulf me and other Rural Affairs representatives. The

cloud was in the form of the new USOM director. James Killen was supposedly brought in to clean up USOM, we had heard, whatever that meant. He
would do much more. He would destroy the original concept of Rural Affairs
as a Vietnamese counterinsurgency program, implemented by them with few
Americans involved. We were available for assistance, but the concept was not
originally set up for Americans to run the program. Killen would destroy this
concept with his bull-in-the-china-shop approach. Along with it, he and USOM
Mission Internal Security (MIS) goons would try to dirty the reputations of
many of us who were involved with Rural Affairs before he made his infamous
entrance into South Vietnam.

My first inkling that something strange was going on was when another
desk was put in my office in the USOM Rural Affairs complex. The explanation
was that there was a shortage of space, and the Vietnamese personnel in USOM
needed a place to finish some accounting work. Besides, I was in Saigon for
only five or six days a month. The Vietnamese accountant employee of USOM
was busy on his calculator for days. I was out of the office most days, but each
time I returned, the accountant would be working away on his calculator.

One day, I asked him what kind of accounting he was doing. He said he was
calculating all the days Rural Affairs personnel collected per diem or living
expenses in the provinces away from Saigon. Per diem in those days was a paltry nine dollars. This included money to be used for hotels, food, and laundry.
In some places it was adequate; in others, it wasn't, but it certainly wasn't an exorbitant amount in those days. When asked whether he had calculated my per diem,
he searched in his records and stated that I had been in the provinces between
twenty and twenty-five days per month average for the past eighteen months.

I had never worked for a government bureaucracy before so didn't think
much about how it operated. However, little did I know, at that time, that this
USOM administration had launched a plan to wipe out Rural Affairs as it was
originally organized and to tarnish the names of as many people connected
with the program as was convenient and possible.

> I don't like pigs or windmills
> Once more I don't like corn
> And anyone working on these two
> I'm gonna trim his horns.
>   I'm gonna trim his horns
>   I'm gonna trim his horns
> And anyone working on these two
> I'm gonna trim his horns.
>
> H. C. Neese, 1965, song lyrics

Two young Vietnamese children

A USOM auditor had an apartment in the same building as I did on 145 Yen Do street in Saigon. We occasionally rode the USOM van to work together and we became somewhat acquainted. One day when I was in Saigon, Bert Fraleigh asked me to come to his office at a certain time for a meeting. As I waited outside the office area to meet Bert, the USOM auditor sat down beside me. I had heard that he was no admirer of Bert or Rural Affairs, so I wondered what he was doing there and why I was invited to the meeting. We exchanged greetings, and Bert's pretty secretary, Co Nga, opened the door for us to enter. As we sat down, the auditor almost floored me with his opening remarks.

"I'm going to tell you something which I will deny if ever asked to repeat it outside this room," he began. "I want you to know that someone in the USOM Mission is out to get Harvey." After our total surprise, he explained what he meant. It seems the MIS people had charged me with going to the Catholic Relief Services and demanding powdered milk, brought in for orphanages, for feeding the thousands of quarantined pigs at My Tho. Also, I had purportedly given permission to the Vietnamese to transfer PL480 corn from Section 201 to 202 (or vice versa) for use in a Montagnard Pig Corn Program. One section was PL480 corn that was supposed to be used for human food, the other for animal feed. There was no difference in the corn, only the numbers on the bags were different, and the bureaucracy said they couldn't be interchanged without stiff penalties.

I was astonished at the accusations because I didn't know what he was talking about. The auditor said he had personally visited the Catholic priest heading up the Catholic Relief Services and asked him if he knew me or if I had ever demanded powdered milk. The priest told the auditor that he had never met me and that I had never contacted him about powdered milk. The auditor said when he reported his conversation to the controller's office, it refused to drop the charges. He continued, saying that employees in the controller's office told him they had the minutes of a meeting stating I had given permission to illegally transfer PL480 corn. Only Bert Fraleigh or someone above his rank could authorize the transfer. I was charged with violating a bureaucratic paper transaction. I was to later learn that USOM Director Killen was really trying to get at Bert Fraleigh, and I was just a pawn to be used, destroyed, and thrown away in the process.

I went to the USOM controller who supposedly had the minutes of the meeting during which I had unlawfully authorized the transfer of corn. I asked the short, dumpy USOM controller to show me the minutes of the meeting that he had. He reluctantly retrieved the document and handed it to me. It was in Vietnamese. I could read it as it stated, "Ong Neese se hoi," or "Mr. Neese will ask," Fraleigh on the possibility of transferring corn to the Montagnard Pig Corn Program. It showed I had not authorized the transfer. I then asked the controller to call his best Vietnamese interpreter there to read the document. The interpreter read it just as I did. The controller sort of stared at me with a blank look, but the charges were never dropped. Somebody was out to get me all right, and I was scared and mad at why it was being done in such an underhanded manner.

The next charge that was made against me came out of the review of per diem checks by the Vietnamese accountant who was sharing my office. I had been with the Pig Corn Program for eighteen months. I averaged some twenty to twenty-five days a month in the provinces, which gave me a minimum of 360 days in the field to that point. One day, amounting to just nine dollars out of $3,240 per diem I had received, raised the eyebrows of the investigators. An airline ticket from Saigon to Ban Me Thuot was illegible. The day the ticket recorded that I left Ban Me Thuot was hard to read—whether it was on, say, the twelfth or the thirteenth. Because the exact date of departure couldn't be read, the assumption was that I left a day early, thereby cheating the U.S. government out of nine whole dollars.

This was unbelievable, and it was happening to me. Was this a USOM-inspired investigation or perhaps something that was learned from the adversaries we were trying to defeat, the communists? I asked myself over and over again, What kind of Americans would prostitute themselves and do this to an innocent countryman?

I found out that other Rural Affairs field personnel were having to answer to phony, trumped-up charges as well. The USOM well driller was charged with turning in phony receipts (USOM later had to reimburse him thousands of dollars he had spent of his own money on the program to keep it going). Another Rural Affairs prov rep was charged with authorizing questionable expenditures in a province because he had frequent lunches with the province chief.[2] The ugliest was a charge of homosexuality against three Rural Affairs province reps. Two of the three had families in Saigon. In the halls of the U.S. State Department, I was told by a USOM official who had seen the classified paperwork that the three were watched daily with binoculars as they sat on the veranda at one of the men's apartments. During the time the spying went on, the document reportedly stated, not once did the three men have female companions (prostitutes) as they relaxed after work. Because of this, the document purportedly surmised they were gay (an offense punishable by dismissal in those days).

These charges dragged on for months, directed against old Rural Affairs personnel. I would later find out when I went to Washington on home leave that eight-by-ten-inch photographs had been made of the airline ticket on which the date of the day I left Ban Me Thuot couldn't be deciphered, along with a photograph of the per diem voucher I had filled out for the trip (copy machines were not yet available). These would be shown to me in Washing-

Children of workers at one of the livestock experiment stations in South Vietnam

ton by USOM security personnel with the explanation that they understood what was going on in the South Vietnam USOM office, but they were helpless to do anything about it. In other words, let stupid people do stupid things but don't interfere with the system or you might be next or get a bad evaluation.

These are examples of the lengths to which some officials of the U.S. government were willing to go to discredit the Office of Rural Affairs and its programs and personnel. Once the people making these decisions were in place, getting them removed before they could do too much damage was out of the question. They just stayed and screwed up whatever they could screw up in the process. Or they didn't do anything but take up valuable space in the meantime. On a grading scale of A to F, much of the USOM, including the director's office and the Agricultural Division, would have gotten an F from any objective observer. And these were the people that were sent to South Vietnam to counter the ever-ingenious, dedicated-to-their-cause Viet Cong?

> The apple of my eye
> Is Aggie AID.
> I like to see them jump real high
> And kiss my ass for me.
>   And kiss my ass for me
>   And kiss my ass for me
> I like to see them jump real high
> And kiss my ass for me.
>
>   *H. C. Neese, 1965, song lyrics*

The USOM Agricultural Division personnel were turning handsprings because Rural Affairs, as it was originally conceptualized, was being dismantled by communist- and Mafia-type actions of the U.S. government. The original Rural Affairs personnel were under siege, not by a communist government but by the U.S. government. As amazing as it may seem, this was happening to dedicated Americans in 1964 in South Vietnam by their own kind.

Personnel in the Agricultural Division of USOM were making snide remarks in their glee at what was happening to Rural Affairs. I was the only one in Rural Affairs who also was required to try to work with the Ag Division. At times it would get to me—such as on those occasions when I would see a certain agricultural adviser in the community church in Saigon on Sundays. With his deep Southern drawl, he talked as if he might have been a part-time preacher in the past. Whenever we met, he would needle me about the attack on Rural Affairs by the USOM administration by asking seemingly innocent questions such as, "Well, Harvey," he would drawl with a smirk on his face, "how is Rural

Affairs these days?" In a moment of frustration and anger in the churchyard one Sunday morning, I shot back, "Not bad, I had a couple of 'em this week!" He and his wife almost fell over from shock. However, he never discussed Rural Affairs or rural affairs with me after that.

The final straw for me, as a U.S. government employee, was done in collaboration with a "friend" in the Agricultural Division who was interviewed by the MIS people. He gave them what might be construed as insignificant information about an employee (me) under ordinary circumstances. But when the MIS people were after you, there wasn't a straw they wouldn't grasp. The acquaintance reportedly told them such things as I didn't take direction well and ran around the provinces unsupervised—a sort of prima donna. Until that point, I didn't know how envious the former friend was of the freedom my boss gave me, plus a higher pay grade.

By some stroke of fate, the classified report of the interview reached the desk of Bert Fraleigh. That evening Bert visited the acquaintance at his residence (I was in the United States on home leave) and asked him if what was in the report was what he had told the MIS goons.

He denied having given the information to MIS as stated, and he told Bert he had been misquoted. Bert then asked him to go to the MIS people and report to them the errors. He said he would. He then condemned Bert for carrying a classified document outside the office safe area, which was considered a breach of security.

Washington on Home Leave

In Washington on home leave in early 1965, I was awaiting word on whether I would return to Saigon. A terse cable finally arrived from USOM stating that "my presence was no longer needed in Saigon." The goon squad of Jim Killen had gotten me as well as others. The people in AID/Washington tried to get me to ignore the trumped-up charges, the photographs of my "misdeeds," and the fact that I was being run out of South Vietnam after helping to develop one of the most successful efforts in the pacification program. I couldn't forget this affront to my honesty and integrity. I also thought of how most of us in Rural Affairs had risked our lives, at one time or another, for what we thought was a worthy cause by the U.S. government. And to be treated like this by a misplaced misfit like Jim Killen who was allowed to do his dirty work was unbelievable.

The way things evolved in South Vietnam, under the USOM administration, Secretary of Defense Robert McNamara, and the military conventionalists, it was almost as if it had been planned to be a losing cause. Nobody wanted to intervene or look for better and more effective ways when things went awry. Even Killen, the USOM director, lasted for some time before he was removed. But not before the American-supported counterinsurgency effort in South Vietnam was transformed into a bureaucratic, barely functional operation in which reporting was the primary objective and assisting the Vietnamese in implementing their program was so far down the list it was no longer important as an objective.

I adamantly and somewhat angrily told AID/Washington that I wanted no more of this organization. I was offered a position in Thailand with another pay grade hike. It was no doubt a type of bribe to keep me quiet as the misdeeds of Killen and his cohorts were starting to crop up in the *Washington Post*. The U.S. government was trying to keep a lid on the character assassinations and false charges by the USOM in South Vietnam. I vowed I would never again work directly for an organization such as AID that would condone character assassinations and deliberate false charges against its employees. And I kept that vow for the rest of my life.

The Women in South Vietnam: A Hidden Bright Spot

There has been very little written on the women of South Vietnam, other than the exploits of Madame Nhu, which were presented mostly on the negative side of the ledger. In one of my programs in the rural areas of South Vietnam, the women were very prominent in agriculture and often were responsible for caring for the improved pigs we provided to the villagers. Many local businesses were owned and operated by women, although the operations might have had masculine-sounding names.

I was always impressed with Vietnamese women's industriousness, dependability, and cheerfulness, sometimes under trying conditions for them. I have often wondered if national conflicts would have ever existed in South Vietnam if the female population was equally represented in the political arena. There is no doubt whatsoever, in my mind, that what stability did exist in South Vietnam during the long, terrible war was due in large part to the hidden bright spot, the women. They kept families together against, at times, almost insurmountable odds. They worked to bring in money. And few, if any, ever had to shoot or maim anyone to keep the steady course they followed.

Hot Dog Barbecue with the Dragon Lady

I met the most famous Vietnamese woman of her time (or infamous, as some would say) in the most unusual circumstances. It was at a hot dog barbecue at the IVS house in Dalat. Here a small group of current and former IVSers and friends decided to barbecue hot dogs a few days before Christmas in 1962. Someone suggested, in jest, that we ought to invite Madame Nhu, who had a vacation home half a block away, to come to the barbecue. (Madame Nhu was the First Lady of South Vietnam, by proxy, because she was the wife of bachelor President Diem's brother Ngo Dinh Nhu, who was also counselor to the president.)

Don Wadley and Dan Leaty promptly went to Madame Nhu's home, knocked on the door, and extended the invitation. To everyone's surprise, Madame Nhu was there and accepted. A half hour later she arrived at the outside barbecue grill, dolled up like Cleopatra. Madame Nhu was quite attractive; she was very pleasant and asked a number of questions, as well as answering some from our group of young people as she barbecued her hot dog. She did ask us to explain what we were doing and what we called what we were doing to the hot dogs. With her limited knowledge of English, she did not seem to have the word "barbecue" in her vocabulary at that time.

I have often wondered if Madame Nhu didn't derive her internationally unforgettable and unforgiven remark (by the news media) about Buddhist clergy barbecuing themselves from that get-together in Dalat. The infamous remark was made during the aftermath of an incident in which a Buddhist

Harvey Neese with Mong Thi Nga, the Vietnamese secretary for the director and associate director of the Office of Rural Affairs

priest set himself afire in a suicide. He was protesting the mishandling of the
Buddhist affair by Madame Nhu's husband and her brother-in-law, the president. Madame Nhu equated the self-immolation to the "barbecuing of a Buddhist monk." This off-the-cuff remark overshadowed all the positive things
Madame Nhu had done for women's rights in South Vietnam, which were
extensive. Madame Nhu was vilified from all quarters of the globe, and she lost
much stature as a proxy First Lady after the callous remark.

Viet Cong Propaganda from U.S. Actions

American combat military personnel who had to fight the war in the jungles of
South Vietnam or were prisoners of the North Vietnamese deserve our highest
sympathy and praise. The conditions in which they lived and died were intolerable and in a place they didn't particularly want to be. They are the heroes of
the Vietnam War. There was, however, another side of the story, the support
troops. There didn't seem to be any cultural-awareness training given to American military enlisted support personnel sent to South Vietnam. Support personnel lived mostly in bloc-rented hotels and other housing in many of the
largest cities of South Vietnam. They did not engage in combat, and their ratio
was approximately seven times the number of combat troops. From observation,
the way many of them acted around Vietnamese women whom they met mostly
in bars was as if they had never seen a human being of the opposite sex before.
Hanging on or wrapping themselves around a young woman in South Vietnam
in public, especially as a foreigner, was culturally unacceptable.

Many of the young Vietnamese women working in bars were there because
of the economic need to supplement their other increasingly meager incomes.
Some were teachers or factory workers. The high inflation caused by the large
amount of dollars brought into the country by U.S. military personnel caused
prices to skyrocket.

The disgust by the Vietnamese people in observing how American enlisted
personnel were blatantly violating their customs is probably what prompted
the outcome of a poll taken on the attitudes of the U.S. military in South Vietnam. This article, titled "Most South Vietnamese want U.S. to leave," was
printed in the *Singapore Straits Times* on 28 August 1970.

Indianapolis (Indiana) Thurs.—Most of the South Vietnamese people
apparently want the U.S. military out of their country, Representative
Andrew Jacobs, Democrat, Indiana, said here yesterday.

His remarks were based on a recent poll taken by the U.S. Command
in Saigon that was "alleged and not denied to have been conducted."

The poll shows "65 percent of the Vietnamese people want the United States to leave their country," said Jacobs. "Only five percent express a contrary view."

We can only speculate how much propaganda value the Viet Cong were able to generate from the actions of American servicemen in their "after hours" activities. Because the Viet Cong were experts at manipulating public opinion to suit their political objectives, a good guess is that they gained considerable propaganda value from this cultural unawareness of servicemen.

What was the conflict about and could it have been avoided? I can only give the perspective of one who traveled and worked in the rural areas of South Vietnam for years when questions are asked about the Vietnam War and what it was all about. Could it have been avoided? I had a good working knowledge of the Vietnamese language and probably met and talked with as many rural villagers as any foreigner in the country did. I was not privy to the high-level intrigues and the squabbles involved with American military officials resisting unconventional tactics in favor of heavy armament, tanks, and the dropping of bombs on a very mobile foe. But I was always out there where the war was being fought.

There was a huge cultural chasm between Vietnamese, especially in rural areas, and many Americans. I believe there must have been a lot of misunderstanding between the U.S. military leaders and their Vietnamese counterparts. Things happened with village people that I couldn't understand, and I dealt with them for years. An example is the time I came to a village to look at some pigs, and I saw a large crowd of people in the village square. I worked my way through the crowd, and in the middle of the square, I saw half a dozen burned corpses, presumably Viet Cong, spread out on the ground. They must have been napalmed. Some of the young children had sticks that they used to poke into the burned flesh. Some villagers were laughing as if it were a joyous occasion. The old folks were egging on the kids to tear off more of the flesh. Needless to say, I was appalled, and the incident is still etched in my mind to this day.

I didn't understand how the villagers could treat mangled and burned bodies so casually and laugh and joke as if it were a birthday or something. I am sure the villagers, if they knew my true feelings of the scene, would have been astounded I took the whole thing so seriously.

It must be remembered, in the final analysis, that the Vietnamese suffered many times more losses than the Americans did. Although some fifty-eight thousand Americans were killed in the war and many thousands were wounded, which are not trivial numbers by any measure, the Vietnamese experienced

Madame Nhu barbecues a hot dog at a Christmas gathering at the IVS house in Dalat, 1962. *Forest Gerdes and Fred Bell*

horrendous death losses estimated by Vietnam authorities in 1995 at more than three million human beings.[3]

Could the conflict have been avoided? That is the question that haunts many of us and will for years to come. From my observation, the people in the countryside, the poor people of South Vietnam, had ample reasons to revolt against the government. There was plenty of corruption, and the peasants were largely ignored by a government that was supposed to help them to improve their lives. The people both feared the Viet Cong and supported them in many ways. However, I believed very deeply that the best opportunity the government of South Vietnam had to combat communism was through economic and political changes.

The counterinsurgency or pacification concept, as it was originally designed, was not given a chance to work because of the tragic ineptitude of the U.S. government in Americanizing and undermining the program. This and the assassinations of Presidents Kennedy and Diem were probably the turning points of the war. After these three acts, it was probably written in the cards that the communists would ultimately triumph

Contrary to what former Secretary of Defense McNamara mentioned in his book, *In Retrospect: The Tragedy and Lessons of Vietnam,* about a lack of knowledge of Asia, there were literally hundreds of Americans in South Vietnam who had worked and lived in the provinces many years before 1965. Many of them could speak Vietnamese. Although they knew the situation in the rural areas where the war was to be fought by American troops, no one wanted to tap their knowledge. It was an arrogant and stupid attitude by American officials that led America into the Vietnam morass with little chance of winning. If political and military leaders had bothered to ask those who knew the situation on the level where the war was to be fought and then took their advice, America might never have blundered into the unwinnable situation.

I have not changed my beliefs in what the peasants really wanted out of life during those terrible, turmoil-filled years. Only America's political higher-ups would not listen. It was too simpleminded for them to think that helping the peasants with improved pigs, fertilizer, or irrigation water would gain their support. That's where they were wrong, and to prove it—just look at the scoreboard.

I would live in Southeast Asia from 1959 to 1975, except for brief periods of home leave and in between jobs, and I would remain in international work for my entire professional career. In closing, I would like to end with a short poem that I wrote in the early 1960s on my observations of the Viet-

namese farmer and his simple desire for one of the most important aspects
of his life.

> There is movement from the west
>   Where blows the hot, dry wind.
> The east with cool breezes to spare
>   Lies dormant and will not send.
> Heat waves cause the land to tremble
>   As if in mortal pain,
> While sparse clouds hover, yet too timid
>   To give forth a bit of rain.
>
> This monotonous war of six months drought
>   Is fought each passing year
> Nothing changes the eternal cycle,
>   Nations, guns or tears.
> Nature, then is still the tyrant—
>   Not ideologies of man,
> For when such thoughts be long forgot,
>   There'll still be no more rain.
>
> Farmers know best of hot season's stress—
>   Of parched and hard earth,
> When water buffalo cannot bathe
>   In a land that is a curse.
> Then come clouds, six months of rain
>   And they can realize
> That Buddha's gift to Vietnamese
>   Is lush, green paddy rice.
>
>   H. C. Neese

Notes

1. See the appendix for a discussion of Frank Tan's involvement with the OSS and Ho Chi Minh during World War II.
2. See John O'Donnell's narrative in this book for a description of his own run-in with AID's internal security staff.
3. The following information is taken from an article in *Indo China Digest* in 1995: "On 3 April, Vietnam News Agency published statistics by the Ministry of Labor, War, Invalids and Social Affairs that disclosed for the first time that 1.1 million communist soldiers had died and 600,000 were wounded in the Vietnam War between 1954–1975. Previous estimates in the West said communist forces lost about 666,000 fighters. Other figures released showed that nearly 2 million civilians were killed in the North and South and an equal number were injured, along with 223,000 South Vietnamese soldiers."

Conclusion

In the preceding chapters, eight individuals who were deeply involved in the struggle against the communist insurgency in South Vietnam have written their personal accounts of what happened during the early days of America's involvement in that country in the early 1960s. During this critical period, between the U.S. commitment to increase support to the Diem administration in 1961 and the introduction of U.S. combat troops in 1965, the fateful decisions were made that led to the tragedy we have come to know as the Vietnam War.

In 1960, America's presence in South Vietnam consisted of a traditional embassy and U.S. Information Service (USIS) staff, a relatively small U.S. Military Assistance Advisory Group (MAAG), and a conventional economic assistance program (U.S. Operations Mission, or USOM), mostly concentrated in the capital of Saigon. With the U.S. decision in late 1961 to increase its support to the Diem administration in its struggle against a communist-led insurgency, the American military placed small advisory detachments at the corps, division, and provincial levels. The economic assistance program was expanded to provide material, funding, and advisory support at the provincial level for the Diem government's Strategic Hamlet Program.

Initially, this expanded U.S. support helped the government and armed forces of South Vietnam to place increased pressure on the Viet Cong. The guerrillas were being pushed back to their base areas, and their mobility was increasingly restricted by the expanding Strategic Hamlet Program and complementary operations. But then, things began to go wrong.

The writers of this book were all in South Vietnam during the 1960–65 period when things started right and then went wrong. They witnessed the initial successes of the counterinsurgency program and then the deterioration of the situation during the Viet Cong counteroffensive and the Buddhist crisis of 1963 and as the Vietnamese government went into a tailspin after the assassination of President Diem. What went wrong? What were the mistakes that led to the tragic decision to introduce U.S. combat troops and Americanize what had been a Vietnamese conflict? Some of the factors were broad and deep-seated; others were specific and immediate. A short synopsis is offered in this concluding chapter.

Highest-Level U.S. Policymakers Do Not Understand

A fundamental, deep-rooted problem was the inability of high-level American leaders such as Secretary of Defense Robert McNamara, Gen. Maxwell Taylor, Ambassador Henry Cabot Lodge, Gen. Paul Harkins, and others to understand and deal with the political, psychological, and economic nature of the struggle with the Viet Cong to win the loyalty of the rural population. In his book, *In Retrospect: The Tragedy and Lessons of Vietnam,* McNamara acknowledges that he "underestimated the power of nationalism to motivate a people (in this case the North Vietnamese and Viet Cong) to fight and die for their beliefs and values."[1] He acknowledges further that he (and other U.S. leaders) failed to "recognize the limitations of modern, high-technology military equipment, forces and doctrine in confronting unconventional, highly motivated people's movements" and to "adapt our military tactics to the task of winning the hearts and minds of people from a totally different culture."[2] He blames this failure in part on "our profound ignorance of the history, culture and politics of the people in the area, and the personalities and habits of their leaders . . . and the fact that there were no Southeast Asian counterparts (as in the case of Bohlen, Kennan and others in our relations with the Soviet Union) for senior officials to consult when making decisions on Vietnam."[3]

How different the outcome in South Vietnam might have been had McNamara and other U.S. policymakers understood and learned from the earlier French experience (as described by George Tanham and others) and sought and heeded the advice of experts such as Major General Lansdale, Sir Robert Thompson, and others, such as those represented by the writers of this book. They understood communist revolutionary warfare from firsthand experience and had been successful in combating it in South Vietnam as well as in the Philippines, Malaya, and elsewhere.

Early in McNamara's tenure as secretary of defense, General Lansdale, who was the secretary's assistant for special operations, was told that he had fifteen minutes to brief McNamara on South Vietnam. Wondering how he could convey the complexities of communist revolutionary warfare in South Vietnam in such a short time, Lansdale decided to put together an exhibit of Viet Cong weapons, such as homemade mortars and rifles, spiked bamboo booby traps, and crude antipersonnel mines. When McNamara appeared for the briefing, Lansdale explained that these weapons characterized the kind of enemy that the United States faced in South Vietnam. McNamara looked puzzled and then became angry, asking why Lansdale was wasting his time with such exhibits, and left the room.[4]

What Lansdale was trying to do was to educate McNamara about how the communists were able to use nationalism and other deeply held aspirations of the people to achieve a high level of motivation among their followers. Thus motivated, the Viet Cong were willing to take on airplanes, artillery, and armored personnel carriers and risk their lives in support of their cause, often armed only with the crude weapons that Lansdale had assembled to show McNamara. Unfortunately and tragically, McNamara never grasped that point during the Vietnam War and only acknowledged it some thirty years later in his book, *In Retrospect*

McNamara and other U.S. policymakers never fully understood the importance of winning over the rural population to deny its support to the communist insurgents. They gave lip service to "winning the hearts and the minds of the people" but didn't have a good grasp of how to do it. There were those such as Col. Tran Ngoc Chau, Gen. Lu Lan, and the other writers of this book who understood that it was essential to win the support of the rural population to isolate and eventually destroy, or bring about the surrender of, the communist-led guerrillas. They also understood and put into action the kinds of programs that would win the support of rural inhabitants. Good examples of successful counterinsurgency programs were the programs initiated by Colonel Chau in Kien Hoa Province and General Lan in Quang Ngai Province.

We believe that these programs were effective in winning over the rural population and isolating the Viet Cong and, if continued and expanded to other parts of the country, could have led to a much different outcome in South Vietnam. Unfortunately, these programs were not supported, as McNamara and other policymakers placed increasing emphasis on the purely military aspects of the struggle. In addition, these successful programs had to contend with the havoc wreaked by Jim Killen in his effort to discredit the original USOM rural counterinsurgency program.

Conventional Thinking in an Unconventional Setting

A continuing and pervasive problem was the tendency of U.S. policymakers (and of those in higher-level military and civilian bureaucratic ranks dealing with South Vietnam) to think of the problems in South Vietnam in strictly conventional terms. This was done despite the fact that it was definitely an unconventional conflict that required an unconventional response.

A good example of this conventional thinking was described in Gen. Lu Lan's account of his experiences as deputy chief of staff for operations and training of the Army of the Republic of Vietnam (ARVN) from 1958 to 1961. During this period, the United States was helping to restructure and equip ARVN. Lu Lan attempted in vain to persuade top American military advisers that ARVN needed a light and flexible-force structure with great mobility and firepower, working closely with the Civil Guard, village Self-Defense Corps, and hamlet militia. Lu Lan's proposed force structure and strategy were based on his years of experience fighting with and against the Viet Minh. The high-level U.S. advisers politely dismissed his suggestions and went on to supply and train a South Vietnamese army based on the American experience in World War II and the Korean War, totally unsuited to the demands of an effective counterinsurgency campaign.

Another example of this conventional thinking was illustrated by a one-on-one session between Colonel Chau and General Westmoreland. Chau suggested many of the same principles, including the use of U.S. forces as a strategic reserve to be called upon when the ARVN needed their support. General Westmoreland listened for a while and then abruptly got up, shook Chau's hand, and left. No action was ever taken as a result of their conversation.

There was a failure of the U.S. and South Vietnamese military to organize, equip, train, and utilize ARVN forces in a manner that would have enabled them to provide active support and render immediate assistance to the hamlet militia under attack by the Viet Cong regular units. In too many cases, this led to the disillusionment and demoralization of the hamlet militia and the Self-Defense Corps. What happened to the Strategic Hamlet Program in Long An Province, as described by Rufus Phillips and John O'Donnell, is an example.

The unwillingness to deal with the insurgency in unconventional ways was a direct result of the ingrained, strongly held conventional bias of many in the U.S. military, particularly at the Saigon headquarters level. By virtue of the strong U.S. advisory role, a similar attitude prevailed within the higher Vietnamese military ranks. In fairness to the U.S. military, we should note that the lower-level U.S. military advisers, in direct contact with the rural population at the provincial level, understood the importance of pacification and winning the hearts and minds of the rural population but were not able to get through to their supervisors in Saigon.

There were a few exceptions to this rule at the higher levels of the U.S. government, such as General Lansdale, who had been successful in carrying out his unconventional approach both in the Philippines, where he assisted in defeating the Huk communist-led insurgency, and in South Vietnam, where he helped President Diem to consolidate his position in 1954 and 1955.

A second exception was President John Kennedy, who was attracted to unconventional responses such as the U.S. Special Forces and the strategic-hamlet approach in South Vietnam. Unfortunately, with his untimely death in November 1963, U.S. policymakers returned primarily to conventional approaches. These were characterized in the military sphere by the introduction of American combat troops and application of a search-and-destroy strategy. They also included the economic assistance sphere and the undermining of the innovative counterinsurgency program by new USOM Director Jim Killen.

These fundamental problems were greatly exacerbated by the failure of U.S. policymakers to understand the critical importance of maintaining leadership continuity in South Vietnam, which led to their support of, or tacit agreement to, the coup against President Diem. The overthrow of Diem led to a leadership vacuum at the highest levels and the ensuing deterioration of the governmental apparatus at all levels. Although there was dissatisfaction with President Diem, and particular unhappiness with his brother and sister-in-law Ngo Dinh Nhu and Madame Nhu, many, if not most, Vietnamese respected Diem as a nationalist and a patriot. They all recognized the critical role that he had played in building the government and holding it together.

U.S. Ambassador Requests General Lansdale

The Buddhist crisis in 1963 led to an increase in anti-Diem sentiment within the country and the faltering of support at the highest levels of the U.S. government. The entire Buddhist crisis might never have happened, or could have been quietly and effectively defused, if President Diem had been able to have the benefit of the advice and counsel of an experienced friend like General Lansdale, whom he trusted and who had been his key adviser during the troubled years of 1954 and 1955.

President Kennedy had considered sending Lansdale to South Vietnam in 1962 to assist President Diem but had been dissuaded by some of his principal advisers.[5] The idea of sending Lansdale to South Vietnam was raised again by Rufus Phillips in his briefing of President Kennedy on 12 September 1963.[6] On 13 September 1963, Ambassador Henry Cabot Lodge sent a personally typed letter to Secretary of State Dean Rusk requesting that General Lansdale be sent to Saigon as the CIA chief of station.[7] Lodge asked that his request be shared with President Kennedy.[8]

In a telephone conversation on 17 September 1963, the director of the Central Intelligence Agency, John McCone, told Rusk that there would be "insurmountable problems" with sending Lansdale to Saigon as chief of station.[9] The objections of the CIA, the Defense Department (McNamara), and the Department of State killed the opportunity of sending Lansdale to advise Diem and with it the possibility of helping extricate the president from the problems caused by his inept handling of the Buddhist crisis.

The inability of U.S. officials to provide timely advice and to persuade Diem to defuse the Buddhist problem was the single most important diplomatic failure of the U.S. government during this critical period. It led to the coup against Diem, the shameful murder of Diem and his brother, and the subsequent deterioration of South Vietnamese government programs. This failure and the subsequent political morass were exacerbated by the strong counterstrike by the Viet Cong and North Vietnamese against the Strategic Hamlet Program.

If Lansdale had been available to interact with Diem in 1963, there is reason to believe, based on his past performance, that he could have worked with Diem to calm the Buddhist turmoil and to ease Ngo Dinh Nhu and his wife out of their high-profile positions in the government. In an account of one of his meetings with President Diem, Colonel Chau discusses the president's inquiry about how Chau would view Diem sending the Nhus out of the country, which confirms the president's willingness to consider such a move.

The Beginning of the End

With the death of President Diem, the governmental apparatus began to break down. U.S. policymakers tried in vain to prop up a series of military leaders who proved to be ineffective. The Viet Cong seized the opportunity presented by the uncertainty of the government forces and hit back hard. With the deterioration of security in rural areas and the discrediting of the counterinsurgency program by Jim Killen and others as described in the sections by Bert Fraleigh, George Tanham, Harvey Neese, and John O'Donnell, the U.S. policymakers began to think increasingly in conventional military terms and of the necessity to take over leadership of the counterinsurgency effort from the Vietnamese.

This unfortunate view led to the decision to commit U.S. combat troops to South Vietnam in early 1965, which was the second tragic mistake made by the United States. If President Diem had been able to continue as president (with advice and assistance from a trusted friend like Ed Lansdale), and if the United States had continued to provide support for a Vietnamese-led counterinsurgency campaign, combining political, psychological, economic, and military elements in a cohesive strategy, there is good reason to believe that there might never have been a need to commit U.S. combat troops and to Americanize the conflict.

We believe that the United States should have held firmly to the position expressed by President Kennedy in his 2 September 1963 interview with Walter Cronkite: "In the final analysis, it is their war. They are the ones who have to win it or lose it. We can help them, we can give them equipment, we can send our men out there as advisors, but they have to win it, the people of Vietnam, against the Communists. . . . All we can do is help, and we are making it very clear, but I don't agree with those who say we should withdraw. That would be a great mistake."[10]

Secretary McNamara echoed this position in his 25 September 1963 interview with Harry Reasoner on *CBS Reports:* "It is important to recognize it's a South Vietnamese war. It will be won or lost depending upon what they do. We can advise and help, but they are responsible for the final results, and it remains to be seen how they will continue to conduct that war."[11]

But then Diem was killed in the coup, Kennedy was assassinated, and the Vietnamese government went into a tailspin. The Viet Cong came on strong, and the United States was forced to introduce combat troops to stabilize the situation. Then, the United States went further and took over the direction of the war effort and the main combat role against the Viet Cong and North Vietnamese.

Experience in other Asian nations demonstrated that the communists could be confronted and defeated, as in the Philippines and Malaya, or held at bay, as in the case of South Korea. We do not believe that North Vietnam would have necessarily lessened its determination to reunify the country under communist rule. We also do not claim that the effort against the Viet Cong and the North Vietnamese might have been won by the South Vietnamese, just that the course of the conflict might have been very different. The South Vietnamese might have continued in a long-term stalemate with the communists or might have fallen eventually to the Viet Cong and the North Vietnamese. But they would have done so on their own (albeit with equipment, advisers, and other support from the United States as advocated by Kennedy and McNamara). This would have been without the commitment of U.S. combat troops and national prestige, which changed it from a Vietnamese war to an American war.

By militarizing and Americanizing the conflict in 1964 and 1965, the United States became bogged down in a full-scale, counterguerrilla war in Asia. The United States took the leadership of the war effort away from the South Vietnamese and undercut that leadership in the eyes of its own highly nationalistic people. This move provided a perfect propaganda vehicle for the North Vietnamese and Viet Cong, who claimed that the United States had replaced the French as the oppressors of the people. As the war dragged on, and resistance to sending young Americans to their deaths in the jungles of South Vietnam increased, American political will waned and then collapsed. We continue to believe that the Vietnam War, as we came to know it, did not have to happen. The mistakes made by arrogant, poorly informed U.S. policymakers from 1961 through 1965 led to the debacle that followed in the next decade.

We hope that these on-the-scene personal accounts will help to illuminate what really happened in South Vietnam in the early 1960s, which paved the way to such a great tragedy for both America and South Vietnam.

Notes

1. McNamara, *In Retrospect: The Tragedy and Lessons of Vietnam,* 322.
2. Ibid.
3. Ibid.
4. Rufus Phillips, personal conversation with Ed Lansdale.
5. In addition to Currey, *Edward Lansdale: The Unquiet American,* 228; and Rust, *Kennedy in Vietnam,* 27; see U.S. Department of State, *The Foreign Relations of the United States, 1961–1963,* vol. 1, *Vietnam, 1961,* 719, which includes the following footnote: "Rostow later wrote that President Kennedy decided not to appoint Lansdale as an adviser to Diem. The reasons, said Rostow, 'lay deep in the American military and the civil bureaucracy. The American ambassador and the ranking general in Saigon—and the departments backstopping them in Washington—did not want another American that close to Diem.'" (Rostow's undated draft manuscript, chapter 34, page 562, National Defense University, Taylor Papers, T-15-71.)
6. See discussion of Rufus Phillips's suggestions to President Kennedy in the meeting on 12 September 1963 described in Phillips's narrative in this book.
7. U.S. Department of State, *The Foreign Relations of the United States, 1961–1963,* vol. 4, *Vietnam, August–December 1963,* 163.
8. Ibid., 205.
9. Ibid., 240–41.
10. McNamara, *In Retrospect,* 61–62.
11. Ibid., 72.

Appendix

America's Involvement in Vietnam

The Colonization of Vietnam

The name Vietnam was given to this Southeast Asian country in an official proclamation in 1802. The country consisted of three regions: Tonkin in the north, Annam in the central region, and Cochin China in the south.

In 1857, the French military attacked Da Nang (or Tourane as it was called at one point) in Annam, or the central lowlands region. By 1867, after ten years of fighting, the French had conquered Cochin China, making it a French colony. In 1883, the French took over Annam and Tonkin. The Vietnamese fought to regain their freedom until 1917, when overt opposition subsided. The French would subsequently occupy and colonize Cambodia and Laos to form a three-country union that was named Indo-China.

The Japanese Invade Vietnam

Japanese military forces moved into Vietnam about fifteen months before the attack on Pearl Harbor in 1941. In a settlement with the French, the Japanese occupying forces recognized some French authority in Vietnam and left the French in charge of local administration and security. During this period, various groups in Vietnam were organizing to overthrow the French colonialists (and at the same time extricate the Japanese from their soil). The leader who emerged from these early nationalists was called Ho Chi Minh. Ho was born Nguyen Sinh Cung in 1892 in the northern part of the country. Subsequently, Ho would use a number of aliases during his career. The organizational bonding agent for the

Some of the material in this appendix comes from conversations Harvey Neese had with Frank Tan between 1997 and 1998.

resistance was the Vietnamese Communist Party. The name would be changed in 1941 to the Viet Nam Doc Lap Dong Minh Hoi, or in English, the Vietnamese Independence League, which would be further shortened to Viet Minh. The Viet Minh would become the primary force of opposition to the French in Vietnam.

First Contacts between United States and Ho Chi Minh

There was an independent private group in Vietnam in 1944 called GBT, which was taken from the initials of the three Allied civilians who made up the group. Their names were L. L. Gordon, a Canadian; Harry Bernard, an American; and Frank Tan, a Chinese American. The three-person group developed a number of French and Vietnamese guerrilla contacts, and its intelligence reports were distributed to all Allied intelligence centers.

The British (who were in India at the time) supplied GBT with funds and equipment, the Chinese provided some personnel, and the U.S. Fourteenth Air Force in China provided additional services. Later GBT received both money and equipment from a U.S. organization, Air Ground Aid Services (AGAS). AGAS provided help in rescuing downed Allied pilots, made contact with prisoners of war, and collected intelligence of Japanese troop movements. At some point, AGAS received financial help from the Office of Strategic Services (OSS), the predecessor to the Central Intelligence Agency (CIA).

The OSS, in Vietnam during the latter stages of World War II, also was attempting to gather intelligence on the Japanese military. During this time, GBT and AGAS, which GBT was transferred to in 1944, had regular contacts with Ho Chi Minh in Kun Ming, China, a guerrilla sanctuary across the Chinese border. Frank Tan (a longtime acquaintance of Harvey Neese) shared some of his personal contacts with Ho Chi Minh during his time in Kun Ming.

Ho, according to Tan, was friendly and outgoing to him and other members of GBT. Tan believes to this day that Ho was a nationalist foremost and a communist for expediency or necessity (to gain support from the outside). Tan once asked Ho if he was a communist. His reply was, "You tell me what a communist is, and I'll tell you whether I am one."

In between the serious business of helping to counter the Japanese military activities in Indo-China, Tan experienced some lighter moments with Ho Chi Minh. In a letter written to Tan when Ho was ill, Ho wanted to wish Tan good health and good luck as they were preparing to leave Vietnam after the atomic bomb was dropped on Hiroshima, foreshadowing the end of World War II. Ho added that he wished Tan would get "a good madame soon." The comment was referring to Tan's bachelorhood, which was not particularly by choice. A girlfriend had recently parted company with Tan, the news of which was relayed to Ho. Ho told Tan that he was fond of a girl once, but when he went off to sea, he put her out of his mind. Ho then encouraged Tan to meet some of the Vietnamese female guerrillas, but Tan told Ho at the time that "unfortunately, none of them seemed interested in getting married."

After the atomic bomb was dropped on Hiroshima, GBT's work was finished in Indo-China, and the three-person group departed. Before Tan left Kun Ming, Ho Chi Minh drafted a letter and asked Tan to carry it to American authorities in Washington. In the letter, Tan remembers Ho had requested that the United States send a team of observers to his encampment to determine whether America would support the aim of removing French colonial rule from Indo-China. Tan took the letter into China and passed it to the U.S. military command. His youth and lack of knowledge of the U.S. bureaucratic system led him to not carry the letter to the United States. Tan never heard what happened to the letter. Ho was known to have sent seven or eight additional letters to the U.S. State Department and to U.S. officials, including the president, trying to solicit support for his cause. None of the letters were ever answered.

On the one side, some believe that Ho Chi Minh, this small, frail Vietnamese with many aliases, was as ruthless and cruel as any leader in modern times. They also believe that his politics and philosophical motivation were formulated solely to gain total control over the Vietnamese masses by any means available. Any contacts with the United States, this side believes, were merely done to use America to further his aims of controlling all the people of Vietnam under the cruel cloak of communism.

On the other side, there are those, including Frank Tan, who believe that Ho Chi Minh was a nationalist first, and his priority in life was to remove the French from Vietnam and all of Indo-China. These same people believe that America might have lost a golden opportunity by not cultivating a relationship with this rather obscure guerrilla leader in the 1940s as he tried so desperately to gain America's sympathy and support for his cause. The question will always haunt us—whether support from America at that crucial time might have helped to peacefully remove the French from Indo-China and possibly bypass the French Indo-China War. And then, dare we even think for a fleeting moment that this also might have been instrumental in avoiding the Vietnam War with U.S. involvement?

Defeat of the French and the Geneva Conference

The French and Ho Chi Minh's Viet Minh forces had fought since the end of World War II. On 7 May 1954, the French, lured into a pitched battle at a place called Dien Bien Phu, were defeated by the Viet Minh despite some $1.4 billion in military aid given by the United States from 1950 to 1954.

The Geneva Conference had been going on from 26 April 1954 until 21 July, when it ended with the signing of the Geneva Accords. In essence, the Geneva Accords separated the opposing forces in Vietnam, on a temporary basis, at the seventeenth parallel. The Viet Minh went north of that parallel, and the French and their supporters occupied the territory south of this line. The Accords stipulated that there were to be nationwide elections held within a short period to determine which political entity would rule the country.

Higher-level U.S. officials voiced their concerns that Ho Chi Minh would run away with any elections held because he was at the apex of his popularity. After all, he had just led an Asian bunch of ragtag guerrillas to defeat a Western world power. One writer of the time, Carl T. Rowan, wrote, "The odds were considered at least eight to one against Diem [Vietnamese leader of the South] and the free world."

A Vietnamese introverted loner, Ngo Dinh Diem, was made the premier of the southern section, or South Vietnam, as it was to be called. He would later be elected president by the people in the South. During this same period in 1954, Col. Edward Lansdale, an American, assembled a small team that included Rufe Phillips, a contributing writer to this book. The team of counterinsurgency specialists was sent by the U.S. government to do what it could to help South Vietnam survive what many believed would be inevitable disintegration. Lansdale had previously and successfully assisted President Magsaysay in the Philippines survive the Huk communist-led rebellion.

The Lansdale team subsequently duplicated the Philippine magic touch by helping Diem's government to survive, and by 1956, the country began to prosper. The team's work included what some termed military and psychological warfare against the Viet Minh, which was supposedly contrary to provisions of the recently signed Geneva Accords. No elections were ever held in the North and South as was agreed at Geneva. President Diem had an innate suspicion and fear of the Viet Minh. The United States agreed with Diem and ignored this provision.

South Vietnam: A Geographical Description in 1960

Vietnam was still divided into two sectors in 1960 at the seventeenth parallel. South Vietnam bordered North Vietnam on the north, Laos and Cambodia on the west, the South China Sea on the east, and the Gulf of Siam on the south.

South Vietnam had some forty-three provinces, or states, which were broken down into districts, villages, and hamlets (this number changed as provinces were split). The southern part of South Vietnam is a large delta, fed by the Mekong River flowing out of Cambodia and Laos. The Mekong Delta is the most productive food-producing part of South Vietnam (or of Vietnam as a whole). Rice, pigs, tropical fruit, vegetables, ducks, and fish are produced in large supply throughout the delta region.

Going north from Saigon, the interior of the country is a mixture of jungles, some rubber plantations, and considerably fewer villages than in the delta region. Vietnamese villages give way to Montagnard areas, where ethnic tribal groups live on a subsistence economy consisting of upland rice, fish from the rivers, and meat and foodstuffs gleaned from the jungle.

Farther north of the jungles of the lower elevation areas are the Highlands. Here the terrain is mostly mountainous jungles, with some intermixed hilly grasslands. This is the home of the largest population of Montagnard tribal peoples. The Highlands border Laos on the western part of South Vietnam and extend all the way to the North Vietnam border.

Along the eastern coast, a narrow strip of lowlands borders the South China Sea the entire length of South Vietnam. Here ethnic Vietnamese live in scattered villages where they subsist on small agricultural enterprises and fishing. The northern part of the lowlands is called Central Vietnam. The Central Vietnam lowlands are traditionally among the poorest regions of the country. Paddy rice production is marginal, fertile land is scarce, and irrigation is not predominant as in the delta region.

The population of both South and North Vietnam was approximately twenty-four million in the early 1960s, of which half was distributed almost evenly between each country.

U.S. Assistance to South Vietnam

Immediately after the signing of the Geneva Accords, America began sending military and economic aid to South Vietnam to stave off a communist takeover. By 1960, the Viet Minh and a southern arm in the South, the National Liberation Front, or the Viet Cong, began an insurgency to undermine the South Vietnamese government. This campaign set the stage for larger U.S. intervention to keep the communists from taking over by force what they had expected to win at the ballot box in 1954. The eight writers contributing to this book discuss the subsequent crucial period, the early 1960s.

Selected Bibliography

Bui Diem. *In the Jaws of History*. Boston: Houghton Mifflin, 1987.

Buttinger, Joseph. *The Smaller Dragon*. New York: Praeger, 1958.

Colby, William. *Honorable Men: My Life in the CIA*. New York: Simon & Schuster, 1978.

———. *Lost Victory*. Chicago: Contemporary Books, 1989.

Cooper, Chester L. *The Lost Crusade: America in Vietnam*. New York: Dodd, Mead & Co., 1970.

Currey, Cecil B. *Edward Lansdale: The Unquiet American*. Boston: Houghton Mifflin, 1988.

Drake, Jeff. "How the U.S. Got Involved in Viet Nam." In VIETNAM VETERANS HOME PAGE [online], 1993. Available from <http://grunt.space.swri.edu/jeffviet.htm>.

Fall, Bernard. *Street without Joy: Insurgency in Indochina 1953–1966*. Harrisburg, Pa.: The Stackpole Co., 1963.

———. *The Two Viet-Nams: A Political and Military Analysis*. London: Pall Mall Press, 1963.

Fenn, Charles. *Ho Chi Minh: A Biographical Introduction*. New York: Charles Scribner & Sons, 1973.

Grant, Zalin. *Facing the Phoenix: The CIA and Political Defeat of the United States in Vietnam*. New York: Norton, 1991.

Halberstam, David. *The Best and the Brightest*. New York: Random House, 1972.

Hilsman, Roger. *To Move a Nation*. New York: Doubleday, 1967.

Joes, Anthony James. *Modern Guerrilla Insurgency*. Westport, Conn.: Praeger, 1992.

Karnow, Stanley. *Vietnam: A History*. New York: Viking, 1983.

Lansdale, Edward G. *In the Midst of Wars: An American's Mission to Southeast Asia*. New York: Harper and Row, 1972.

McMaster, H. R. *Dereliction of Duty*. New York: HarperCollins, 1997.

McNamara, Robert S. *In Retrospect: The Tragedy and Lessons of Vietnam*. New York: Times Books, 1995.

Mecklin, John. *Mission in Torment*. Garden City, N.Y.: Doubleday, 1975.

Newman, John M. *JFK and Vietnam*. New York: Warner Books, 1992.

Race, Jeffrey. *War Comes to Long An: Revolutionary Conflict in a Vietnamese Province*. Berkeley: University of California Press, 1972.

Rust, William J. *Kennedy in Vietnam: American Vietnam Policy, 1960–1963*. New York: Charles Scribner & Sons, 1985.

Shaplen, Robert. *The Lost Revolution: The U.S. in Vietnam, 1946–1966*. New York: Harper and Row, 1969.

Sheehan, Neil. *A Bright Shining Lie: John Paul Vann and America in Vietnam*. New York: Random House, 1988.

Tanham, George K. *Communist Revolutionary Warfare: The Vietminh in Indochina*. New York: Frederick A. Praeger, 1961.

———. *War without Guns: American Civilians in Rural Vietnam*. New York: Frederick A. Praeger, 1966.

Thompson, Sir Robert. *Defeating Communist Insurgency: The Lessons of Malaya and Vietnam*. New York: Frederick A. Praeger, 1966.

———. *No Exit from Vietnam*. New York: David McKay Co., 1969.

U.S. Department of State. *The Foreign Relations of the United States, 1961–1963*. Vol. 1, *Vietnam, 1961*. Washington, D.C.: U.S. Government Printing Office, 1988.

———. Vol. 2, *Vietnam, 1962*. Washington, D.C., 1990.

———. Vol. 3, *Vietnam, January–August 1963*. Washington, D.C., 1991.

———. Vol. 4, *Vietnam, August–December 1963*. Washington, D.C., 1991.

———. *The Foreign Relations of the United States, 1964–1968*. Vol. 1. *Vietnam, 1964*. Washington, D.C., 1992.

Valeriano, Col. Napoleon D., AFP (retired), and Lt. Col. Charles T. R. Bohannan, U.S. Army (retired). *Counter-Guerrilla Operations: The Philippine Experience*. New York: Frederick A. Praeger, 1962.

Warner, Denis. *The Last Confucian: Vietnam, Southeast Asia, and the West*. Baltimore: Penguin Books, 1964.

Winters, Francis X. *The Year of the Hare: America in Vietnam, January 25, 1963–February 15, 1964*. Athens, Ga.: The University of Georgia Press, 1997.

Index

Agency for International Development (AID): and counterinsurgency effort, 25; role of advisers, 93–94; and Strategic Hamlet Program, 27; structure of, 93–94; and U.S. Operations Mission (USOM), 93; in Vietnam, 96

Air Ground Aid Services (AGAS), 290

Albertt, Charlie, 164

Alsop, Joseph, 226

American mistakes: Americanization of war, 235, 282, 287; conventional aid programs, 19; failure to support Ngo Dinh Diem, 17, 23–24 286; failure to understand Civic Action, 23; failure to understand communist revolutionary warfare, 175, 236; failure to understand need for support of local people, 283; failure to understand unconventional (guerrilla) warfare, 5, 83, 166, 282, 283; inadequate leadership training, 166; introduction of combat troops, 228, 236, 282, 286; support of coup d'état plot (1963), 228, 235, 285; support of Ngo Dinh Nhu, 18; support of secret political party, 18; undermining of counterinsurgency effort, 235, 286

Ames, John, 226

An Giang Province, 126

An Xuyen Province, 100

Army of the Republic of Vietnam (ARVN), 4, 46, 199; bombing raids on villages, 39, 40–41; and coup d'état plot (1963), 3, 44; engagement with Viet Cong forces in Quang Ngai Province, 148; failure to protect rural people, 50, 87, 106, 111, 128, 225; importance of the people's support, 148–49; and John Paul Vann, 219; and people-first strategy, 43; reaction to temple attack, 3, 43; reorganization of, 20; role in counterinsurgency effort, 86; role in local defense, 19, 99; role in pacification and reoccupation, 19; and Rural Affairs, 106; structure of forces, 83, 143; training by United States, 142, 145, 284; troop behavior, 15, 38–41, 168; use of U.S. military advisers, 142; U.S. *versus* Vietnamese military strategy, 143, 200

Bao Dai, 10, 62, 63, 134, 142

Bao Long, 63

Barrows, Leland, 22

Ba Xuyen Province, 33

Bell, David, 51, 117, 171, 231

Bernard, Harry, 290

Big Minh. *See* Duong Van Minh

297